# Crisis in Christology:
# Essays in Quest of Resolution

### Edited by William R. Farmer

Sold and distributed in the U.S.A. by
Dove Booksellers
30633 Schoolcraft Road, Suite C
Livonia, Michigan 48150

Sold and distributed in the U.S.A. by
Dove Booksellers
30633 Schoolcraft Road, Suite C
Livonia, Michigan 48150

ISBN: 0-9648151-3-3

Manufactured in the United States of America.

# ACKNOWLEDGEMENTS

**The Manhood of Jesus in the New Testament** by C.F.D. Moule was first printed in **Christ, Faith and History**. It is reprinted here with the permission of Professor Moule and Cambridge University Press.

# GREAT MODERN DEBATES, A Series

## Roy Abraham Varghese, General Editor

**Volume One:**
Artificial Intelligence and the Human Mind
Edited by Joseph Mellichamp, Introduction by Daniel Robinson

**Volume Two:**
New Arguments for the Existence of God
Edited with an introduction by William Lane Craig

**Volume Three:**
Crisis in Christology: Essays in Quest of Resolution
Edited with an introduction by William R. Farmer

# TABLE OF CONTENTS

# SERIES EDITOR'S PREFACE

## Roy Abraham Varghese, Series Editor

The defining paradigm of much twentieth century thought, from the standpoint of belief, has been skepticism, the flight from faith. The seeds sown in the Enlightenment have blossomed into an impenetrable jungle of positivist presuppositions and reductionist methodologies. Science, philosophy and even theology have moved away from the frame of reference of religiously significant affirmation.

But a change appears to be in the making. In the latter part of this century there has been an undercurrent of activity in mainstream academia suggestive of a more considered view of things if not a change in direction. Serious thinkers born and brought up in the cradle of disbelief are now skeptical of skepticism, critical of the critics.

In modern philosophy the question of God has returned to the conversation. "In a quiet revolution in thought and argument that hardly anyone could have foreseen only two decades ago, God is making a comeback. Most intriguingly, this is happening ... in the crisp, intellectual circles of academic philosophers," began a famous story in *Time*. ["Modernizing the Case for God," *Time*, April 7, 1980, p.65]. In modern science, supposedly the central font of skepticism, the question of God had never really gone away. Some of the greatest creative scientific geniuses of this century — Einstein, Heisenberg, Schroedinger, Plank — retained a religious view of reality. The bestselling scientific book of the century, **A Brief History of Time** by Stephen Hawking, explored the implications of modern science for theology and contemporary scientists like Paul Davies continue this exploration in their works.

The **GREAT MODERN DEBATES** series, a project of *Truth, A Journal of Modern Thought,* is a chronicle of these developments with first hand reports from many of the participants themselves. The first two volumes in the series, **Artificial Intelligence and the Human Mind** and **New Arguments for the Existence of God**, considered central questions of science and philosophy with papers from thinkers on various sides of the conceptual divides. Volume One, **Artificial Intelligence and the Human Mind**, explored the question of whether homo sapiens is a complex computer or a union of body and mind with proponents of both points of view presenting their positions. Contributors to Volume One included Daniel Robinson (Georgetown), Marvin Minsky (M.I.T.), neuroscientist Nobel Prize winner Sir John Eccles, Douglas Lanat (Microelectronics and Computer Consortium), John Beloff (University of Edinburgh), J.R. Lucas (Oxford), Hans Moravec (Carnegie-Mellon) and Joseph Mellichamp (University of Alabama). In Volume Two, **New Arguments for the Existence of God**, the theme of discussion was the existence of God and here theists and atheists offered their respective arguments. Contributors to this volume included William Lane Craig (Louvain), Alvin Plantinga (Notre Dame), William P. Alston (Syracuse), Illtyd Trethowan (Downside Abbey), C. Stephen Evans (St. Olaf College), Hugo Meynell (University of Calgary), Richard Swinburne (Oxford), John Leslie (University of Guelph), H.D. Lewis (University of London), Antony Flew (University of Reading), Kai Nielsen (University of Calgary), Paul Kurtz (State University of New York, Buffalo, editor, *Free Inquiry*) and H.P. Owen (University of London).

**Crisis in Christology: Essays in Quest of Resolution** is volume Three in the **GREAT MODERN DEBATES** series. In this anthology the series turns from the philosophical and the scientific to the historical and the theological. The positive trends in science and philosophy have their parallels in modern theology as well. On the one hand, the field of biblical studies has more often than not been antagonistic to traditional theological affirmations. On the other hand, as the current volume shows quite clearly, not a few major mainstream biblical scholars are looking beyond skepticism to a positive re-appraisal of age-old affirmations.

# INTRODUCTION

## William R. Farmer

This book is an anthology of christological essays, which have been selected with a particular purpose in mind. Namely, to focus attention on a long-standing crisis in christology, now re-emerging in a radically new form. This purpose has been achieved by selecting a set of occasional essays composed during the late eighties and early nineties which, when arranged as they are, discloses certain developments in the world of theological scholarship that bear on the question of the direction in which christology is headed as we near the end of the second millennium and prepare to enter the opening decade of the third. No one of these essays was originally composed with this specific purpose in mind. But it is this which has dictated the final choice and arrangement of these particular studies.

Like many anthologies, this volume has matured over a period of time, and the story of its conception, development and birth is worth telling. One cannot say that the nature of this anthology was fully understood at the time the first essays were composed. In fact, as the editor responsible for the selection, redaction and arrangement of these essays I was not brought into the picture until the process of producing this volume was well underway. Credit for initiating this process goes to Roy Varghese, whose most recent publishing venture is an intriguing book about God entitled, *Cosmos, Bios, Theos* which he has co-edited with Henry Margenau, Eugene Higgins Professor Emeritus of Physics and Natural Philosophy at Yale University, published by Open Court, 1992 (second printing 1993, third printing 1994). Included among the seventy scientists who contributed to that anthology are twenty-four Nobel Prize winners. Roy Varghese is also the publisher of *Truth: A Journal of Modern Thought*, which features the publication of seminal essays on "great modern debates."

Varghese was influenced by the "myth and truth debate" that took place over a decade ago in Great Britain. He sensed that an important christological debate was underway. This led him to conceive and execute a plan to bring together a set of scholars in Dallas, Texas to read and discuss papers on the present state of christology. I myself, though living in Dallas, had no knowledge at that time of this conference which took place in a local hotel.

Some time after this conference ended and all the papers that were to be considered for publication were assembled, Varghese contacted me to see whether I would consider assuming the responsibility of bringing these papers into publishable form. After reading the essays, I could perceive a certain coherence that united many of them, a coherence that was worthy of note, and worthy of whatever effort would be required to see the volume through to publication. In a word, the essays as a whole struck a responsive chord; amid all the contemporary sounds of clanging cymbals there was a harmony uniting certain of these essays that rang true to my experience. I recall a distinguished theologian from the University of Chicago who came to Southern Methodist University in the sixties to help celebrate the publication of Schubert Ogden's *Christ Without Myth*, saying, "Deep down inside, each one of us wants to be orthodox." That struck me as a remarkable concession, coming as it did from a very liberal theologian. However, if it is true that deep down everyone "wants to be orthodox," why is it that there is so much apparent evidence to the contrary? One thinks, for example, of the well-publicized Jesus Seminar and the work of one of its prominent members Dominic Crossan. The latter, on dubious grounds, regards a second century "Gospel of Peter" as in some respects a more reliable gospel than any the Church has included in its canon. While Crossan finds considerable authentic Jesus material in the church's gospels, and in his own way is a case in point that deep down we all want to be orthodox, his idiosyncratic judgment that one stratum of the Gospel of Peter served as the source for all the canonical passion narratives serves to skew his portrait of Jesus.

One can also mention the Society of Biblical Literature Presidential address by James M. Robinson who concluded his presentation with the claim that there are now two ways to understand the origins of Christianity. There is that understanding which comes through a scientific reconstruction of early Egyptian Christianity largely based upon the Nag Hamadi manuscripts. Then there is another understanding which comes through a study of the New Testament. Each of these understandings, said Robinson, is equally valid.

Over the past seventeen years, I have attempted to live in accordance with the notion that "study of the Bible as literature and study of the Bible as scriptural canon can and should advance together."[1] This has become an increasingly difficult balancing act. As the editor of this volume, I continue to walk that tight rope.

The difficulty I face increases each year as leading advocates of the practice of studying the Bible as literature become ever more insistent that a distinction between canonical and non-canonical literature has lost all meaning. This insistence is based largely on a lack of understanding of how and why the biblical canon was formed, and is bound up with a tendency to blend the ideology of civil religion with the theology of the Church. The failure of scholars to recognize the extent to which they remain indentured to an outdated and bastardized critical tradition handed down from highly trained nineteenth century university-based servants of state *interesse* is a major factor leading to "false consciousness" in contemporary theological and biblical scholarship[2]. In other words, those like Holtzmann who were consecrated as saints by their admiring and dependent progeny (e.g. Kümmel) were not in fact saints, at least not so far as the reliability of their most esteemed work is concerned[3].

On the night Jesus was delivered up, by asking his disciples to remember his words and deeds on that occasion, he took a step that set in motion the survival of a humanly imperfect and yet divinely guaranteed record of his teaching and saving death, which record in developed forms comes to expression in the Church's four gospels, all of which tell a story not told in any but these four gospels. This story represents the unfolding of God's salvific purpose for the nations as Jesus appropriated and enfleshed it in and for himself and his followers from "Moses and the Prophets," focusing on Isaiah and within that book particularly on chapter 53.

There is nothing surprising about the fact that Jesus has been subjected to all sorts of historical scrutiny beginning with the Hellenistic opponents of Christianity and continuing through the Age of Enlightenment up to our own times, culminating with Bultmann's judgment that the Lord's Supper, one of the definitive and most firmly attested traditions of the Church, is a "cult legend." This is a natural consequence of the fact that God has truly become a man and thus had to become the subject of historical investigation and be made vulnerable to all the vagaries of human skepticism[4]. We will never know how many academic blunders have been committed by unwitting scholars in the name of being "rigorously scientific," which often means just being free to advocate, with little or no concern for the consequences, any conclusion, however unlikely, if only it serves to demonstrate that the scholar is open to conclusions which work against the interests of faith. This, I take it, is close to what Durwood Foster has in mind when he writes about historiography as a discipline from which faith may expect both positive clarification as well as *threatening obfuscation* of its essential concerns [underlining mine W.R.F.].

The nineteenth century quest for the historical Jesus started out with great optimism to find the real Jesus behind the crust of ecclesiastical dogma. But this quest ended with a Jesus who was inadequate either to sustain faith or to explain its origin. For awhile many German New Testament scholars advocated simply explaining the Church's kerygma, while avoiding the problem of the historical Jesus not only as an impossible but also as a theologically illegitimate enterprise. Yet, most English-speaking scholars never gave up on the need for researching the historical Jesus. Eventually, within some circles of German New Testament scholarship the quest for the historical Jesus reemerged in the form of a "New Quest." However, the advocates of this New Quest (which quickly found its champions in the English-speaking world), realized that all the documents about Jesus are expressions of the faith of the early Church and that one must take this into account in any historical inquiry. Nevertheless, many representatives of the New Quest have tried to by-pass the faith of the Church and have attempted to understand the New Testament documents without even conditionally appropriating the faith of the New Testament authors.

In fact, it is the historical method itself that requires that one try to approximate the "world" of an author in order to understand the writer's intention in writing the document[5]. If the researcher is not tuned-in to the faith of the author, that person is similar to a tone-deaf person who tries to understand and evaluate a piece of music[6]. Thus, for many of its representatives the New Quest ended in a similar fiasco as had the old Liberal Quest: the New Questers created a Jesus who resembled only too well the world (and the intentions) of the researcher and had very little to do with the historical figure of Jesus of Nazareth.

What distinguishes the essays in this volume, is the effort of their authors to take seriously the faith of the Early Church as a hermeneutical tool that tunes-in the researcher to an understanding of the teaching, the deeds, the suffering, death and resurrection of Jesus. Of course the historians in this volume have a great deal of regard for historical criticism: they recognize their duty to ascertain—with appropriate degrees of probability—the historicity of what pertains to the figure of Jesus of Nazareth. However, they are all open to the larger perspective of faith in which the enigma of the full figure of Jesus, with all its historical components included, receives its intelligibility and significance.

The essays in this volume by Brian Hebblethwaite, Klaas Runia, R. T. France, Nikolaus Lobkowicz, James Dunn, Earle Ellis, David Martin, and Paul Johnson, were all originally included among the larger set of papers shown to me be Varghese. A paper by the late C. F. D. Moule was also included, but by special arrangement with his permission another of his essays, more appropriate to the editor's vision for the volume was substituted. The essays by Peter Stuhlmacher, Ben F. Meyer, Martin Hengel, and Roch Kereszty were commissioned by Varghese on the recommendation of the editor. Three years were spent negotiating the publication of the resulting set of essays with different university presses . Final editorial approval was given by a distinguished Catholic university press, but on the grounds of financial stringency, the "limited readership" for the volume dictated a negative publishing decision. Meanwhile, the public need for the anthology was growing with each passing year. Finally the decision was made. We would abandon our search for a university press publisher and return to our original plan to publish the essays as an edition of *Truth*.

But now there was a further reason for delay. The Jesus Seminar at long last published its *magnum opus, The Five Gospels*. Its considerable merits not withstanding, this book so fully documents the impasse among the adherents of so-called "standard" gospel criticism, that it occurred to Varghese to suggest that N. T. Wright be asked to assess critically for our anthology the work of the Jesus Seminar. The editor agreed.

Meanwhile, the editor turned to Durwood Foster for a contribution. Foster is a systematic theologian who has long been interested in the question of the relevance of the historical Jesus for Christian faith. For many years he has played a leading role in theological circles on the west coast of the United States where the Jesus Seminar, though drawing strength from elsewhere, finds significant support. As one would expect from a theologian whose vocation calls upon him to identify as much consensus as possible in contemporary biblical exegesis for the sake of providing theological guidance to the Church, Foster's perception of the Jesus Seminar is considerably different from that of N. T. Wright. Foster's own intellectual history is influenced by the experience of the Church on the western side of the Atlantic more than is that of N. T. Wright, who responsibly represents the life of the Church on the eastern side of that great divide while maintaining a lively dialogue with scholars in Canada and the United States. While Foster is well read in European theology, his orientation is also deeply sensitized by inter-faith dialogue, especially with Buddhists. His essay complements and supplements in a meaningful way the majority view of most of the contributors whose theological roots are more European. None of this is intended to blunt the trenchant criticism of the methodology of the Jesus Seminar made by N. T. Wright The essays by Wright and Foster do not contradict one another; they serve to put the reader in a position to make a more balanced evaluation of the Jesus Seminar than if the reader had only one or the other to go by.

Finally, a paper read at the AAR/SBL meetings in Chicago in November 1994 by Adrian Leske caught the attention of the editor. With Leske's agreement his work has been included. This paper puts a certain finishing touch on an underlying argument that serves to unite the volume as a whole, an argument that both points to and presupposes the unity of the Bible.

All essays in this volume have been given their respective places out of a concern to enhance the value of each. The volume closes with an essay that gathers up into itself much of what is of enduring value in the volume as a whole. It is not a summary essay. It is, however, well suited for pointing thoughtful readers forward to work yet to be done.

I am convinced that each reader who takes sufficient time will find many hours of rewarding reading in this anthology. Each author has his own distinctive contribution to make. Doubtless many readers, for reasons of their own, will read these essays in varying orders. But those who seek to understand the volume as a whole, as a book that has been put together with a purpose, will not ignore how this book begins and ends, and will also read each essay with some consideration for its context (i.e. what precedes it and follows it in the volume as a whole). For example, "Christ and the Ideologies" has been deliberately placed before "The Five Gospels," so that the reader can be sensitized to the role of ideology in the Jesus Seminar. At the same time, I have intentionally placed Foster's essay immediately after that by N. T. Wright so that the reader can have the benefit of two quite different perceptions of the work of the Jesus Seminar back-to-back so to say.

The reader has every right to ask how an editor who rejects the priority of Mark and the existence of Q can endorse essays by authors who continue to accept these ideas. The answer is that in contrast to the results of the Jesus Seminar, whose members' work is profoundly dependent upon these ideas, the essays in this anthology are free from any decisive dependence upon either the theory of Marcan priority or belief in the existence of Q. For example, R. T. France, in his effort to trace the development in New Testament christology, makes no attempt to deal with Q. By way of contrast, members of the Jesus Seminar, like Crossan, make Q basic to what they have to say about New Testament christology[7].

The solid historical achievements of the New Testament scholars contributing to this anthology provide a consideration that favors following a methodological procedure which avoids relying on the Two Source research paradigm to the extent it would be relied on were the critic confident of its validity.

Prof. James Robinson, has a point when his position leads him to say that Q is the most important Christian document we have. For if the Q, which he and his colleagues are so painstakingly reconstructing, ever actually existed and was received as scripture by some early Christians, then it should be an early source that can take us back to Jesus in a very significant manner. In this case, the absence of any emphasis upon the death and resurrection of Jesus in Q presents a special problem for anyone who is a serious student of Christian origins and at the same time wants to advocate the reliability of the Two Source hypothesis. The facts hardly fit the hypothesis. For example, the very early pre-Pauline tradition that Paul received and passed on to his churches contradicts the conclusions reached by those who reconstruct an image of the early Jesus from their study of Q and Thomas[8].

This is not a trendy anthology. Even with the timely essays by N.T. Wright and Durwood Foster, no claim is made that the reader of this anthology is being brought up-to-date as of the year of publication. Nor does this volume belong to the "end of the century" genre, where authors are invited to review a period of time which only artificially relates to the life of the Church (despite my reference to the third millennium in the opening paragraph of this introduction). As the essays of Brian

Hebblethwaite and others make clear, in important respects this is an anthology of essays that takes the measure of a long-term crisis for Christianity, a crisis centering on the question of the reliability of Church teaching. Hebblethwaite takes us back to 1977 with the publication of **The Myth of God Incarnate**, and then on back to 1921 with the Girten Conference. Nikolaus Lobkowicz takes us back to 1941 with Rudolph Bultmann's famous lecture on de-mythologizing the Bible and then on back to Hegel. Durwood Foster takes us back to 1892 with Martin Kähler's work and then on back to Schleiermacher's hermeneutical lectures of 1827. And so it is with many of our authors.

The point is that taken together the authors of these essays wish us to see the present crisis of skepticism within its historical context. How far back they go, in their effort to give the reader a proper historical perspective, varies from author to author. Some go back to the period preceding World War I, others go back behind Hegel to Herder and behind the Germans to Descartes, Spinoza, and Hume. This is a very rich collection of essays. The overall argument is well grounded, and it amounts to this: the evidence properly assessed supports the view that, as from the beginning, Christians are prepared to give reasons for the faith they profess. Christians disagree to be sure. And this set of authors may not have everything right. But the special merit of this anthology is that it serves to indicate where the weight of evidence lies on the main question before us: "Was the death of Jesus redemptive, and does the message of that redemption remain the central message of the Church, and the world's best hope?"

Modern skepticism has a long history not unrelated to the kind of questioning to which Christian doctrine has been subjected from critics since the second and third centuries. There is always the temptation to think that the crisis in our own day is worse than those which have come before. But that appears unlikely. For example, there was a time when it was seriously argued that Jesus never existed. But as Paul Johnson notes, few would make that claim today. Why not? The answer is given in these essays. There is sound historical evidence not only for his existence but also for much more. How much more? And how does the more that we can know bear on the question of christology? As these essays indicate, what can be known today serves to correct contemporary error and to move the Church forward in the direction of a more adequately orthodox christology, improved in its formulation and enriched by the experience and reflection of exegetes, theologians, church historians, historians of doctrine, and sociologists, both men and women[9].

In order to give the reader a proper perspective it is important to emphasize that the scope of this anthology is limited. For example, it is not enriched by the experience and reflection of modern experts in moral theology, practical theology, liturgy, feminism or racism not to speak of ecology. That calls for another volume of essays which will spell out how sound worship, pastoral work, ethics and politics flow from the Church's christology. We have attempted to attend to first things. We have struck at the root of the problem. If the reigning christology which informs the homily is unsound, the homily will be unsound, and there will be no basis for Christian hope. This underscores the need for this book, its limitations not withstanding. A moral theology based upon an inadequate christology can only sow confusion.

While the interests of faith in Jesus of Nazareth have brought together in this anthology scholars of various theological traditions, the converging results of their work may confirm a real, though imperfect, ecclesial unity among them. The energizing center of all ecumenical work is, after all, our common faith in Christ.

## NOTES

1. cf. Farmer in "Symposium on Biblical Criticism," *Theology Today*, January 1977, p. 361.
2. cf. Farmer. "The Social History of Marcan Priority," *The Gospel of Jesus: the Pastoral Relevance of the Synoptic Problem*. Westminster/ John Knox, 1994.
3. cf. Meijboom, Hajo Uden. "An Appraisal of Holtzmann's Contribution," *A History and Critique of the Origin of the Marcan Hypothesis 1835-1866.: A Contemporary Report Rediscovered*, John J. Kiwiet (trans.). Mercer University Press, 1993. See also, Stoldt, Hans Herbert. *Geschichte und Kritik der Markus-hypothese*. Vandenhoeck & Ruprecht, 1977. English translation by Donald L. Niewyk, *History and Criticism of the Marcan Hypothesis*. Mercer University Press, 1980. David Peabody answers the attempt of C. M. Tuckett to defend the work of Holtzmann in "Chapters in the History of the

Linguistic Argument for Solving the Synoptic Problem....," *Jesus, the Gospels and the Church*. E. P. Sanders (ed.). Mercer University Press, 1987, p. 47-67.

4. From an orthodox perspective, one might remark that it can appear to be a strange and rarely considered result of the Incarnation that the Son of God, when he became human, delivered himself not only into the hands of the Pharisees, Saducees and Roman authorities, but—what at times may appear even more humiliating—into the hands of scholars and, in particular, of historians.

5. cf. D. Farkasfalvy. "In Search of a 'Post-Critical Method' for Biblical Interpretation of Catholic Theology," *Communio* 13, 1986, p. 288-307.

6. cf. D. Farkasfalvy, *ibid.*.

7. In my opinion, there is no important point made by any of the authors in this anthology that depends upon Mark having been the first gospel or upon there ever having been a Q source. On the other hand, some of the most important points that are made by the authors of these essays would be significantly strengthened by any source hypothesis that dispenses with Q and/or recognizes the foundational character of Matthew. For example, the case is argued in several of these essays that, contrary to what Bultmann and others have concluded, christology begins with Jesus himself. This case can be strengthened if one is able to dispense with Q, and if one can accept the Gospels of Matthew and Luke as more basic for understanding the earliest stage of Christian history than is the Gospel of Mark.

8. That there is a problem for the adherents of the Two-Source hypothesis at this point is attested by the fact that reputable scholars like John Kloppenborg, Migaku Sato and Werner Kelber have addressed the topic in writing.

9. When I consider the magnitude of the task of doing justice to all that is important going on in the world of theological scholarship today, this editor is chagrined and humbled by the fact that none of the contributions to this volume comes directly from the growing ranks of the "excluded" who until now have had little influence on the christological discussion witnessed to in this anthology. As the essay by Durwood Foster makes clear, this is a reality that is certain to give way to change as the voices of the oppressed become ever more articulate and ever more powerful. I think particularly of voices I have personally heard and taken to heart, those of Gustavo

Gutierrez, Elsa Tamez, Jon Sobrino, Teresa Okure, James Cone, Elaine Wainwright, Luise Schottroff, Elisabeth Schuessler-Fiorenza, Cain Felder and many others perhaps less well known, but no less worthy to be heard. When the voices of these theologians are heard sympathetically and taken into account in the ongoing dialogue, I am convinced that the weight of their scholarship will in balance in new and unexpected ways serve to strengthen the case for the essential reliability of the New Testament witness. By way of contrast, I view the path being courageously pioneered by the most prominent Thomas/Q scholars as a railroad disappearing into a desert of contemporary gnosticism.

# 1

# THE MYTH AND TRUTH DEBATE

## Brian Hebblethwaite

The stir caused, in 1977, by the publication of **The Myth of God Incarnate** was in some respects surprising, in others not so surprising. It was surprising in that advocacy of a non-incarnational Christology was hardly a new thing in the theological or even in the wider Christian world. Papers read at the Girton Conference of the Modern Churchmen's Union in 1921 had advanced very similar views, and a number of post-second-world-war books on the person and work of Jesus Christ, putting forward what came to be known as a 'degree' Christology, already pointed in the same direction. And some strands of popular Christianity, appealing to Jesus primarily as a teacher and an example, had for a long time provided grass-roots support for playing down the divinity of Jesus Christ as an essential element in Christian faith.

On the other hand, the reaction was not surprising, given the publicity with which **The Myth of God Incarnate** was launched, bringing to a much wider audience than, say, that of those who knew about the Girton Conference of 1921, the fact of Christian theological rejection of the classical Christian doctrine of the Incarnation. It was also not surprising, given the importance accorded to the doctrine of the Incarnation in Anglican theology at least since the time of Liddon and Gore. Bishop Stephen Sykes, formerly of Cambridge University, has drawn attention to the fact that this Anglican incarnational theology was very much a late nineteenth century and twentieth century affair; but I doubt if we should really think of it in such restricted terms, even if the doctrine of the Incarnation was not emphasised so much in earlier times and in other communions, where other doctrines, such as that of justification, were given the central place. After all, the Christologies of Luther and Calvin, to say nothing of Aquinas, were firmly incarnational and firmly within the classical tradition.

One of the striking things about the theological, critical, response to **The Myth of God Incarnate**, certainly in England, was the wide range of theological and ecclesiastical backgrounds from which the critics of **The Myth** came. **The Truth of God Incarnate**, to which I contributed, contained essays by evangelicals, central Churchmen, a liberal and a Roman Catholic. The seven critics (of whom again I was one) matched against the seven authors of **The Myth** in the Birmingham colloquium which led to **Incarnation and Myth: the Debate Continued** were all scholars schooled in biblical and doctrinal criticism. It could hardly have been less like a conservative backlash. And it is precisely the non-fundamentalist critical response to **The Myth** which I wish to describe and take a little further.

First let me offer a thumb-nail sketch of the kind of position advanced in **The Myth**. There were of course some marked differences between the authors of **The Myth** themselves, between the historical scepticism of Dennis Nineham, for example, and Don Cupitt's conviction of our ability to recapture and share the religion of Jesus. Frances Young stood out from her co-authors with her moving affirmation of the way God shares in all our sufferings, as supremely in the Cross of Jesus. Nevertheless they were all seven agreed that, despite popular misapprehensions, 'myth' was a good word to use to characterise talk of the Incarnation or of the divinity of Jesus Christ, since in their minds such talk could not possibly be literally true. Rather such talk must be interpreted as a way of bringing out the religious importance of the man Jesus to the Christian and indeed, so the majority of the authors of The Myth held, to all mankind. So 'myth' was not a negative or pejorative term. Rather, as the editor, John Hick explained, myth is a way of capturing and expressing figuratively the profound importance of the man Jesus as the supreme Mediator (or one of the supreme mediators) of God to men and women on earth.

It was clear from the book itself and from our discussions, that four factors in particular were impelling these theologians in the direction of this non-incarnational Christology. In the first place was the conviction, born of the application of historical critical methods to the New Testament writings, that the Church's traditional doctrine of the Incarnation was a later development, unsupported by the earliest texts themselves. In the second place was the suspicion that talk of one who is both God and man is incoherent, in that it attempts to combine the logically incompatible concepts of divinity and humanity. In the third place was the conviction that all that matters in Christianity, its essential features, could be secured in terms of a non-incarnational Christology. The doctrine of the Incarnation, in other words, was not a necessary part of Christian belief. And finally, there was the strong conviction, found particularly in the editor, John Hick's, own contribution, that the classical Christian doctrine of the Incarnation was a great, if not the greatest, stumbling block to the development of a viable 'global' theology of religion, that could do full justice to and give due weight to all the world religions. That this last consideration was indeed of major significance can be illustrated by the fact that soon we were all deluged with copies of a small book, entitled **About 'The Myth of God Incarnate.' An Impartial Survey of its Main Topics**, by Abdus-Samad Sharafuddin, published in Jeddah, Saudia Arabia, in 1978, welcoming ecstatically the removal, from the Christian side, of the immense barrier between Christianity and Islam, which the doctrine of the Incarnation had always been.

In this paper I wish to consider these four grounds for advancing a non-incarnational Christology, concentrating particularly on the third and the fourth.

About the first consideration, the alleged paucity of historical evidence for the belief that Jesus of Nazareth was in fact the incarnate Son of God, I shall not say much; there are New Testament scholars and historians who can assess this matter much more professionally than I can. I will simply observe that in order to present New Testament Christology in non-incarnational terms, one has to give excessive preference to initial, half-formed, reactions to the life and death of Jesus and their aftermath; one has to depreciate the insights of Paul, John of Patmos, the author of the letter to the Hebrews and the author of the fourth Gospel; and above all, one has to explain away the Resurrection. And I must add the point that I have argued elsewhere, in an essay included in my collection, **The Incarnation** (Cambridge 1987), that these questions cannot be regarded and discussed as questions of historical evidence alone. The doctrine of the Incarnation is about an event which undoubtedly had historical aspects and implications. It could not possibly be true if there were no such person as Jesus of Nazareth, if he had been of a wicked or even mediocre nature, if he had not died on a cross, if his death had not been followed by some remarkable claims and the astonishingly rapid emergence of a new faith and a new religious tradition. All these are in principle falsifiable truth-conditions of the doctrine of the Incarnation. But the Incarnation, if indeed it happened, was a

3

trans-historical act of God, a coming into history from beyond history, and, by the same token, it involved the taking of Jesus Christ, as it will the taking of us all, beyond history into the resurrection world. Now these are not historically verifiable claims. Our access to their truth cannot possibly be by historical scholarship alone. In a word, it must also be by participation in the life and worship of the Body of Christ, the Church, and by reflection on the moral, spiritual and rational sense which incarnational belief makes of the world and life in the world.

On the logical coherence of the doctrine of the Incarnation I will simply observe that in order to demonstrate incoherence, one would have to show conclusively that the concepts of God and man are logically incompatible, as are those of circle and square. Needless to say, this has not been done and cannot be done. I have to admit that my own remarks on this topic have been largely negative and agnostic. We do not have the kind of access to God's essence that would enable us to reject the possibility of his living out from a centre in his own infinite being a finite human life on earth, and of raising that finite life to be the permanent focus of divine-human encounter for all eternity.

I wish at this point to pay tribute to the book, **The Logic of God Incarnate** by T. V. Morris, which appeared in 1986. We are all in Professor Morris's debt for the rigour and clarity with which he has defended the coherence of the doctrine of the Incarnation. In particular he has put forward powerful arguments against all versions known to me of the incoherence thesis. Moreover he has produced a detailed defence of the idea that the infinite divine mind of God the Son could very well contain the finite human mind of Jesus of Nazareth, without being contained by it. On this view, the divine and human consciousnesses are consciousnesses of the same person in different modes. Of course it is only the infinite mind of God that could thus at the same time exercise its own omniscience and also channel itself through the limited cognitive powers of a human mind.

I do not think that Professor Morris has said the last word on this subject. I myself would hold that there is more to be said for the logic of reduplicative propositions, as they have been called, than Professor Morris allows. It seems to me to be preferable to say that qua divine Christ exists from all eternity, but qua human he came to be in time as Jesus of Nazareth, than to say that Jesus existed from all eternity. In other words I am not happy with Professor Morris's insistence on the indiscernibility of identicals in this unique case. Furthermore, in a later section of this paper I shall wish to argue against Professor Morris that far more is involved in the Incarnation than the containing of a human range of consciousness within the divine consciousness of God the Son. Hence I shall wish to maintain my opposition to the possibility of multiple incarnations. This point, however, is best discussed in connection with the problem of other religions, the fourth of the factors that I singled out as prompting in the authors of **The Myth** a non-incarnational Christology.

My own contribution to the myth and truth debate was chiefly concerned with the third of these factors, the view that Christianity's essential features can be maintained without the doctrine of the Incarnation. I remain convinced that this is not the case. Five key elements in the Christian religion would, I still believe, be lost to us if we were seriously and consistently to take the non-incarnational path.

The first key element that would be lost, in my opinion, is the very special and uniquely personal sense in which God reveals himself to us by coming amongst us as one of us. This closeness of God to us, his own personal presence to us this side of the divide between infinite and finite, Creator and creation, is a very precious and irreplaceable gift. Certainly, God reveals himself in many other ways, in other religions as I shall explain below, by his universal Spirit present in the created world, and at special moments to particular individuals too. But a burning bush, a figure high and lifted up, a chariot of fire, and even a still small voice, none of these things are the same as the incarnate Son, in whom the fullness of godhead dwells, full of grace and truth, embodying in person the love which is God and God's love for the world. For God comes close to us in and as this particular individual Jesus of Nazareth. It is his life, teaching and deeds, and his death and resurrection that manifest who God is, what God's character is and what his attitude to us and will for us are. It is simply no use, after the Incarnation, saying that the infinite, eternal, source of all there is is beyond personality; for he has revealed himself as personal and as love. Other religions speak of God as personal and loving, and they are right. But Jesus Christ is the person who God is and his love is God's love.

All these things would be lost if Jesus of Nazareth were one or even the greatest of the human representatives or mediators who, from their own experience of God's love, tell us about God's love. We learn more of God from God's presence and his very self than we do from words about God spoken by even his most faithful servants.

It is perfectly true that we do not see and hear and talk with Jesus of Nazareth face to face as the disciples did. But, as I shall shortly be concerned to stress, it is precisely because Jesus Christ is not solely a figure from the past but a present and living Lord that we can and do meet him through his spiritual and sacramental presence here and now. That can only be true of one who is more than just a human figure in history. Nevertheless the one whom we encounter in the Spirit now is none other than the one we read of in the Gospels. So the revelation retains for us too the intensely personal form it had for Peter and James and John.

This then is the first thing that would be lost if we decided to adopt a non-incarnational Christology: our knowledge of God in person.

The second key element that would be lost is the consequential trinitarian understanding of God that distinguishes Christian theism from all others. Once again, other contributors will be spelling out this aspect of belief in Jesus Christ as God and man. I will restrict myself to pointing out how non-incarnational Christology tends to go with virtual unitarianism, as is clear from the writings of both Professor Maurice Wiles and Professor Geoffrey Lampe, and that there are deep problems with unitarianism which demand a richer conception of deity as containing within itself relations of love given and love received. For the idea of God, modelled on an isolated individual, is deeply unsatisfactory, religiously speaking. God's love, on such a view, depends entirely upon his creation of an object to love. It makes no sense to speak of a unitarian God as being love. It is for this reason that rational theology, quite apart from revelation can speak of the need to postulate relation in God. Professor R.G. Swinburne, in a recent book, *The Christian God,* has pressed this argument further, suggesting that not only sharing but co-operating in sharing is involved in the very concept of love, and that therefore we must postulate not only two but three relational poles in the one supreme God who is Love. Be that as it may, for the whole Christian tradition, experience of Christ and of the Spirit has driven revealed theology in a firmly trinitarian direction and this too would be lost if we were to demythologise the Incarnation.

The second thing that would be lost, therefore, is our understanding of God as, in himself, love.

The third key element that would be lost is the conviction that Jesus Christ is alive and experienced today as a living Lord, encountered in prayer and sacrament, and with whom we are one, here and now, in his Body the Church. This sense of the presence of Christ to the believer is a great deal more than belief that Jesus of Nazareth, like all God's personal creatures, is raised through death to the life of heaven. Not even the most catholic faith in the communion of saints and prayers for the dead is comparable, in existential force, to the conviction of countless Christians down the ages that they can worship Christ and pray to him as a real presence in the bread and wine of the Eucharist, in the heart of the believer at prayer, and in the neighbour's need. It requires incarnational Christology to enable us to believe that God's life and omnipresence are mediated to us through Christ's risen life and omnipresence by his Spirit. All this is of the essence of historical Christianity.

The third thing that would be lost, therefore, is experience of Christ as the living Lord.

The fourth key element that would be lost is the peculiarly Christian understanding of the way in which our God confronts and overcomes the world's suffering and evil. It is one thing to hold that God is with us in the depths of suffering, grieving over the pains of his children and bestowing the resources of his Spirit to enable us to bear and overcome the evil. It is another thing to hold that God subjects himself to suffering and dereliction, in letting himself, in the person of the Son, be crucified. For, despite Christianity's insistence on man's own responsibility and freedom for what he does and for what he makes of God's world, the Creator is, ultimately speaking, responsible for the world's being and nature, including our vulnerability to suffering and evil. An incarnational Christology enables us to see the Creator taking that responsibility upon himself and rendering himself vulnerable to the world's ills in a way that goes far beyond sympathy and help. Moreover it is by this self-identification with us in human suffering and death that God draws us into oneness with himself and turns us into fellow heirs and inheritors of the Kingdom. I do not wish to defend a substitutionary theory of the Atonement at this point, since it makes no moral sense to say that God requires a death before he can forgive. On the contrary, God's forgiving love is manifested and acted out in the Passion and Death of Christ, on the incarnational view. However, there is a sense in which Christ does stand in our place, taking the burden of suffering and evil on himself and drawing its sting. There is a vicarious self- sacrificial act here by our God himself, which wins our response of gratitude, repentance and faith, and opens up the way to our sanctification in and through the gift of the Spirit of God who is at the same time the Spirit of this self-same, now risen, Christ.

So the fourth thing that would be lost, if we decided to adopt a non-incarnational Christology, is our ability to see Christ's cross as God's cross in our world, whereby both God's own moral credibility and his way of overcoming evil is acted out and revealed.

The fifth key element that would be lost is the eschatological conviction of the Christians that, in the end, it is in and through the risen Christ that God will sum up all things in the consummated life of heaven. Thus Dante's vision at the climax of the **Paradiso** of a human figure in the heart of God, symbolises Christianity's recognition of Jesus Christ as permanently now the human face of God, who will be God to us and God with us — Emmanuel — to all eternity. Similarly, in the more social eschatological imagery of the communion of saints and the perfected Kingdom of God, the Christian hope envisages a Kingdom where Christ is King and pictures the saints as gathered round the Lamb upon the throne. I shall return to this question of the eschatological centrality of the risen Christ for all creation, when I turn to the final factor behind the non-incarnational Christology of **The Myth**, the problem of other religions. For the moment I am drawing attention to the way in which Christianity's Christ-centred eschatology would be completely lost if we take the non-incarnational path.

A Christianity without these five key elements — our personal acquaintance with God in Christ, our understanding of the trinitarian God who is Love, our experience of Jesus as the living Lord, our participation in God's overcoming of evil by the Cross, and our conviction of the eschatological centrality of the risen Christ — would be a very different Christianity from that which we have inherited from nearly two thousand years of Church history. It is hard to believe that the essence of Christianity can be maintained in non-incarnational terms.

I turn now to the problem of Christianity and other religions - the forth main factor impelling the authors of **The Myth of God Incarnate** and especially its editor, to renounce the traditional Christian doctrine of the Incarnation. I have already mentioned the fact that this doctrine constitutes a major stumbling block for our Muslim — and, we may add, our Jewish — friends, and certainly, if Christian incarnational soteriology is held to imply the condemnation of men and women of other faiths to eternal loss, a sense of moral outrage at this doctrine is entirely justified. John Hick is quite right to say that the God of love revealed in Jesus Christ cannot possibly be thought to have restricted his saving encounter with mankind to a single stream in history or to a single segment of the human race. But it does not follow from this perfectly valid point that the Christian doctrine of the Incarnation must be abandoned. For it is in no way entailed by the doctrine of the Incarnation that, other religions of mankind have no revelatory or salvific worth, or that their adherents are lost eternally. On the contrary, to draw such a conclusion shows an extraordinary blindness to *what* has been revealed in Jesus Christ.

Certainly it is incumbent upon Christian theology to give a plausible account, from its own incarnational perspective, of God's dealings with the human race throughout history and all over the globe. We need to see the religions of mankind not only as man's constant search for God but as the providential means by which God makes himself known to all his human creatures. There is no need for Christians to depreciate the faith and spirituality nurtured in the various religions, partial and incomplete as all historically and culturally moulded forms of the religious life undoubtedly are. But if the history of religions has in fact reached a climax in the Incarnation of God's Son, within the matrix of a specially chosen people and tradition of faith, and if that Incarnation has the moral, spiritual and rational force that I have claimed for it, initiating a new level of union between God and man, with implications for all eternity, then what a Christian global theology has to do is not to go back on its own best insights but offer an all- embracing account of the significance of Jesus Christ for all men and women, including men and women of other faiths. Attempts at such an inclusivist view of Christ have already been made — by Karl Rahner, for example, with his theory of 'anonymous Christians.' We are to look for Christ, the eternal Son and universal Logos of creation, already at work in other contexts than that of explicit recognition and response. I think there is some merit in this theory. For my own part, I hope for further opportunities beyond death, in further phases of God's creative plan, for those whose experience of God has been shaped in other streams of life, to grow into the knowledge and love of Christ as indeed *the* human face of God. That is to say, I look for an eschatological resolution of the problem of Christianity and other faiths.

It is in this connection that I find myself wanting to defend the uniqueness of the Incarnation and to reject the possibility of multiple incarnations, left open by Professor Morris. I have argued above that the man Jesus is the human face of God. Now God the Son is not two faced or many-faced. His very self and essence all divine were present amongst us in and as the man Jesus. It was not only the mind or consciousness of Jesus that was contained in the infinite mind of God the Son. His character and personality as well manifested in human terms the very nature of God as Love. Two or more different human persons could not *be* the one divine Son. Christians believe that the course of human history was shaped and moulded in such a way as to allow this unique self-presentation of the divine within the structures of creation to take place. Moreover, as also argued above, the risen Christ took his humanity for ever into God and remains the human face of God for all eternity. His eschatological significance, as well as his revelatory significance, rules out the possibility of multiple incarnations.

If, as Professor Morris suggests, the Son of God could have become incarnate more than once, but as a matter of fact came only once, then the Christian inclusivist global theology of religions, adumbrated above, comes under very great strain. Its picture of the whole history of religions, reaching its climax in the Incarnation, whose effects are then held to be universal and all-embracing in their scope, loses its point.

For, if the asymmetry which the Incarnation, including its preparation and effect, introduces into the history of religions was not a necessary feature of God's fullest revelation and gift of himself for our salvation, then the question arises, why did he only come once? We can only make sense of the fact of the many non-incarnational religions in the history of mankind if we suppose that the Incarnation was necessarily unique and that therefore other modes of access to the divine — inevitably, on this view, less full and complete than that of Jesus Christ — have been vouchsafed to those segments of humanity which, in the nature of the case, could not be receivers of the incarnate one during his earthly sojourn. The scandal of particularity is only intelligible on the supposition that that is how things had to be, if God himself, in the person of his Son, was to come amongst us as a man.

The myth and truth debate has had the very positive and beneficial effect of making us reflect on the centrality and significance of the doctrine of the Incarnation in the Christian religion. I have tried in this essay to explain its centrality and significance. We can be grateful to the authors of **The Myth** for giving us the opportunity to think these matters out and to see, with fresh eyes, how central and significant that doctrine indeed is.

# Crisis in Christology

# 2

# "CONTINENTAL" CHRISTOLOGIES

## Klaas Runia

The history of theology in some ways resembles the motion of the pendulum of a clock. The one moment it goes in one direction, but when it cannot go further it returns and moves in the other direction. I was reminded of this image when I looked again at what happened in the doctrine of Christ during this century.

In the first quarter of the century Liberal Theology was dominant. In its final consequences, as we find them e.g. in the theology of Adolf Harnack, the Son dropped entirely out of the Gospel. In his book, **What is Christianity?**, Harnack condensed the whole Gospel into one sentence: 'The Gospel, as Jesus proclaimed it, has to do with the Father only, not with the Son.'[1] Naturally, the pendulum could not go any further here and so we see it return and go in the other direction.

This becomes particularly clear in the **Church Dogmatics** of Karl Barth. In the very first part he states that a church dogmatics must, of course, be christologically determined. In fact, dogmatics can regard itself only as 'fundamentally Christology.'[2] In this first part, which deals with the doctrine of the Word of God, Barth takes his starting point in the central statement of the Christology of the Ancient Church, that is, the belief that God becomes one with man in Jesus Christ, who is 'very God and very man.'[3] He fully accepts the decisions of Chalcedon and their implications for the doctrine of the Trinity. In this first part he does not go beyond Chalcedon, since here he fully concentrates on the person of Christ. Later on, in the fourth part of his **Church Dogmatics**, which deals with the doctrine of reconciliation, the approach is somewhat different, because now he continually speaks of the person and the work of Christ in their unbreakable inter-relationship. Although even now he fully adheres to Chalcedon, the emphasis changes. He no longer speaks of Jesus Christ as very God and very man, full stop, but as the One 'who is (1) very God, that is, the God who humbles Himself, and therefore is the reconciling God, (2) very man, that is, man exalted and therefore reconciled by God, and (3) in the unity of the two the guarantor and witness of our atonement.'[4] One could say: Chalcedon loses its abstractness, because the two natures are related to the two states and the three offices. He is very God and very man in his mediatorial work. Yet even so Chalcedon itself is fully adhered to.

In the years immediately after World War II the pendulum begins to swing again into the other direction. In his programme of demythologizing Bultmann concentrates everything upon the cross of Jesus, which is the great 'eschatological event' in which the divine redemption took place. The person of Jesus Himself, however, fully disappears behind the horizon. As early as 1926 Bultmann had already stated: 'We can, strictly speaking, know nothing of the personality of Jesus.' But this does not really matter, for it is not the historical Jesus that concerns us, but the 'kerygmatic Christ.'

Again, as was to be expected, a reaction started, this time among Bultmann's own former students. In 1954 Ernst Kasemann wrote an article on 'The problem of the historical Jesus,'[6] in which he accused his former teacher of docetism! Kasemann and some of his colleagues believed that it is possible to penetrate into the pre-Easter stratum of the Gospels, where we can discover 'Jesus' own implicit christological selfunderstanding.'[7] Nearly all the post-Bultmannians tried to put this selfunderstanding into one comprehensive formula. Ebeling spoke of Jesus' 'faith,' Fuchs of his 'behaviour' (German: Verhalten), Paul Van Buren of his 'freedom.' But whatever formula they used, they were all agreed that it is possible to say something about the historical Jesus and his selfunderstanding. They were also agreed that, if we want to develop a Christology, we have to start with the historical Jesus Himself. Or to put it in another way: we have to start 'from below.'

This New Quest for the Historical Jesus, however, even though it was a great improvement compared with Bultmann's view, did not really proceed beyond the rather vague notion that the Christ of faith is the man Jesus of Nazareth in whom God has acted decisively for man's redemption. The question still remained open: But who is He? Is He what the New Testament proclaims Him to be: the Son of God? Is He what the ancient creeds profess Him to be: *vere Deus* and *vere homo*? These questions were bound to come back. And indeed the pendulum started to swing again.

One of the first to tackle these questions in a new way was Wolfhart Pannenberg in his book **Jesus - God and man**.[9] I have no time even to summarize his argument.[10] It must suffice to say that his Christology, which starts 'from below,' through the perspective of the resurrection and seen in the context of Jewish apocalyptic, comes very close to the classical doctrine of Christ and even issues in a full-fledged doctrine of the Trinity. The same is true of Jurgen Moltmann's Christology, which he has expounded in his book **The Crucified God**.[11] Again there is no time to summarize the content of the book.[12] His main questions are: who is God in the cross of the Christ who is abandoned by God, and what does this mean for the liberation of man in general? From this perspective he develops his Christology within the framework of the trinitarian being of God. It appears to be a Christology that proceeds from the starting point of Chalcedon: Jesus is vere Deus and vere homo. At the same time he goes beyond Chalcedon. To him the cross is more than the revelation of the Trinity; it is itself a trinitarian event, that is, an event within the very Trinity itself: God is forsaken by God.

## Alternative Christologies

Unfortunately we must limit ourselves to these few brief remarks. But it is clear, I trust, that both Pannenberg and Moltmann still move within the framework of Chalcedon and of the classic trinitarian conception of God. In this sense they are *not* representative of the new mood in European theology, which became manifest at the end of the sixties and throughout the seventies, and was evidenced by a clear and consistent rejection of Chalcedon and its doctrine of the two natures of Christ united in the person of the Son, that is, the second Person of the Trinity. The starting point of the new Christologies is that Jesus is man, and no more than man. H. Berkhof, who himself is a representative of this new approach, mentions three objections to the solution of Chalcedon: (1) the doctrine of the Trinity here moves in the direction of tri-theism; (2) the historical Jesus, conceived an-hypostatically, that is, without a human person as the ground of his existence, begins alarmingly to look like God dressed up as a man or like a composite being, half God and half man; (3) this speculative doctrine cannot possibly be the content of the church's proclamation, the less so because this speculative accentuation is missing in the proclamation of the New Testament itself. For all these reasons it is necessary to look for an alternative solution.

It is striking to see that this search for an alternative Christology is going on in both Roman Catholic and Protestant theology. In fact, there seems to be a growing consensus at this very point. In spite of the individual differences, they are all agreed that we have to take our starting point in the man Jesus (in other words, we have to start 'from below') and that we have to take his true humanity absolutely and utterly seriously.

The Roman Catholic Dutch theologian Piet Schoonenberg acted as a pioneer in this new Christological venture.[13] His starting point is a twofold conviction: (1) Jesus is a unity in Himself; (2) He is a real man. At the same time, however, He is quite different from us because of his unique relationship with God. But what kind of relationship is it? Chalcedon answered: He is God and man at the same time, the Godhead being the ground of existence of the humanity. Schoonenberg rejects this, for then Jesus would not a real man. We should not think in terms of God *and* man, but of God *in* man. Jesus as the Christ is the man who is completely filled with and guided by the indwelling Word and therefore is 'the eschatological man,' who already stands in the final consummation and is the bringer of salvation, life, freedom, love and sonship.[14] It is obvious that this Christology is quite the opposite of that of Barth, Pannenberg and Moltmann. Here all emphasis is on the humanity of Christ. Whatever we may have to say about Christ (and we have to say a great deal about Him, according to Schoonenberg), principally and essentially He is and remains man. The basic thrust of Chalcedon with its two natures in the one divine person is rejected. Jesus Christ is a unity in his absolute humanity. His uniqueness is found in the unique indwelling of the Word of God in his humanity, but this does not break up the essential unity of his humanity. Schoonenberg is one of the most outspoken Roman Catholic advocates of this alternative Christology, but he is certainly not the only one. Several other leading Roman Catholic theologians of our day move along similar lines. It may not always be so obvious in their case, because they also try, at least formally, to adhere to the formulations of the ancient councils, but they can do this only by a vigorous process of reinterpretation. In most cases they do not really differ from Schoonenberg. I am thinking here in particular of the Christologies of Edward Schillebeeckx (a former colleague of Schoonenberg in the Roman Catholic University of Nijmegen)[15] and of Hans Küng.[16] Both are very influential, for their books have gone through many editions and have been translated into various languages, including English. Both Christologies have much in common. They both start 'from below,' but at some stage encounter the divine mystery which is manifest in Jesus' words and deeds. They both try to do justice to the teaching of Chalcedon and even claim to succeed in this, yet they do not really go beyond a functional, that is, revelational Christology. The most Schillebeeckx can say is that 'in the man Jesus the revelation of the divine and the disclosure of the true, good and truly happy humanity perfectly coincide in one and the same person'[17] and the most Küng can say is that 'the true man Jesus of Nazareth is for faith the real *revelation* of the *one true God.*'[18] Consequently the doctrine of the Trinity is also interpreted functionally (that is, in terms of revelation) rather than essentially (that is, in terms of divine essence).

So far I have dealt with Roman Catholic theologians only, but the new approach to Christology is not restricted to them. Some of the leading Protestant theologians follow the same road and are even more outspoken. Not encumbered or inhibited by the claims of an infallible tradition, they are even more willing to reconsider the traditional Christology and venture upon new pathways.

The most important specimen of the new alternative Christology among Protestant scholars is, I believe, the book **Christian Faith** by Hendrikus Berkhof.[19] The chapter on 'Jesus the Son' is perhaps the most penetrating analysis and re-interpretation of the traditional Christology that has appeared in recent years. In the first section Berkhof states that there are actually four possible approaches in the Christology: (1) 'from behind' — here we see Jesus in line with the Old Testament; (2) 'from above' — here we see how in Him the creative Word of God becomes a historical human life; (3) 'from below' — here we see Him as human being in the context of his time; (4) 'from the future' — here we see what He brings about in the history of this world. All four approaches are necessary and complementary. Berkhof himself prefers to start 'from below,' that is, with the historical Jesus. He is well aware of the fact that historical-critical research cannot bring to light the divine mystery of Jesus the Christ, but he also believes that, if there is such a mystery, we shall come across it at some stage of our research and then we shall have to look for a different, more deeply penetrating approach. Having made this choice, Berkhof proceeds to examine the New Testament sources

**17**

and concludes that Jesus himself was convinced that in his own person the Kingdom of God's grace was already present, a conviction that rested upon his most intimate relationship with God. At this moment Berkhof switches to the approach 'from behind' and sees Jesus as the fulfillment of God's covenant with Israel: He is pre-eminently the obedient and therefore beloved covenant partner. As the true man He is the faithful covenant partner, who in his radical covenant obedience achieves the definitive, eschatological salvation for all the others. Therefore He is called the 'Son of God.' But Jesus is not simply a continuation of the old covenant with Israel. A new beginning was necessary, and so Berkhof comes to the third approach, that 'from above.' Jesus is the Son par excellence. He is that not as the fruit and climax of human religious and moral purity, but in virtue of a unique and new creative act of God. In a new creative act God Himself calls Jesus into existence as the perfect covenant partner, the New Man, the eschatological man. This man is not a composite being, partly human and partly divine. He is in every respect a human 'I' (here Berkhof fully agrees with Schoonenberg), but at the same time this human 'I' is completely (that is, to the utmost capacity and to the farthest corners of his being) and voluntarily penetrated by the divine 'I.' In Jesus we have a new union of God and man, far beyond our experience and imagination, and so we can indeed say that in Jesus God Himself comes to us, in order that He may save us by Him.

It is clear that this Christology of Berkhof is far removed from the older liberal views, which were all basically humanistic and had no place left for real salvation. For Berkhof (and all the others) Jesus is indispensable as the Saviour. In a certain way Berkhof also advocates a 'high' Christology. He can even say: 'God was in Jesus.' And yet, however 'high' the language he uses maybe, he always stops short of calling Jesus God's Son in an ontological sense. There is in Jesus a divine secret, but it is not the secret of his own divinity!

## Evaluation

Unfortunately time does not permit me to evaluate these alternative Christologies at any length or depth. It is quite obvious that they all grapple with the secret of Jesus' being, just as the Council of Chalcedon did. At the same time it is also clear that, inspite of their respect for Chalcedon, they all reject its 'solution' and opt for quite a different

Christology. What they offer is not a further explication, not even a re-interpretation of Chalcedon, but a revision of or, better still, an alternative to Chalcedon. But this raises a host of questions.

In the first place we must ask whether it is really possible to go back behind Chalcedon and even behind Nicea, and to start all over again. Admittedly, neither Nicea nor Chalcedon is a divinely revealed Word of God. Both are human attempts to express the secret of Jesus who is the Christ. The words and the terms used by these councils are not inspired nor sacrosanct. The church has never claimed that we may not say it in other words. But at the same time the church has always believed — and this is true of the whole Catholic Church in all its various branches and confessions — that the real secret of Jesus' being was described in the words of Nicea: very God and very man and that it was safeguarded in the four so-called negative statements of Chalcedon. Both the unity (the one person of the divine Son) and the duality (the two natures) were thus confessed. The question we have to put now is: is it really possible to go behind this and retain the real secret? Is it really possible to take a different road, a road that leads to a functional, revelational Christology only, without proceeding to an essential, ontological Christology?

In the second place, there is the exegetical question. Do the new alternative Christologies really do justice to the New Testament witness in its entirety? We do not deny that there is a great variety of Christological statements in the New Testament. But what is amazing is the underlying unity in all this diversity. In each document the message is that in Jesus Christ God has come to this world in order to save it. Actually *all* Christological statements in the New Testament are high. *All* writers, one way or another, put Jesus on the side of God. Paul writes to the Corinthians that God Himself is acting in the death of Christ: 'God was in Christ reconciling the world to himself' (II Cor. 5:19). In the Gospels we read that Jesus forgives sins (Mark 2:1-12; Luke 7:36-50), and the amazing fact is that He does this not 'on behalf of' God, but in his own name and on his own authority. This same absolute authority also comes through in the emphatic way he uses the word 'I.' He does not only ask people to accept his message but also his person. He urges them to acknowledge Him before men (Matt. 10:32) and to lose their life 'for his sake' (Matt. 16:25). He openly identifies Himself with God and God with Himself: 'He who receives Me, receives Him who sent Me' (Matt. 10:40). Wherever we read in the New Testament, we encounter this high

Christology. As a matter of fact, we find the highest christological state-ments already in the earliest writings, namely, the very first letters of Paul. In less than twenty years after the death and resurrection of Jesus a full-fledged Christology appears to be present already. Such a rapid development can be explained only by the impact Jesus himself must have made on his followers.[20] They must have been deeply impressed, not only by what He said and did, but also by who He was. Now it cannot be denied that the advocates of the alternative Christologies are also deeply impressed by what Jesus said and did and was. Yet they cannot really accept the high christological statements of the New Testament. Time and again they feel that they have to reinterpret them. The pas-sages that speak of Jesus' pre-existence are re-interpreted in such a way that they no longer speak of a real pre-existence. The high titles ac-corded to Jesus, in particular the title 'Son of God,' are entirely explained against the Jewish or Hellenistic background of those days and the pos-sibility that in the case of Jesus they received an altogether new mean-ing is not really considered. But can one in this way ever do justice to the New Testament witness about Jesus? Is Chalcedon, in spite of its technical and rather philosophical language, not much closer to the se-cret of Jesus as witnessed to in the New Testament? Apparently some of the authors of the new Christologies seem to be increasingly aware of this problem. It is striking that both Schoonenberg and Berkhof in later publications or in later editions try to move closer to the language of Chalcedon. Schoonenberg begins to speak of a reciprocal 'inter-penetra-tion' of the person of Jesus and of the Word.[21] In later editions of his **Christian Faith** Berkhof tries to 'upgrade' Jesus and moves increasingly in the direction of a kind of 'divinization' of Jesus. Yet they both con-tinue to reject the idea that Jesus is both God and man. Even though, according to Berkhof, Jesus' human 'I' is fully and exhaustively perme-ated by the 'I' of God and one can speak of 'a new union of God and man, far beyond our experience and imagination,' Jesus remains a man and never becomes more than a man. In other words, although Schoonenberg and Berkhof move closer to Chalcedon, the fundamental difference re-mains. It is not 'very God *and* very man,' but at the most 'very man,' fully and exhaustively permeated by 'very God.'

Finally, there is also the dogmatical question. An alternative Christology, as presented in our day, is not an 'innocent' affair. Christology is the heart of all theology, and a drastic change in this doctrine will have far-reaching consequences for the rest of our theology. I think first of all of the doctrine of the Trinity. If Jesus is only 'true man,' there is no place left for the idea that God is triune in his innermost being. At the most one can speak of an 'economic' or a 'revelational' Trinity, but one can no longer speak of an 'essential' or 'ontological' Trinity.[22] But, of course, the consequences are not limited to the doctrine of the Trinity. In his review of **The Myth of God Incarnate** John MacQuarrie rightly says: 'Christian doctrines are so closely interrelated that if you take away one, several others tend to collapse. After incarnation is thrown out, is the doctrine of the Trinity bound to go? What kind of doctrine of the atonement remains possible? Would the Eucharist be reduced simply to a memorial service? What a rewriting of creeds and liturgies, of prayer books and hymn books, even of Holy Scripture, would be demanded!'[23] But even this is not all. One could mention other points as well. If the alternative Christologies are right, we can no longer speak of Jesus as the self-revelation of God, but at the most as a revelation of God. The distinction between Jesus and Moses or the great prophets would no longer be essential, but gradual at the most.

I do indeed believe that much is at stake here. In the doctrine of Christ we are not dealing with just a theoretical problem. The Fathers of the Early Church fought the christological battle, because they believed that the Gospel itself was at stake. And I believe they were right. The divinity of Christ is not a dispensable 'extra' that has no real significance for our salvation. On the contrary, our salvation depends on it. We can be saved by God only. I do not deny that the advocates of the new alternative Christologies also see Jesus as their Saviour and Redeemer. There are no traces of the older liberal theology, that regarded Jesus only as a great Teacher and Example. Yet I also believe that this new Christology moves in a direction that can easily lead (or perhaps is even bound to lead) to such deviations. If Jesus is no longer the Eternal Son of God, who 'for us men and for our salvation came down from heaven... and was made man' (Nicene Creed), if He is only the 'true man' who is the Pioneer and Forerunner, then the deepest safeguards against a moralistic transformation of the Gospel are removed.[24]

The seriousness of the situation should not be underestimated. The present-day developments in Christology are not just variations on the classical theme, but they mean a restructuring of the entire Christian faith. The consequences are far-reaching. The message of the church will become quite different, both within and outside the church. The discussion with the synagogue and the mosque will change completely. The question must even be asked whether the church will not become one of the many movements or sects within Judaism. Of course, the new Christologies also claim that Jesus is the God-given Messiah. But some Jewish scholars are prepared to accept even this. Pinchas Lapide, for instance, is prepared to call Jesus the Messiah of the Gentiles. Admittedly, this is also as far as he is willing to go. Jesus is *not* the Messiah of the Jews. But one could nevertheless say that the main barrier has been removed. Jesus is no longer the Son of God in the ontological sense of the word. He is the eschatological prophet (Schillebeeckx), the perfected covenant man, the new man, the eschatological man (Berkhof). These are expressions pregnant with meaning. But they can easily be incorporated into Jewish thinking, without changing the essence of it. At any rate they do not exhaust what the New Testament writers tell us or what the great Councils of the ancient church confessed. One finds, as in a nutshell, the whole Christology of the New Testament in Paul's words to the Corinthians: 'The grace of our Lord Jesus Christ who, though he was rich, yet for your sake became poor, so that by his poverty you might become rich' (2 Cor.8:9). There is not a trace of mythological thinking here. The words are plain and clear: He who was rich became poor for our sake, so that by his poverty we might become rich. It was this very Christology that was upheld by the church both at Nicea and Chalcedon.

## NOTES

1. *Op.cit.*, 1901, 147. Already in his **History of Dogma** (E.T. 1900) he had severely criticized the Logos-doctrine and described it as a pagan, metaphysical invasion in the sphere of the Christian faith, by which the truly human picture of Christ is petrified and mutilated. Likewise he severely criticized the decisions of Chalcedon, in particular the bald negative statements (Vol.IV, 1961, 222).
2. Barth, *CD* I, 2, 123.
3. *Op.cit.*, 125f.
4. *Op.cit.*, IV, 1, 79.
5. R.Bultmann, **Jesus and the Word**, 1926, 147.
6. Available in English in Kasemann's **Essays on New Testament Themes**, 1964, 15-47. ,

7. Reginald H. Fuller, **The New Testament in Current Study**, 1962, 49.

8. Cf. Fuller, op.cit., 142.

9. Original German title: **Grundzuqe der Christologie**, 1964. E.T. in 1968.

10. Cf. my book **The Present-day Christological Debate**, 1984, 33-38.

11. Original German edition in 1972, E.T. in 1973.

12. Cf. my book, *op.cit.*, 38-46.

13. Cf. P.Schoonenberg, **The Christ**, 1972. The original Dutch edition dates from 1969. The second part, called 'God and Man, or God in Man' was originally prepared as a contribution to the multi-volume Roman Catholic standard work on systematic theology, called **Mysterium Salutis**, but the editorial committee rejected it asinsufficiently orthodox and replaced it by a contribution by Dietrich Wiederkehr, whose views are much more in line with those of Barth and Pannenberg.

14. Cf. my book, *op.cit.*, 48-52.

15. See his books **Jesus, the Story of a Living One**, 1974 (624 pages!); **Justice and Love, Grace and Liberation**, 1977 (904 pages!); and **Interim Story about Two Books on Jesus**, 1978 ('only' 151 pages). Cf. further my book, op.cit., 53-58 and John Bowden, **Edward Schillebeeckx - Portrait of a Theologian**, 1983.

16. See his books **On Being a Christian** 1978 (first German edition in 1974), 437ff. and **Does God Exist?** 1980 (first German edition 1978), 677ff. Cf. also my book *op.cit.*, 58-65.

17. Schillebeeckx, **Interim Report**..., 144.

18. Kung, **On Being a Christian**, 444.

19. E.T. published in 1979. The original Dutch edition was published in 1973. Berkhof was for many years professor of systematic theology in the State University of Leyden. Cf. further my book, op.cit., 71-77.

20. Cf. C.D.F.Moule, **The Origin of Christology**, 1978, 135.

21. Cf. P.J.A.M. Schoonenberg, 'Spirit Christology and Logos Christology' in *Bijdraqen* 38 (1977), 350-375. Cf. also my book, op.cit., 50ff.

22. Cf. Berkhof, op.cit., 330-337. The combination of the three names is 'a summarizing description of the covenantal event.... The Father is the divine partner, the Son the human representative, the Spirit the bond between them and therefore the bond between the Son and the sons whom he draws to the Father. Can we say then that we have here "one essence in three persons"? No, there is here one event that happens from God...'(331). Together with us God is in-

volved in a process. 'The trinitarian event arises from the very nature (essence) of God and leads to it. In that sense is the Trinity natural (essential) for God. It describes how God, according to his eternal purpose, extends and carries on in time his own life so as to share it with man. The Trinity is thus not a description of an abstract God-in-himself, but of the revealed God-with-us' (332). It is evident that Berkhof does his utmost to tie the trinitarian event to the being of God. Yet he cannot, of necessity, go beyond a 'revelational' Trinity.

23. **The Truth of God Incarnate**, edited by Michael Green, 1977, 144.
24. Cf. Schillebeeckx' personal creed in my book, *op.cit.*, 113, 114.

# 3

# AN HISTORIAN LOOKS AT JESUS

## Paul Johnson

Christianity, like the Judaism from which it sprang, is an historical religion, or it is nothing. It does not deal in myths and metaphors and symbols, or in states of being and cycles. It deals in facts. It presupposes a linear flight in time, through a real universe of concrete events. It sees humanity as marching, inexorably, from an irrecoverable past into an unprecedented future. The march is not haphazard. It proceeds according to a divine plan, in part revealed to us. Christians believe that certain other, specific historical events will occur, bringing humanity's sojourn in this world to a climax. Then, to use Shakespeare's phrase, 'time must have a stop.' Thereafter, the Christian's perception of the timeless world of eternity — the non-historical after-life — is much less clear. But the Christian notion of historical time is very definite, and central to the faith. Jesus, the son of God, was born of a virgin, at a particular time and in a specific place. He was God and man. He was crucified for our sins, but rose again the third day. The incarnation and the resurrection are not metaphors but actual, historical events. A man or woman cannot reject their historicity and remain a Christian. To accept the message of Christ, the teaching, the ethics, the example, the human perfection of Christ, is not enough. It is necessary to accept the Godhead as well as the manhood, to believe that the incarnation and the resurrection actually occurred. Without them, Christianity is nothing — it becomes a mere fantasy, a delusion.

That being so, there must inevitably be a certain tension between the study of history and Christian theology, and that tension must be particularly acute, it would seem, in the heart and mind and soul of a Christian historian, or an historian who is a Christian. Do the demands of the craft, the science of history take precedence over the requirements of the faith? Is it possible for a Christian historian to explore the truth of Christianity, to examine its specific historical claims, with the requisite degree of detachment? In the years just before and just after the First World War, it was common among historians, particularly German ones, to assert that Christian faith and true historical scholarship were incompatible, and that the sceptical and critical methods the historian must employ were inevitably destructive of the unqualified assent the Christian must make to the central claims of his religion.

It is a fact that historical scholarship, in its broadest sense, is liable to be far more destructive of religious claims than advances in the physical sciences. The conflict between exact knowledge and religious faith is epitomised and dramatised in the case of Charles Darwin and the **Origin of Species**. It was made the occasion of a celebrated debate, in 1860, at the annual meeting of the British Association for the Advancement of Science, in Oxford, when the local Bishop, Samuel Wilberforce, met the Darwinist Professor T. H. Huxley in frontal conflict. The issue was reduced to a ludicrous level by Benjamin Disraeli, who put it to the electoral public: 'Is man an ape or an angel? Now I am on the side of the angels!' But as Darwin always tried to point out in the din of argument, there was no necessary incompatibility between the truth of his theory and Christianity. He died a believer. He is buried in Westminster Abbey. The much more serious threat to religion in the 19th century came from the historical reconstruction of remote antiquity made possible by the findings of geologists and archaeologists. This was far more erosive of faith, particularly among clergymen, than anything Darwin discovered because it destroyed, beyond serious argument, the traditional or fundamentalist, chronology of the Old Testament. It was the fossil rather than evolution that undermined confidence in the Bible as the divinely-inspired source of truth — to the point when one theologian, in desperation, was driven to assert that fossils were the work, not of time, but of God, who had put them there for his own mysterious purposes! The work of demolition of the pre-historians appeared to be reinforced by ever-more critical examination of the Biblical texts, both of the Old and New Testaments, which gave them later and later datings, removing them further and further from the events they purported to describe, and presented them, not as the work of eye-witnesses and recorders of fact, but of ecclesiastical ideologues, rewriting the past for their own dogmatic purposes.

Against this background, many Christian historians lost their nerve and their judgment. An historian, above all people, ought to take a long view, to exercise the patience of one who deals not in daily headlines and mere years, but in centuries. But the Christian historians of the 19th and early 20th centuries often, alas, took a short view. An interesting case was that of William Stubbs, an excellent historian who was really the founder of the scientific study of medieval history in Oxford. But Stubbs was also the bishop of that city, and felt it his duty to limit lines of historical inquiry in the interests of religious orthodoxy. Victorian society was convulsed by Ernest Renan's brilliant and imaginative reconstruction of Jesus's life, **La Vie de Jesus,** published in 1863. Stubbs boasted, in a public lecture, of his first meeting with the popular historian John Richard Green. 'I knew,' he wrote, 'by description the sort of man I was to meet: I recognised him as he got into the (railroad) carriage, holding in his hand a volume of Renan. I said to myself, "If I can hinder, he shall not read that book." We sat opposite and fell immediately into conversation.. He came to me (at my house) afterwards, and that volume of Renan found its way into my waste-paper basket.'

This is really a pretty disgraceful story. Stubbs had never properly examined Renan's book and condemned it unread; moreover, he persuaded another historian to do likewise — one historian, as it were, corrupting another. And it was all so unnecessary, if one takes the long view! No one now takes Renan's book seriously, or indeed reads it at all, except as an historical curiosity — as much a part of the Victorian religious scene as, say, Moody and Sankey or Cardinal Newman's **Apologia pro Vita Sua**. For the study of history moves on, remorselessly, like time itself. Today's sensation becomes tomorrow's irrelevance. The bestseller of one decade becomes the embarrassment of another. The revolutionary theory which convulses the academic world gets cut down in the next age to an ironic footnote.

A Christian historian must have confidence not merely in his Christian faith, but in the process of history itself. One thing we have learned, or ought to have learned, in two thousand years of Christianity, is that the emergence of Christian truth is not a finite but an indefinite and continuous process. Revelation is not static but dynamic. And that is exactly how history operates too. No one age knows the whole historical truth. Indeed, in any one age the history we accept will be incomplete, misleading, even in some respects actually false. We have to take the long view that the unfolding of historical truth is progressive, never-ending, and that it will terminate only with humanity itself. For a Christian to seek to interfere with the unfolding of historical truth is as foolish as for him to try to stop the process of revelation.

When we discussed this point at school, my history master, a wise and learned Jesuit, used to remind me of Jesus's saying, recorded by the evangelist John, Chapter 14:6: 'I am the way, the truth and the light.' It was Jesus himself who identified his work and revelation with truth, and Christianity, properly considered, ought to be seen as co-extensive with truth. There is no inherent conflict between truth and faith: they are one. Hence Christianity, by identifying truth with faith must teach — and in its enlightened form does teach — that any interference with the truth is immoral. A Christian with faith has nothing to fear from the facts. A Christian historian who draws the line limiting the field of inquiry at any point whatever is, indeed, admitting the limits of his faith. He is also repudiating the nature of his religion in its progressive revelation of truth . So the Christian, according to my understanding, should not feel himself inhibited in the smallest degree from following the line of his inquiries — the line of truth — whithersoever it may lead. Indeed, I would say he is positively bound to follow it. He should, in fact, be freer than the non-Christian, who tends to be precommitted by his own rejection of Christian truth.

If I can interpose a personal note, I found I had to think all these things out for myself when I first embarked on my **History of Christianity**. I am a Christian, and my faith is the most precious thing I possess. But my faith, like anyone else's I think, is vulnerable, brittle, fragile. When I started work on that book, I feared to damage my faith. But I drew courage from my belief that, in the long term, Christian truth and historical truth must coincide, and in the event my faith emerged from writing the history of Christianity not damaged but strengthened and reinforced. Such a history is marked by the folly and wickedness of leading Christians on almost every page, but I came to realise, in studying the account, that men have done evil not because of their Christianity but despite it — that Christianity has been, not the source of but the supreme, often the sole, restraining factor on mankind's capacity for wrong-doing. The record of the human race with Christianity is daunting enough. But without its restraints, how much more horrific the history of these last 2,000 years must have been!

I am often reminded, in considering the restraints of the Christian faith, of a famous story concerning the novelist Evelyn Waugh. That superbly gifted but curmudgeonly and occasionally extremely malevolent writer sometimes gave the impression that he positively enjoyed inflicting pain, by the sharp and wounding things he said to people, even without provocation. He was once asked a hard question by a brave woman. 'Mr. Waugh,' she said, 'how can you behave as you do, and still remain a Christian?' Waugh replied to her, with grim sincerity, 'Madam, I may be as bad as you say, but, believe me, were it not for my religion, I would scarcely be a human being.'

It is now a solid part of my belief, both as a Christian and an historian, that true religion, by which I mean religion based upon Judaeo-Christian revelation, is the essential mitigating factor in human depravity. Earlier this year I completed work on the book I designed as a companion volume to my history of Christianity, which I have called **A History of the Jews**. Of course this has a much longer time-span, nearly 4,000 years — about three-quarters of the period during which mankind has had any real claim to be called civilised. I approached this book in exactly the same spirit in which I began writing about Christianity: I intended to follow truth wherever it led. This experience also confirmed my faith, but in a rather different manner. The story of the Jews, over nearly four millennia, is profoundly tragic, and often horrifying: quite how horrifying can only be appreciated fully by one who is actually familiar with the whole history. The faith of the Jews, and their destiny — their predicament — are obviously connected. It is therefore easy to conclude that Jewish faith is the source and cause of their misfortunes. And in all ages, many Jews — perhaps most — have at times felt their faith to be burden, to be carried through life with many groans and sights — sometimes an almost unbearable burden. But to conclude from this that their religion has been, for the Jews, a kind of curse, is a very superficial viewpoint, which any historian of the Jews quickly learns to discard. For their history, as I discovered, shows beyond any doubt, that the faith of the Jews, and their practise of it, has been the source of profound happiness for many generations, in the midst of endless oppressions and sufferings; it has been the dynamic, too, of the remarkable achievements of this small people, so disproportion to their numbers. Without their faith, the Jews would never have existed. And had they abandoned their faith, they would soon have lost their identity and merged without further trace into the background of the Middle East, long before they had the opportunity to figure on the world scene.

The study both of Christianity and of Judaism illustrates the thesis that, in reconciling faith and truth, it is necessary to take the long view. The critical study of the Bible goes back at least to the time of Marcion in the 2nd century AD, who sought to differentiate between the more acceptable and less acceptable portions of the New Testament. The rejection of the Bible as a dependable historical record, and the denial that Providence has even actively intervened in human affairs, dates from the time of Spinoza, in the mid-17th century. Spinoza's writings effectively laid down the principles of modern biblical criticism. For the best part of 250 years, the general thrust of historical study into the dating, composition, form and content of both the Old and the New Testament was all in one direction: to present both as didactic rather than historical documents, dealing with myths rather than events and, even where the events purportedly described had some foundation in fact, presenting them through the distorting lens of much later fanaticism. This process reached its culmination in the decade or so before 1914, when it was quite common in academic circles to present the entire Old Testament, except for a few fragments, as a tendentious compilation of priests written in post-Exilic times. The Book of Genesis, in particular, was pure myth: Abraham and the other patriarchs had never existed, but were mythic figures representing, if anything, collective tribal personalities. The Gospels were similarly dismissed as late productions written generations after the happenings they claimed to describe; some German scholars seriously advanced the view that Jesus had never existed at all, as a man, let alone as God.

In the seventy or so years since that low-water mark in the historicity of the Judaeo-Christian tradition, the tide of faith, driven by the force of historical and archaeological scholarship, has been flowing back again. The careful and scientific examination of sites which figures in the history of the ancient Near East, and perhaps even more so, the recovery of ancient texts which has been the consequence of archaeological work, have on balance tended to rehabilitate the Bible as a record of actual events. In fact, the more we discover about the ancient Near East, the more we tend to trust the truthfulness of the men who compiled the Pentateuch. For instance, the patriarchs have reemerged as actual historical figures. The process began in the 1920s, when Sir Leonard Woolley discovered Ur itself, whence Abraham came, found the great ziggurat which plainly inspired the story of the Tower of Babel, and discovered evidence that rescued the Flood story from the realm of pure myth. Thanks to the work of W.F. Albright and others, it gradually became possible to anchor the patriarchal narratives in the Middle Bronze Age and to give approximate datings to many of the events described in Genesis. Those who continued to deny the historicity of the Pentateuch were forced back onto the defensive and obliged to insist, with logical absurdity, on higher or rather totally different standards of proof for Old Testament assertions as opposed to those in purely secular records — the academic equivalent of Christian fundamentalism.

Still more strikingly, French excavations at the ancient palace of Mari and the American excavations of ancient Nuzi produced vast quantities of cuneiform tablets — over 20,000 dating from the 15th century BC in Nuzu alone — which illuminate the social and legal background to the patriarchal narratives.

Many of the events they described, which once baffled commentators and strengthened the view that these tales were pure myth — the proposal, for instance, for the adoption of Eliezer as heir-presumptive to Abraham, the latter's negotiations with Sarah, the transfer of a birthright from Esau to Jacob, the binding-power of a deathbed blessing and disposition of property, Rachel's theft of her father's household gods, Jacob's contractual relations with Laban — all of these turn out to be common legal practice as illustrated repeatedly by the recovered records of these ancient cities.

Again, the process whereby the Hebrews first settled in ancient Palestine, sojourned in Egypt, and then conquered Canaan, has been brought, bit by bit, over the past half century, into the lighted circle which is how illuminated, if still only dimly, by archaeology. Some of the events in the books of Exodus and Joshua, once dismissed by biblical critics as entirely imaginary, have now been confirmed by the work of such scholars as G.E.Wright on ancient Shechem, Kathleen Kenyon at Jericho, J.L. Starkey at Lachish, Yidael Yadin at Hazor, James Pritchard at Gibeon, to mention only five outstanding cases. As we move onto the age of the first Jewish commonwealth, the kingdom of David and Solomon, it becomes possible to correlate Old Testament events with other ancient Near Eastern sources, notably Egyptian, where absolute datings are possible, so that we can, for instance now assert with complete certainty that Solomon died in the year 925-6 BC. Miss Kenyon's brilliant work at Jerusalem, and excavations at the so-called 'chariot-cities' of Hazor, Gezer and Megiddo, fill in the background to the great Davidic kingdom. Indeed, it is now possible to see much of the historical writing contained in the books of Samuel, Kings and Chronicles as constituting the finest and most dependable history in all the ancient world, on a level with the best work of the Greeks and sometimes superior even to Thucydides.

The recovery of ancient texts, both tablets and papyrus, continues. We are now accustomed to discovering, translating and interpreting state and private archives in excavated cities of the ancient Near East. The dry sands of Egypt yield written fragments from time to time, both of secular records valuable for cross-reference to biblical texts, and of very early versions or copies of sacred writings. The sectarian library we call the Dead Sea Scroll has so far yielded about 600 volumes, including the entire text — and of course by far the earliest text we possess — of the Book of Isaiah, which many would agree is the most beautiful book in the entire bible. These and other discoveries allow us to fill in the background to the life and mission and beliefs of Jesus Christ in a way which would have astonished poor Renan. The archaeological illumination of the New Testament is proceeding. From 1969, Professor Avigad began excavating the houses or palaces of the priestly aristocratic families which in Jesus's day controlled the Temple. Pilate's residence has now been identified. About the same time, archaeologists recovered the bones of a crucified man near the Old City of Jerusalem so that it was possible, for the first time, to discover exactly how the crucifixion of Jesus was carried out — which again makes sense of the New Testament record.

The late-19th early-20th century notion that the New Testament was a collection of late and highly imaginative records can no longer be seriously held. No one now doubts that St Paul's epistles, the earliest Christian records, are authentic or dates them later than the AD 50s. Most scholars now date the earliest gospel, the so-called 'Q' not later than about 50AD; Mark 65AD; Matthew and Luke from the 80's or 90's, John not later than 90-100. Some scholars, notably the late Dr. John Robinson, put them considerably earlier: Mark possibly as early as 45 AD, only a decade and a half or so from Christ's passion; Matthew between 40 and 60; Luke 55-60, and John possibly as late as 65AD plus, but possibly as early as 40. The very latest New Testament scholarship is moving in the same direction.

I doubt if there is any serious scholar alive now who would deny Jesus's historical existence. Indeed he is much better authenticated than many secular figures of antiquity whose existence no one has ever presumed to question. The earliest fragments of the New Testament go back a surprisingly long way. In the Jon Rylands library in Manchester, England, there is a papyrus fragment of St John's Gospel which contains parts of Chapter 18:31-3 on one side, and Chapter 18:37-38 on the other, evidently part of a very early codex, or book of sheets bound together in a volume. The hand-writing style is not later than 140AD, and could be as early as 110AD. If we consider that Tacitus, for example, survives in only one medieval manuscript, the quantity of early New Testament manuscripts is remarkable. The earliest complete texts, in the Codex Vaticanus, in Rome, and the Codex Sinaiticus, in London, date from the first half of the 4th century; but there are altogether about 80 papyrus fragments from the 2nd to the 4th centuries, 270 unical manuscripts on vellum dating 300 to 100 AD, and over 4,000 upper-and lower-case 'minuscule' manuscripts dating from 1000 AD to 1500 AD. Moreover, the process of recovering early fragments continues. More are sure to emerge, and there is even the possibility of us discovering an early Christian library on the lines of the Qumran scrolls. What is clear beyond doubt is that whereas, in the 19th century, the tendency of history was to cast doubt of the veracity of Judaeo-Christian records, and to undermine popular faith in God and his Son, as presented in the Bible, in the 20th century it has moved in quite the opposite direction, and there is no sign of the process coming to an end. It is not now the men of faith, it is the sceptics who have reason to fear the course of discovery.

However, the historian, whether he be a Christian or not, must emphasise that the vindication of the New Testament records, as authentic documents describing actual events, concerning a real man, does not in any way 'prove' that he was God too, and that the incarnation and resurrection actually occurred. All that it establishes is that men and women who lived at and shortly after the time, believed these things. Christianity remains, will remain and I think must remain a matter of faith. The historical process cannot by its very nature establish the truth of Christianity: all it can do, and what it now does, is remove the obstacles to faith, and place the Christian notions in a plausible context.

But an historian, looking at Christianity and the phenomenon of Jesus, is entitled to say something more about the content and significance of Christianity, and this is my final point. He is entitled, I think, to warn against a worldly interpretation of Jesus Christ's message. When Jesus said that his kingdom was not of this world he meant exactly that, and he was warning his followers not to place any political construction on his mission. Anyone who studies the history of the Jewish people in the century or so before Christ, during his lifetime, and in the decades which followed his death, will understand why he found it necessary to give such a warning.

The saviour figure or Messiah was a characteristic Jewish notion, for Judaism is not only an historical but an historicist religion, radiating portents of impending and dramatic events, particularly during periods of crisis and suffering. But though the Messiah was often mentioned, it was never clear what the Messiah was, of what exactly he was supposed to do. He might be a saviour-king, like Saul, David or Zedekiah — or even a friendly foreigner like the Persian King Cyrus. He was supposed to come from the line of David. One psalm calls him the son of God, though the Hebrew kings had never claimed divinity. He was supposed to live among the people, die and be exalted, and so bear away their sins — though again the Hebrew monarchs had never claimed to embody their people. Sometimes he was not called a King, but the Son of Man, the Servant of the Lord, the Seed of the Woman, the Suffering Servant. But he might be interpreted not as an individual at all, but as a symbol for the collective faithful of Israel, the true 'remnant' of the just.

Not surprisingly, the Jews became confused about the Messiah. When they thought of this being, they naturally thought of Kingship, leadership, political change, revolution, the end of the Roman occupation, the coming of some sort of physical, actual Kingdom of which God approved. When Herod the Great heard that the Christ was born, he reacted violently, as to a threat to his throne and dynasty. A Jew who heard a man claim to be the Messiah automatically assumed he had to do with a political if not also a military programme. That was the assumption behind the preparations for action described in the Qumran war-scroll. The Roman authorities, the Sanhedrin, the Sadduccees, the Pharisees, the common people all, in varying degrees, thought a Messiah would come to overthrow the existing order — a Messiah who preached fundamental change would be talking not in spiritual or metaphysical terms but of actual government, and real taxes, and everyday justice in the here and now.

Now here were the elements of a great deception and a thundering anti-climax, because Jesus was not that kind of Messiah at all. His mission was the one adumbrated in the famous Chapter 53 of Isaiah — he was the 'tender plant,' the 'despised and rejected of men,' the 'man of sorrows,' who would be 'wounded for our iniquities, bruised for our transgressions,' one who was 'oppressed and afflicted and yet he opened not his mouth.' This Messiah would be indeed the 'suffering servant,' who would be 'taken from prison and from judgment,' 'brought as a lamb to the slaughter,' would make his grave with the wicked and be 'numbered with the transgressors.' He was not a danger to any existing order or a particular throne or clerical bureaucracy or ruling class — at least in the immediate and direct sense. He was not a mob leader, a demagogue, a populist, a guerilla chieftain. He was talking, it is true, of freedom. But it was not the freedom of Republican Rome, the freedom, within a firm framework of orderly government, to move, trade and worship where and as you willed. Not was it the kind of freedom the Jewish priesthood demanded — freedom to carry out the demands of the Law without external interference. It was, rather, the internal freedom of the conscience at ease with itself, the spiritual and intellectual and emotional freedom acquired by the conquest of the passions and the self, the 'freedom men find in Christ' later preached so eloquently by St Paul. This new freedom could not be measured in terms of frontiers and forms of government, and it would be won not by military victory but by the degraded sacrifice of the Messiah himself. Moreover, it would be offered not merely to Jews but to all mankind in accordance with the prophecy of Isaiah: 'In thee shall all families of the earth be blessed.'

Hence, in the context of the politics and the apocalyptic religion of his time, the entire movement and mission of Jesus ended in shattering bathos. When it came to the point he repudiated popular Messianism completely. The authorities sighed with relief and dispatched him without hesitation or compunction. The mob was disappointed. The cry, 'Crucify him!' was, perhaps, prompted by disgust and disillusionment as much as by anything else. So the Messiah had not come to liberate the Jews, but to preach self-sacrifice and resignation to all! That was not the message the Jews in the street had been expecting or wanted. At the time, only a handful of Jews saw the point.

The victory of Christianity lay in the fact that, in time, the tiny handful swelled into a mighty multitude, and that this steady and eventually overwhelming growth was secured not by the power of the sword or by the efficiency of political organisation, but by virtue of example and by the appeal of words. That wholly unmilitary and unpolitical conquest fills the historian with wonder and awe, for it is unique in antiquity; unique, I think, at any age. It is what differentiates Christianity, in its early, most authentic stages, from any other comparable phenomenon. It suggests, too, a lesson for today which perhaps an historian ought to pass on.

Christianity is not a simple but a complex faith, and I think deliberately so. It was so right from the start, for Jesus Christ was aiming not at a particular group of people — as he certainly would have done, had he been a militant and populist — but at all. Hence the general nature, one might almost say the universalism, of his message. What St Paul made explicit was already implicit in Christ's teaching. This was a creed in which all types of men and women, not just all nations and races but all casts of mind, could find meaning. In its very ambiguities lies its strength, for it is open to a variety of interpretations. Men and women have always found, and were intended to find, different signals in his gospel. Jesus was giving mankind, then and for a long future, not one matrix, but a whole series of matricies of conduct — he was thinking of the contemplative, the mystic, the devout; but also of the men and women of action; he spoke to the Marthas, as well as the Marys; he had something to say to the centurion and the man of property, as well as the poor; he honoured the hermit, but he preached also a relentless gospel of work and he appealed to the achievers. 'Seek and ye shall find!' — it is all there, for all of us, whatever be our nature or our aim. No type of human personality goes to the words of Jesus Christ and comes away empty handed. He is, truly, all things to all men.

But all these roads, which Christ indicated, are routes to the next world, not this. What Christianity is not about, what it never has been about, what it never can be about, is politics. That was the mistake made by the Jewish elites, and the Jewish mob, in Jesus's own lifetime. It is a mistake many have made since, in all ages, not least in our own. It is, I think, the commonest mistake made by Christian elites today. 'My kingdom is not of this world.' Those seven words go to the heart of the Christian faith. The truth of Christ is not a truth about worldly Utopias. It is not a mandate for socialism or capitalism or democracy or kingship or social welfare. When Satan took Jesus to the high mountain and showed him the kingdoms of the world — and Jesus rejected them and told

Satan to be gone — he was rejecting the worldliness not only of wealth and privilege but the worldliness of systems and ideology, the worldliness of political programmes and politicised theology and of morals preached to attain political ends, however speciously high-minded they may be. When an historian looks at Jesus Christ and Christianity, his final conclusion must be, I think, that Jesus was not concerned with this world at all, except in so far as it forms a threshold to the next; and that Christianity is, quite literally, *like nothing on earth*.

# Crisis in Christology

# 4

# JESUS CHRIST AND MODERN SOCIOLOGY

## David Martin

I have to begin by working myself out of a job. I cannot deal with the theme 'Jesus Christ and modern sociology.'

Let me explain. In the first place there is no such animal as modern sociology. I do not mean to suggest that some sociology may not be old-fashioned, musty and market by its time, but there is nothing we can point to which represents a major revolution in sociological thinking. Sociology began with Ibn Khaldun and with Vico's 'New Science,' and above all with the Scottish Enlightenment over two centuries ago. Indeed it is no great exaggeration to say that sociology was the invention of Scottish clergy. But those beginnings have never been overturned in some intellectual revolution. Those beginnings were the revolution and they offered to humankind a certain kind of novel perspective on the way we see and understand the construction and constitution of our social world. The revolutionary questions posed at that time were How is society? What is society? Why is society? The new perspective offered saw human beings as creators of culture and created by culture, as involved in patterns of power and rank and custom, as players of roles and incumbents of roles, as shaped by membership in nation or profession or class.

Since then the new perspective has been amplified and become popular, even to the extent of informing subjects like history, including the history of the earliest Christianity. It has permeated so widely that some New Testament scholars now discuss with great speculative ingenuity which distinct social groups may lie behind what they see as the varied elements in the New Testament, and hypothesise about the crucible of social conflict and turbulence out of which Christianity emerged. They see Christianity as a social movement, to be understood sociologically.

But that change is not the consequence of a new kind of thinking which can be labelled modern sociology. There is no modern sociology in the sense that there is a modern physics and a modern biology. There is simply this perspective on the world originally devised in Edinburgh over two centuries ago by a couple of clergymen, and constantly enriched and developed since. That fact about sociology is very important. Sociology is a way of looking, which advances in richness, comprehensiveness, and depth, but which does not experience a 'modern' revolution, a radical shift of paradigm, a massive revision.

Having said that let me go on, still perhaps easing myself out of a job, by saying that sociology can have nothing whatever to say about the Incarnation. Sociology might consider the long-term impact of Jesus Christ on human history, or analyse the struggles between groups which surrounded this or that formulation of Christian doctrine, but it cannot trespass directly on who He is. You may remember the conclusion of Schweitzer's Quest of the Historical Jesus' where Schweitzer says that those who follow Him will *find out* who He is. Sociology is not concerned with that *kind* of finding out. It may identify Christ as a bearer of charisma, that is, as anointed by a powerful grace, but the Incarnation is not within its scope. You cannot even imagine a sociological argument the conclusion of which triumphantly vindicates or disproves the Christian claim concerning Christ.

The question now is whether I have declared myself totally redundant so far as this conference is concerned. The answer is 'not quite.' I have some considerations I want to urge. One of these considerations concerns the limits of sociology which I've already indicated with respect to the Incarnation. Allow me to touch on a very important instance of limits to sociology. It is this. You cannot on the basis of sociology come to a philosophical position which holds all theological and moral affirmations to be relative. Philosophical relativism does not follow from social (or cultural) relativism. Of course it is perfectly possible to adopt a relativistic attitude for all kinds of reasons, but logically you cannot derive a philosophic relativism from the facts of social relativity.

In case we are now lost in a fog of words let me clarify. We observe that beliefs and moral standards arise in particular social contexts to which they relate. There may be, for example, a connection between the existence of a moral standard which permits infanticide in response to the problem of overpopulation. The practice of murdering infants becomes understandable in *relation* to the particular circumstances of a given society. It does not follow that this relation between social circumstance and moral standard makes a moral objection to murdering babies a matter of mere opinion. Likewise one might show a relationship between my being born of Methodist family in SW London and my current beliefs, and likewise show a relationship between the current beliefs of another scholar and *his* background in a Christian Science home in N.E. Boston. But so what? Does that mean that we cannot discuss the truth or otherwise of Christian Science or Methodism? We are, in part, creatures of our social time and place, nurtured in a particular culture. Nevertheless the question of truth and of criteria for truth supervenes.

Take the mass murder of the Jews by the Nazis . Does the fact that both Nazis and Jews were shaped by social circumstances forbid us to go beyond social relativism and say 'That is *wrong*?' It follows that if moral standards can be faulty then theologies also can be mistaken. I would argue then that there is no logical step from cultural relativity to theological and moral relativism, and I would add further on other grounds that the relativistic position is in any case intolerable. Of course, there are those who believe that to say anything is ever wrong or mistaken is to be intolerant. I for one have to admit that I do not see myself obliged to be tolerant of murdering babies or Jews in order to exhibit a proper liberal openness of mind, and in particular I am convinced that the attempt to base this openness of mind on sociological premises constitutes a logical mistake.

I am agreeably reinforced in this position by some remarks of Professor John Polkinghorne in his book 'The Way the World Is.' John Polkinghorne till recently held the chair of Mathematical Physics at Cambridge prior to taking holy orders and he comments succinctly that the entry of sociological factors into one's understanding of the world does *not* imply the exit of truth from it.

But maybe I am still out of a Job, because the argument I have just made is philosophical argument, not a sociological one. However I want now to go on to an observation which is more properly sociological. The observation is linked to the point about our understanding being rooted in time and cultural place. An event such as the Incarnation and a doctrine such as the Incarnation do not come about in human history like unanticipated meteorites intruding from outer space. Nothing *drops* from heaven, including the gospel. A sociologist assumes that there must be a context within which the Incarnation may be conceived. Saying that I mean simply what every theologian or student of the *Bible means when he speaks of a preparation of the gospel. The vocabulary of the sociologist will, of course, be somewhat different. What for the believer (as believer) represents prophecy or inspired visions of what is to come, is for the sociologist (as sociologist) the setting of a scene, the preparation of a soil, even perhaps the accumulation of potentialities. But there is no problem here. The theologian says that the Divine Word can only be spoken (and acted) when the language has been built up within which it can be understood. The sociologist says that events have not occurred in a historical vacuum. Either way the tutelage of Israel is necessary and inevitable.

And this 'consideration' of mine may be extended a little. When the cultural language has been built up the final word will not appear entirely novel. The last word in the crossword is already very strongly implied. Theologians have sometimes vexed the ordinary believer, and even vexed themselves, by suggesting that much in Christianity is not original. Yet — to change the metaphor — capstones are central. The reality is that so many elements have to be built up, and so much material assembled from different sources, before all can be locked into the perfect arc of truth. There has to be a 'fullness of time' before anyone can answer the question 'Whom do ye say that I am?' Truth is realised in slow epiphanies, in divine 'showings' within a frame already in place. Anything less organic would be monstrous, mechanical, and abhorrent.

Just now I referred to the building up of a crossword which lacked only one or two vital clues. So far as Christianity is concerned — and here inevitably I shift towards the language of faith — the last word in the crossword is the word of the cross. The cross piece lies at the centre of the pattern. It is the semaphore or code in which God transmits to us, and transacts for us, the message of His love. The cross is His coded message, His sign language, His seal and signature.

At this point I may seem to be completely given over to the language of faith. Yet there is a sociological commentary or elucidation of that language. Sociology looks for codes and sign languages in order to open them up. It cannot comment on the validity of the message but perhaps it can help decipher the signs. Perhaps. Or perhaps not. Let us see.

I am going to conclude by a commentary on the sign, offering maybe a small post-script to scripture, tracing the deep structure of hope.

Christianity is, I've suggested, a sign-language: these things 'shall be a *sign* unto you.' We trace the sign and translate the code.

The code as I understand it is transmitted in the last supper and in the final sacrifice. That supper and that sacrifice are one and the same last and final act. The common elements in both are breaking and offering. The breaking and the offering constitute a meal. What else do you do at a meal but break and offer, break and offer, break and offer? Hold just for a moment to that.

To break and to offer is to unite the whole company of the guests who attend the table. The sharing out is incorporation in the fraternity. It is an act of inclusion. But no fraternity can be incorporated and constituted without cost. The unity of humankind around the common table has from the very first been broken. The hand of man has turned against the hand of man; all hands are stained with the blood of broken fellowship. So that primal, primæval, breakage has to be reversed, by hands which receive the hurt and bear the cost. The cost of breakage will be borne in the breaking of a body and in the shedding of blood. The codebook tells us that 'without the shedding of blood is no redemption,' meaning that there can be no recovery, no restitution, no reversal without the total gift of God's essence and His very self.

So the gift that is proffered and the body which is broken is God in Christ: He is both giver and gift, He who offers up and He who is offered, at-once priest and victim. And with the making and the tracing of the sign - the fracture and the offering - He is sacramentally present, made known in the breaking of bread. So we bring together a gift and a presence. The offering is a present; the offering also makes Christ present under and by a sign; and the offering is a re-presentation, or 'representation' of the last acts of Christ at the supper and on the cross. It re-enacts and re-presents; it does not repeat what was done 'once for all.'

I have used the word 'enact' and now I will change that to the word 'gesture.' The cross and the supper are the divine gesture, evoking in us a response. The sign-language asks for a reception. And that is signified and sealed in our reception of the gift. We *ingest* the broken body, and it makes us whole. The breaking has healed the terrible brokenness in ourselves; the fracture of the body of Christ has restored the fracture in our souls and the breakage in our fellowship one with another.

And in so doing it has reversed the law of sin and death, bringing life and immortality to light. As breakage makes whole, so death brings immortality to light. Those who respond to the gesture by ingesting the body of the Lord receive into themselves the medicine of immortality and the resurrection presence. They are united in their risen and triumphant Head, taken with Him into godhead, made one with the Father. They have communicated with each other and with God: by the making and receiving of sign-language and of gestures.

Just as the sign-language of 'breaking' reverses and cancels all breakages, in the soul and in the fellowship, so it looks back and forward. It looks back and forward because it stands at the crux, the crossing-point. This is the last feast of an old order and testament, and the first feast of a the new order and new testament. The law and Moses are cancelled and completed by the force of Christ. As the old order and old testament looked back to the glorious liberation of the whole people of God by Moses from bondage under the sign of blood and of the slaughtered Lamb, so the new order and new testament is celebrated by a looking forward to a liberation of the whole people of God under the great seal of the Lamb who was slain and who is worthy to receive all honour and blessing. Here we arrive at the conclusion of the great code: the mysterious sign of the Lamb who is in the midst of the throne and who is the sole light of the heavenly city, New Jerusalem. This completes the mystery, and there is no more to be said except 'Amen' and 'Amen.'

What I have just written has not, of course, been sociology. I have rather tried to reuse the language and imagery of the Bible in a concentrated form. Nevertheless I have wanted to bring out the meaning of what might otherwise seem a strange ceremony in which people mysteriously take bread and wine and understand it as the body and blood of Christ, and as His presence with them. They call themselves communicants and I have aimed to show what is being communicated simply by making a slight shift from the theological language of 'sign' to the idea of 'sign-language' or crossword or semaphore or code. I have achieved a marginal increase in distance, such as the sociologist needs for seeing things differently, by speaking of the Bible as a 'code book' and of Christianity as the 'Great Code.' The literary critic may do precisely the same thing as did Northrop Frye recently in his book **The Great Code**. In other words I have deployed the full panoply of Christian language but shifted the field of understanding to what is known technically as semiotics, the science of reading signs and breaking codes.

Further than that I have used another contemporary mode of understanding, structural analysis. Just as semiotics runs parallel to the theological language of 'sign' so structural analysis runs close to the theological language of typology.

Structural analysis tries to locate the key elements in what is being said or done and I did that by appealing to human universals: division and unification, gift and reception. Everything turned around those mighty oppositions: break, unite; give, receive. The unity of man with man is broken: humankind must once more be in solidarity. The unity of man with God is sundered: God and man must once more be at one. The unity of our souls is severed by sin: we must be inwardly healed and restored. And that reunification demands a cost commensurate with the loss: the brokenness of our condition can only be met by the brokenness of God Himself. His brokenness feeds our brokenness as pure gift. So the great reversals begin: from breakage to unity, from sin to redemption, from death to life. It is all summarised as the broken and slaughtered Lamb takes His place at the centre of the throne and of the heavenly city.

All that is a kind of secondary commentary, informed I hope by ways we have of understanding sign and structure. I could go on, of course, to analyse the significance of the *table* as the centre of this sacrificial and redemptive drama. I could give a commentary on the gestures which priest or minister uses and which are part of the table manners belonging to God's board. Why do we clean our hands and hearts before partaking of his supper? How do we comport ourselves to make the transition to God's presence? All that is unnecessary to my purposes here. I have simply endeavored to come as close as I can to the heart of the mystery using such modes of understanding as I have.

My concluding remarks must return to a very general point about the limits of sociology. A sociologist may attempt a preliminary analysis of sign and structure; he may elucidate the means whereby humankind crosses thresholds, especially the threshold of the divine presence. He may go further to enquire how re-enactments of redemptive sacrifice made around a table establish fraternity but build into various other solidarities, even divisions of human society. But it is no part of the proper task of a sociologist to define the fundamental acts and re-enactments of religion as really 'at bottom' *nothing but* expressions of fraternity and of social solidarities which have been diverted through a transcendent frame. If he once claims not only to see what is involved in a celebration of the death and presence of Christ but also to see *through* it to undergirding processes which alone are real or which are capable of realization only in political practice, then he has gone beyond sociology. If he goes on to claim that this transcendent and illusory diversion can be overcome by earthly communion inefficacious political action he does so on grounds which are inherently philosophical. He has, in philosophical language, *reduced* a realm of meaning to other elements which are raw, real and ontologically secure.

To do that implies that nothing can be dome in and for itself, standing valid quite apart from ascertainable consequences in the political sphere. Yet religion affirms precisely an act perfect and efficacious in and of itself, whatever it may also demand in terms of how we treat with each other personally and politically. If I may state my own philosophical position: the redemptive act, the offering, is a summary statement of the universals of our condition valid in and for itself. Were I in prison facing immediate death (were I, that is in precisely the same situation as that summarised and celebrated in the Eucharist) my offering of the holy meal would still be efficacious and not drained away in some other category. It would stand 'before God.' It would belong with those acts which human beings may do up against the last things with nothing further *of consequence* to contemplate.

What I am trying haltingly to say has to do with rebutting the philosophical nihilation of our acts unless they contribute to some political programme. It is important for our humanity that we hold fast the capacity to stand 'before God' and none else. Deprived of that access, reduced to forces and pressures or philosophically circumscribed by what is to count as 'real' and 'correct' political practice, we have no 'standing' at all as humans. It appears to me, as a reflective human being, not as a sociologist, that the last acts of Christ, his offering of his body in bread and wine and on the cross, stand efficacious 'for us men and for our salvation' in and of themselves.

# 5

# THE MANHOOD OF JESUS IN THE NEW TESTAMENT

## C.F.D. Moule

A modern Christian investigator necessarily comes to the study of the New Testament with certain questions in his mind which might not belong to a non-Christian, or even to a Christian if he lived in another period. It is impossible to disabuse oneself of such questions: one can only try to be aware of them, and to be ready to accept the possibility that, if they are not New Testament answers, or, if they are essentially modern questions, there may be no answers from any period of antiquity. Conversely, it is possible to pay too little attention to antiquity. An investigator who, while tolerably proficient as a New Testament scholar, is not professionally expert in the subsequent history of Christian doctrine, may be insufficiently acquainted with certain important facts - not least the subtleties of ways in which his own questions may already have been asked (albeit probably in a different form), and answers may already have been given in the past. The manhood of Jesus is a subject in which such drawbacks may be particularly great, in view of the wide range of the answers that have been thrown up by the continual debate over this question. In any case, even a master of the entire story might well be disposed to ask whether human insight could ultimately improve on previous attempts, subtle and less subtle, to express the mystery in terms of various attempts, conceptions of Godhead and of human personality. Some of these attempts are reviewed in — to adduce just one example — J. McIntyre's **The Shape of Christology** (1966). If there is any new formulation over and above these classic attempts, it is likely to spring from some of the new insights of psychology, sociology, and anthropology: which only emphasizes the limitations of one who approaches the question from the modern world but with only the equipment of a New Testament specialist.

Thus, it is with modern questions inevitably in mind, and yet with a necessarily insufficient grasp of the entire story up to and including the modern era, that a New Testament investigator who is not professionally equipped in the history of Christian doctrine has to go to work: and it is necessary to emphasize this limitation and bring it out into the open, if this study is to take its proper place in the total investigation. This being said, we proceed as best we can. In any case, the manhood of Jesus is only one facet of christology; and this investigation touches on only a few arbitrarily selected aspects of New Testament thought about the manhood of Jesus. It takes three paradoxes in New Testament convictions about Jesus — his humiliation and exaltation, his continuity with and discontinuity from the rest of humanity, and the individuality and yet inclusiveness of his person — and shows that no christological statement that bypasses these or simplifies them away is true to New Testament ways of thinking. Also, an attempt is made to find some basis, not indeed for resolving these paradoxes, but at least for bringing their opposite poles into some mutual relationship.

# I

Perhaps a suitable starting-point in the discussion of the paradox of humiliation and exaltation is the observation that Phil. ii. 5-11 probably has nothing to do with so-called 'Kenotic' theories of the incarnation, despite its frequent use as the key text for them. By 'Kenotic' theories are meant attempts to explain the human limitations suffered by the divine Son of God in terms of a deliberate act of self-emptying, as though the pre-existent Son of God voluntarily emptied himself of divine prerogatives for a time, in order to share to the full the human lot, and resumed his full capacities only after the death on the cross. Against this, it has been widely recognized that it is none of the intention of Phil. ii. 5-11 to explain anything. Rather, it has come to be interpreted as simply a statement, an assertion in pictorial language, about the supreme humility of one whose pre-existent divine dignity enhances the greatness of his condescension. But for my part — and this is my reason for starting from this passage — I am inclined to join the minority of interpreters who go still further and identify, rather than contrast, the so-called condescension with the so-called dignity, this underlining a divine paradox which stands every human scale of values on its head. I agree[1] with those who interpret **harpagmos** not, concretely, as 'something worth snatching,' but, abstractly, as 'the act of snatching' (i.e., virtually, 'acquisitiveness'), and who render the phrase in which it occurs in some such way as: 'Jesus did not reckon that equality with God meant snatching: on the contrary, he emptied himself...' This would mean that, whereas ordinary human valuation reckons that God-likeness means having your own way, getting what you want, Jesus saw God-likeness essentially as giving and spending oneself out. If this is really the intention of the passage, then the participial phrase usually rendered, in a concessive sense, as '**though** he was in the form of God' might even, perhaps, have been intended, rather, in a causative sense: precisely **because** he was in the form of God he recognized equality with God as a matter not of getting but of giving. Of course there is no denying that the 'pattern' of Phil. II. 5-11 as a whole is the pattern of descent followed by ascent, humiliation followed by exaltation: it is, as it were, a V-pattern — from heaven to the depths and up again (or, as some aver, up to an even higher status than before — which would require a pattern more like a square-root symbol !). But that, I believe, need not prevent our seeing, at the same time, a straight line pattern in it, by which height is **equated** with depth, humiliation is **identified** with exaltation. Indeed, the very paradox of the truth lies in the fact that what, in ordinary human estimation, is a V-pattern of descent followed by ascent is, in the eyes of God, a straight line of equation: the two diagrams, therefore, positively need to be there together, if the paradox is to be expressed. 'He was rich, yet for your sake he became poor' (II Cor. VIII. 9) can be glossed by 'penniless, we own the world' (II Cor. VI. 10). And, whether or not this is a true exegesis of the Philippians passage, the paradox of the conflicting diagrams is demonstrably present in St. John's famous 'exaltation' (hupsoun), which is, at one and the same time, an uplifting in shame on the cross and an uplifting in the glory of accomplishing God's will; and, indeed, this motif informs a great deal of New Testament thinking, as we shall see.

If, then, this is genuinely an insight of the New Testament, we may state at least one finding of supreme importance for the understanding of its estimate of the manhood of Jesus, namely, that (at least in certain passages) it recognizes what is ordinarily called 'emptying' as really 'fulfilling': kenosis actually is plerosis; which means that the human limitations of Jesus are seen as a positive expression of his divinity rather than as a curtailment of it:

'Jesus divinest when thou most art man!'[2]

This is a principle which is undoubtedly borne out in aesthetic experience. Anybody will recognize, for instance, that creative art involves an acceptance, and a positive use, of limitation. A craftsman in wood has to know all about the grain and the capacities of the wood he is working with, and, by accepting them and working within them, he exploits them in such a way as to express himself to the full as a craftsman in wood-carving.[3] So God the creator, when working in humanity, may be expected to express himself most fully, so far as the idiom of that medium goes, by accepting the human range of capacity and exploiting the human medium to the full. This is no more self-emptying than it is complete self-fulfillment in a given medium. It would be positively inartistic, it would be limiting and less than creative, to go contrary to the nature of the chosen medium. Fulfillment in any given medium and on any given level of expression involves acceptance and full affirmation of the medium and the level. On that showing, it is arguable that 'emptying' is a positively misleading description of the activity.

But, if the artistic quality of craftsmanship is fulfilled and enhanced by acceptance of the characteristics of the chosen medium, it is, admittedly, true that this does also mean foregoing the scope that some other medium might offer (although any 'medium' must, by definition, offer some limitation). There is, it must be granted, an 'emptying,' a kenosis, in respect of scope, even if this is in the interests of the 'fulfillment,' the plerosis, of artistic skill. It is possible to recognize a change of 'status,' even if not of character. It is thus legitimate if the kenoticists speak of incarnation as limitation in this sense, while insisting on the continuity of undiminished moral attributes — as it were absolutely divine artistry, in a miniature. Besides, since the human imagination likes to work in spatial metaphors, it is only natural if, from time to time, this creative fulfillment-by-self-limitation, this complete fulfillment of the creator's nature by the positive affirmation of a given element, is spoken of in terms of the creator's condescending 'descent' into a 'lower' sphere and his abandonment of 'lofty' status, and if fulfillment in a given medium is described as 'emptying,' as though qualities belonging to a higher region had to be jettisoned. But it would be a mistake if it were imagined that such language implied a deliberate renunciation of possibilities, as in so-called kenotic theories. Anything so contrived or artificial would simply be inappropriate to the Christian conviction that, as God expresses himself through every medium and fills everything, so the incarnation is God's natural filling of this particular area, as natural as the filling of a cavity by water which pours into it, following its contours until it is full. Viewed in this way, the incarnation is a positive filling, not a negative emptying; and, as such, it should, strictly speaking, constitute nothing for surprise, as though it were something incongruous with God's majesty, however much it may be a theme for adoring wonder, as congruous with God's eternal, generous self-giving. However, when God is conceived of as omnipotent, it is easily forgotten that the omnipotence of a personal God is exhibited (to quote the collect) 'most chiefly in showing mercy and pity,' and that the omnipotence of a creator God is shown precisely in creative self-limitation. Consequently, religious writing often expresses surprise that so lofty a being can stoop so low. There is, no doubt, an intended paradox in the prophet's utterance:

Thus speaks the high and exalted one,
whose name is holy, who lives for ever:
I dwell in a high and holy place
with him who is broken and humble in spirit,
to revive the spirit of the humble,
to revive the courage of the broken (Isa. I VII.15)

And the same paradox runs through St John's gospel. E. Kasemann, it is true, has brilliantly put the case for virtually eliminating the paradox, and regarding St John's gospel as a docetic document.[4] The dominant theme, he maintains, is the glory of Jesus: he is the glorious, preexistent son of God who bestrides the world like a colossus. To be sure, the phrase 'the Word became flesh' does occur; but what sets the tone is the phrase which follows hard on its heels: 'we saw his glory.' The unquenchable glory of the divine is what dominates. Despite the passion narrative and the occasional bow to a conventional gospel of humiliation, this is not really a theologia crucis but an only thinly disguised theologia gloriae. In a vigorous reply,[5] G. Bornkamm is able to show that this selection of what is to be deemed the dominant note does not do full justice to the gospel's dialectic. It is impossible simply to ignore the paradox without doing violence to the gospel as a whole. There is no denying that the fourth evangelist allows himself sometimes to draw a very docetic picture; but then he also contradicts it. The truth seems to be that he simply states both facts — Jesus is the pre-existent Son of God, the unique Son who shares God's glory; yet also, Jesus is the one who accepts human limitations; and he does not bring them into anything like a unified system. If Jesus asks a question not for information but to test a disciple (John vi. 6) — a very docetic portrait - yet also he has to escape and hide, like any mortal, when his life is prematurely threatened (viii. 59, xii. 36). The gospel simply has it both ways and does not make any very obvious reconciling gesture. But, while the human mind needs the paradoxical form to express the truth, it does also crave a reconciling factor; and if there is any factor at all that makes for something like a unifying and organizing of the two extremes, it is the filial relationship. The Son's absolute and unique oneness with the Father is shown precisely in his submitting to the Father's will: 'I and the Father are one' (x. 30) precisely because 'the Father is greater than I' (xiv. 28). That is, Jesus exhibits the nature and character of God in the only way in which they can be absolutely and perfectly exhibited in the context of human behaviour, namely in such a relationship as properly belongs to man over against God, the relationship of glad and willing filial obedience. To this extent the paradox of glory and humiliation, of equality and subordination, is resolved in that relationship of perfect intimacy and identity of purpose which expresses itself in perfect obedience. Oneness of will is expressed in subordination of will, freedom in constraint.

Perhaps this may be said to be true — if only by implication — of the Epistle to the Hebrews also, which is equally notorious for its violent juxtaposition of the paradoxical extremes. If, in the prologue, Jesus is 'the Son who is the effulgence of God's splendour and the stamp of God's very being' (i. 3), yet it is equally true that 'son though he was, he learned obedience in the school of suffering' (v. 8). One would need to alter that last phrase, 'though he was,' onto 'precisely *because* he was,'[6] in order to bring it into line with the insight which belongs to Phil. ii. 5-11 if it is interpreted in the manner proposed; and this the Epistle to the Hebrews never does. Nevertheless, the underlying theme of sonship might, if it were explicitly exploited in this way, provide a unifying principle.

Thus, Professor John Knox is probably right when he maintains[7] that the New Testament writers believed firmly in the humanity of Jesus but never properly reconciled this conviction with the twin conviction of his divinity; but possibly he might give more credit than he does to the filial relationship as a clue to the understanding of this conflict.

## II

But the crux of the incarnational question is perhaps more precisely identified in another paradox, namely, the paradox of continuity and discontinuity. According to New testament writers, the humanity of Jesus is both continuous with and discontinuous from that of the rest of mankind. By 'the humanity of Jesus' in this context we mean (if we follow a line of thought which is specially clear in the Pauline writings but is not unrepresented elsewhere) his 'generic' humanity, his being the entire human race — Jesus as 'Adam.'[8] It is evident that the New Testament writers firmly believed that Jesus' humanity in this sense — Jesus as inclusive of humanity — was continuous with our humanity. If Jesus did not 'belong' to humankind, men and women would not find new life in him. The principle later formulated by Gregory of Nazianzus in the much-quoted phrase 'what Christ has not assumed he has not healed'[9] is certainly implied in such phrases as the following:

"For if the wrongdoing of that one man brought death upon so many, its effect is vastly exceeded by the grace of God and the gift that came to so many by the grace of the one man, Jesus Christ." (Rom. v. 15b)

"...by sending his own Son in a form like that of our own sinful nature, and as a sacrifice for sin, he has passed judgement against sin within that very nature." (Rom. viii. 3b)

"...that he might be the eldest among a large family of brothers." (Rom. viii. 29b)

"For since it was a man who brought death into the world, a man also brought resurrection of the dead. As in Adam all men die, so in Christ all will be brought to life." (Cor.xv.21f.)

"...one man died for all and therefore all mankind has died. His purpose in dying for all was that men, while still in life, should cease to live for themselves, and should live for him who for their sake died and was raised to life." (II Cor. v. 14bf.)

"It was clearly fitting that God for whom and through whom all things exist should, in bringing many sons to glory, make the leader who delivers them perfect through sufferings. For a consecrating priest and those whom he consecrates are all of one stock; and that is why the Son does not shrink from calling men his brothers, when he says, 'I will proclaim thy name to my brothers; in full assembly I will sing thy praise'; and again, 'I will keep my trust fixed on him'; and again, 'Here am I, and the children whom God has given me.' The children of a family share (kekoinoneken) the same flesh and blood; and so he too shared (meteschen) ours, so that through death he might break the power of him who had death at his command, that, the devil; and might liberate those who, through fear of death, had all their lifetime been in servitude. It is not angels, mark you, that he takes to himself, but the sons of Abraham. And therefore he had to be made like (homoiothenai) these brothers of his in every way, so that he might be merciful and faithful as their high priest before God, to expiate the sins of the people. For since he himself has passed through the test of suffering, he is able to help those who are meeting their test now." (Heb. ii. 1 0ff.)

But on the other side of the paradox is a affirmation of a newness and sinlessness which mark a distinction between Christ's humanity and ours.[10] It is true that sinlessness is a negative quality for which there could be no direct evidence, and that, in any case, the explicit affirmations of Christ's sinlessness in the New Testament are all part of the expression of a belief, reached, no doubt, through experience, in his Saviourhood rather than being part of a discussion of the quality of his manhood as such: his sinlessness is an aspect of his proved ability, whether as an unblemished sacrifice or under some other figure, to rescue us from sin. But it nevertheless constitutes a New Testament conviction about the character of his manhood. Here are the chief passages:

"Christ was innocent of sin, and yet for our sake God made him one with the sinfulness of men, so that in him we might be made one with the goodness of God himself." (II Cor. v. 21)

"...Tested every way, only without sin." (Heb. iv. 15b)

"The price was paid in precious blood, as it were of a lamb without mark or blemish - the blood of Christ." (I Pet. i. 19)

But perhaps even more significant is the association of newness and the idea of new creation or new birth or a new beginning with Jesus. Here are the chief passages:

"The old leaven of corruption is working among you. Purge it out, and then you will be bread of a new baking. As Christians you are unleavened Passover bread, for indeed our Passover has begun; the sacrifice is offered - Christ himself." (Cor. v. 7)

"When anyone is united to Christ, there is a new world (ktisis); the old order has gone, and a new order has already begun." (II Cor. v. 17)

"Circumcision is nothing; uncircumcision is nothing; the only thing that counts is a new creation (ktisis)!" (Gal. vi. 15)

"...His is the primacy over all created things. In him everything in heaven and on earth was created... He is, moreover, the head of the body, the church. He is its origin, the first to return from the dead (prototokos ek ton nekron)..." (Col. i. 15b, 16a, 18a)

"He it is who sacrificed himself for us, to set us free from all wickedness and to make us a pure people marked out for his own." (Tit. ii. 14)

"...the first-born from the dead (ho prototokos ton nekron)..." (Rev.i.5)

"...the prime source of all God's creation (he arche tes ktiseos tou Theou)." (Rev. iii. 14b)

All these phrases in different ways bear witness to a conviction that with Jesus a new humanity had begun — as human as the old, but not sinful like the old.[11] And it is possibly this distinctiveness and newness, coupled with a conviction about the continuity, that led Paul to use the ambiguous word *homoioma* which is capable of implying both identity and also resemblance without identity. In Rom. viii. 3 the phrase *en homoiomati sarkos hamartias* might mean 'in what was exactly like sinful flesh' or 'in what only resembled sinful flesh.' The English Jerusalem Bible adroitly renders 'in a body as physical as any sinful body' but the French seems to reproduce the ambiguity of the Greek: 'dans une chair semblable a celle du peche.' Similar doubt attaches to homoioma in Phil. ii. 7.[12] At any rate, it is this conviction of newness and a fresh start that, no doubt, is involved also in the idea of virgin birth. Without discussing the historicity of the virgin birth, or the objection that it does for the modern mind precisely what it was intended by the New Testament writers not to do, it is evident that, to the ancient mind at least, it meant that Jesus, if truly man, was yet, as truly, a new kind of man, free from the entail of human sinfulness. It bears witness to the same end of the paradox in Christian conviction as that for which the 'newness' passages stand.

But if both ends of the paradox are there — both the continuity and the discontinuity — we ask (exactly as we did in relation to the paradox of humiliation and exaltation) whether there is anything that brings them together inside an intelligible system. One point at which any tentative answer to this question may be reasonably tested is the attitude of New Testament writers to Christ's temptation. One widely agreed characteristic of real humanity is that it has genuinely free will, and that the temptation to use that will contrary to God's will should (at least at some stage) have exercised a genuine attraction. Therefore, if Christ's humanity was real and continuous with ours, then there must have been something in him which consented to temptation,[13] in which case was he not sinful? Alternatively, if there was nothing in him that consented to temptation, then the temptation cannot have been real: he was incapable of sin and not genuinely human. Now Heb. iv. 15 asserts that Christ was indeed tempted, yet without sin. In view of our notions of temptation, is this simply a bleak affirmation of an insoluble paradox, without the shadow of an attempt to bring it into a plausible unity? I wonder whether, once more, it may not be to the filial relation and the quality of loyalty which it implies that we must look for some sort of an answer. Filial obedience means loyalty. The perfect Son is undeviatingly loyal to the Father's purposes. But what does loyalty mean, in human personality? Does it not mean a steady and undeviating 'set' of the will's current? In a desperately long battle, a soldier may yearn with every muscle in his weary body to gain the relief of desertion; but it is possible for him, at the same time, never to deviate a hair's breadth from the steady 'set' of the current of his loyalty to his country or his cause. Physically — even mentally — he may consent to the relief he longs for; but the 'set' of his will remains constant in its direction. In another context, and by way of another example, one might say that this 'set' of the will will negate what might otherwise have been 'looking lustfully on a woman' (Matt. v. 28).

So, perhaps, it may be with the humanity of Jesus. He is involved in all the circumstances of normal humanity: whether by heredity or not, at least by reason of belonging to a sinful society, he is involved in extreme temptations to 'desert.' He is involved also in circumstances where to choose any course is necessarily to do harm to somebody (for instance, by breaking his mother's heart or precipitating the downfall of a disciple). But that does not necessarily mean (does it?) that the 'set' of his loyalty was not undeviatingly in the direction of God's will, nor that he could not make, with absolute perfection, the right response to those particular circumstances. This conception of response makes it seem to me incorrect to suggest that, because Jesus' physical and mental constitution must have been particular and not general or 'average,' therefore he cannot have been perfect. Perfection of response is, in any human situation, necessarily quite particular. But the 'scandal of particularity' does not prevent a new perfection coming into existence — a perfection of response in given circumstances: for a Jew, of Jesus' constitution, in the social and political circumstances, of his day and country, his response (so the New Testament writers seem to say) was absolutely in line with God's will. And this absoluteness, though within the narrow limits of the particular, represents a newness of relationship within the old, spoilt humanity. To respond to him is, therefore, to be brought inside a new creation.[14]

But of course the questions arise: Is this a newness of degree only or also of kind? One can only reply, to the first, that the newness is something which Christians believed they could not have by their own efforts. It was 'given,' and no amount of striving could achieve it. In that sense, the perfection of Christ's response was an 'intrusion,' if you like, from outside. It did not simply 'emerge,' as by evolution: it was a gift from 'above,' a new 'creation.' And yet it was achieved within the circumstances of humanity at that time and in that place. It was genuinely from within, in man, in flesh like ours. And, secondly, while of course it is impossible to demonstrate that such absolute perfection existed, the point is that to conceive it in terms of response does offer a way of relating the absolute to the particular and the relative, if the evidence of Christian experience seems to require such a postulate. I doubt if we can get much further than simply the recognition that both the perfection and the relativity have to be affirmed if we are to do justice to Christian experience. But if there is any unifying factor, it will be in terms of personal relationship and filial loyalty and 'the paradox of grace.'[15]

## III

But the relation between the divine and the human is not the only major paradox created by the interpretation of Christian experience in the New Testament. Another concerns the relation, in the manhood of Jesus, between the individual and the corporate. Later christological thought has formulated the problem in terms of the question, was Jesus a man or was he Man?, and the late D.M. Baillie is among the writers who have come down decisively in favour of the view that, since Jesus was undoubtedly a man, it is impossible to identify him, as is done by such as R.C. Moberly, with Mankind.[16] But it is clear that at any rate Paul recognized Christ as 'Adam,' that is, as Man, in some collective sense, as well as knowing him as an individual figure of history. I have attempted elsewhere[17] to present a summary analysis of Paul's subtle use of the preposition *en* followed by a designation of Jesus. I have also tried to show that, although Luke and John, with their much more individualistic tendency, do not share Paul's language in this respect (despite John's striking use of *en*), the recognition of Christ as an inclusive personality seems to be implied, for Christians of the New Testament period generally, by their sacramental practice. There is not space here for a repetition of these studies in detail: but it seems difficult to escape the conclusion that the New Testament reflects a conviction that Jesus was both an individual of history and a corporate, inclusive personality - a body, in whom Christians found themselves limbs. And it seems, therefore, that experience of Jesus Christ, from the first days until now, confronts us with a paradox that has to be accepted, whether or not it is capable of any sort of resolution. C.H. Dodd states the matter clearly as follows (his references are to St John's gospel):

He was the true self of the human race, standing in that perfect union with God to which others can attain only as they are incorporate in Him; the mind, whose thought is truth absolute (xiv. 6). Which other men think after Him; the true life of man, which other men live by sharing it with Him (xiv. 6, 20, vi. 57).

It is clear that this conception raises a new problem. It challenges the mind to discover a doctrine of personality, which will make conceivable this combination of the universal and the particular in a single person. A naive individualism regarding man, or a naive anthropomorphism regarding God, makes nonsense of the Johannine Christology. Ancient thought, when it left the ground of such naive conceptions, lost hold upon the concrete actuality of the person. It denied personality in man by making the human individual no more than an unreal 'imitation' of the abstract universal Man, and it denied personality in God by making Him no more than the abstract unity of being. A Christian philosophy starting from the Johannine doctrine of Jesus as Son of Man should be able to escape the impasse into which all ancient thought fell, and to give an account of personality in God and in ourselves."[18]

It may be questioned whether the Johannine use of that particular term, 'the Son of Man,' is itself so characteristic of the doctrine to which reference is here made; but that is a detail. The main point stands - that in Jesus a new problem is presented, and a new hope arises. The problem is constituted by one who, although a vividly portrayed individual, yet turns out also to be more than individual - an inclusive personality, the species *novus homo*. The hope is that this opens up new possibilities of (as C.H. Dodd puts it) giving an account of personality in God and in ourselves - and of entering into the resulting experience. And it is relevant both to the problem and to the hope that in the New Testament there is reflected a new way of experiencing the Spirit of God. For Christians, 'the Holy Spirit' (their most usual description of the Spirit of God) was the Spirit of God's unique Son reproducing in them the intimate trust and obedience which Jesus himself had shown (Mark xiv. 36, Rom. viii. 15, Gal. iv. 6). This means that the attitude of the individual, Jesus, is multiplied by as many times as there are Christians: it becomes available in plurality; so that whereas Christians find themselves 'in' Jesus Christ (as their more-than-individual environment, as the body of which they are limbs), yet each one, individually, finds himself indwelt by the Holy Spirit and thus possessed of (and possessed by) the individuality of Jesus. Somewhere in the Christian experience of the Holy Spirit through Jesus Christ lies the new synthesis of individuality and corporeity: the paradox of the incarnation, while it remains intellectually insoluble, is this put into effect in experience.

## IV

To conclude: the New Testament states paradoxes about the manhood of Jesus without successfully reconciling them into a rationally coherent system; and it seems probable that the incarnation has to be recognized as of such a character as to impose this insoluble tension on the human mind. If there are any pointers towards a unification and a resolution of the paradox of continuity and discontinuity, they seem to be in the direction of something in terms of will and of personal relationship, and of a perfection of response on the part of Jesus to particular circumstances — a perfection such that the result is seen and experienced as a new and creative event, rather than merely a better example than anything that had gone before.

And, as for that other paradox, of the individual and the corporate, it may be that the resolution is in the experience of the Holy Spirit. According to the predominant usage in the Pauline epistles, Christians are in Christ but the Holy Spirit is in Christians.[19] And the Holy Spirit in Christians enables them to utter the cry of intimacy and obedience, 'Abba, your will be done!' which the individual, Jesus of Nazareth, uttered in his lifetime. Somewhere here, perhaps, lie the roots of that subtle relation between the individual and the corporate which, whether it can be explained or not, is certainly one of the phenomena of christology.

As was said at the beginning, the topics of this sketch have been arbitrarily selected out of an endless range of problems; but there is no doubt that the manhood of Jesus is among the most pressing of christological questions; and, within that area, the paradoxes here briefly considered are of decisive importance in New Testament thought.

# NOTES

1. See my essay, 'Further Reflexions on Philippians 2:5-11' in **Apostolic History and the Gospel, Biblical and Historical Essays** Presented to F.F. Bruce, eds W.W. Gasque and R.P. Martin (1970), pp. 264ff.
2. F.W.H. Myers, **Saint Paul** (1902), p. 16.
3. Cf. a description of Schroeder's art, in a concert programme (King's College Chapel, 11 July 1970), which refers to the texture of a partita composed by him as 'notable for that artistic economy of means which is the hallmark of a composer who understands the instrument's strengths as well as its limitations.'
4. **The Testament of Jesus** (1968).
5. 'Zur Interpretation des Johannes-Evangeliums' in Geschichte und Glaube I (Gesammelte Aufsatze III), 104ff.
6. Curiously, Hebrews itself, at xii: 7, uses a line of argument in which suffering is associated with sonship; but even there, the point is not quite the one here in question.
7. **The Humanity and Divinity of Christ** (1967), passim.
8. This leaves unasked (at least in so many words) such thorny questions as whether the humanity assumed by Christ was sinful before the assumption.
9. Epistola 101.7 (P.G. 37, 181), *to gar aproslepton atherapeuton*.
10. The other half of Gregory's terse epigram (see above) was: 'but what has been united with God is saved,' *ho de henotai to(i) theo(i), touto kai sozetai*.
11. Cf. Iren. adv. Haer. III 21.10 (Harvey p. 120), where the question is asked why, if God wanted to make a new beginning, he did not again take dust from the ground, but, instead, caused the fashioning to be made from Mary; and the answer given is *hina me alle he plasis genetai, mede allo to sozomenon e(i), all' autos ekeinos anakephalaiothe(i), teroumenes tes homoiotetos;* i.e., (apparently) 'in order that the fashioning [in question — that is, the making of the new humanity in Christ] should not be different [from the original fashioning of the first Adam], and that what was saved should not be different, but that he himself [i.e. the original Adam] should be recapitulated, with the likeness [to the original Adam] preserved.' In F. Sagnard's edition, in **Sources Chretiennes** (1952),

p.373, the Latin text is: Vt non 'alia' plasmatio fieret neque 'alia' esset plasmatio quae saluaretur, sed eadem ipsa recapitularetur, seruata similitudine; and his translation (p.374), taking plasis as concrete: 'C'est pour que cette oeuvre ainsi faconnee ne fut pas autre que la premiere et qu'il n'y en eut pas une autre a etre sauvee, mais que ce fut exactement "la meme," "recapitulee," en respectant la ressemblance.'

12. The other occurences of *homoioma* in the New Testament are Rom. i. 23, v.14., vi.5, Rev. ix.7. Relevant also is *homoiotes* in Heb. iv. 15; but none is quite conclusive for our purpose.

13. See e.g., Knox, op cit. p.47.

14. Cf. a brilliant passage about Christ's temptations in Austin Farrer's **Lord I Believe** (1962), pp.44ff., including the following: 'The essential point here is that we should see in what the impossibility of his sinning lay. If it lay in the virtual fixing of his choices before he made them, then indeed he had no temptations, nor was his life a human life at all. But suppose it lay in a perfect trust reposed by him in his Father, assuring him that in all the unseen possibilities and sudden temptations of the coming time, his Father's power and Spirit would not fail him? ... Certainly there was something fixed and inflexible about him, but it was not a pattern of moral choice forestalling all surprises, it was divine Sonship, filial love, absolute dependence, entire derivation' (pp.46f.).

15. D.M. Baillie, **God was in Christ** (1948), ch.v.

16. Op. cit. ch. iv.

17. **The Phenomenon of the New Testament** (1967), ch. ii.

18. **The Interpretation of the Fourth Gospel** (1953), p.249.

19. See **The Phenomenon of the New Testament**, loc. cit. and references there to M. Bouttier.

# 6

# DEVELOPMENT IN NEW TESTAMENT CHRISTOLOGY

## R. T. France

## I. "Evolution" or "Development"?

In 1977 two books on Christology were published independently in Britain. The first, a symposium entitled, **The Myth of God Incarnate**,[1] attracted a lot of publicity, perhaps more on account of the provocative nature of its title than for any major contribution to scholarly discussion. The second, less noticed at the time, is likely to prove of more long-term significance: **The Origin of Christology** by C.F.D. Moule.[2]

Moule's primary aim is to call attention to, and to challenge, an assumption which underlies much recent christological discussion, and of which in fact **The Myth of God Incarnate** provides an obvious example. He characterizes this as a theory of "**evolution**," as opposed to one of "**development**" which Moule himself offers as an alternative. The terms chosen may not be the most helpful, particularly in circles where the word "evolution" has emotive connotations in quite a different connection, but the point is crucial.

In Moule's own words, the "evolutionary" approach is "the tendency to explain the change from (say) invoking Jesus as a revered Master to the acclamation of him as a divine Lord by the theory that, when the Christian movement spread beyond Palestinian soil, it began to come under the influence of non-Semitic Saviour- cults and to assimilate some of their ideas"; the result was the rise of new christological categories derived from non-Christian mythology, which were alien to the original character and teaching of Jesus. Moule's "developmental" approach, by contrast, "is to explain all the various estimates of Jesus reflected in the New Testament as, in essence, only attempts to describe what was already there from the beginning."[3]

This is, to my mind, one of the most important issues in current christological debate. Was the increasingly sophisticated christology of the New Testament authors (and still more of subsequent Christian discussion) due to the addition of new ideas which substantially changed the underlying understanding of Jesus, or was it simply working out more explicitly what was already there? In what sense can Jesus the Son of God, the second Person of the Trinity, be recognized to be the same person as the historical Jesus of Nazareth? Is there a discernible continuity between them, and if so, how is the development of the more theologically explicit language and thought to be explained?

That there **was** a development is clear enough. To take the most extreme case, the use of the word "God" to describe Jesus is very rare in the New Testament, and occurs almost exclusively in what are generally agreed to be the later writings (with the one remarkable exception of Romans 9:5).[4] And in almost all these passages there is hot debate over either the original reading of the text or the syntactical analysis which allows the word **theos** to be construed as referring to Jesus (or in some cases on both points at once!).[5] The gospels (even the Gospel of John) do not portray Jesus as claiming in so many words that he was God, and in this they have historical verisimilitude on their side — the picture of the carpenter of Nazareth walking the hills of Galilee proclaiming "I am God" is not one which rings true to the monotheistic culture of first-century Palestine. As a public relations exercise it would have been a guaranteed disaster. And yet a generation or two later Christians, including those of Jewish background, were beginning, however hesitantly, to use such language. Is it then necessary to see this remarkable change as the result of influence from pagan mythological ideas about "the gods come down to us in the likeness of men" (and therefore as totally lacking in "factual" correspondence with what was actually true about Jesus)? Or was there something "already there" in Jesus which, however, veiled in its expression at the time, made it inevitable that eventually he would be described in some such terms?

The terms used would, of course, vary depending on the cultural and linguistic background of the writer; and indeed the immediate semantic value of a term such as "son of God" would also differ from one reader to another. New ideas and experiences, in theology as anywhere else, have to be expressed in terms which have not previously been used in quite the same way, and which may carry different connotations depending on the reader's background. In the process of exploring the significance of Jesus many different categories were used, some of which proved to have more lasting value than others.[6] At first, these were mainly Jewish categories, since it was among Jewish Christians that the process of development began. But as the Christian message began to be preached in a wider context, new terms came to be used. In the following centuries Greek philosophical categories came to be adopted as the chief currency of christological debate, a process which culminated in the "orthodox" christological formulations of the great councils, in which the language of the New Testament has been left far behind. But even in the New Testament itself it is possible to discern the beginning of this development, as for instance in John's adoption for the first time of what became a central term in patristic debate, when he described Jesus as the **Logos**, a term which will be understood differently depending on whether you come to it from the background of Old Testament thought about the "word of Yahweh" or from a Greek philosophical school which sees **logos** as the governing principle of the universe.[7]

The question we need to ask is whether such terms and categories of thought, whether Jewish or pagan, are themselves the source of the christological ideas they are used to express, to the extent that the content of the christology is determined by the linguistic and conceptual apparatus available, or whether they are rather, in Martin Hengel's helpful analogy,[8] to be seen as "building material" available to the early Christians for the construction of a christology which derived its content not from any existing model, but from the new events, experiences and teaching which had come to them in the life and ministry of Jesus.

## II. A Sample Area: Christological Development in the Gospels

In the necessarily brief compass of this paper, I cannot discuss this question of "evolution v. development" with regard to the whole of the New Testament. But we may appropriately focus on the gospels, for there we find both an ostensible portrait of the beginnings of Christianity in the ministry of Jesus, and also at the same time some indication of the subsequent development of thought about him, at least in the explicit reflections of the evangelists themselves, but also in what we can discern of the development of the traditions between the events recorded and the incorporation of them into the finished gospels.

In this connection it has been usual to deal separately with the Synoptic Gospels and with John, since it is generally recognized that the process of development has gone much further in the case of John, resulting in a more explicit presentation of Jesus as the son of God who came from heaven and will return there. In more recent scholarship, however, this difference has been understood more as one of degree than of kind, in that all the evangelists, not just John, are seen to have their own christological tendencies which affect the way they present their material; there is a Marcan Jesus, a Matthean Jesus and a Lucan Jesus as well as a Johannine Jesus, and all these portraits in their differing ways reveal the features of the son of God displayed in the person of Jesus of Nazareth. At the same time there is an increasing tendency to recognize in John a more historically grounded tradition, to a large extent independent of that found in the Synoptics, but none the less reliable for that.[9] John may have carried out a more thorough and consistent process of christological interpretation in the way he has presented Jesus' life and teaching, but he is not therefore to be dismissed as having lost touch with the historical reality of Jesus. The distinction between John and the Synoptics tends therefore to be less sharply drawn than it used to be.

## (a) The Messiahship of Jesus in the gospels.

For the earliest Christian preachers, working in a primarily Jewish context, one of the main points to be established was that Jesus was the **Messiah**. Indeed during his ministry we are told that this was a question regularly canvassed by those who encountered him. All the gospels, in differing degrees, focus on this question, and Matthew's overriding concern with the theme of "fulfillment" in Jesus clearly relates to this issue. How far, then is it possible to discern a development in this area?

Discussion of Jesus' Messiahship frequently begins with William Wrede's theory of the "Messianic Secret."[10] For Wrede, Mark's presentation of Jesus as Messiah was not a development from Jesus' own claim, but a falsification of it. It was the belief of the early Christians (as a result of the resurrection) that Jesus had been the Messiah which caused them both to attribute falsely to Jesus a claim to that effect and to explain its absence from the tradition (as well as the embarrassing failure of the Jewish establishment to accept him as Messiah) by the theory that Jesus deliberately suppressed any public acknowledgment of this supposed role during his pre-Easter ministry. Even the apparently very basic concept of Jesus as the Messiah is then, on this theory, not the result of development of what was "already there," but rather represents the "evolution" of a new and alien category.

It would be possible (though not perhaps very convincing) to isolate the specific occurrences of the word **Christos**, and to set these aside as unhistorical elements in the tradition. But the issue of "Messiahship" involves much more than the usage of the title itself. Some of the most central elements in the gospel narrative presuppose that a messianic claim was involved. The accounts of Jesus' baptism and temptation focus on the distinctive role he was to fulfill as the one upon whom the Spirit came, and whose identity was declared in terms of Isaiah 42:1 and Psalm 2:7.[11] The feeding of the 5,000 takes place in an atmosphere of messianic expectation, and indeed it is hard to see how a ministry such as Jesus exercised could fail to evoke the sort of response indicated in John 6:14-15, where the people hail Jesus as "the prophet who is coming to the world" and attempt to force him into the role of "king." The retreat to Caesarea Philippi and the teaching about the coming suffering both of Jesus and his followers which is associated with it would make little sense without Peter's use of the title **Christos** as the focus of Jesus' subsequent "re- interpretation." The involvement of the "messianic" figures Elijah and Moses is fundamental to the account of the transfiguration (and that of Elijah at other points in the tradition as well). The entry to Jerusalem is viewed by all four gospels as amessianic demonstration, and it is hard to see what other meaning it could have had in earlier tradition. Jesus' demonstration in the temple is also best seen as conveying a similar message.[12] The trial of Jesus before the Sanhedrin climaxes in the question of his alleged claim to be the Messiah; if that is eliminated, or if Jesus refused to acknowledge the alleged claim, what was the basis of his conviction? The subsequent Roman trial clearly depends on a charge of seditious intention, focused on the title "King of the Jews"; it is agreed that it was on such a charge that Jesus was executed, and it is hard to see how Wrede's non-messianic Jesus could have attracted that fate.

These are among the more prominent aspects of the story of Jesus which make little sense without at least an implicit messianic claim, and it would be a very bold critic who would attempt to discard all such stories as unhistorical at least in their essential outline. There is, of course, an element of reluctance or of reinterpretation about Jesus' response to overtly messianic language in some of these stories,[13] but that may tell us more about the possible connotations of **Christos** in popular Jewish thought than about Jesus' own view of his role.

In fact the title **Christos** itself is not the main basis for asserting Jesus' "messianic consciousness." This is found rather in the subtle way in which the idea of the fulfillment of Old Testament hope in Jesus' coming and through his ministry is woven into the tradition at many levels. Incidents such as the sermon at Nazareth (Luke 4:16-30) and the reply to John the Baptist (Matthew 11:4-5) depend on this idea, as does also the fundamental summary of Jesus' preaching in Mark 1:15 etc. The centrality of the coming of the kingdom of God in Jesus' preaching must raise the question of the status of the one who brings it. A similar force derives from the frequent mention of Jesus' unique authority, particularly when that authority is seen in a sovereign declaration of the will of God which dispenses not only with the traditions of the scribes but also with the generally understood sense of the Old Testament itself.

Many more such indications of a "messianic" element in Jesus' teaching and activity could be listed. Several of the sayings and incidents involved would be disputed by some scholars as historical records of what Jesus actually said and did, but the case is strong enough to survive a good deal of skepticism over individual items. The impression is very firmly embedded in the tradition of a Jesus who, whether he used or welcomed the title **Christos** or not, spoke and acted as the one in whom God's eschatological purposes were coming to fulfillment (and that is what **we** mean by "the Messiah," even if the term **Christos** itself may have carried more specific and less desirable connotations for Jesus and his contemporaries).

On such grounds it may reasonably be concluded that the use of messianic language for Jesus is a clear case of the sort of "development" Moule is arguing for. The title **Christos** itself is far more evident in the post-Easter preaching of the church and in subsequent Christian writing than it seems likely to have been during Jesus' ministry. It emerges apparently as a newly established theme in Christian preaching as a result of the resurrection (Acts 2:36), and the title about which Jesus' own attitude seems to have been at least ambivalent now becomes central to what his followers have to say about him. But this is not a matter of foisting onto Jesus after his death a role which he himself would have repudiated (as the "evolutionary" approach would insist), but of expressing openly and unequivocally a perception which had been implicit in Jesus' own presentation of his mission but which it would have been premature (and politically undesirable) to express in such terms while he was still on earth.

Moule, having reached such a conclusion from his brief discussion of the title "Christ," concludes drily: "This is an absurdly old-fashioned conclusion, but the question is whether it does not still fit the evidence."[14] I believe that it does, and that it thus provides a paradigm case of how "development" (in Moule's sense of the word) operated in New Testament christology.

## (b) Jesus as the Son of God in the gospels

The preceding discussion may seem scarcely relevant to today's Christological debates. It is not Jesus' Messiahship that is under discussion today, but the claim that he is to be understood as "more than human," a claim often encapsulated in the title "Son of God." Indeed even in ancient christological discussion this was so, as the title "Christ," while not explicitly put aside, became increasingly less central to the discussion, particularly as Christian thought moved more outside Jewish circles. It remained one of the given factors rather than a matter for debate.

It has become customary to distinguish between "functional" and "ontological" aspects of christology. In terms of that distinction the question of Jesus' Messiahship is primarily a functional question, a matter of the role he had to fulfill, while the centre of interest soon became, and has remained, rather the ontological question of who he **was**. The two are of course inseparable:[15] the role he could fulfill depends on who he was, and who he was is likely to be discerned primarily through what he did. But in so far as the distinction can properly be drawn, "Son of God" promises to be a more relevant title than "Christ" for the "ontological" questions on which today's christological debate is focused. It is possible, to be sure, that "son of God" could have carried no more ontological implications than "Messiah" for some of Jesus' contemporaries, if, as is increasingly being recognized, it was a title which might be used in at least some Jewish circles for the Messiah.[16] It is certainly true that in both pagan and Jewish circles such phrases could be used of people who, either by office or by character, were felt to have a special relationship with a god or gods, without necessarily implying any doubt about their being themselves "merely human."[17] But it is clear that the New Testament usage of the title implied more than that, and formed a crucial element in the church's ultimate confession of the divinity of Jesus.

Is it then possible to trace in the case of such language the same sort of development which we have seen in the use of messianic categories? Was there anything in the life and sayings of the historical Jesus which might appropriately give rise not only to the use of the title "Son of God" but also to the implication of his being "more than human"?

A central issue here must be the clear difference in perspective between the Gospel of John and the other canonical gospels with regard to the sort of language Jesus used about himself. The Johannine Jesus not only refers to himself as "Son of God" or "the Son" some 25 times, and to God as "Father" some 120 times, but his teaching develops a consistent view of his unique relationship with God which, for all its acceptance that "the Father is greater than I," nonetheless finds its appropriate culmination in such sayings as "I and the Father are one" and "he who has seen me has seen the Father." While the other gospels have a few sayings of Jesus which reflect a similar self-understanding (and a greater number of places where others refer to Jesus as "Son of God'), there can be no doubt that we have here a specifically Johannine emphasis. From this most modern scholarship has concluded that the Gospel of John is not the place to look for information about the historical Jesus.

But here the concept of "development" is again important. It is one thing to recognize that John presents a more "developed" christology, in the teaching ascribed to Jesus as well as in the evangelist's own assertions, but quite another to assume that therefore there was no historical basis for this christology in the teaching of Jesus. We have already noted that Johannine scholarship in the last thirty years or so has swung markedly back towards a recognition that John had independent and valuable sources of information, and that therefore when he differs from the other gospels it may not necessarily be because he is reading back later beliefs into the story of Jesus. A few years ago this trend reached its remarkable climax in the posthumous publication of J.A.T. Robinson's book, **The Priority of John**,[18] which argues not necessarily that John's was the first gospel to be written, but that it is the "closest to source," in that its presentation of Jesus reflects the most reliable information on what Jesus was really like, so that it should have "procedural priority" in our reconstruction of the historical Jesus. Thus instead of taking the Synoptic portrait as our primary framework into which Johannine material must somehow be made to fit, we should work the other way round. Robinson's argument includes (though it does not entirely depend on) the conclusion that the author of the gospel was John the son of Zebedee, so that his primary source of information is his own reminiscences as one of the very closest of Jesus' disciples throughout his ministry. In that case, Robinson argues, we have every reason to be confident that John "got it right -historically and theologically.'

It is hardly surprising that so unfashionable a view has as yet received little welcome in the scholarly world. Robinson's own earlier experience had warned him to expect this.[19] But such a radical challenge to the accepted consensus coming not from a dogmatic conservatism but from a full and fresh reconsideration of the evidence deserves to be taken seriously, however uncomfortable its wider implications for our conception of Christian origins. In that case, the Johannine Jesus may have a lot more to tell us about what Jesus of Nazareth actually said and believed about himself than is generally admitted.[20]

But in any case the relation between the Synoptic Jesus and the Johannine is not one of total discontinuity. The assertion of a unique relationship[21] in the statement that "No one knows the Son except the Father and no one knows the Father except the Son" (Mt. 11:27; Lk. 10:22), which is sometimes said to be too "Johannine" to fit in a Synoptic gospel, is not alone. The declaration of Jesus' special status as "Son of God" is central tot he Synoptic accounts of his baptism, and the subsequent temptation as recorded by Matthew and Luke focuses on this newly declared relationship, "If you are the Son of God ..." The repetition of the same declaration at the transfiguration would serve only to reinforce this conviction. It emerges most obviously in Jesus' use of the name "Father" in addressing God (Mk. 14:36, using the Aramaic term Abba), a use which is not confined to John's gospel, and which has long been recognized as one of the distinctive features of Jesus' approach to God when contrasted with what we know of contemporary Jewish piety.[22] It even comes to public expression in Jesus' choice of the figure of the owner's only son to represent his own role in the parable of the tenants in the vineyard (Mk. 12:1-12), a choice daring enough to provide a plausible basis for the High Priest's inclusion of the title "the Son of the Blessed" in his challenge relating to Jesus' alleged claims (Mk. 14:61). Even the assertion, potentially embarrassing for a high christology, that there is something Jesus does not know (Mk. 13:32) is expressed in such a way as to locate himself as "the Son" in a position in the ascending order between the angels and God.

All that is obvious on the surface. A belief that Jesus neither thought nor spoke of himself as the Son of God involves the rejection of more than the Johannine testimony. But to focus attention solely on the title "Son of God" is perhaps to miss the strength of the case that all the gospels, not just John, present Jesus as conscious of a "more than human" status. We have noted already the impression of a unique authority which comes across in many aspects of Jesus' ministry: people leave everything and follow him, accepting his demand for total allegiance even at the expense of the closest family ties; he declares the will of God with a sovereign assurance, "not like their scribes," frequently using his distinctive formula "Amen, I say to you';[23] his power over illness and even over the forces of nature is displayed in many remarkable miracles, and even the demons are unable to resist his authority. We are frequently told that people were "amazed" at what they heard and saw, and asked "Who is this?" None of this, of course, in itself requires us to believe that Jesus was anything more than a very remarkable man who was closely in touch with God. But there are times in the stories of Jesus' ministry when such a view begins to seem inadequate. Sometimes Jesus seems to assume the right to exercise what are specifically divine functions. His response to the theologically correct comment that only God can forgive sins is not to retract his claim to do so, but to prove it by a miracle (Mk. 2:1-12; cf. Lk.23:43). He gives rest to those who accept his yoke, a gift offered in Jewish though only by the divine wisdom (Mt. 11:28-30; cf. Ben Sira 51:23-27). His words, like those of God, have eternal validity (Mk.13:31; cf. Is. 40:8). He will be the one who determines people's final destiny, and the basis for the decision will be their relationship with him (Mt. 7:21-23). He is the final judge, the king in an eternal kingdom (Mt. 25:31ff). To accept or to reject him is to accept or reject God (Mt. 10:40; Lk. 10:16). Such language does not constitute a formal claim to be divine. Some of it may be seen as no more than a rather exaggerated expression of the consciousness of a prophetic commission. But it is at least suggestive of something more far reaching in Jesus' self-consciousness.

This suggestion is strengthened when we notice some of the ways the Old Testament is used in Jesus' recorded teaching. That he should refer to Old Testament messianic hopes as fulfilled in his ministry is not so surprising in the light of what we have seen above. But sometimes he takes up passages which refer to God himself, not to a messianic figure, and uses these equally naturally as if they refer to himself. Thus his mission "to seek and to save the lost" (Lk. 19:10) echoes Ezekiel's prophecy about God himself as the shepherd (Ezek.34, esp. vv.16,22), while his defense of the children's praise of him is based on a Psalm about how God is praised (Mt. 21:16;cf. Ps.8:2). He is the stone on which people stumble, taking up an image for God in Isaiah 8:14f (Lk. 20:18). He identifies John the Baptist as the returning Elijah of Malachi 3:1; 4:5f, whose role it is to precede the coming of God himself to judgement (Mk. 9:12f; Mt. 11:10,14). The portrayal of himself as judge in the final assize is modelled on a group of Old Testament visions of God himself coming as judge (Mt. 25:31ff; cf.Dan. 7:9f; Joel 3:1-12; Zech. 14:5).[24] None of this is argued out, it is simply taken for granted that such language is appropriate to Jesus, just as he seems to feel no difficulty in portraying himself in some of the parables in roles which are typically in the Old Testament descriptions of God himself - the shepherd, the bridegroom, the sower.[25]

Jesus' chosen "title" by which to refer to himself seems to have been "the Son of Man." Later Christian thought has typically taken this term as an indication of his humanity, and so has contrasted it with "Son of God." It is reasonably clear, however, that whatever the original lexical value of the phrase "a son of man," the relevant background for Jesus' distinctive self-designation as "the Son of Man" is to be found in the vision of "one like a son of man" in Daniel chapter 7, a passage from which Jewish thought was already beginning to develop the expectation of a heavenly deliverer.[26] In the view of some recent scholars it is not going too far to claim that far from conveying the opposite to "Son of God," Jesus' choice of "the Son of Man" is intended to convey something of the same connotations, a claim summed up in the title of Seyoon Kim's monograph, **The "Son of Man'" as the Son of God.**[27]

What we have been considering are indications, sometimes subtle and uncertain, but perhaps the more impressive for their very unobtrusiveness, that Jesus was conscious of a status which was "more than human." He did not call himself "God" — how could he? But if even some of this material is a genuine reflection of how Jesus spoke and thought, we have here at least the raw materials to enable us to discern a self-consciousness that forms a solid basis for the church's subsequent confession that Jesus was in a unique sense "Son of God," a confession which in due course found its proper expression in the worship of Jesus as God.

We have often been warned of the danger of attempting a psychological analysis of Jesus. It is a necessary warning, but I do not believe that it prohibits us from taking notice of such hints in the accounts of Jesus as we have been considering. James Dunn boldly reopened the question in his book **Jesus and the Spirit**.[28] The first part of the book is devoted to "the Religious Experience of Jesus," and within this section there is an important discussion of Jesus' awareness that he was the Son of God.[29] Jesus knew that he was God's son, Dunn argues, not just in the sense that any religious man might make such a claim, but with a distinctive intimacy which must be called unique, to the extent that other people's sonship is in some way dependent on his. To claim this as evidence of a metaphysical "divine consciousness" is, Dunn believes, to outrun what we may responsibly conclude from the gospels, since he is not prepared to use the Gospel of John as a source for what the historical Jesus actually said and did. But even so, there is here, we may reasonably suggest, a firm foundation in the self-consciousness of the historical Jesus on which the later development of more explicitly metaphysical language could be built. If, with John Robinson, you are prepared to give more historical credence to the Gospel of John, that foundation is significantly strengthened.

## III The Nature of Christological Development

We have considered only two sample areas of christological development, and those only in relation to the gospels. If we could have taken our study further through the rest of the New Testament the importance of this concept of development would have become much more evident.[30]

This study suggests that we are wrong to look in the accounts of the ministry of Jesus for the overt expression of metaphysical truths about the nature of his relationship with God in a way which might be appropriate to theological discussion at the end of the first century (still less for statements of Chalcedonian orthodoxy!), and that the absence of such language is no cause for doctrinal embarrassment. However great Jesus' own awareness of his unique status, it is surely to be expected that the extent to which he might give it open expression must be governed by the likely understanding (or rather misunderstanding) of such language on the part of those who heard him, whether friends or enemies. We have to reckon too with the fact that the accounts of what Jesus said and did have come down to us through his followers who themselves must have experienced a growth in their own awareness of the implication of what was said. No doubt the impact made on them by Jesus was striking and immediate, but there is no reason to imagine that their christological understanding was fully formed at the first encounter. Indeed the gospels give us plenty of evidence that the process was slow and painful for them, and that it was not until after the resurrection that the full truth of what they had heard and seen began to come home to them. Even then, it is no surprise that Peter's speech at the first Pentecost is far from the theological sophistication of the later writings of Paul. Such a gradual process of deepening understanding is what might reasonably be expected, and the New Testament does not dispel that expectation. This is not to suggest of course a rigid scheme whereby succeeding stages of christological understanding can be located at fixed points along an inexorable line of chronological development, so that the more "primitive" is necessarily to be seen as earlier than the more "sophisticated," in much the same way that Old Testament scholars used to attempt to date the presumed sources of the Pentateuch by their supposed place along an evolutionary line from the vivid anthropomorphism of "j" to the dry scholasticism of "P." Life is not as simple as that, and we do well to heed B.C. Butler's dry comment that "The parish magazine is not necessarily of earlier date than the **Summa Theologica** of St. Thomas."[31] There is therefore no place for the dogmatism which will not allow Paul to express more "developed" theological ideas simply because he was writing in the 50's, earlier than the generally agreed date for the writing of any of the gospels. But of the fact that the New Testament does include both more and less "developed" christological formulations there can be no doubt, and it should be no surprise therefore that the sayings of Jesus in the gospels do not use the language of Hebrews 1:1-3 or of the prologue of John.

The nature of the development is sometimes expressed in terms of the distinction mentioned earlier between functional and ontological aspects of christology. At first, on this understanding, Christians thought of Jesus only, or at least primarily, in terms of what he had done, as the Messiah or the Saviour. It was only later that they began to realize that in order to fulfill these functions Jesus must have been more than an ordinary man, and so ontological christology came onto the scene. It may be questioned, indeed, how far a concept of Jesus as Saviour could ever have existed without at least a rudimentary realisation that this was a role beyond the scope of a mere man. But the progression from functional to ontological interest is one which seems to correspond in general to the way religious experience may be perceived to develop. The development will not stop there, of course, but one ontological question will lead to another, so that the development from the christology of the New Testament to the patristic formulations of the doctrine of the Trinity was a necessary next step - you could not confess Jesus as the eternal Son of God without having to go further and ask what this confession does to your monotheistic presuppositions.

It may be more appropriate, however, to formulate the nature of the development more in terms of the experience of the first Christians as this came to be expressed in their worship. Recent christological discussion, through concentrating mainly on the titles and explicit theological formulation found in the New Testament, may be in danger of missing the more fundamental evidence for a developing attitude to Jesus expressed in worship, which was itself the seedbed out of which the christological titles and formulations grew.[32] Those who at a very early date after the resurrection were "calling on the name of our Lord Jesus Christ" (1 Cor. 1:2), a practice reflected in the early Aramaic prayer "Maranatha" (1 Cor. 16:22), who in what is probably a pre-Pauline hymn had already come to revere him as the "Lord" to whom is due the worship exclusively reserved for God (Phil. 2:9-11, echoing Is. 45:22f), were in their worship giving expression to a conviction about the nature of Jesus which may not yet have come to formal christological expression, but which must inevitably lead them in that direction. The development of christology is, then, on this view, not a matter of abstract intellectual speculation but of the translation into more theological formulations of convictions which were already fundamental to the worshipping life of the Christian community. In opposition to the currently fashionable search for models outside the Christian community which they gratuitously adopted in their desire to clothe the figure of Christ with appropriately noble attributes, this view finds the origin of the high Chrisology of the NT within the Christian context, as the religious experience and worship of ordinary men and women (not necessarily speculative theologians) came to be focused on Jesus of Nazareth. Christology then arose out of the attempt to give appropriate expression to what they had already come to know to be true in their experience.

I have tried elsewhere[33] to sketch out this approach to New Testament christology as finding its source in the worship of Jesus. It seems to me to supply a necessary context for christological thought which is lacking when the study is restricted to titles and formal statements(34). If it is true that worship preceded and gave rise to theology, rather than vice versa, the origin of that experience which is expressed in worship lies much further back than the supposed influence of non-Christian cults on Christian thought in the context of the Gentile mission. It goes back to the beginning of the church's distinct existence as the body of those who worship Jesus. And that means, as we have seen argued in Moule's concept of "development," that the high christology to which New Testament writers eventually gave expression was in essence "already there" in the beginning.

It was there in the impact that Jesus made on those who saw and heard him; it was there in the religious experience into which he led them, as they found that in coming to him they found a new relationship with God; it was there in the paradoxical compulsion to attribute divine honours in their worship to a man whom they had known before his death and resurrection as an itinerant preacher in Galilee. For Jesus' first followers were Jews, to whom the very thought of offering worship to a human being was abhorrent (cf. Acts 10:25f). The fact that nonetheless during the brief period between Jesus' resurrection and the writing of Paul's letters the worship of Jesus had become the distinctive feature of this largely Jewish group points to some influence more potent than a mere desire to imitate pagan myths. There was something "already there" in the life and teaching of the historical Jesus which led them to take this remarkable step, with all the doctrinal problems it was bound to cause. It is, I believe, in this irresistible impact of Jesus himself that we must find the origin of christology.

# NOTES

1. J. Hick (ed.), **The Myth of God Incarnate** (London: SCM, 1977).
2. C.F.D. Moule, **The Origin of Christology** (Cambridge University Press, 1977).
3. *Ibid* pp.2-3. An interesting brief discussion by E.L. Mascall, **Jesus: Who He Is and How We Know Him** (London: Darton, Longman & Todd, 1985) strongly endorses Moule's perspective, but goes on to suggest that the same "development" which Moule traces only within the New Testament may be found continuing also through the christological discussions of the patristic church and beyond.
4. For a full discussion of the textual and translation problems posed by Romans 9:5 see B.M. Metzger, "The Punctuation of Rom.9:5" in B. Lindars & S.S. Smalley (ed.), **Christ and Spirit in the New Testament: In Honour of C.F.D. Moule** (Cambridge University Press, 1973) 95-112. Metzger concludes that the passage does describe Jesus as "God." An even earlier example would be found in 2 Thes. 1:12, if the text were translated (as the Greek syntax suggests) "our God and Lord Jesus Christ'; it is however possible, even if less natural, to construe it as referring to two persons, "our God and the Lord Jesus Christ," and the other expression is felt to be so remarkable in a very early letter of Paul that commentators regularly opt for the latter rendering (or deny the Pauline authorship of 2 Thessalonians!).
5. The relevant passages are usefully assembled and discussed by A.W. Wainwright, **The Trinity in the New Testament** (London: SPCK, 1962) 53-74 and by R.E. Brown, **Jesus: God and Man** (New York: Macmillan, 1967) 6-28.
6. R.N. Longenecker, **The Christology of Early Jewish Christianity** (London: SCM, 1970) chapter II considers a variety of "distinctive imagery and motifs" (such as "The Name," "The Righteous One," "The Shepherd and the Lamb," "The Rejected Stone') which were explored in the earlier days of christological development, but tended to drop out of use, particularly in non-Jewish circles.
7. The background of the term *Logos* as a christological title has often been discussed. For a good recent survey see J.D.G. Dunn, **Christology in the Making** (London: SCM,1980) 215-230.
8. M. Hengel, **The Son of God** (ET. London: SCM, 1976) 57.

9. This movement in Johannine studies was described in and important paper by J.A.T. Robinson as "The New Look on the Fourth Gospel," originally read at the Oxford conference on " The Four Gospels in 1957," and reprinted in Robinson's **Twelve New Testament Studies** (London: SCM, 1962) 94-106. One of the most influential works was C.H. Dodd, **Historical Tradition in the Fourth Gospel** (Cambridge University Press, 1963). For a more recent survey see S.S. Smalley, **John, Evangelist and Interpreter** (Exeter: Paternoster, 1978). Robinson's last work, which will be noted below, takes this trend to new lengths.

10. W. Wrede, **Das Messiasgeheimnis in den Evangelien** (1901), eventually published in English as **The Messianic Secret** (London: James Clarke, 1971). For subsequent discussion see the articles collected in C.M. Tuckett (ed.), **The Messianic Secret** (Philadelphia: Fortress, 1983), especially Tuckett's own introductory survey.

11. J. Jeremias proposes that there is no echo of Ps. 2:7 in Mark 1:11, and that Is. 42:1 supplies the only significant background. His view is discussed in detail by I.H. Marshall, **NTS 15** (1968/9) 326-336.

12. For the messianic significance of the "Cleansing of the Temple" see e.g. B.F. Meyer, **The Aims of Jesus** (London: SCM, 1979) 197-202; E.P. Sanders, **Jesus and Judaism** (London: SCM, 1985) 61-76.

13. See e.g. the reaction of Jesus to the titles "Messiah" and "King of the Jews" in Mark 8:27-33; 14:61-62; 15:2. For the affirmative force of the formula "You have said," but with an element of reluctance or circumlocution, see D.R. Catchpole, **NTS 17** (1970/1) 213-226.

14. **The Origin of Christology**, 35 (concluding a discussion on pp. 31-35).

15. O. Cullmann, **The Christology of the New Testament** (ET. London: SCM, [2]1963), especially 315-331, argues that "Functional Christology is the only kind which exists" (326). W. Pannenberg warns on the contrary of the danger of the approaching christology from the perspective of soteriology, **Jesus - God and Man** (ET. London: SCM, 1968) 38-49. In response to Pannenberg, A.E. McGrath, **Theologische Zeitschrift** 42 (1986) 222-237, asserts the inseparability of christology from soteriology.

16. For the possibility that "son of God" was an accepted title for the Messiah see e.g. Longenecker, **The Christology of Early Jewish Christianity** 93-99.

17. For non-Christian use of "son of God" see e.g. Hengel, **The Son of God** 21-56; more briefly, Dunn, **Christology in the Making** 13-22.

18. J.A.T. Robinson, **The Priority of John** (London: SCM 1985).

19. Robinson's equally ground-breaking study **Redating the New Testament** (London: SCM, 1976) has been largely ignored by New Testament scholarship. It may be suggested that this was because its conclusions would involve too drastic an upheaval in this accepted framework of thought. Robinson wrily comments on his own experience on this connection: "One must always beware of the tendency of the critical establishment to close ranks against anything that disturbs its fundamental presuppositions." (**The Priority of John**, 10).

20. It should be noted, however, that Robinson's high view of the reliability of John does not lead, as might be expected, to a high christology, since he argues in his final chapter that not even this gospel may be properly interpreted as teaching the incarnation of a pre-existent being.

21. J. Jeremias, **New Testament Theology, Part One: The Proclamation of Jesus** (ET. London: SCM, 1971) 59-61 argues that "the son" and "the father" here are not specific "titles" but merely convey a general statement about human relationships. Even if this were so, it is hard to see what other sense such a "parable" might be intended to convey in this context than to claim a special relationship between Jesus and his Father - the same point would be made, but by analogy rather than by a direct statement.

22. The well-known argument by J. Jeremias, **The Prayers of Jesus** (ET. London: SCM, 1967) 11-65 that Jesus' use of the term **Abba** as an address to God in prayer marks his awareness of a unique relationship has been heavily contested (notably by G. Vermes, **Jesus the Jew** [London: Collins, 1973] 210-213) but remains intact. See the assessment by J.D.G. Dunn, **Jesus and the Spirit** (London: SCM, 1975) 21-26. and more recently (with specific reference to Vermes" arguments) **Christology in the Making** 26-29. J. Barr, 'Abba isn't "Daddy,"' JTS 39 (1988), pp. 28-47, has shown convincingly that Abba is not a specifically childish form of address, as preachers often assert, but does not (and does not intend to) disprove Jeremias' basic argument for the originality of Jesus' use of the term.

23. J. Jeremias, **The Prayers of Jesus** 112-115.

24. For these and other such passages in the Synoptic Gospels see my **Jesus and the Old Testament** (London: Tyndale, 1971) 150-159 ("The Assumption of the Role of Yahweh').

25. For a fuller list of such features in the parables (some of which are of more questionable relevance) see P.B. Payne, "The Authenticity of the Parables of Jesus" in R.T. France & D. Wenham (ed.) **Gospel Perspectives II** (Sheffield: JSOT, 1981) 338-341.

26. In view of the complexity of scholarly discussion on the title "the Son of Man" in general and the interpretation and use of Daniel 7:13 in particular it is bold to risk so firm a statement! A recent full discussion of the subject, however, moves strongly in the direction of identifying the "one like a son of man" in Daniel 7:13 as a transcendent, heavenly being, who replaces the traditional concept of a human Messiah: C.C. Caragounis, **The Son of Man: Vision and Interpretation** (Tübingen: Mohr, 1986) 35-81.

27. Seyoon Kim, **"The "Son of Man"" as the Son of God** (Tübingen: Mohr, 1983). Cf. Moule, **The Origin of Christology** 25-27.

28. J.D.G. Dunn, **Jesus and the Spirit: a Study of the Religious and Charismatic Experience of Jesus and the First Christians as Reflected in the New Testament** (London: SCM, 1975).

29. *Ibid*, 11-40, 62-67. Cf. more briefly Dunn's **Christology in the Making**, 22-33.

30. Moule's presentation of his case for a "developmental" view of New Testament christology is derived in fact mainly from outside the gospels, with special reference to the letters of Paul.

31. B.C. Butler, **The Originality of St. Matthew** (Cambridge University Press, 1951) 171.

32. *Cf.* the remarkable statement of M. Hengel, **The Son of God**, p. 2, on the christological development in the 30s and 40s of the first century: "One is tempted to say that more happened in this period of less than two decades than in the whole of the next seven centuries, up to the time when the doctrine of the early church was completed."

33. "The Worship of Jesus: a Neglected Factor in Christological Debate?" in H.H. Rowdon (ed.) **Christ the Lord: Studies in Christology Presented to Donald Guthrie** (London: IVP, 1982) 17-36. A parallel argument was developed independently by R.J. Bauckham, "The Worship of Jesus in Apocalyptic Christianity," **NTS** 27 (1980/1) 322-341. See also the recent work of L. Hurtado, **One God, One Lord:**

**Early Christian Devotion and Ancient Jewish Monotheism** (London: SCM, 1988), which explains the "binitarian mutation" within Jewish Christianity as arising out of the worship of Jesus as "a second object of devotion alongside God." A forthcoming book by Douglas de Lacey, **The Mediator: On the Christology of Saint Paul**, proposes a similar view; ch. 1 is entitled "Faith before Doctrine."

34. For some cautionary comments on the danger of restricting Christology to a study of titles, see L.E. Keck, **NTS** 32 (1986), pp. 368-370: "To reconstruct the history of titles as if this were the study of Christology is like trying to understand the windows of Chartres Chathedral by studying the history of coloured glass."

# 7

# THE SYNOPTIC GOSPELS AND HISTORY

## E. Earle Ellis

The four NT Gospels are virtually the only source for our knowledge of the acts and teachings of the earthly Jesus.[1] They are received by the Christian church as the work of inspired writers, apostles and prophets, who were guided by the Spirit of God to give a true portrayal and interpretation of his life and work, and they are also historical documents whose origin and formation can be investigated and in some measure discovered. Written some time after Jesus' death and resurrection, they have been subjected to careful and prolonged study to determine their background and the degree to which they accurately reflect his preresurrection ministry. The historical investigation of the Gospels has taken mainly taken four routes, (1) the attempt to identify underlying documents (known as 'source criticism'), (2) the attempt to identify individual literary units and analyse their formation and character (known as 'form criticism'), (3) the attempt to trace changes in these units during their transmission prior to their use by the Evangelist (known as 'tradition criticism') and, finally, (4) the attempt to identify changes that each Evangelist himself made in composing his Gospel (known as 'redaction' or 'composition criticism') Each of these avenues of research is perfectly legitimate but, as in other areas of historical reconstruction, the results arrived at are heavily influenced if not determined by the world-view with which the historian approaches the texts and by his other historical and methodological assumptions.[2]

## I

An assumption that may be addressed at the outset is the view, still held in some quarters, that history writing is an objective science in which the historian is a neutral observer and evaluator of probabilities. This view has been effectively discredited by such writers as Carl Becker, H.S. Commager and, for biblical history, Alan Richardson,[3] and its fallacies illustrated again in the work of John Kenyon on critical historians in Britain.[4]

As Bernard Lonergan[5] and others have reminded us, the term 'history' may be employed in two senses, that which is written and that which is written about. It is history in the former sense that is presented to us both by the Evangelists and by modern historians of early Christianity. Such history is by its very nature interpretive and modern historians, including of course the present writer, are no less subjectively involved in their reconstructions than the Evangelists were in theirs. As one who very early had to contrast the history of the War between the States received at my grandmother's knee and in Jefferson Davis' **The Rise and Fall of the Confederate Government**[6] with that presented, for example, by Charles A. Beard in the public school text-books of my high school years, I later read the diverse accounts of the ministry of Christ and historicity of the Gospels by, say, F.W. Farrar, C.H. Dodd and B. Gerhardsson[7] on the one hand and D.F. Strauss and R. Bultmann on the other with a distinct sense of *deja vu*.[8]

The subjectivity inevitably involved in the reconstruction of the past does not, of course, diminish the importance of a proper method or excuse us from criticizing historical reconstructions that are demonstrably defective in this or other respects. A currently widespread view of the origins of the Gospels with its skeptical attitude toward their historicity seems to me to warrant such criticism, specifically, (1) in its misrepresentation of its own confessional presuppositions as a scientific or critical stance, (2) in its misuse of historical method and (3) in its mistaken historical and literary assumptions.

1.  The historical study of the Gospels has been marked for the past two centuries by a cleavage in world-views, characterized on the one side by deism and on the other by Christian theism or, in the categories of H. Thielicke, by Cartesian and non-Cartesian assumptions.[9] In the mid-twentieth century it was dominated in many circles by a Cartesian, that is, rationalistic approach for which R. Bultmann was probably the most influential representative. Regarding history and the natural world as a closed continuum of cause and effect 'in which historical happenings cannot be rent by the interference of supernatural transcendent powers,[10] Bultmann dismissed, and indeed on a priori grounds had to dismiss, large portions of the Gos-

pels as later mythological creations. On the same grounds he had to limit the 'authentic' sayings of Jesus to those he regarded as originating in Jesus' earthly ministry since no exalted Lord could, in fact, speak to and through the Gospel traditioners and Evangelists. These attitudes and conclusions which Bultmann and other rationalist historians represented as 'scientific' and 'critical' were in fact only the expression and predetermined result of their world-view, that is, their philosophical and thus ultimately confessional commitments.

2.  Other questions of method are not unrelated to these philosophical assumptions, for example, the assignment of the 'burden of proof' in determining whether a particular episode in the Gospels originated in the preresurrection mission of Jesus and the criteria by which its preresurrection origin could be established. The proposed criteria were (1) an episode's attestation in more than one Gospel, (2) its lack of so-called 'developed,' that is, postresurrection tendencies, (3) its dissimilarity from the idiom or ideas found in contemporary Judaism or early Christianity and (4) its coherence with other Gospel material thought to be authentic. Some of the criteria raise certain probabilities and some simply beg the question, but none of them produce any 'assured results.'[11] As the critiques of M. Hooker and E.L. Mascall have pointed out, the conclusions drawn from them were 'very largely the result of (the scholar's) own presuppositions and prejudices.'[12] Moreover, the criteria received an importance beyond their due from the assumption, adopted by E. Käsemann and others, that the Gospel accounts should be regarded as postresurrection creations unless proven otherwise.[13] Does this view of the burden of proof accord with good historical method?

According to E. Bernheim's classic text on historical method the historian has the two-fold task of testing the genuineness and demonstrating the nongenuineness of his sources.[14] Applied to the Gospels this means, as W.G. Kümmel has rightly seen[15] that the historian must not only test the preresurrection origin of a Gospel account but also must demonstrate that any part of the Gospel materials is created in the postresurrection church since the Gospels present their accounts in the context of the preresurrection mission of Jesus. In a word good historical method requires that a Gospel passage be received as an account of Jesus' earthly ministry unless it is shown that it cannot have originated there.

## II

Under the influence of R. Bultmann and M. Dibelius[16] the classical form criticism raised many doubts about the historicity of the Synoptic Gospels, but it was shaped by a number of literary and historical assumptions which themselves are increasingly seen to have a doubtful historical basis. It assumed, first of all, that the Gospel traditions were transmitted for decades exclusively in oral form and began to be fixed in writing only when the early Christian anticipation of a soon end of the world faded. This theory foundered with the discovery in 1947 of the library of the Qumran sect, a group contemporaneous with the ministry of Jesus and the early church which combined intense expectation of the End with prolific writing. Qumran shows that such expectations did not inhibit writing but actually were a spur to it. Also, the widespread literacy in first-century Palestinian Judaism,[18] together with the different language backgrounds of Jesus' followers — some Greek, some Aramaic, some bilingual — would have facilitated the rapid written formulation and transmission of at least some of Jesus' teaching.[19] Finally, the factor that occasioned writing in early Christianity, the separation of the believers from the teaching leadership, was already present in the teaching of Jesus who had groups of adherents in the towns of Galilee, Judea and probably on the Phoenician coast, the Decapolis and Perea. There are good grounds, then, for supposing not only that the traditioning of Jesus' acts and teachings began during his earthly ministry, as H. Schürmann has argued,[20] but also that some of them were given written formulation at that time.

Secondly, the early form criticism tied the theory of oral transmission to the conjecture that Gospel traditions were mediated like folk traditions, being freely altered and even created ad hoc by various and sundry wandering charismatic jackleg preachers. This view, however, was rooted more in the eighteenth century romanticism of J.G. Herder[21] than in an understanding of the handling of religious tradition in first-century Judaism. As O. Cullmann, B. Gerhardsson, H. Riesenfeld and R. Riesner have demonstrated,[22] the Judaism of the period treated such traditions very carefully, and the New Testament writers in numerous passages applied to apostolic traditions the same technical terminology found elsewhere in Judaism for 'delivering,' 'receiving,' 'learning,' 'holding,' 'keeping,' and 'guarding,' the traditioned 'teach-ing.'[23] In this way they both identified their traditions as 'holy word' and showed their concern for a careful and ordered transmission of it. The work and word of Jesus were an important albeit distinct part of these apostolic traditions.

Luke (1:2ff.) used one of the same technical terms, speaking of eye-witnesses who 'delivered to us' the things contained in his Gospel and about which his patron Theophilus had been instructed. Similarly, the amanuenses or co-worker-secretaries who composed the Gospel of John speak of the Evangelist, the beloved disciple, 'who is witnessing con-cerning these things and who wrote these things,' as an eyewitness and a member of the inner circle of Jesus' disciples.[24] In the same connec-tion it is not insignificant that those to whom Jesus entrusted his teach-ings are not called 'preachers' but 'pupils' and 'apostles,' semi-technical terms for those who represent and mediate the teachings and instruc-tions of their mentor or principal.[25]

A third fundamental axiom of classical form criticism is also histori-cally doubtful, that is, that the geographical and chronological frame-work of the Gospels was wholly the creation of the traditioners and Evan-gelists. The Gospels are not chronologues, of course, and the Evange-lists feel free, as did the Roman historian Suetonius, to organize their presentation on thematic or other lines. However, if C.H. Dodd's sche-matic framework of Jesus' ministry is not fully acceptable,[26] K.L. Schmidt's views are much less satisfactory.[27] Among other things Schmidt drew too sharp a dichotomy between editorial and traditional elements in the Gospels and did not recognize that the Evangelists' editorial ar-rangements' such as the journey to Jerusalem in Luke (9:51-19:44) — are often simply a reworking of received traditions.

If the early form criticism built upon a poor foundation, is there a better explanation of the origin and formation of our Gospels?

## III

An acceptable reconstruction of the formation of the Gospels must take into account both first-century Jewish attitudes toward the trans-mission of religious traditions and the charismatic, prophetic character of the ministry of Jesus and of the primitive church. With respect to the former B. Gerhardsson's conception of a controlled transmission of Gospel traditions marked a clear advance beyond the earlier form criticism, but his rabbinic analogy was unable to account for the kind of alteration and elaboration of Gospel traditions that one observes even when comparing one Gospel with another. Indeed, the traditioners and Evangelists seem to handle Jesus' word with the same kind of freedom that they use another type of 'holy word,' the Old Testament scriptures. Their conduct in this respect is best explained by a prophetic consciousness.

Jesus viewed himself[28] and was perceived by others[29] to be the bearer of the prophetic Spirit, and he promised the same Spirit to his followers.[30] Already in his earthly ministry the apostles were sent on their missions of teaching, healing and exorcisms in the role of prophets whether, as J. Jeremias has argued, the Spirit was already conferred on them[31] or, perhaps not very different, whether the Spirit of Jesus was active in their use of his name. It is clear in any case that the Gospel traditioners included themselves among those who according to Mt 5:12, 13:11, Lk 21:15 and other passages fulfilled a prophetic role both in their preaching and persecution and also in their writing as 'wise men and scribes,' that is, scripture teachers.[32] This prophetic consciousness best explains their boldness and confidence both in their christological contemporization of Old Testament texts and in their similar treatment of the holy word of Jesus.

There are few if any historical or literary grounds to suppose that the Gospel traditioners created events in Jesus' life or, indeed, that they mixed to any great degree oracles from the exalted Jesus into the Gospel traditions. If a proper historical critical method is followed, proper presuppositions observed and the practices of first-century Palestinian Judaism considered, the Gospels of the New Testament will be found to be a reliable presentation and faithful portrait of the teachings and acts of the preresurrection mission of Jesus.

## NOTES

1.  There is a brief reference to his ministry by the first-century Jewish historian, Josephus (**Antiquities** 18, 63f = 18, 3, 3), and a few additional sayings of the earthly Jesus recorded elsewhere in the New Testament (e.g., Acts 20:35) and in other sources (cf. J. Jeremias, **Unknown Sayings of Jesus**, London 1958).

2. I address these questions in more detail in E. E. Ellis, 'Gospel Criticism: A Perspective on the State of the Art,' **The Gospel and the Gospels**, ed. P. Stuhlmacher, Grand Rapids 1991, 26-52.

3. C. Becker, **Detachment and the Writing of History**, *Atlantic Monthly* CVI (Oct 1910), 524-536; H.S. Commager, **The Study of History**, Columbus OH 1966, 43-60; A. Richardson, **History Sacred and Profane**, London 1964, 83-183.

4. J. Kenyon, **The History Men**, London 1983.

5. B. Lonergan, **Method in Theology**, New York 1972, 175.

6. J. Davis, **The Rise and Fall of the Confederate Government**, 2 vols., London and Cranbury NJ 1958 (1881).

7. F.W. Farrar, **The Life of Christ**, London 1912; C.H. Dodd, **The Founder of Christianity**, London 1971; idem., 'The Framework of the Gospel Narrative,' *New Testament Studies*, New York 1953, 1-11; B. Gerhardsson, **Memory and Manuscript**, Lund 1961.

8. D.F. Strauss, **The Life of Jesus**, London 1902 (1835); R. Bultmann, **Jesus and the Word**, London 1935.

9. H. Thielicke, **The Evangelical Faith**, 3 vols., Grand Rapids 1974-81, I, 30-173.

10. R. Bultmann, **Existence and Faith**, New York 1960, 292 (German text: *Theologische Zeitschrift* 13, 1957, 411f.); cf. *idem*, 'New Testament and Mythology,' **Kerygma and Myth**, London 1953, 7 (German text: 18).

11. Cf. Ellis (note 2), 30f.

12. M. Hooker, 'On Using the Wrong Tool,' *Theology* 75 (1972), 581; cf. *idem*, 'Christology and Methodology,' *NTS* 17 (1970-71), 480-487; E.L. Mascall, **Theology and the Gospel of Christ**, London 1977, 87-97.

13. E. Kasemann, 'The Problem of the Historical Jesus'(1954), **Essays on New Testament Themes**, London 1964, 37 (German text: **Exegetische Versuche und Besinnungen I**, Gottingen 1960, 205). He was followed by the Anglo-American writers, N. Perrin (**Rediscovering the Teachings of Jesus**, London 1967, 39) and J.M. Robinson, (**A New Quest of the Historical Jesus**, London 1959, 38.) The latter is critiqued by R.P. Martin, 'The New Quest of the Historical Jesus,' **Jesus of Nazareth: Savior and Lord**, ed. C.F.H. Henry, Grand Rapids 1966, 25-45.

14. E. Bernheim, **Lehrbuch der historischen Methode**, New York 1965 (1908), 332; cv. Langlois and C. Seignobos, New York 1966 (1898), 157 are more sceptical.

15. W.G. Kümmel, **Dreissig Joehre Jesus Forshung**, (1950-1980), Bonn 1985, 28f. *Theologische Rundschau* 31 (1966), 42f.

16. R. Bultmann, **History of the Synoptic Tradition**, New York(5) 1963 (1921); M. Dibelius, **From Tradition to Gospel**, New York(2) 1965 (1919).

17. Cf. E.E. Ellis, 'New Directions in Form Criticism,' **Prophecy and Hermeneutic**, Tubingen and Grand Rapids 1978, 237-253; *idem* (note 2), 39-43; Stuhlmacher (note 2), 2f.

18. Cf. Josephus, **Against Apion** 2, 204 = 2, 25: The Law 'orders that (children) should be taught to read...;' cf. *idem*, **Antiquities** 12, 209 = 12, 4, 9; Philo, **Embassy to Gaius** 115, 210. Further, see R. Riesner, **Jesus als Lehrer**, Tubingen 1988, 112-115.

19. Jesus had hearers and doubtless some converts from Syria (Mt 4:25), the Decapolis (Mt 4:25; Mk 3:8; 5:20; 7:31), Tyre and Sidon (Mk 3:8; 7:24, 31; Mt 15:21; 6:21).

20. H. Schürmann, 'Die vorösterlichen Anfange der Logientradition, ' **Traditionsgeschichtliche Untersuchungen**, Düsseldorf 1968, 39-65; *idem* **Jesus**, Paderborn 1993, 380-397.

21. J.G. Herder, **Vom Erlöser der Menshen** (Riga 1796); *idem*, **Von Sohn Gottes** (Riga 1797) reprinted in *idem*, **Sämtliche Werke** ed. B. Suphan, 33 vols., Hildesheim 1994 (1877-1913), XIX, 197, 213f., 417f., cited in W.G. Kummel, **The New Testament: the History of its Problems**, Nashville 1972, 79-83.

22. 0. Cullmann, 'The Tradition,' **The Early Church**, London 1958, 55-99; B. Gerhardsson, **The Origins of the Gospel Traditions**, Philadelphia 1979; H. Riesenfeld, **The Gospel Tradition**, Philadelphia 1970, 1-29; R. Riesner, **Jesus als Lehrer**, Tubingen [4]1995.

23. Rom 6:17; 16:17; I Cor 11:2, 23; 15:3; Phil 4:9 Col 2:6ff. II Thess 2:15; 3:6; II Tim 3:14; Tit 1:9; II Jn 9f.; Jude 3; Rev 2:13, 24. Cf. Aboth 1:1; Philo, **The Worse Attacks the Better** (quod det. pot.) 65-68; W. Bacher, **Die exegetische Terminologie der judischen Traditionsliteratur**, 2 vols. in 1, Darmstadt 1965, I, 94ff.; II, 234f. *et passim*.

24. Jn 19:35; 21:24f.; cf. 13:23; 18:15f.; 19:26f.; 20:1-10; 21:7, 21-23. Cf. J.A.T. Robinson, **Redating the New Testament**, London 1976,

298-311. *Pace* S.S. Smalley, **John: Evangelist and Interpreter**, Nashville(3) 1984, 80ff. and R.E. Brown, **The Gospel According to John**, 2 vols., Garden City NY 1970, I, ci-cii, who distinguish the Evangelist from the Beloved Disciple.

25. On parallels with other rabbis and their disciples and other Jewish usage cf. Mk 2:18 = Lk 5:33; K.H. Rengstorf, TDNT I (1964/1933), 413-443; IV (1967/1942), 431-455.

26. C.H. Dodd, 'The Framework of the Gospel Narrative'(1932), **New Testament Studies**, New York 1953, 1-11.

27. K.L. Schmidt, **Der Rahmen der Geschichte Jesu**, Darmstadt 1964 (1919).

28. Mt 13:57 = Mk 6:4 = Lk 4:18, 24; 13:33f.; Jn 4:44; cf. Mt 12:28 = Lk 11:20.

29. Mk 6:15; 8:28; cf. 8:11; 14:65 = Mt 26:67f. = 22:63f.; 24:19.

30. Mt 10:19f. = Mk 13:11 = Lk 21:15; 12:12; Jn 7:38f.; 14:17f.,26; 16:7; cf. Mt 3:11 = Mk 1:8 = Lk 3:16.

31. J. Jeremias, **New Testament Theology**, London 1971, 79. Cf. Mt 10:1; Mk 6:7, 30; Lk 9:1f.; 10:9, 17.

32. Mt 13:52; 23:34; cf. Lk 11:49ff. Cf. Philo, **On the Giants** 5, 22; idem, **On the Unchangeableness of God** 1, 3: prophet = wise man.

# Crisis in Christology

# 8

# CHRIST AND THE IDEOLOGIES

## Nikolaus Lobkowicz

When Roy Varghese called me up and asked me to present to this symposium a lecture on "Christ and the Ideologies," I accepted his invitation without much hesitation. Only much later, when I began pondering what exactly I should say and how I could best organize the subject, did I realize that the latter is surrounded by a number of didactic and/or methodological difficulties. Three of them are important enough at least to be mentioned by way of introduction.

This symposium unites an audience representing several Christian denominations. This entails the problem that if we were to go into the details of our faith, there would be many issues about which we would disagree. It is of course true that most of these disagreements would concern ecclesiology, that is, issues concerning the Church, the nature of Church offices, and the sacraments, rather than Christology, that is, our Lord himself. Nevertheless some of them may have and probably do have an immediate bearing upon Christology. On the one hand, disagreements even on ecclesiology are disagreements on what our Lord intended; and what he intended throws light on what or rather who He was, and is. More importantly, the disagreements between the denominations are usually rooted in the role they ascribe to Holy Scripture as well as in the way in which their traditions, or Churches, expect us to read it; and everything we know about our Lord, and in fact everything we believe, is directly or indirectly rooted in Holy Writ. It is therefore — and this is the first difficulty, a didactic one — quite likely that in one case or another I shall implicitly defend Christology against ideological encroachments which to some of you might seem more important, or less important, than they do to me or, in general, to a Catholic, which I am.

The second difficulty concerns the notion of ideology. In general, 'ideology' is defined as a system of thought with strong political implications and a considerable socio-political impact, a system of thought which, in addition, hides some interest, be it individual, class-bound, national or in another general way political. This notion of ideology is extremely vague, reaching from profoundly Christian to radically atheist conceptions. Marxism-Leninism, or socialism, or capitalism are certainly not the only ideologies in this sense; when in the fourth century Eusebius of Caesarea tried to establish a connection between the Roman Empire as founded by Augustus and the rule of Christ over his faithful and indeed the heavenly kingdom, this was also in a sense an ideology.

Now it would seem possible to take one contemporary ideology after another and to ask about each of them what they have to say about Christ. It would be a somewhat tedious method, since we are surrounded by hundreds of ideologies, many of them closely interlinked, but it would be a possible approach, even though nothing like a systematic conspectus of ideologies seems to exist. After some reflection, however, I have decided to choose another approach, which seems to me more direct and pertinent. In so doing I assume what our common faith tells us, namely that Jesus Christ was both man just as we are men, that is, living in a certain place at a certain time, and the second divine person, the Son of God, equal in all respects to God the Father and the Holy Spirit. Having assumed this and feeling that the basic definition of what this means was given at the Council of Chalcedon, I will look for contemporary ideas minimizing either the divine nature and ultimate personality of Christ or his human nature. As a consequence I shall consider not only ideologies in the proper sense of the term but also conceptions which consider themselves Christian theologies. After all, today it has become possible even within the framework of a Department of Theology, to defend notions that Christ was not God, or that God is dead, or that he never existed. I shall therefore be under the obligation in each case to explain why I consider such conceptions ideological, in which case "ideology" will mean no less and no more than a misconception or an error due to some preconceived idea about what is real. I admit that this approach is much more risky than the first-mentioned alternative, in particular, since I am a philosopher, not a theologian; at the same time, however, it seems to me much more direct, pertinent and therefore exciting than the first.

Finally, in preparing this lecture I was confronted with the difficulty that very little literature exists on the subject I am to treat. To put it more precisely, a great deal has been written about it but usually not in a systematic way. All competent treatments of Christian dogmatics and many treatments of exegesis will of course, when explaining a Christological tenet, point out that this or that author, or this or that doctrine, denies what Christianity believes or the author maintains. In most cases, however, such treatments are not interested in the doctrine or ideology in question but merely wish to underline, exemplify or articulate an aspect of the Christian creed.

Therefore, I would like to emphasize that my treatment cannot be in any way exhaustive. I can only exemplify some basic trends, and even their enumeration will probably be far from satisfactory. In addition, I shall mostly refer to German authors, since I am not very familiar with the more recent theological literature in the United States. There is, however, one excuse that I venture to submit for this last imperfection: over the last one hundred and fifty years German theology, in the past mainly Protestant, for about thirty years also Catholic, has had a tremendous impact on Christian theologians all over the world. To give a very simple example, Latin American Liberation Theology is of very German origin; the Latin American theologians defending it are clearly wrong when they maintain that their kind of theology is an "original Latin American contribution" to international theology. After all, Karl Marx was a German, and the basic theological ideas in connection with him have been developed by German Protestant authors such as Jürgen Moltmann, and German Catholic authors such as Johann Baptist Metz.

Before I proceed, I should like to add another reflection. Someone might object that however interesting the topic I have been asked to discuss and the approach I have chosen might be, they center around problems that are subtleties, having little to do with what "normal Christians" actually believe. After all, very few Christians have studied the Christological discussions and councils of the fourth and fifth centuries; most Christians seem to be satisfied with simply believing that in some mysterious way Christ was the Godman or the Mangod, and feel uneasy when they are expected to clarify this mystery with sophisticated notions. It seems to them a disrespectful nosiness. And in a sense they are perfectly right: if Christology had a purely theoretical end, if its aim were simply curiosity or a desire for conceptualization, it would never be adequate to the fundamental Mystery of our Salvation.

But this is not how Christology came about, and it is not why a subject such as "Christ and the Ideologies" is worth treating today. On the one hand, the Christological definitions of the early Church, like in fact all dogmas, were responses to implicit or explicit errors; this is true even of the two Mariological dogmas of the Catholic Church, which were very consciously promulgated to counteract materialistic tendencies in our times. In the verbal promulgation of the dogma of the Assumption, Pius XII used a phrase not found in the written documents: explaining the reasons for the promulgation, he used the word *ad damnandum materialismum dialecticum*, to condemn the Marxist heresy of Dialectical Materialism. Even today, ideological misrepresentations of our faith are of considerable interest to us; they help us to clarify, in our own minds as well as towards others, what it is that we believe. After all, it would not be very apostolic if we were to reply to someone inquiring about our faith and asking us what we Christians mean by the statement that Christ is both man and God: "Now look, on the one hand it is a mystery and on the other hand it means just what it says." Of course it is a mystery and we shall never be able to explain more about it than why it is not self-contradictory and thereby nonsense. However, by explaining, by means of sometimes very sophisticated concepts, why it is not nonsense we also explain exactly what it is that we believe in. To believe in something that cannot be rationally explained does not condemn us to not being able to say something reasonable about what it is that we maintain.

On the other hand, concern with Christology has something to do with our love for Jesus Christ. If I love someone I want to learn as much from him about himself as I can. If this someone is, for example, a girl, I may not feel a particular need to plumb the depths of ontological or metaphysical searches. In all likelihood, she will be a human being of the opposite sex, and that's it. But Christ is an infinitely more profound subject. Someone really loving Him wants to know who He is, even if this requires delving into considerable depths. And, in fact, even with human loved ones we quickly delve into metaphysical issues; we consider, for example, the possibility that we might lose them through death and ask ourselves: Will that be all there is to it? Actually people falling profoundly in love with each other sometimes even consider the possibility that they are destined for each other. And immediately the question arises of what this could mean. Love is not as unintellectual or even anti-intellectual as many today maintain.

Let me now come to my subject. The most radical way of discarding Christ consists in saying that he never existed. In view of the fact that the oldest letters of St. Paul were written no later than in the fifth decade of the first century, relying on oral sources going back to the first ten years after Christ's crucifixion, that the Gospel of St. John was written in the first century, and, last but not least, that Christ is mentioned by the Jewish historian Josephus as well as by the Roman historian Tacitus, and possibly also by Suetonius, this claim has become very rare today.

However, since the claim that Christ never existed was made by some critics at the end of the 19th century, it is taken up in Soviet Marxism-Leninism. Thus in the 17th volume of the **Great Soviet Encyclopaedia**, published in 1952 you will find under "Jesus": "Name of the mythical founder of Christianity, see Christ" (p.523); and in the 46th volume, published in 1957, under "Christ": "mythical founder of Christianity, to have been born in the Palestine town of Bethlehem, to have taught a new religious doctrine in Judea, Galilee, Samaria and other places, to have died on the cross and, according to the Christian teaching, to have risen from the dead, see Christianity" (p.364). According to the article "Christianity" in the same volume (p.352-362), Christianity emerged in the second half of the first century "according to our Chronology" and was the expression of the class struggle in the "Eastern provinces of the Roman Empire" (p.23). In a similar vein, the **Dictionary of Philosophy** by M. Rosenthal and P. Yudin, the English translation of which was published in Moscow in 1967, says under "Christianity": "The main thing in Christianity is the teaching of the mythical man-God Jesus Christ, the son of God, who descended from heaven to earth, underwent suffering and death, and then rose from the dead to redeem people from original sin" (p.75). Amusingly enough, under "Buddha" the same book supposes that the founder of Buddhism not only existed but also "expressed the protest of the common people against the Brahman religion" (p.60). In 1969, the Institute of Philosophy of the Soviet Academy of Science began publishing the **Filsofskaya Entsiklopedya**, an encyclopaedia of philosophy in several volumes; as it contained a number of quite competent articles and even took notice of Western critics of Marxism-Leninism, Western scholars hailed it as a major achievement. But even in this publication, on p.249 of the 2nd volume, Christ is treated as a "mythical founder"; referring to a Russian translation of a German book published in 1939, the encyclopaedia claims that the "non-historicity" of Jesus Christ may be considered demonstrated today; even bourgeois scholars, it says, maintain it. This does not, of course, prevent Soviet ideologists from occasionally referring to the Bible, just as we would sometimes refer to Greek mythology or to the wisdom of Zarathustra. Such references, however, are almost always thoroughly negative. During the debate on the deployment of strategic rockets in Europe, Soviet journals did not, it is true, criticize the Sermon on the Mount, but this was because the West European peace movements appealed to it. As soon as this cause was lost for the Soviets, however, even this biblical text was again criticized. On July 30 of this year [1986], the official Soviet youth journal *Komsomolskaya Pravda* published an article claiming that the Sermon on the Mount is utterly uninteresting since it merely repeats what the Old Testament had already said. Interestingly enough, the articles on Jesus Christ in Soviet dictionaries and encyclopaedias do not quote any of the "classics" of "Marxism-Leninism." Marx and Engels, and later Lenin, wrote quite a number of pages on Christianity, but there seem to be almost no statements by them on Christ Himself. This amounts to saying that Marxism-Leninism, by claiming that Christ did not even so much as exist, simply repeats what was claimed by some West European atheists towards the end of the 19th and the beginning of the 20th centuries.

Today, this claim seems extremely primitive to us; as far as I can see, no serious scholar of our times would want to support it. But we should not overlook the fact that it is only a radicalization and simplification of a claim which is indeed widespread among Western scholars, even among exegetes. Though today no serious scholar maintains that the existence of Jesus Christ is a myth, there are many scholars considered to be serious who, in various degrees of subtlety, suggest that this or that feature of Christ as transmitted by Christian tradition is not historical and therefore a myth. In fact, a very large proportion of modern exegesis is tacitly governed by the principle that things which do not occur in our experience could not have happened in Christ's lifetime. The whole trend of "demythologizing the Gospel" has to be explained in this way: as miracles do not happen and, in particular, as people who have died do not return among the living, all of Christ's miracles and above all his resurrection cannot be but a myth. However, as "demythologizations" can go hand in hand with a belief in Christ's divinity, I will return to it later.

At this point I would instead like to discuss a group of contentions which presuppose that, though Christ did exist, he was obviously nothing more than an extraordinary man comparable to, for example, Socrates. As we shall see, such ideas can be accompanied by a profound dislike of as well as by a deep admiration for Christ, just as someone might like or dislike the figure of Socrates.

A typical example of someone disliking Christ is Rudolf Augstein, the editor of the highly influential German monthly *Der Spiegel*. His book **Jesus Menschensohn**, (Jesus, Son of Man), published in Munich in 1972 is interlarded with insults, most of which, however, are not addressed to Jesus himself but to Christians and their Churches. The explicit aim of his book is to describe Christians as either idiots or hypocrites or opportunists, and probably all three at the same time; their churches, above all the Catholic Church, which according to Augstein still has an important social influence in Germany, do nothing but influence elections, prohibit the pill, stimulate guilt complexes, produce tensions and stabilize "structures of domination." Therefore, Augstein wants to prove that all Christian churches "appeal to a Jesus, who never existed, to doctrines which he did not teach, to powers which he did not confer, and to a being the Son of God, which he himself did not consider possible and did not lay claim to " (p.7). His method is a thoroughly incompetent summary of all the difficulties which modern exegesis has raised for almost 2000 years; even so leftist a theologian as Dorothee Solle criticized the book by writing: "Take 100 exegetes from the last 50 years, chop their results as finely as possible, in fact in half lines, sieve out as irrelevant all results aiming at genuineness or significance, and stir into the whole a stale mayonnaise of the magazine *Der Spiegel*. The book's salad is boring" (*Die Zeit*, Nov. 10, 1972). It is difficult to discover what Augstein really wants to say about Jesus. On the one hand, he claims that we know virtually nothing about him; on the other hand he qualifies him as a crank and a wrong-headed fellow. The historical Jesus is someone utterly insignificant, a claim which led Solle to ironically remark: "Nobody can understand why this pale Jesus, this artificial product of traditions before him and legends after him should have had an absolute significance for so many people" (ibid.). Nevertheless, this odd book is worth mentioning: Augstein is a well-known person, he writes well, he sums up many different ideas of modern exegesis, and he is full of resentment. A thoroughly frustrated cynic, he concludes his book by saying, "Rational reappraisal did me good and it is necessary for society" (p.427).

In addition, Augstein's book illustrates an intellectual strategy which is quite widespread today, namely to approach Jesus by disclaiming most or everything of what Christian tradition tells us about him. Two other examples are Joel Carmichael's **Life and Death of Jesus of Nazareth**, published in the 1960's, as well as a similar book by the German Johannes Lehmann, **Jesus Report**, published in 1970. Both books assume that the Gospels are a misinterpretation of what Jesus was; Lehmann's book carries the subtitle "A Record of a Falsification." According to Carmichael, Jesus was a political zealot, who even had an armed force, occupied the Temple, was then betrayed, arrested, condemned and executed as a rebel. According to Lehmann, who calls Jesus "Rabbi J," he was an Essene who applied to himself the teaching about the Messiah and fought for the political liberation of his country from the Romans. Both authors claim that it was St. Paul who changed the story of Jesus' life past recognition. "The triumph of Paul meant the definitive extinction of the historical Jesus; the historical Jesus has been handed down to us encased in Christianity like a gnat in a piece of amber" (Carmichael, retranslation from German translation, Munich 1965, p.282). In the same vein, Lehmann suggests that the historical Rabbi J has nothing to do with Christ as Christians preach him; he would never have become a member of a Christian church.

Neither Carmichael nor Lehmann belongs to those who dislike the historical Christ, but, just like Augstein, they do dislike the Christians. The reason why these and similar books have had an important impact is that they denounced what Christians say, and, in particular, the churches teach. Thus they unveil an important, because widespread ideological tendency: to discredit the Christian churches detested because they have a hold upon people. Secondly, these books are examples of what one might call "elevated journalism" used to calumniate Christianity. Finally, they illustrate the tendency to describe Christ from the point of view of a preconceived idea, usually a political one. Christ the political rebel has become a very influential notion, which can be used by any political ideology. To Marxists who do not deny his historical existence outright, Christ was a fighter for the oppressed just as Spartacus was;

for the Nazis he was a fighter for the purity of Aryans (see e.g. H. Hauptmann, **Jesus der Arier**. Ein Heldenleben. Munchen 1930, p.6: "it became a certainty to him (i.e. Jesus) that only the Aryan man is created by God according to the image of the Father, that only he, according to the Father's will, is the legitimate Master of the Earth"); for Freemasons he is a fighter for a vague deist humanism. All these approaches, of course, presuppose that the Gospels are thoroughly unreliable; usually it is St. Paul who is considered responsible for their falsification.[2]

The strategy of discrediting the Churches by describing Christ as completely different from what Christians believe about him has also become a popular gimmick among novelists. The great model is of course the story of the Grand Inquisitor as told by Ivan in Dostoyevsky's **The Brothers Karamasov**. Yet while Dostoyevsky's Christ is without any doubt the Son of God returning to his church, which in the end rejects him just as the Jews did, the Jesus of contemporary novelists is usually a Prince Charming coming from somewhere or nowhere, informing his faithful (who reject him) as well as unbelievers (who hail him) about what the author of the book considers the ideal way of life. Usually, it is an easygoing life in a world in which all suffering stems from repressive ideals or power hungry authority. An example of this is the well-written, though superficial novel **Jesus in Osaka** by the German novelist Gunter Herburger. His Jesus comes from the future and is described as a clearcut contrast both to a "Jesus from Rome" and a "Jesus of Nazareth." He leaves the Christians and joins the beatniks and other subculture groups. He is a Jesus who sings and plays, is cheerful, lighthearted and even roguish; he wants to liberate his friends to love and life, to reconcile happiness and prosperity, to overcome the religion of popes, capitalists, and the cross. He is a newcomer among men, who wants to teach them a better way of life (cf. **Jesus von Nazareth**, ed. F.J. Schieres, Mainz 1972, p. 122 ff.). A number of novels of this kind have been published over the last few years. Some of them play with the stylistic trick of alienation, describing Christ as someone saying and doing what he said and did according to the Gospel, but in preposterous modern circumstances. The aim can be either to show how far removed we are from what Jesus wanted or to suggest that Jesus' teaching is preposterous, because unworldly. Quite often such contrasts are sought for purely aesthetic motives; Christ then serves as an instrument of surrealism as, for example, in the German movie Das Gespenst (The Ghost), in which he turns into a snake creeping into the bed of a nun or annoys the police by collecting dog faeces in the street. This film has been condemned as blasphemous by many German Christians but could not be forbidden, since the German constitution guarantees the "freedom of art." The difficulty, aesthetic as well as political, of such novels and films consists in the fact that they seem to contain a message but nobody, least of all the author himself, can say what it is, as in Jean Cocteau's beautiful and mysterious film, La Belle et la Bete (Beauty and the Beast). One is tempted to say that Christ is simply an impossible subject for novels and films; they are either syrupy stuff, like most Hollywood productions, or else adulterations. However, the fact that this is not universally true is indicated, for example, by the justly famous novel **Listy Nikodema** by the Polish novelist Jan Dobraczynski, who narrates the story of Jesus by constructing a series of letters written by the Pharisee, Nicodemus, to his former teacher. Similar novels have been written by genuine Christian visionaries, as in the case of Katharina Emmerich, the early 19th century nun whose visions were collected by the Romantic poet, Clemens Brentano, or more recently the monumental **Il poema dell' Uomo-Dio** by the Italian female mystic, Maria Valtorta (though there are good reasons not to consider her ten volumes an expression of what the Church calls personal or private revelations).

A very different interpretation of Christ is to be found in a group of authors who may be described as dissident Marxists. Usually they are former Communists, often children of Catholic, sometimes also Protestant families, who became Marxists of the Stalinist vein, often held important positions in the Party, were appointed specialists for the dialogue with Christians, became engrossed in the study of the Christian tradition and were in the end expelled from the Party because they became too fascinated with Christianity. The most famous examples are the Czech Milan Machovec, who, after a prominent Party career, is today an organist in Prague; the Frenchman Roger Garaudy, a former member of the Central Committee, who a few years ago became a Moslem; the Italian Luigi Lombardo-Radice, who, as far as I know, still remains a member of the Italian Communist Party; in his earlier years the Pole Leszek Kolakowski, who, while still an orthodox Communist, became a very competent specialist in Catholic spirituality in the 16th and 17th centuries, and today teaches at Oxford; and finally the German Ernst

Bloch, who left Eastern Germany in the 50's, became Professor of Philosophy at the West German University of Tübingen and through his book, **Das Prinzip Hoffnung** (The Principle of Hope), was one of the most important sources of the so-called "Political Theology" of Jürgen Moltmann and Johann Baptist Metz, who in turn have strongly influenced the Latin American "Liberation Theology." All these authors have in common that they express a deep admiration for Christ: although he is for them no more than a man, his new teaching about charity is considered so remarkable that he turns out to be someone very unusual. As Garaudy puts it: "With Christ for the first time in the History of Mankind there resounds a call for a human community which knows of no frontiers, for a totality which includes all totalities"; for Garaudy "the admirable idea of Christian love, according to which I can realize myself only in and through others, is the highest notion that man can have of himself and of the meaning of his life" (J. Garaudy, J.B. Metz, K. Rahner, **Der Dialog**, Frankfurt 1966). It is therefore understandable that some of these authors, e.g. Bloch, Machovec and Lombardo-Radice, speak in connection with Christ even of "transcendence": in a mysterious way, Christ transcends what people usually are. Of course, for them he does not transcend them towards God, for all the authors mentioned have remained atheists, with the exception of Garaudy, who in the end joined a mystical trend in Islam. Christ's transcendence, according to these authors, is a historical one; he transcends what at his time and even in our times was and is possible towards a future which, these authors usually add, can only come through Marxism. In this sense Machovec concludes one of his essays by quoting Luke 24,23: "Were not our hearts burning within us when he spoke to us on the road?." Christ becomes a kind of a symbol of what man and mankind could be if only they would fully develop their potentialities. All these authors, all of them philosophers, fascinated many Christians in the 60's and 70's. For many decades, Western philosophy had practically never spoken of Christ; and now the most radical of the atheists were speaking about him with such admiration, with almost religious fervour. What usually escaped those who hailed the authors in question was the fact that the latter's interpretation of Christ is in its own way preposterous. Garaudy, when raving about the admirableness of Christ, explicitly speaks of his life and death. When we read the Gospel, we certainly get the impression that Christ preached love and died out of love for us; yet if we do not add that he died out of obedience to the Father, it becomes very difficult to say wherein this love is supposed to consist. After all, Christ did not sacrifice himself for the defense of the oppressed or to save the lives of his disciples; his dying for mankind makes sense only if we know that he is not just man but also God and that therefore his death has a very special significance. Thus this Marxist interpretation of Christ, obliging as it may sound to a Christian, is merely another version of the claim that Christ was a social rebel; after all, Christ was condemned and crucified because he claimed to be God, not because he fought for certain social groups or because he preached love. On the other hand, the quasi-mystical way in which these dissident Marxists speak of Christ suggests that they are doing something very dubious from the point of view of simple methodology; this is particularly obvious in Machovec and Bloch. They see Christ as believing Christians see him and then proceed to eliminate everything properly theological. This is not an honest approach even from an atheist point of view: either one sees Christ from a strictly historical, as it were empiristic bias, or else one sees Him as a Christian does. You can hardly have it both ways.[3]

Before I come to Hegel who, to my mind, is ultimately behind these Marxist interpretations, I want to add a few words on a kind of Christology which, though it is considered theological, is nevertheless strongly influenced by an implicit ideology. I choose as the most striking example so-called "demythologization," a concept which is connected with the theology of Rudolf Bultmann who, in a famous lecture given in 1941, claimed that the primary task of contemporary theology was to demythologize the Bible, and who later had an enormous influence on exegesis in general. It is important to see that Bultmann's aim was very different from what Marxist-Leninists aim at when they describe Christ as a myth. There is indeed a long rationalist tradition, starting in the 18th century, which tries to show that the whole of the New Testament is the product of collective enthusiasm in the original Christian community rather than a description of historical events; the most famous 19th century examples are David Friedrich Strauss and Ernest Renan. The decisive motive of this rationalist exegesis was to discredit the Gospel as myth; by showing that the Gospel is a myth, they wanted to demonstrate that it cannot be considered true. The Marxist-Leninist claim that even the historical existence of Christ is but a myth is no more than an ultimate radicalization of this tendency. Bultmann, on the contrary, was far from wanting to discredit Christian faith; in fact, he personally was a quite pious Christian whose sermons must have displayed considerable depth. By speaking of "demythologization," he certainly on the one hand wanted to distinguish between what happened historically and what the primitive Christian community made of it; however, while the rationalists concluded from the idea that the evangelical reports were merely a product of the enthusiasm of the first Christians that Christian faith had thus been falsified, Bultmann argued that myth is the proper way of speaking of things divine. In other words, the Gospel tells us about a Christ who never acted in the way in which it describes him; nevertheless, what the Gospel says it "true" since revelation is not a historical report but a way of saying how God acts in history. In other words, Bultmann gave the predicate "mythical" a positive sense, suggesting that the Gospel message expresses a truth relevant to us.

The best example of how this works is Bultmann's interpretation of the Resurrection. On the one hand, it seems clear to him that Christ died a violent death, was buried and, therefore, to put it bluntly, his body rotted like the bodies of all the dead; from an empirical point of view, nothing more happened. On the other hand, the Apostles had an experience which revealed to them the meaning of Christ's death on the cross. According to Bultmann, we have no real way of saying whether this revelation was subjective or objective; personally, Bultmann seems to be inclined to consider it an objective revelation in the sense that Christ had, without anything happening in the world, overcome death. But this in turn means only that belief in the Resurrection is nothing other than belief in the cross as an event of salvation, in the cross as the cross of Christ," and that "the Easter event (das Osterereignis) is nothing other than the rising of faith in the Resurrected Christ (an den Auferstandenen)" (**Kerygma and Mythos**, Berlin 1948 ff., 11, 46 ff.).

This is all very Germanic, since profoundly unclear. It becomes understandable only if we presuppose two things. On the one hand (and in this respect Bultmann certainly is right) Christ's resurrection is not what one might call an "ordinary miracle": Christ does not return from the grave in the way Lazarus did but is transfigured; his resurrection is not a press item that anyone can go along and verify after publication; Christ appears only to those who believe in him. As, for example, Aquinas saw very clearly, the Resurrection was an object of faith even for the Apostles: "Resurrecting, Christ did not return to ordinary life as we all know it, but to an immortal life appropriate to God; therefore, his resurrection as such was not witnessed by people, but made known by angels" (S.Th.III, 55,2).

On the other hand, however, Bultmann (and with him a great number of contemporary exegetes) share the prejudice of the rationalists that certain things simply do not happen in this world: virgins do not have children, medically unexplainable healings do not occur, the dead do not rise to life. This is very clearly an ideological assumption: the modern scientific conception of the world is upheld at all costs, even God cannot and certainly does not act contrary to it. The difference between Bultmann, and with him a great number of contemporary theologians, on the one hand, and the rationalist, mostly atheist exegetes of the 18th and 19th centuries, on the other hand, consists in nothing more than that the latter considered this assumption an argument against Christian belief while the former seek, with greater or lesser success, an interpretation of Christian faith that offers a basis for coping with reality as it is currently perceived.

This "interpretation" operates with a sort of an intellectual trick, the roots of which go back to Hegel. The trick consists in saying that although preternatural things do not happen in nature, they may and do happen in the mind, and in adding that such mind-happenings may be "true" in a more genuine sense than statements about events in the world. Now in this lecture I cannot possibly enter into the details of Hegel's philosophy. By some, e.g. Walter Pannenberg, he is considered a sort of a Lutheran Aquinas; others consider him, e.g. Franz Gregoire, an atheist. Although I clearly incline towards the second opinion, the question is too involved to be discussed here. The following brief remarks must suffice. One way of summing up Hegelianism consists in saying that according to it Nature precedes Mind, but Mind becomes an antecedent of Nature as soon as it emerges. At first, this sounds preposterous; perhaps it becomes somewhat clearer if you imagine, first, that individual human minds are nothing but particular expressions of *the* Mind, and second, that *the* Mind is identical with the various forms of human culture. That Nature precedes Mind, but Mind becomes prior to Nature as soon as culture develops means then that Nature becomes for us a dimension of culture as soon as culture develops. As cultural beings we know of nature only through culture, although we know that nature is its basis. This implies, however, that what ordinary man considers real events which, after having happened, can be interpreted, evaluated, and so on, are not truly distinct from their interpretation or evaluation. We have no access to reality except through our culture-bound interpretation of it, reality is its cultural interpretation by man. To the obvious objections that we do after all argue about the legitimacy of interpretations and that we can do this only if we have specific standards, Hegel would reply that culture develops in a definite way in a definite direction (that of the progress of freedom) which thereby becomes the standard.

I do not want to argue about the very involved question of the extent to which this view has some truth to it. For the purpose of this lecture it may be enough to point out that if one takes it seriously, it does imply that it is not important whether Christ really is the Son of God and whether he really was resurrected. For the idea to become true it is enough to know that the community of his disciples developed this idea as a notion that influenced world history. What really happened does not count, for belief in the idea, by becoming a cultural forceful phenomenon renders it, as it were, real. Thus it is that the same Hegel with respect to whom there is disagreement as to whether he even believed in the existence of a personal God can write paragraphs about Christ which sound profoundly Christian. To Hegel, Christ is "the hinge, on which world history turns" (**Werke** XI, 410); "Christ has appeared, a man who is God, and God who is man; thus peace and reconciliation have accrued to the world" (ibid., 416). At the same time, however, if one reads the pertinent passages in Hegel's **Philosophy of Religion** and also in many other of his works, a very strange doctrine emerges, which, it seems to me, has, in many direct and indirect ways, influenced a great number of modern exegetes. On the one hand, Hegel seems to adhere to a doctrine of the Trinity reminiscent of the heresy of Sabellius in the 3rd century A.D., which since the late 17th century, probably in connection with the philosophy of Spinoza, has been called "Modalism"; according to this doctrine the three divine persons are nothing but three different modes (*modi*) in which God reveals himself: in so far as he remains invisible, God is the Father; in so far as he becomes man, he is the Son; in so far as he sanctifies men, he is the Holy Spirit. This kind of doctrine has received some attention in recent times, since Jürgen Moltmann has accused both Karl Barth and Karl Rahner of implicitly defending it (**Trinität und Reich Gottes**, 1980, 155,166), whereupon Walter Kasper retaliated by accusing Moltmann of a "tritheism" (**Der Gott Jesu Christi**, 1982, p.360). If one assumes, which is probably the correct interpretation of Hegel's theology, that to Hegel God is merely a sort of a logical structure of the world which becomes aware of itself (and thus something like a person) in the minds of men, one can describe his theology as a "dynamic modalism." In this respect, then, the unity of the Divine and the Human in Christ was nothing but a breakthrough in, and of, world history, through which God for the first time became aware of himself as God. On the other hand, such an interpretation is corroborated by what Hegel says about Christ as a "historical individual." It is blatantly apparent how little Hegel is interested in Christ as he was before he died. As Hegel puts it, as an individual person Christ is nothing but a "passing moment" (XI, 417), who becomes what he truly is through his death and resurrection. For after resurrection, according to Hegel, Christ is the Holy Spirit, who in turn is nothing other than the theological self-awareness of the Christian community. Since Hegel understands his own philosophy as a "spiritual expansion" (**Enzyklopädie** 1829, ed. Nicolin-Poggeler, 25) of the Christian faith, that is, as a kind of theology, and since for him philosophy casts in articulate notions what religion can express only in symbolic language, one arrives at the rather preposterous claim that, in the last analysis, Christ viewed in his ultimate fulfillment is Hegel's own philosophy. Considering Hegel's assumption, however, this claim is not as preposterous as it may sound. As a concrete person in history, Christ is no more than a beginning. Of course, this is so, since he is a man. But through his claim to be God, he is the first man in whom God becomes aware of himself as God. Yet the self-awareness of both God and the universe finds its fulfillment in philosophy, of which, by a quirk of history, Mr. Hegel is the ultimate representative and occasion.

Now I do not want to argue whether or not Hegel may be described as an ideologist; in one sense he is one of the most ingenious philosophers since Aristotle. What I wish to claim, however, is that Hegel's Christology is highly ideological. Its most striking, but in a way also most influential feature, is its vagueness, the way in which it obscures the Christian claims by mixing truth and error.

The most far-reaching step by which a Christian believer may oblige an exegete consists in admitting that the disciples fully realized who Jesus was only after Easter and Pentecost, i.e. only then answered for themselves the question asked in Mark 4:41: *tis ara outos estin*, "Why, who is this?," a question implying "Why, what kind of person is this?" (cf. F. Muffner in L. Scheffczyk, ed., **Grundfragen der Christologie Heute**, Freiburg 1975, 79 ff.). They certainly would have answered this question differently before Easter and Pentecost. But this cannot mean, as Hegel, and with him much of modern exegesis, thinks that only after Easter and through the event of Pentecost did Christ become what we believe about him. The effect of the Easter event and the inspiration of Pentecost is an interpretation of what the disciples had witnessed and now remembered; an interpretation which would have been completely different and indeed impossible if the disciples' memories had not suggested to them what the Gospel tells us. In other words: however true it may be to say that their post-Easter faith was different from their pre-Easter faith, the ultimate impetus to their post-Easter faith came from what they witnessed before Easter. It is simply preposterous to claim that through some kind of experience at Easter the disciples came to believe about Jesus something that did not correspond to what they had experienced while he was among them. Yet this is precisely what many contemporary exegetes influenced by Hegel would suggest: although Jesus may have been a thoroughly unusual fellow, he — so they imply — certainly had none of the supernatural characteristics ascribed to him by the Gospel. If anything truly extraordinary did happen, it happened in the minds of the disciples. In other words, revelation consists in the experiences of Easter and Pentecost, not in Christ himself.

It hardly seems necessary to emphasize what the ideological premise of this kind of exegesis is: events such as those related in the Gospel — the virgin birth, the angels singing in heaven, the changing of water into wine, the various healings, the confrontation with demons that had taken possession of mortals, the resurrection of Lazarus and other dead, the resurrection of Christ himself — simply do not happen. None of us has ever witnessed events of this kind; so why should they have happened in Christ's times?

Strangely enough, this attitude seems psychologically compatible with the admission that Christ was somebody divine, even God in person. This strange combination of a reduction of the historical Christ to a mere man, of Christology to Jesuology, with the admission of the central claim of Christian faith, that of Christ's divinity, has its parallel in a notion of prayer quite common among Christians today. They will argue that prayers may indeed be granted, but only with respect to spiritual events or those in the mind. God may influence our thinking and thereby possibly also our behaviour, but he does not change anything in nature. Similarly, Christ may have been the Son of God, indeed even somehow been aware of it, but he could not possibly have made things happen which in our world do not happen and, in particular, he could not have effected something that cannot be explained except by direct divine intervention disrupting the sequence of inner-worldly causality. Of course one has to admit that, however ideological this approach may be (simply because it does not grant God the power he has), it includes a concern that must be taken seriously. Most of contemporary theology has difficulties in admitting that Christ may have acted in the way God acts; if he did so it happened either in the order of grace, that is, behind the veil of the empirical, or else in the minds of the disciples, as a special experience granted to them. The disciples may have "experienced" that Christ is someone of divine origin, but they could not have seen it in the sense in which St. John says: *kai etheasametha ten doxan autou*, "and we have *seen* his glory" (1,14). On the other hand, however, it would be wrong to deny that parts of the Christian tradition often succumbed to the temptation to minimize Christ's humanity. Although one knew that in Christ the Divine Word had assumed a human nature, it seemed irreverent to take this too literally. If I am not wrong, in recent times it has been above all Christ's consciousness and self-awareness that was (and still is) at issue. We feel that, being God, Christ must have been constantly and continuously aware of his being God; but how could one be a man and at the same time know that one is God? Or the other way round: how could the disciples possibly see Christ's splendour and majesty when he was truly man? There is the constant temptation to think of Christ's humanity as an outward appearance, an illusion, a veil which one has to push aside in order to see who Christ really was.

In a sense, this is also an ideological influence on Christology. Its premise is that God cannot become one of his creatures, that he cannot be "made flesh" (John,1,14). Yet this is precisely what we are invited to believe. Christ is not, as some theologians would seem to suggest today, someone who gradually made up his mind to have a special relationship to God and therefore a special mission; he is not, as a German bishop by a slip of the tongue recently put it, one of us who received the distinction of becoming the Son of God. But neither is he God who only appears to be a man; centuries of intellectual effort, probably the most difficult task ever given to human beings, have tried to clarify this point. And yet part of the reductionism which tends to reduce Christ to a mere man cannot be explained except by admitting that we often succumb to the temptation to act as if Christ were not a man in the full sense of the term.

Let me conclude by referring to a completely different dimension of the subject of my lecture, "Christ and the Ideologies." Whereas I have in fact tried to sketch how ideologies of our time view Christ, I could also have tried to say what from the point of view of Christ ideologies are. This would have been a very speculative lecture, since ideologies have not to date been a *locus theologicus*. Yet there is one issue worth mentioning at the end of my paper: the reason why Christian faith cannot be treated as an ideology is that, in the first place, it is not a doctrine. Of course, our faith does have doctrinal elements. But prior to these in the most fundamental sense it is a commitment to someone, to a person. To be a Christian means to follow Christ: not because he discovered a special way of human life like Buddha, or because he found a special wisdom like Confucius, or because he had some kind of a revelation like Mohammed, but because of what, and above all who, He is. The revelation we Christians possess does not lie primarily or even mainly in what Christ teaches, but in who He is. He himself is the revelation of what we need to know about things divine. For this, and only this reason, it is so urgently important to know who Christ is, what His intention was, how He viewed things, what He wanted us to see in Him.

Those of you who have read Evelyn Waugh's **Brideshead Revisited** or seen the impressive television film based on the book will remember a number of strange dialogues conducted by Catholics in it. In the last scene, as the old Lord dies, there is a lengthy discussion as to whether and why Extreme Unction is necessary or desirable and whether the dying man must still be alive in order to receive it. For Catholics who saw the film this discussion had something eerie about it. It reminded them of the time when Catholics felt that they knew the exact answer to every question, that one only had to look up the catechism to find it. Now I am far from wanting to minimize the doctrinal element in the Christian faith, including that of the Catholic Church, which, according to the Constitution **Lumen Gentium** (8) of the Second Vatican Council, is the community which Jesus Christ put into Peter's hands by saying "Feed my sheep" (John 21,17). And I felt that the Episcopal Synod gathered in Rome in December 1985 was well advised in considering the need for a new catechism to teach the faithful in an unambiguous way what they have to believe if they want to merit being called Catholics. Still, it is undeniable that we Catholics have sometimes been tempted to confuse the unambiguous teaching of the Church, as it administers the *depositum fidei* on behalf of Jesus Christ, with theology. However important and indispensable theology may be, it is not revelation, but a purely human endeavor with no guarantee of being guided by the Holy Spirit. I am a great admirer of Aquinas and like to read and re-read him: but he himself knew quite well what we Catholics sometimes forgot, namely that his admirable synthesis is something thoroughly human and, therefore, like all things human, historical, perishable, not "the real thing." Educated Catholic laymen, perhaps even more than theologians, have sometimes forgotten to draw a sharp line between what he and other great men of the ecclesiastic tradition said and revelation. Thus we may sometimes have been in danger, in Christology as well as in other issues, of becoming ideological. Of course, Aquinas or, for that matter, St. Augustine or Cardinal Newman or Karl Rahner or Urs von Balthasar, were and are not ideologists. But even what clearly is not ideology may become ideological if it is thoughtlessly repeated. One repeats it, since it is so clear and simple and obviously transparent, like Gothic cathedrals. But Gothic cathedrals are human products as well. The only revelation which, in spite of Christ's being a man in the fullest sense of the term, is in no way human is Christ himself and what the Holy Spirit teaches us about him, be it through the Gospel, or the binding teaching of his mystical body, the Church. Therefore, and with this I wish to conclude my lecture, it is Christ himself, and in the end only He who guarantees that our faith is not ideology — a person whom we follow, not a doctrine.

## NOTES

1. That Engels belonged to those who at least doubted the historical existence of Christ is suggested by at least two writings of the 1880's, see his article published at the occasion of Bruno Bauer's death in 1882, "Bruno Bauer und das Urchristentum," Marx-Engels, **Werke**, East-Berlin 1961 ff., XIX, 297 ff., here 298; and "Das Buch der Offenbarung," ibid., XXI, ff., here 10-11 ("Christianity came about in a way thoroughly unknown to us ..."). In the early writings of Marx,

Christ is mentioned in a symbolic way several times, also with reference to Bruno Bauer, e.g.; "As Christ is the mediator on whom man unburdens all his own divinity and all his religious ties, so is the state the mediator to which man transfers all his unholiness and all his human freedom," ibid., I, 353 ("Zur Judenfrage"); in the same vein, K. Marx, **Grundrisse der Kritik der politischen Okonomie**, East-Berlin, 1953, 237. Karl Kautsky, too, suggested that if Christ existed at all, he was a proletarian revolutionary, see his **Ursprung des Christentums**, 1908.

2.  According to a very old tradition that was still familiar to Origen in the first half of the 3rd century A.D., the name of the prisoner whom Pilate offered to the mob in exchange for Jesus was also "Jesus"; Barabbas, after all, means simply "Son of Abbas" (cf. Mt. 27,1; Mk.15,1; Lk.23,1; Jn.18,40). And what is imputed to Christ when he is described as a revolutionary is, in fact, the same as what Barabbas was charged with; according to the Jewish historian Flavius Josephus, the leaders of the rebellion against the Romans were *lestai*, which is the Greek expression used by St. John when he writes that Barrabas was a robber (*lestes*). As Cardinal Ratzinger put it recently, to describe Jesus as a political revolutionary means once more to opt for Barabbas against Jesus (J. Ratzinger, *Internationale Theologische Zeitschrift*, Xl (1986) 3, 413.

3.  A careful analysis of various Neomarxist authors on Christ is found in Virgilio Melchiorre, "L'interpretazione neomarxista di Gesù," Autori vari, **Icona dell invisibile**, Milano 1981, 101-182. Besides those mentioned, Melchiore analyses the Italian Fernado Belo, the Slovak Vitezslav Gardavsky, and the German Leo Koffler.

# Crisis in Christology

# 9

# FIVE GOSPELS BUT NO GOSPEL: JESUS AND THE SEMINAR

A Critique of the *The Five Gospels: the Search for the Authentic Words of Jesus*, new translation and commentary by Robert W. Funk, Roy W. Hoover and the Jesus Seminar (New York: Macmillan, 1993)

## N. Thomas Wright
## Lichfield Cathedral, England

## 1. Looking for Jesus

People have been looking for Jesus for a long time, but never quite like this. The 'Quest of the Historical Jesus' has been proceeding, in fits and starts, for two hundred years. Its story has often been told;[1] in recent years there has been a flurry, not to say a flood, of writing about Jesus, and debates of all sorts, about every aspect of the evidence, and every conceivable reconstruction of Jesus' life, teaching, work and death, have been running to and fro.[2] Most of this writing has been produced by individual scholars, working independently. But in the last few years a new corporate venture has emerged, attempting by a process of discussion and voting to arrive at an answer to the question: 'What Did Jesus Really Say?' This group has called itself 'The Jesus Seminar,' and among its many recent publications one stands out as a kind of flagship: *The Five Gospels*, published late in 1993 by Macmillan (though emanating from the Seminar's own publishing house, Polebridge Press). This is the subject of the present chapter.

No doubt there are at least as many opinions about the 'Jesus Seminar' as the Seminar itself holds about Jesus. Passions, in fact, already run high on the subject, and may run higher yet before the storm abates. Some of the Seminar's members treat any questioning of its work like a slap in the face — though not with the turning of the other cheek, as one might have thought considering that that saying received the rare accolade of a red vote (meaning authentic: see below).[3] In other quarters, one only has to mention the Seminar to provoke a wry smile, or even guffaws of laughter. At a packed and high-profile meeting of the Society of Biblical Literature's 'Pauline Theology' seminar in 1991, the person in the chair — one of the most senior and respected of North American biblical scholars — rejected a call for a vote on the subject that had been under discussion, by simply saying 'This ain't the Jesus Seminar.' This was greeted with laughter and applause in about equal measure.

So what is the Jesus Seminar up to, and what should we think about it? It has now completed many years of detailed and painstaking work, and, though it may well all deserve discussing, there is no space here to go into its many products, with all their presuppositions, methods, decisions, and results.[4] I have, in any case, written about all that elsewhere.[5] I want in this essay to concentrate on *The Five Gospels*, the book towards which all else was preliminary.

The 'five gospels' in question are (in case anyone was in doubt) Mark, Matthew, Luke, John and Thomas. The inclusion of the last of these will still raise one or two eyebrows, though it is by now well known that the Seminar takes kindly to Thomas, not least because of its apparent similarity with (some reconstructions of) the hypothetical source 'Q' — and, as we shall see, the portrait of Jesus which it appears to support. More striking is the technique with which the Seminar's results are displayed. The old 'red letter testaments' picked out all the words of Jesus in red; this one accords that status to the favoured few among the sayings, those which the Seminar voted as highly likely to emanate from Jesus himself. The rest of Jesus' sayings are set in pink, gray and black, on a rough sliding scale of the probability and improbability of their coming from Jesus; I shall discuss the precise nuances of the colors presently. Each saying, story, or group of sayings/stories is then commented on, and the reasons for the voting are explained, sometimes briefly, sometimes up to a few pages. The text is broken up from time to time by 'cameo essays' on key topics (the kingdom of God, the son of man, and so forth). The text is attractively laid out, with diagrams and occasional pictures. Everything is presented about as clearly as it could be; nobody, from highschool student upwards, could fail to see what was being said. All in all, it is a substantial product, and whatever one thinks of the actual results, it clearly represents a great deal of hard labour.

## A New Translation

Six features of the book call for general comment right from the start. First, it uses what the Seminar has called 'The Scholars Version' [sic] — its own translation of the four canonical gospels and Thomas. This is an attempt to represent, in colloquial American, the original flavour of the Greek. Now it is our turn to be slapped in the face:

> Although Jesus was indignant, he stretched out his hand, touched him, and says to him, "Okay — you're clean!"[6]

> The king came in to see the guests for himself and noticed this man not properly attired. And he says to him, "Look pal, how'd you get in here without dressing for the occasion?"[7]

> When Jesus noticed their trust, he said, "Mister, your sins have been forgiven you."[8]

I have no objection to colloquial translations — though one might have thought this would be the People's Version, not the Scholars.' What I do find somewhat objectionable is the dismissive tone of the introduction, which explains that other versions are 'faintly Victorian' and set a context of 'polite religious discourse suitable for a Puritan parlour.'[9] The New Revised Standard Version comes in for particular criticism; one suspects that its main fault in the eyes of the SV translators is that it is a lineal descendant, on one side of the family at any rate, of the old King James Version, which, as we shall see, represents all that the Seminar abominates by way of American religion. The authors make great play of the fact that, unlike most bible translations, this one both includes the non-canonical Thomas and is not authorized by any ecclesiastical or religious bodies. Instead, pompously, 'The Scholars Version is authorized by scholars.'[10]

## Present and Absent Friends

But, second, which scholars? Seventy-four names are listed in the back of the book, and there have been other members, quite influential in earlier stages of the debate, who are not explicitly mentioned here.[11]

Some of them are household names in the world of New Testament Studies: Robert Funk himself, the driving force behind the entire enterprise, whose earlier work on the Greek grammar of the New Testament is universally recognised as authoritative; Dominic Crossan, whose combination of enormous erudition, subtlety of thought, and felicitous writing style have rightly ensured him widespread respect; James Robinson, whose work on the Nag Hammadi texts has placed the entire discipline in his debt; Marcus Borg, Bruce Chilton, and Walter Wink, all of whom have made distinguished and distinctive contributions to the study of Jesus in his context (and to much else besides); Ron Cameron, whose forthright and provocative writings on Thomas and related topics are rightly famous; John Kloppenborg, one of the leading specialists on the hypothetical source 'Q.' In any list of contemporary North American biblical scholars, all these would find a place of honor.

But one could compile a very long list of North American New Testament scholars, including several who have written importantly about Jesus, who are not among those present, and whose work has had no visible impact on the Seminar at all. The most obvious is Ed Sanders, whose work, massive in its learning, and almost unique in its influence over the present state of scholarship worldwide, seems to have been ignored by the Seminar — except for one tiny particular, and that precisely where Sanders is at his weakest.[12] Another figure whose work has been totally ignored is Ben F. Meyer, who has more understanding of how ancient texts work in his little finger than many of the Jesus Seminar seem to have in their entire word-processors, and whose writing on Jesus is utterly rigorous, utterly scholarly, and utterly different in its results from anything in the volume we are considering.[13] So, too, one looks in vain for members of the teaching faculties of many of the leading North American colleges and universities. There is nobody currently teaching at Harvard, Yale, Princeton, Duke, McGill, or Stanford. Toronto is well represented; so is Claremont (not least by its graduates); several Fellows of the Seminar have doctorates from Harvard. But where is the rest of the guild — those who, for instance, flock to the 'Historical Jesus' sessions at the annual meeting of the Society of Biblical Literature? They are conspicuous by their absence.

No doubt some within the Seminar would suggest that this comment is academic snobbery, but they cannot have it both ways. The Jesus Seminar is in something of a cleft stick at this point. On the one hand, the members are determined to present to the general public the findings which 'scholars' have come up with. Away with secrecy, and hole-in-a-corner scholarship, they say: it is time for scholars to come out of their closets, to boldly say what no-one has said before. They must, therefore, present themselves as the pundits, the ones in the know, the ones the public can trust as the reputable, even the authorized, spokespersons for the serious tradition of biblical scholarship.[14] But, on the other hand, they lash out at the 'elitism' of their critics within the broader academic world[15] — while saying on the next page that attacks on members of the Seminar have tended to come from 'those who lack academic credentials.' Sauce for the goose and sauce for the gander: either academic credentials matter, in which case the Seminar should listen to those who possess them in abundance and are deeply critical of their work, or they don't matter, in which case the Seminar should stop priding itself on its own, over against the common herd. The attitude to critics expressed in this book reminds me of John 7.49: in the Scholars Version, it reads 'As for this rabble, they are ignorant of the Law! Damn them!.' It becomes apparent that the work we have here does not represent 'scholars,' as simply as that; it represents *some* scholars, and that mostly (with some interesting exceptions) from a very narrow band within a broader community which is itself, after all, only one narrow band among serious contemporary readers of the Gospels worldwide.[16]

These comments about the make-up of the Seminar highlight a point which must be clearly made before we go one step further. Though this book claims, on every page, to speak for all the Fellows of the Seminar, it becomes increasingly apparent that it comes from the Seminar's Chair, Robert W. Funk (R. W. Hoover is named as co-author, though there is no indication of which author drafted which parts). Dissentient voices are, of course, recorded in the reporting of voting patterns. But it would be a mistake to saddle all, perhaps even most, of the Fellows with the point of view, and the arguments, that we find on page after page. Only occasionally is this really acknowledged. In the bibliography, for instance, one of Marcus Borg's books is listed, with the comment 'It goes almost without saying that he didn't vote with the majority on every issue.'[17] One suspects that that is something of an understatement. In the present essay, therefore, I am discussing the work of Funk and Hoover, not necessarily that of other Fellows; we may note, though, that the whole layout and intent of the book predisposes the reader — not least the non-academic reader, who is clearly in view — to assume that the verdicts reached are those of 'scholars' in a much broader sense.

## A Driving Agenda

There is, thirdly, a further agenda involved at this point, which is, one may suspect, the major force which motivates the project in general and several (though by no means all) of its members. They are fundamentally antifundamentalist. Listen to these wonderfully objective, value-free, scholarly comments, taken from the book's introduction:

> Once the discrepancy between the Jesus of history and the Christ of faith emerged from under the smothering cloud of the historic creeds, it was only a matter of time before scholars sought to disengage [the two] ... It is ironic that Roman Catholic scholars are emerging from the dark ages of theological tyranny just as many Protestant scholars are reentering it as a consequence of the dictatorial tactics of the Southern Baptist Convention and other fundamentalisms.[18]

> With the council of Nicea in 325, the orthodox party solidified its hold on the Christian tradition and other wings of the Christian movment [sic] were choked off.[19]

There are only two positions allowed, it seems. One must either be some kind of closed-minded fundamentalist, adhering to some approximation of the historic creeds of the Christian church; one notes that this lumps together Athanasius, Aquinas, Barth, Pannenberg and Moltmann along with the TV evangelists who are among the real targets of the polemic. Or one must be non-judgmentally open to the free-for-all hurly-burly of Gnosis, Cynicism, esoteric wisdom, folklore and so on represented by various groups in the first three centuries — and to the baby-and-bathwater methodological skepticism adopted by the Seminar.[20] The strange thing is that there are several members of the Seminar itself who represent neither point of view; has the author of this introduction forgotten who some of his colleagues are? Unfortunately, as we shall see, this either-or has so dominated the landscape that a great many decisions of the Seminar simply reflect a shallow polarisation which has precious little to do with the first century and, one suspects, a great deal to do with the twentieth, not least in North America. One suspects that several members of the Seminar do not actually *know* very many ordinary, non-fundamentalist, orthodox Christians. Would it be going too far to venture the supposition that more than one leading member of the Jesus Seminar is doing his (or her) best to exorcize the memory of a strict fundamentalist background? Unfortunately, the attempt to escape from one's own past is not a good basis for the attempt to reconstruct someone else's.

This question has another aspect to it which must be noted carefully. It is now endemic in North American Biblical Studies that very few practitioners have studied philosophy or theology at any depth. Such study, indeed, is sometimes regarded with suspicion, as though it might prejudice the pure, objective, neutral reading of the text. Leave aside for the moment the impossibility of such objectivity (see below). The real problem is that if one is to discuss what are essentially theological and philosophical issues, in terms both of the method required for serious study of Jesus and of the content and implications of Jesus' proclamation, one really requires more sophistication than the Seminar, in this book at least, can offer. This will become apparent as we proceed.

## Which Gospels?

The fourth introductory point concerns the treatment of the different 'gospels.' As I said, it is now commonplace to treat the book known as the Gospel of Thomas alongside the canonical gospels. If we are studying the entire gospel tradition, this is clearly mandatory. The Seminar is to be congratulated for pushing this fact into the public eye (and for the marvellous work of producing study texts of a large number of relevant documents which had not been easily available hitherto). But, when all is said and done, huge questions remain about the relevance of Thomas for the study of Jesus. By no means all students of it agree with the majority of the Seminar in placing it early and independent of the canonical gospels.[21] If members of the public are interested in knowing what 'scholars' think, they ought to be told fair and square that diagrams in which a hypothetical first edition of Thomas is placed in the 50s of the first century are thoroughly tendentious, and belong out on a limb of current scholarship.[22]

In particular, we should not accept without question the assumption that Thomas, and for that matter fragments like the Egerton papyrus, are (or belong to) *gospels*. It all depends what you mean. Thomas does not call itself a 'gospel.' Nor, for that matter, do Matthew, Luke and John; and the opening note in Mark ('The beginning of the gospel of Jesus Christ') may well refer, not to the book which then follows, but to the events which it purports to record. The meaning of the word 'gospel' in the first two centuries of the Christian era is, in fact, quite controversial;[23] sufficient to note here that to call Thomas, and for that matter 'Q,' 'gospels' is to make quite a far-reaching decision. It is to say that these works are to be regarded as *proclamations* about Jesus, of the same sort as the four better-known 'gospels,' despite the fact that they do not narrate the story of Jesus, do not (for the most part) proclaim him as Messiah, do not tell of his death and resurrection — do not, in fact, do the very things which seem, from the Pauline evidence, to be what the earliest Christians regarded as 'gospel.' Bringing Paul into the picture at this point is of course itself controversial, but not nearly so much as making Thomas contemporary with him.[24]

I suggest that nothing would be lost, and a good deal of clarity regained, if, instead of referring to Thomas, and indeed 'Q,' as 'gospels,' and thereby supposing that they record the theology of an entire group within very early Christianity, we see them as what they are (supposing for the moment that 'Q' ever existed): collections of sayings. Calling them 'gospels' obscures the obvious difference of genre between them and the four ordinarily so called. In an attempt to gain a hearing for different supposed presentations of Jesus, the current fashion distorts precisely that sort of literary analysis that 'scholars' ought to favour.

In fact, although *The Five Gospels* prints all of John as well as the others, it is clear that John is regarded a priori as having little or nothing to do with Jesus himself. This, indeed, is one of the Seminar's vaunted 'seven pillars of scholarly wisdom.'[25] But here we see quite sharply, what we shall observe in more detail presently: the Seminar's method has not been to examine each saying all by itself and decide about it, but to start with a fairly clear picture of Jesus and early Christianity, and simply run through the material imposing this picture on the texts.

## All Cats are Gray in the Dark

A note, next, on the color-coding of the sayings. This is clearly meant to convey a definite and precise meaning. The 'ordinary reader,' browsing through *The Five Gospels*, picks up quite quickly that red or pink is a quite rare accolade, that black is common, and that gray, close enough (it seems) to black, also dominates at several points. The book's cover reflects something of this balance, with a small red box on a large black background, and in the small red box the words 'WHAT DID JESUS RE-ALLY SAY?.' It seems fairly clear that red denotes what Jesus said, black what he did not, and that pink and gray are softer variants on these two.

Not so simple, however. The voting system was quite complex:[26] there are two cumbersome sets of 'meanings' for the four colours, and an intricate system of numberings for the votes, which were then averaged out. This means that in any given case, especially in relation to pink and gray, the color on the page does *not* represent what 'scholars,' even the small selection of scholarly opinion represented in the Seminar, actually think. A pink vote almost certainly means that, on the one hand, a sizeable minority believed Jesus actually said these words, while a substantial minority were convinced, or nearly convinced, that he did not. Most, in fact, did not vote pink; yet that is what appears on the page. (I am reminded of the notorious fundamentalist attempts to harmonize how many times the rooster crowed when Peter denied Jesus. One of the only ways of doing it is to say that the rooster crowed, not three, but *nine* times. Thus a supposed doctrine of scriptural inerrancy is 'preserved' — at the enormous cost of saying that what actually happened *is what none of the texts record*.) Thus, the Jesus Seminar could print a text in pink or gray, *even though the great majority of the Seminar voted red or black*. The colors, especially the two middle ones, cannot be taken as more than an averaging out of widely divergent opinion. It is perfectly possible that the color on the page, if gray or pink, is one for which nobody voted at all.

In particular, the gray sayings conceal a very interesting phenomenon. Spies on the Seminar report that in some cases the gray verdict could be seen as a victory — for those who, against the grain of the Seminar, think Jesus might well have said the words concerned. Take Luke 19.42-4 for an example. This stern warning about the coming destruction of Jerusalem fits with an 'apocalyptic' strand of teaching which, in almost all other cases, the Fellows of the Seminar voted black by a substantial margin. But on this occasion a paper was given arguing that the words could indeed have been spoken by Jesus. Enough Fellows were persuaded by this to pull the vote up to gray — a quite remarkable victory for those who voted red or pink. Seen from within the Seminar, where a good number start with the assumption that virtually no sayings go back to Jesus himself, gray can thus mean 'well, maybe there is a possibility after all...' Seen from outside, of course — in other words, from the perspective of those for whom the Seminar's products, particularly this book, are designed — it conveys a very different message, namely 'probably not.'

Another example of this occurs in the summary account of the vote on Matthew 18.3 ('If you don't do an about-face and become like children, you will never enter Heaven's domain'). The following is typical of literally dozens of passages:

> The opinion was evenly divided. Some red and a large number of pink votes, in favor of authenticity, were offset by substantial gray and black votes. The result was a compromise gray designation for this version and all its parallels.[27]

Or again, in dealing with the parable of the Two Sons, and the subsequent saying (Matthew 21.28-31a and 28.31b):

> Fifty-eight percent of the Fellows voted red or pink for the parable, 53 percent for the saying in v. 31b. A substantial number of gray and black votes pulled the weighted average into the gray category.[28]

Without using a pocket calculator, I confess I cannot understand how, if a majority in each case thought the saying authentic or probably authentic, the 'weighted average' turned out to be 'probably inauthentic.' A voting system that produces a result like this ought to be scrapped. The average reader, seeing the passage printed as gray, will conclude that 'scholars' think it is probably inauthentic; whereas, even within the small company of the Seminar, the majority would clearly disagree.[29]

In evaluating the color scheme, therefore, it is important not to think that consensus has been reached. The Seminar's voting methods and results remind one somewhat of Italian politics: with proportional representation, everybody's votes count to some extent, but the result is serious instability. Gray and pink sayings are like the smile on the politician's face when a deal has been struck between minority parties; the informed observer knows that the coalition is a patched-up job, which will not stand the test of time. The reader, particularly the reader outside the scholarly guild, should beware. This volume is only a snapshot of what some scholars think within one particular context and after a certain set of debates. But even the snapshot is out of focus, and the colors have been affected by the process of development. This may be fine if what one wants is an impressionistic idea of the state of play. But the Seminar promises, and claims to offer, much more than that. It claims to tell the unvarnished truth. And therein lies the sixth and final point for comment at this stage.

## Jumping on the Bandwagon
## after the Wheels Came Off

Perhaps the deepest flaw in terms of apparent method is that this book appeals constantly, as does all the literature of the Jesus Seminar, to the possibility that by the application of supposedly scientific or 'scholarly' criteria one will arrive at a definite answer to the question as to what Jesus actually said. This jumps out of the very cover of the book: the subtitle ('The Search for the Authentic Words of Jesus') has the word 'authentic' underlined, and the sub-subtitle, 'What did Jesus Really Say?' is clearly intended to emphasize the 'really.' The whole enterprise seems to offer the possibility of objective certainty, of methods which will produce results as watertight as $2 + 2 = 4$.

The puzzle about this is that it buys heavily into exactly the sort of positivism that is now routinely abandoned by the great majority of scholars working in the fields of history and texts — including by several members of the Jesus Seminar themselves. The idea that by historical investigation one might arrive at a position of unbiassed objective certainty, of absolute unconditioned knowledge, about anything, has been shot to pieces by critiques from a variety of points of view. All knowledge is conditioned by the context and agenda of the knower; all reconstructions are somebody's reconstructions, and each 'somebody' sees the world through their own eyes and not their neighbour's. This is so widely acknowledged that one would have thought it unnecessary to state, let alone to stress. The positivistic bandwagon got stuck in the mud some time ago, and a succession of critics, looking back to Marx, Nietzsche and Freud but now loosely gathered under the umbrella of postmodernism, has cheerfully pulled its wheels off altogether. This, of course, has not filtered through to the popular media, who still want to know whether something 'actually happened' or not. The Jesus Seminar, in its desire to go public with the results of scholarship, has apparently been lured into giving the public what it wants, rather than what scholarship can in fact provide. As the previous discussion about voting and color-coding makes clear, the one thing this book cannot offer is an answer to the question on its front cover. All it can do is to report, in a manner that will often mislead the ordinary reader, what some scholars think Jesus may have said.

At this point some members of the Seminar will want to protest. They know very well that positivism is a dead-end street. They fully appreciate that most of the color-codings, especially the pink and gray, are compromise solutions hiding a good deal of debate and uncertainty. Unfortunately, such subtleties were totally lost on whoever wrote the blurb on the back of the book, which encourages the average reader, for whom the book is designed, to assume that the colors in the book provide certain, objective, copper-bottomed, positivistic answers:

> Did Jesus really give the Sermon on the Mount? Is the Lord's Prayer composed of his authentic words? *THE FIVE GOSPELS* answers these questions in a bold, dynamic work that will startle the world of traditional biblical interpretation. . . In pursuit of the historical Jesus, [the scholars] used their collective expertise to determine the authenticity of the more than 1,500 sayings attributed to him. Their remarkable findings appear in this book. . .
>
> Only those sayings that appear in red type are considered by the seminar to be close to what Jesus actually said. . . **According to the Seminar, no more than 20 percent of the sayings attributed to Jesus were uttered by him. . .**[30]

Underneath the rhetoric about making the results of scholarship generally available, therefore, we find a new form of an old divide between the scholars and the simple folk. The introduction to this book castigates those scholars who 'knew' of the problems about finding the historical Jesus (not to mention the Christ of the church's faith), but who kept these 'findings' from the public, who wanted to have their fragile faith confirmed. The Seminar claims to have bridged this divide. But then the Seminar, whose members clearly know that their own work is culture-conditioned, and that the color-coding system repeatedly hides compromise and serious disagreement, keeps these facts from its own public, which wants to have *its fragile faith in positivism* supported and confirmed. At this meta-level, encouraging the reading public to think that the old Enlightenment bandwagon is still rolling along, when in fact the wheels came off it some time ago, is just as irresponsible as the preacher who hides from the congregation the fact that there are serious questions to be faced about the origin and nature of early Christianity.

This is not to say, of course, that all 'results' of Jesus-scholarship are tenuous and uncertain. There is such a thing as genuine historical knowledge, and it does allow us to make definite claims about Jesus. But it is not to be attained by the route of positivism, still less by the dubious method of vote-taking within a small circle of scholars. It is to be attained by the route of critical realism — a historical method which proceeds, not by atomistic discussion of isolated elements, but by the serious process of hypothesis and verification, during which the perspective of the historian is itself taken into account. I have written about this elsewhere.[31] A good many scholars are pursuing this path to a lesser or greater extent. The Jesus Seminar has chosen not to do so.

# 2. Towards a New Portrait

The introduction to the book contains a lengthy section (16-34) setting out the 'rules of written evidence' and 'the rules of oral evidence' which the Seminar formulated and adopted for use in its work. There are thirty-six of these 'rules.' But again and again throughout the book, the 'rules' boil down to three guiding principles which are wheeled out almost *ad nauseam* as the justification for accepting, or more usually for rejecting, a particular saying or set of sayings.

These three actual guiding principles may be formulated as follows. First, the Seminar in fact presupposes a particular portrait of Jesus. Second, the Seminar adopts a particular, and highly misleading, position about eschatology and apocalyptic, particularly about the kingdom of God; this too was presupposed. Third, the Seminar assumes a particular picture of the early church, especially its interest in and transmission of material about Jesus. In each case there is every reason to reject the principle in question. We must look at each in turn.

## Jesus the Distinctive Sage

As we just saw, the explicit intention of the Seminar was to examine all the sayings and vote on them one by one, allowing a portrait of Jesus to emerge slowly and bit by bit. Thus, for instance, the editors can speak of Matthew 7.16b, which was voted pink, as being placed 'into the red/pink database *for determining who Jesus was*' (157, emphasis added). But what has in fact happened is exactly the reverse. For the majority of Fellows at least, what comes first is an assumption about who Jesus really was, which is then used as the yardstick for measuring, and often ruling out, a good many sayings.

This assumption focusses on the portrait of Jesus as a 'traveling sage and wonder-worker' (128). Sayings can be assessed according to whether they fit with this.[32] The Fellows, or at least their spokespersons in this volume, somehow know that Jesus is a 'reticent sage who does not initiate debate or offer to cast out demons, and who does not speak of himself in the first person' (265). On this basis they feel able to make judgments about sayings which, since they make Jesus do some of these things, cannot be his. As a reticent sage, Jesus 'did not formally enlist followers' (284); he used secular proverbs, having 'perhaps acquired his knowledge of common lore from itinerant philosophers who visited Galilee while he was growing up' (287). He does not, however, quote the Hebrew scriptures very often (376, 380), so that when we find such quotations attributed to him, they almost certainly come from the early church, which, unlike Jesus, was very concerned to understand his work in the light of the scriptures.

As a reticent sage, Jesus did not, of course, predict his own death (94; 208; and very frequently); still less did he refer to himself in any way as Messiah or Son of God (75; 312; and regularly). Among the reasons given for this latter assumption is the remarkable argument:

Jesus taught that the last will be first and the first will be last. He admonished his followers to be servants of everyone. He urged humility as the cardinal virtue by both word and example. Given these terms, it is difficult to imagine Jesus making claims for himself... unless, of course, he thought that nothing he said applied to himself.[33]

What the writers seem to ignore is precisely that Jesus *taught* these things. By what right? Even at the level of teaching, Jesus' words carry an implicit self-reference. When we put even a small amount of his teaching into its first-century Jewish context (see below), it was inevitable that questions should be asked about who he thought he was; and virtually inevitable that he would reflect on such a question himself. Instead of this context, however, the Seminar's spokespersons offer one that may perhaps be thought just a little anachronistic:

Like the cowboy hero of the American West exemplified by Gary Cooper, the sage of the ancient Near East was laconic, slow to speech, a person of few words. The sage does not provoke encounters... As a rule, the sage is self-effacing, modest, unostentatious.[34]

Jesus, then, was not aware that he had a specific mission to carry out (70). He did not organise 'formal missions' (311). He was not 'given to institution building' (213). The older liberalism was right after all: Jesus' teaching was about being nice to people, not about warning them of punishment in store for the wicked (170, 181, 289f., 320, and frequently).[35]

In particular, when Jesus did speak it was almost always in pithy, subversive, disturbing aphorisms. (This, of course, was the presupposition for the Seminar's whole enterprise, of breaking up the text into isolated sayings and voting separately on them.) Thus, in rejecting Luke 22.36-7, the editors comment: 'there is nothing in the words attributed to Jesus that cuts against the social grain, that would surprise or shock his friends, or that reflects exaggeration, humor, or paradox... [thus] nothing in this passage commends itself as authentically from Jesus' (391). Proverbs that 'are not particularly vivid or provocative' or which 'do not surprise or shock' 'belong to the stock of common lore and so are not of Jesus' invention' (157). It is admitted that Jesus could have used such proverbs, but again and again they attract a gray or black vote.[36]

The Seminar claims, then, that a portrait of Jesus 'begins to emerge' from their work at certain points (340). Not so. The portrait was in the mind all along. It is, for the most part, a shallow and one-dimensional portrait, developed through anachronistic parallels (the laconic cowboy) and ignoring the actual first-century context. Its attractive and indeed sometimes compelling features, of Jesus as the subversive sage, challenging the status quo with teasing epigrams and parables, has been achieved at the huge cost of screening out a whole range of material which several of the leading Jesus-scholars around the world, in major, serious and contemporary works of historical reconstruction, would regard as absolutely central. By far the most important of these is the material often designated 'apocalyptic'; and, within that, Jesus' announcement of the kingdom of God — or, as the Seminar often puts it, 'heaven's imperial rule.' The rejection of this material is the largest and most central presupposition that the Seminar bring to their entire work, and it deserves a separate section.

## The Resolutely Non-Apocalyptic Jesus

The most thoroughgoing way in which the Seminar applies the criterion of dissimilarity, according to which Jesus stands out from his surrounding context, is in relation to apocalyptic. Here this reader at least had a strange sense of *déjà vu*. Two decades ago Klaus Koch wrote a book describing, among other things, what he called 'the agonised attempt to save Jesus from apocalyptic.'[37] Albert Schweitzer, at the turn of the century, had described Jesus as an apocalyptic visionary; many theologians after Schweitzer found this too much to stomach, and neatly extracted Jesus from his surrounding Jewish, and apocalyptic, context. This was normally done for apologetic motives: if Jesus predicted the end of the world, he was wrong, and this has serious implications for Christology.

The Jesus Seminar, of course, harbours no such motive. Instead, it has a different one, no less all-pervading: Jesus must not in any way appear to give sanction to contemporary apocalpytic preaching, such as that on offer in the fundamentalist movements against which the Seminar is reacting so strongly. Jesus must not, therefore, have supposed that the end of the world was at hand, or that God was about to judge people, or that the Son of Man (whom the Seminar persist in misleadingly calling the Son of Adam) would shortly 'come on the clouds.' All these things form the scriptural basis for much stock-in-trade fundamentalist preaching; the Seminar therefore wishes to rule them out of court.[38] The older flight from apocalyptic was designed to save orthodox Christianity; the newer one is designed to subvert it.

But, though the motive is different, the effect is the same. Although John the Baptist is described as 'the precursor and mentor of Jesus' (128), Jesus' own ministry and message were utterly distinct. John pronounced apocalyptic-style warnings of impending judgment; Jesus did not. Likewise, the very early church (though not the Seminar's hypothetical early Q, and not Thomas) reinterpreted Jesus' sayings in an apocalyptic style which distorted Jesus' own intention. Thus Matthew 10.7, in which Jesus tells the disciples to announce that 'Heaven's imperial rule is closing in,' is an 'apocalyptically oriented summary,' which 'was probably inherited from John the Baptist and adopted by the early Christian movement, including Matthew's community,' but which 'was not, however, the point of view of Jesus'(168). So, too, the warnings of judgment on cities that rejected the disciples are 'alien to Jesus, although not to the early disciples, who may have reverted to John the Baptist's apocalyptic message and threat of judgment, or they may simply have been influenced by apocalyptic ideas that were everywhere in the air'(169).

Stated as baldly as this, the agenda is exposed for what it is: a further agonised attempt to rescue Jesus from contamination with the dreaded 'apocalyptic.' By what means do the Seminar know, a priori, that Jesus so firmly rejected something which was 'everywhere in the air,' which was absolutely central to the work of John, who is acknolwedged as Jesus' 'precursor and mentor,' and which was fundamental, in some shape or form, to all forms of early Christianity known to us — except, of course, to the Thomas collection? (We had better leave the doubly hypothetical 'Early Q' out of account, since the only reason for inventing a non-apocalyptic 'Early Q,' when so many 'apocalyptic' sayings are in the Matthew/Luke parallels upon which the 'Q' hypothesis rests, is the very assumption we are examining, that Jesus and one strand of his followers did not make use of this world of thought.) If almost everyone else thought and spoke like that, how do they know that Jesus did not?[39] The answer is that they do not. This 'conclusion' was, in their phrase, 'in the air' from the inception of the Seminar. It was a starting-point, not a result. It may even, we may suspect, have been one of the reasons why the Seminar came into existence in the first place.

But this view of apocalyptic, and of Jesus' participation in it, can be controverted again and again by serious study of the first-century phenomenon which goes by that name. I have argued in detail elsewhere, in line with a fair amount of contemporary scholarship, that 'apocalyptic' is best understood as a complex metaphor-system through which many Jews of the period expressed their aspirations, not for other-worldly bliss, nor for a 'big bang' which would end the space-time world, but for social, political and above all theological liberation.[40] This enables us to affirm that Schweitzer and others were absolutely right to see Jesus as part of apocalyptic Judaism, while denying Schweitzer's unhistorical notion (shared, of course, by fundamentalists) that apocalyptic language was designed to be taken literally. The Seminar is fighting a shadow.

In particular, the language of the Kingdom of God has been studied in great detail by scholars with far more awareness of the first-century Jewish context than is evident in the present book.[41] There is no sign that this scholarship has been even noted, let alone taken seriously, by the Seminar. Instead, there is a persistent and muddled repetition of outdated and/or naive points of view:

> Mark 13 is an apocalypse (an apocalypse tells of events that are to take place at the end of history. In Mark's version, the end of history will occur when the son of Adam appears on the clouds and gathers God's chosen people from the ends of the earth). This and related themes make Mark 13 sound much like the Book of Revelation...
>
> A notable feature of early Christian instruction is that teaching about last things (termed *eschatology*) occurs at the conclusion of the catechism or manual of instruction. Paul tended to put such matters toward the close of his letters, for example, in 1 Thess 5:1-13 and 1 Corinthians 15. In the second-century Christian manual known as the Didache, instruction in eschatology also comes last, in chapter 16.
>
> Mark thus appropriately makes Jesus' discourse on last things his final public discourse...[42]

> An apocalypse is a form of literature in which a human agent is guided on an otherworldly tour by means of visions. On that tour, the agent learns about a supernatural world unknown to ordinary folk, and the secrets of the future are also revealed. . .
>
> The so-called little apocalypse assembled by Mark in chapter 13, and copied by Matthew and Luke, is not actually an apocalypse in form. But it has the same function. . .[43]

The comment about Paul shows, as clearly as anything else, the shallow and largely spurious level of analysis employed here. Paul is just as capable of talking about (what we call) 'the last things' at other points in his letters; e.g. 2 Corinthians 5. And the whole statement — it is hardly an argument — is designed to minimize the role of 'apocalyptic' in the gospel accounts, isolating Mark 13 and its parallels from the rest of the text, in a way which, as the last comment quoted tacitly admits, does great violence both to that chapter and to the rest of the synoptic tradition.[44]

It is with discussion of the kingdom of God (or whatever it is to be called; 'Heaven's Imperial Rule' does have the virtue of jolting or confronting a contemporary reader in a way that 'kingdom of God' has largely ceased to do) that the problem is focussed most clearly. The 'cameo essay' on the subject (136-7) is extremely revealing; and what it reveals is a string of misunderstandings, prejudices, and false antitheses.

The essay sets out four categories. First, there is the preaching of John the Baptist. Second, there are sayings of Jesus which speak of God's rule as future. Third, there are sayings of Jesus which speak of God's rule as present. Fourth, there is a passage from Paul. Already there are problems. (a) The passage quoted from John the Baptist (Matt. 3.7, 10) does not mention the kingdom of God, and in any case would be regarded by many as a later formulation, not necessarily giving us access to John himself. (b) The main passage quoted as an example of sayings of Jesus about God's future rule is Mark 13.24-7, 30, which again does not mention the kingdom of God, but speaks instead of the son of man coming on the clouds. (c) One of the passages quoted as illustrating sayings of Jesus about God's rule as present is Luke 11.2, which is the petition from the Lord's prayer, here translated as 'Impose your imperial rule.' If this indicates that the kingdom is already present, why is one commanded to pray for it as though it were not yet here? (d) The single passage quoted from Paul is 1 Thessalonians 4.15-17, which says nothing about the kingdom of God, but speaks of the dead rising, the Lord descending, and the living Christians being caught up in the air. There are, of course, passages in Paul which speak explicitly about the kingdom of God, and in some that kingdom is a present reality (e.g. Romans 14.17). The only reason I can imagine for quoting 1 Thessalonians 5 in this context is that the author of the essay is assuming an equation between 'future kingdom of God' and 'end-time apocalyptic events,' and taking passages about the latter, which fundamentalists have interpreted in a particular way (e.g. the 'rapture') as expressions of this 'apocalyptic' view of the kingdom. But each stage in this line of thought is quite unwarranted. Indeed, the author of the essay more or less agrees with the fundamentalist interpretation of the key texts, in order then to dismiss them as indices of Jesus' mind.

The discussion which follows the citation of these texts poses an utterly spurious either-or:

> Does this phrase [kingdom of God] refer to God's direct intervention in the future, something connected with the end of the world and the last judgment, or did Jesus employ the phrase to indicate something already present and of more elusive nature?
>
> The first of these options is usually termed apocalyptic, a view fully expressed in the book of Revelation, which is an apocalypse.

Here we have it: 'apocalyptic' is, more or less, 'that which fundamentalists believe about the end of the world.' The author seems to imply that the fundamentalists have actually read some of the texts correctly. So much the worse for the texts; clearly the Seminar is going to take a different view, which will involve ditching those wicked 'apocalyptic' ideas and setting up its own alternative. But if this loaded argument functions like a shopkeeper putting extra weights onto the scales, what follows is the equivalent of leaning on them with both elbows:

> Did Jesus share this [apocalyptic] view, or was his vision more subtle, less bombastic and threatening?

> The Fellows. . . are inclined to the second option: Jesus conceived of God's rule as all around him but difficult to discern. . . But Jesus' uncommon views were obfuscated by the more pedestrian conceptions of John, on the one hand, and by the equally pedestrian views of the early Christian community, on the other.

As we saw before, Jesus seems to have been radically different from his 'predecessor and mentor,' and was radically misunderstood by almost all his followers from the very beginning. In particular, despite the other passages (e.g. 7) in which the authors regard Paul as the great Hellenizer, or gnosticizer, of the gospel, they wheel him out this time as another representative of Jewish-style apocalyptic:

> The views of John the Baptist and Paul are apocalyptically oriented. The early church aside from Paul shares Paul's view. The only question is whether the set of texts that represent God's rule as present were obfuscated by the pessimistic apocalyptic notions of Jesus' immediate predecessors, contemporaries, and successors.

'Apocalyptic,' then, is unsubtle, bombastic, threatening, obfuscatory, pedestrian, and pessimistic — and shared by everybody from John the Baptist through to the early church, apart from Jesus himself. This picture is then fitted into the broader old-liberal agenda, as follows: future-kingdom sayings are about judgment and condemnation, while Jesus instead offered forgiveness, mercy, and inclusiveness.[45] The evidence adduced to support this astonishing piece of rhetoric — and this remarkably old-fashioned, almost pre-Schweitzer, view of Jesus — is the existence of texts about the kingdom as a present reality, such as Luke 17.20-21, 11.20, and Thomas 113. In addition, the parables are supposed to represent the kingdom as a present, rather than a future, reality. The Jesus Seminar therefore voted 'present-kingdom' sayings pink,[46] and 'future-kingdom' sayings black. It was as easy as that.

I have to say that if I had been served up this 'cameo essay' by a first-year undergraduate, I would quickly have deduced that the student, while very ingenious, was unfamiliar both with some of the basic secondary discussions of the topic,[47] and, more damaging still, with the meaning of the primary texts in their first-century context. The determination to rule fundamentalism off the map altogether has so dominated the discussion (if not in the Seminar itself, at least in this apparently authoritative interpretation of its work) that texts of great subtlety and variety have been forced into a tight and utterly spurious either/or and played off against one another. It would be one thing to find a student doing this. When two senior academics do it, after having gone on record as saying that 'critical scholars practice their craft by submitting their work to the judgment of peers,' while 'non-critical scholars are those who put dogmatic considerations first and insist that the factual evidence confirm theological premises,'[48] the uncomfortable suspicion is aroused that it is the latter category, not the former, that describes the work we have in our hands. Sadly, this suspicion can only be confirmed by the bombastic, threatening and utterly pedestrian nature of the discussion itself.

There is, of course, a good deal more to be said about the kingdom of God in the teaching of Jesus. There is need for much discussion and careful reconstruction. This, however, cannot be the place for it. We conclude that, when it comes to the central theme of the teaching of Jesus, the Seminar, at least as reported in this volume (and with dissentient voices drowned out by the voting averages and by those who voted black for everything on principle), allowed itself to make its key decisions on the basis of an ill-informed and ill-advised disjunction between two ill-defined types of kingdom-saying. The entire history of debate this century on the subject of Jesus and eschatology goes by the board. It is one thing to disagree with the line of thought running, broadly, from Schweitzer to Sanders. It is something else to ignore it altogether. Eschatology and apocalyptic, and 'kingdom of God' within that, has here been misunderstood, misanalyzed, and wrongly marginalized.

Two tail-pieces to this discussion. First, the effect of the Seminar's portrait of Jesus at this point is to minimalize his Jewishness. The authors claim, of course, that Jesus was 'not the first Christian' (24); that is, he does not belong to the Christian movement, but (presumably) to Judaism. But only minimally — if the Seminar's analysis of 'kingdom of God' were to be accepted. Quite unintentionally, of course, the Seminar has reproduced one of the most dubious features of the older liberal picture of Jesus. Judaism only appears as the dark backcloth against which the jewel of Jesus' message — not now as a *Christian* message, but as a subversive, present-kingdom, almost proto-gnostic, possibly-Cynic, laconic-cowboy message — shines the more brightly. We do not actually know anything about wandering pagan philosophers whom Jesus might have met in the days of his youth. There is no evidence for them. But they are brought in of necessity; otherwise one might have to admit that Jesus' language about the kingdom of God was thoroughly Jewish, and belonged within the Jewish setting and aspirations of his day.

At the same time, the authors are clearly anxious not to play Jesus off against 'Jews.' They are very much aware that some allegorical readings of Jesus' teaching have produced tragic consequences for Jewish-Christian relations (234). They are so coy about using the word 'Jew' that they insist on saying 'Judean' instead — even, amusingly, when the Jews in question are mostly Galileans, not Judeans at all (e.g. 168). But they seem unaware that, within our own century, the attempt to paint Judaism as a dark, pessimistic, bombastic, pedestrian religion, expecting a great and cataclysmic final judgment, and to paint Jesus as having countered this by offering (the supposedly unJewish message of) mercy and love and forgiveness, has itself generated tragic consequences.

Second, there are all sorts of signs that the authors, representing some but surely not all of the Seminar, simply do not understand how first-century Judaism, in all its plurality, works. The discussion of 'hallowed be your name' in Matthew 6.9 implies that there is a paradox in Jesus using the form 'Abba' and then asking 'that the name be regarded as sacred' (149). There may, no doubt, be a paradox there, but not at that simplistic level. The point of asking that the divine name be hallowed is, as has very often been pointed out, that the name is hallowed when the people of God are vindicated, rescued from their enemies. This discussion is sadly typical of many points where quite basic perspectives on central texts seem to be ignored altogether. Thus, for instance, we read that Luke 23.31 ('if they do this when the wood is green, what will they do when it is dry?') is enigmatic, which is undoubtedly true. But then, when the authors say 'no one knows what it means, although it, too, must have something to do with the fall of Jerusalem' (395f.), one wonders if they bothered to check any of the major commentaries.

In particular, the authors offer (242) a brief discussion of first-century Pharisaism, in order to substantiate the Seminar's decision to cast black votes for most of the sayings in Matthew 23. They repeat uncritically the line which Sanders took from Morton Smith, though there was never much evidence for it and always plenty against it: the Pharisees were based in Judaea, not Galilee, so Jesus may not have come into contact with them or even known much about them (242, 244).[49] This is backed up in a way which neither Sanders nor Smith suggest: 'The teachings of the rabbis in Jesus' day were all circulated by word of mouth; it was not until the third century C. E. that rabbinic traditions took written form in the Mishnah.' This last statement is of course true, but totally irrelevant, implying as it does that word-of-mouth circulation would be a casual, inefficient, uncertain thing, so that, lacking written texts, Jesus would not have known much about Pharisaic teaching. As we shall see presently, however, in a substantially oral culture, oral teaching will have circulated far more widely, and far more effectively, than written texts.

The authors further suggest that the Pharisees became the dominant party after the fall of Jerusalem, and that 'at the council of Jamnia, in 90 C. E., the Pharisees laid the foundations for the survival of Judaism in its modern form — rabbinic Judaism.' Meanwhile, even in the last quarter of the first century, the 'emerging church, in its Palestinian and Syrian locales, was still largely a sectarian movement within Judaism.'

All this comprises so many half-truths and inaccuracies that one is tempted to wonder whether it is worth reading further in a book supposedly about the first century.[50] It is highly likely that the Pharisees were already very influential, quite possibly the most influential group, within the pluriform Judaism of the pre-70 period. The group that became dominant after 70 was one variety of Pharisees, namely the Hillelites, over against another variety, the Shammaites. But even this was not achieved overnight; it was only with the collapse of the second revolt, in 135, that the shift of influence was complete. In addition, our knowledge of the council of Jamnia is very nebulous; its date and achievements are very uncertain. The later rabbinic traditions about it are, most likely, far more heavily overlaid with subsequent reinterpretations than almost anything we find in the gospels. To use it as a fixed point for establishing early Christian material is like a hiker taking a compass bearing on a sheep. Finally, we do not actually know very much at all about the church in Palestine and Syria in the last quarter of the century. What we do know is that a sharp division between the church, precisely in Palestine and Syria, and Pharisaic Judaism of the more zealous (i.e. Shammaite) variety had already taken place *in the first five years after Jesus' death*. We know this because of Saul of Tarsus, alias the apostle Paul, who, for neither the first nor the last time, puts a spoke in the wheel of the Jesus Seminar's speculative reconstructions of early Christianity.

Lest all these criticisms be misunderstood, I should stress: there is nothing wrong with trying to popularize the results of scholarship. Quick overviews of complex issues are necessary in such work. But popularization sometimes reveals crucial weaknesses which a more highflown and abstract language would have masked. So it is in this case. Serious contemporary research on first-century Judaisms by no means rules out the possibility, which must then be decided (and interpreted) on quite other grounds, that Jesus did come into sharp confrontation with the Pharisees. What the discussion tells us is that the Seminar, or at least its spokespersons in this book, are not to be trusted to know their way around the details of the first century, which they are supposed to be describing.[51]

## Oral Culture, Storytelling, and Isolated Sayings

The third driving principle behind a great many of the Seminar's decisions can be stated quite baldly.[52] It is assumed that only isolated sayings of Jesus circulated in the earliest post-Easter period. Unless a saying can be conceived as having enough intrinsic interest and, as it were, staying power to survive being passed on by word of mouth, all by itself and without any context, we can assume that it cannot be original to Jesus. Words of Jesus which fail this test, and which occur within more extended narratives, are simply part of the storyteller's art, or of the evangelist's theology.[53] This is, at its heart, an assumption about the nature of early Christianity.

Examples of this principle in operation could be picked from almost anywhere in the book's 500 and more pages. Here are some taken at random:

> The words ascribed to Jesus in this story [rebuking winds and wave, Mk. 4.35-41] would not have circulated independently during the oral period; they reflect what the storyteller imagined Jesus would have said on such an occasion.[54]

> The stories Mark has collected in chapter five of his gospel contain words ascribed to Jesus that are suitable only for the

occasion. They are not particularly memorable, are not aphorisms or parables, and would not have circulated independently during the oral period. They cannot, therefore, be traced back to Jesus.[55]

The words ascribed to Jesus [during the healing of the blind man in Mk. 8.22-6] are the invention of the evangelist. Because they are incidental dialogue and not memorable pronouncements, they would not have been remembered as exact words of Jesus.[56]

Jesus' public discourse is remembered to have consisted primarily of aphorisms, parables, or a challenge followed by a verbal retort. Matt 4:17 does not fall into any of these categories.[57]

The remarks quoted from Jesus [in Mt. 8.5-13] are intelligible only as part of the narrative and could not have circulated as a separate saying apart from this narrative context. They were accordingly voted black.[58]

The words attributed to Jesus in the story of the feeding of the crowd all belong to the narrative texture of the story. They cannot be classified as aphorisms or parables and so could not have circulated independently during the oral period, 30-50 C.E. As a consequence, they cannot be traced back to Jesus, but must have been created by the storyteller.[59]

The basis for these judgments is found in the extended discussion of oral memory and tradition in the introduction (25-9). It is impossible, without quoting the entire section and discussing it line by line, to show the extent of the misunderstandings it reveals. Though the authors regularly refer to oral cultures, the only actual examples they give come from a very non-oral culture, that of their own modern Western world.[60] Referring to what Thucydides says about making up speeches to suit the occasion (27) is not to the point; the speeches in question tend to be longer by far than any of Jesus' reported discourses, even the Sermon on the

Mount and the Johannine 'farewell discourses.' In any case, Thucydides was a man of learning and letters, and to that extent less representative of a genuinely oral culture.

The theory that sayings, aphorisms, memorable oneliners, and sometimes parables are the things that survive, whereas stories *about* Jesus, with his words embedded within them, do not, is clearly promulgated with one eye on the results. 'It is highly probable,' we are told — this, recall, at the introductory level, before we have examined a single saying! — that the earliest layer of the gospel tradition was made up almost entirely of single aphorisms and parables that circulated by word of mouth, without narrative context — precisely as that tradition is recorded in 'Q' and Thomas.[61]

With the evidence thus well and truly cooked in advance, it is not surprising that the portrait of Jesus-the-quizzical-sage 'emerges' from the subsequent discussion. It could not help doing so. The theory about what sort of material survives in oral tradition, I suggest, was designed to produce exactly this result.

Against this whole line of thought we must set the serious study of genuinely oral traditions that has gone on in various quarters recently.[62] Communities that live in an oral culture tend to be *storytelling* communities. They sit around in long evenings telling and listening to stories — the same stories, over and over again. Such stories, especially when they are involved with memorable happenings that have determined in some way the existence and life of the particular group in question, acquire a fairly fixed form, down to precise phraseology (in narrative as well as in recorded speech), extremely early in their life — often within a day or so of the original incident taking place. They retain that form, and phraseology, as long as they are told. Each village and community has its recognised storytellers, the accredited bearers of its traditions; but the whole community knows the stories by heart, and if the teller varies them even slightly they will let him know in no uncertain terms. This matters quite a lot in cultures where, to this day, the desire to avoid 'shame' is a powerful motivation.

Such cultures do also repeat, and hence transmit, proverbs and pithy sayings. Indeed, they tend to know far more proverbs than the orally starved modern Western world. But the circulation of such individual sayings is only the tip of the iceberg; the rest is narrative, narrative with embedded dialogue, heard, repeated again and again within minutes, hours and days of the original incident, and fixed in memories the like of which few in the modern Western world can imagine. The storyteller in such a culture has no license to invent or adapt at will. The less important the story, the more adaptation may be possible; but the more important the story, the more the entire community, in a process that is informal but very effective, will keep a close watch on the precise form and wording with which the story is told.

And the stories about Jesus were nothing if not important. Even the Jesus Seminar admit that Jesus was an itinerant wonder-worker. Very well. Supposing a woman in a village is suddenly healed after a lengthy illness. Even today, even in a non-oral culture, the story of such an event would quickly spread among friends, neighbours and relatives, acquiring a fixed form within the first two or three retellings and retaining it, other things being equal, thereafter. In a culture where storytelling was and is an art-form, a memorable event such as this, especially if it were also seen as a sign that Israel's God was now at last at work to do what he had always promised, would be told at once in specific ways, told so as to allow the overtones of fulfilment to be clearly heard, told so that it would be not just a celebration of a healing but also a celebration of the kingdom of God. Events and stories of this order are community-forming, and the stories which form communities do not get freely or loosely adapted. One does not disturb the foundations of the house one is living in.

What about detached aphorisms, then? Clearly, a memorable saying is a memorable saying, and could circulate independently. But what about sayings which sometimes have a context and sometimes not? I suggest that the following hypothesis is far more likely than that proposed by the Seminar.[63] It was only later, when the communities had been scattered through external circumstances (such as sundry persecutions, and the disastrous Jewish War of 66-70), that individual memorable sayings, which might very well have enjoyed a flourishing earlier life *within various narrative settings*, would become detached from those settings and become 'chreiai,' isolated pithy sayings with minimal narrative context, such as we find (of course) in Thomas, and also to some extent in Luke. It is heavily ironic that the reason often given for supposing Luke's version of 'Q' to be earlier than Matthew's is that Luke's versions of 'Q' sayings are more chreia-like, while Matthew's are more embedded in Jewish, and often in narrative, contexts. Unless one had been fairly well brianwashed by the idea that Jesus-traditions consisted originally of non-Jewish, detached sayings, and only in the second generation acquired a Jewish setting, complete with scriptural overtones and so forth, the most natural historical hypothesis here would have been this: that Jesus' earliest hearers, being Jews, eager for their God to act in their present circumstances, would have told stories about him in a thoroughly Jewish way, with scriptural echoes both deliberate and accidental. Then, later on, the church which was leaving the tight storytelling communities, and going out into the Hellenistic world, would find it easier to detach sayings from their original narrative context and present them, like the sayings of wise teachers in the Greco-Roman world, as isolated nuggetts of wisdom.

The Jesus Seminar's view of oral tradition is thus based, not on the most likely historical hypothesis, but on the same view of the distinctive Jesus that we have seen to dominate their whole picture. Jesus would not have quoted scripture;[64] he did not share, or address, the aspirations of his contemporary Jews; he did not even follow the line taken by his 'precursor and mentor.' Nothing much memorable ever happened to him, or if it did we do not know about it. He was not involved in incidents which made a deep impression on the onlookers, causing them to go at once and tell what they had seen over and over again, with the anecdote quickly fixing itself into a pattern, and the words of Jesus, including incidental words, becoming part of that regularly repeated story. He never spoke about himself (the more one thinks about this suggestion, the more absurd it becomes); his conversation consisted only of subversive, teasing aphorisms. He must, in short, have been a very peculiar human being (as one Fellow of the Seminar pointed out to me, a Jesus who always and only uttered pithy aphorisms would start to look like some of the less credible cinematic Jesuses). Such a person would in fact be quite maddening. More importantly, as a historian I find it incredible that such a Jesus could have been a significant historical figure. It is not at all clear why people would have followed him, died for him, loved him, invented rich and powerful stories about him, and (within an almost incredibly short time, and within a context of continuing Jewish monotheism) worshipped him.[65]

Perhaps the greatest weakness of the whole construct lies just here. In order to sustain their home-made view of Jesus, the authors of this book, and presumably a fair number at least of Fellows of the Jesus Seminar, have had to invent, as well, an entire picture of the early church out of not much more than thin air. Sometimes they have borrowed other people's inventions, but they, too, are based on little or nothing. Paul, as we have seen, is the one major fixed point in early Christianity; we know he was active, travelling, preaching and writing in the 40s and 50s, but we do not know anything at all, with the same certainty, about almost anyone else. We do not know that 'Q' even existed; notoriously, there is a growing body of opinion that holds that it did not (though one would never guess this from reading *The Five Gospels*), even as there is a growing body of opinion, represented strongly within the Jesus Seminar, that expounds ever more complex theories about its origin, development, historical setting, and theologies. Of course, once scholars are allowed to invent whole communities at will, anything is possible. Any jigsaw puzzle can be solved if we are allowed to create new pieces for it at a whim. But we should not imagine that historical scholarship built on this principle is of any great value.

# 3. Conclusion

Let me be quite clear, in bringing the discussion to a close, on several points at which misunderstandings of what I have said might perhaps arise.

First, I have no quarrel with the enterprise of publishing as much of the early Jesus-material as possible, from both canonical and non-canonical sources, and bringing every scrap of possibly relevant evidence into full play. Indeed, I am deeply grateful for the immense labor and effort that members of the Seminar have expended to enable all of us involved in the search for Jesus to study these texts more easily. But, as with recent controversies about the Dead Sea Scrolls, the Seminar should be wary of suggesting that those who find the canonical material to be more reliable than the non-canonical are part of a conspiracy of silence, inspired by thoroughly non-historical motives, i.e. by the desire for some form of closed-minded traditional Christianity. Frankly, *both* the desire to 'prove' orthodoxy *and* the desire to 'disprove' it ought to be anathema to the serious historian. The first of these is, of course, the way to what is normally called fundamentalism; the second, taken by at least some (and they are clearly influential) in the Jesus Seminar, is no less closed-minded, and in fact fundamentalist, in practice. Hatred of orthodoxy is just as unhistorical a startingpoint as love of it.

Second, I have no quarrel with popularization. I totally agree with Robert Funk that the results of scholarship are far too important, on this of all questions, to be confined to the classroom and library. I will go further. The Jesus Seminar, in this and in several other of its publications, has done as good a job of popularization as any scholarly group or individual I have ever seen. Its charts, diagrams, tables, layout, and so forth are exemplary. I am not, in short, in any way a scholarly snob, who wants to keep the discussion within a charmed circle. My problems lie elsewhere. The thing which is thus being often brilliantly communicated, especially in *The Five Gospels*, is not the assured result of scholarship. It is a compromise of pseudo-democratic scholarship, based on principles we have seen good reason to question, employing methods that many reputable scholars would avoid, ignoring a great deal of very serious (and by no means necessarily conservative) contemporary scholarship, making erroneous and anachronistic assumptions about the early church and its cultural context, and apparently driven by a strong, and strongly distorting, contemporary agenda. There was no point in popularizing all this. One should only popularize scholarship when it has passed the test this book itself suggests: submitting work to the judgment of peers (34). For what it is worth, my judgment is that *The Five Gospels* does not pass the test. Any non-scholar reading this book is likely to be seriously misled, not only about Jesus, but about the state of serious scholarship. This is culpably irresponsible.

Third, I repeat what I said early on: I have no quarrel with the scholarship of many members of the Seminar. Some I am privileged to count as friends, and I trust that what I have said here will not put that friendship in jeopardy. From within the Seminar, as we saw, several of the discussions, not least some of the votes that ended up gray, must appear as highly significant, points of potential advance in understanding. Several Fellows have done sterling work in persuading others within the Seminar to adopt, or at least to allow for, views other than their original ones; pulling votes up from black to gray may indicate, for many, an opening of an otherwise closed mind. From within certain circles in the North American academy, this is quite a significant achievement. From outside the Seminar, however, the present volume cannot but appear as a disaster, for which the individual Fellows cannot and must not be held responsible, since they did not write it. The two authors of this book are men whose work in other fields I admire and have used a good deal: Funk's Greek Grammar is always close at hand, and Hoover's work on a key Greek term used once by Paul is foundational, I am persuaded, for the correct understanding of a much controverted and hugely important passage.[66] But they, as the named authors, must unfortunately bear responsibility for this, the flagship work of the Jesus Seminar. It does them no credit. Indeed, it obscures any good work that the Seminar itself may have done.

Fourth, and perhaps most importantly of all: I agree completely with the Seminar that the search for Jesus in his historical context is possible, vital, and urgent. I am as convinced as they are that if the church ignores such a search it is living in a fool's paradise. What is more, my own study of Jesus leads me to think that 'conservative' and 'orthodox' Christianity, in the twentieth century at least, has often, indeed quite regularly, missed the point of Jesus' sayings and deeds almost entirely. But the way to address this problem is not, and cannot be, the way taken by the Jesus Seminar. One cannot tackle serious historical problems by taking them to bits and voting on the bits one by one. The only way forward must be the way of serious historiography; and one may search *The Five Gospels* from cover to cover in vain for such a thing. There are a good many people engaged in serious historical study of Jesus at the moment, but the Seminar in its corporate identity (as opposed to some of its individual members) cannot be reckoned among their number.

Fifth, in conclusion, I question whether the Jesus proposed by *The Five Gospels* constitutes, or offers, good news, i.e. 'gospel,' at all. The main thing this Jesus has to offer, it sometimes appears, is the news that the fundamentalists are wrong. Some of us believed that anyway, on quite other grounds. Aside from that, Jesus becomes a quizzical teacher of wisdom, to be ranged alongside other quizzical teachers of wisdom, from many traditions. No reason emerges as to why we should take this teacher any more or less seriously than any other. It is not clear why even a sustained attempt to follow his maxims, his isolated aphorisms, should offer hope in a world threatened by ecological disasters, nuclear holocausts, resurgent tribalisms — and, for those insulated from such things in certain parts of the Western world, the moral and spiritual bankruptcy of materialism. The whole point of calling gospels 'gospels' was, I suggest, that they did contain reason for hope, good news to a world that badly needed it.

*The Five Gospels*, in other words, systematically deconstructs its own title. If this book gives us the truth about Jesus, about the early church, and about the writing of the five books here studied, there is no gospel, no good news. There is only good advice, and we have no reason for thinking that it will have any effect. Many members of the Jesus Seminar would disagree strongly with this conclusion, but this book does not give us any means of seeing why. In any case, those who persist in seeing the Seminar's portrait of Jesus as somehow good news are bound to say, as the book does on almost every page, that Matthew, Mark, Luke and John got it all wrong, producing their own variations on the pedestrian, bombastic, apocalyptic, and essentially fundamenalist worldview. If the Seminar insists on retaining the word 'gospels' in the title, then, it is the word 'five' that is deconstructed: all one is left with is Thomas and, of course, the doubly hypothetical 'Early Q.'

From a historical point of view it might of course be true that there is no good news to be had. Christianity as a whole might simply have been whistling in the dark for two thousand years. Subversive aphorisms may be the only comfort, the only hope, we have. But this question must be addressed precisely *from a historical point of view*. And, when all is said and done, *The Five Gospels* is of no help whatever in that task. There is such a thing as the serious contemporary search for Jesus in his historical context. This particular book makes no contribution to it.

## Bibliography

Bailey, K. E. (1983 [1976, 1980]). *Poet and peasant / through peasant eyes*. Grand Rapids, Mich.: Eerdmans.

Bailey, K. E. (1991). Informal controlled oral tradition and the synoptic gospels. *Asia Journal of Theology*, 5(1), 34-54.

Barbour, R. S. (Ed.). (1993). *The kingdom of God and human society: Essays by members of the scripture, theology and society group*. Edinburgh: T & T Clark.

Beasley-Murray, G. R. (1986). *Jesus and the kingdom of God*. Grand Rapids, MI: Eerdmans.

Borg, M. J. (1984). *Conflict, holiness and politics in the teachings of Jesus. Studies in the Bible and Early Christianity*, 5. New York/ Toronto: Edwin Mellen Press.

Boucher, M. (1977). *The mysterious parable: A literary study*. Catholic Biblical Quarterly Monograph Series, no. 6. Washington: Catholic Biblical Association of America.

Caird, G. B. (1965). *Jesus and the Jewish nation*. London: Athlone Press.

Charlesworth, J. H. (1988). *Jesus within Judaism: New light from exciting archaeological discoveries*. London: SPCK.

Chilton, B. D. (Ed.). (1984). *The kingdom of god in the teaching of Jesus*. London and Philadelphia: SPCK and Fortress.

Chilton, B. D. (1987 [1979]). *God in strength: Jesus' announcement of the kingdom*. Sheffield: JSOT Press.

Chilton, B. D. (1992). *The temple of Jesus: His sacrificial program within a cultural history of sacrifice*. University Park, Pa.: Pennsylvania State U. P.

Crossan, J. D. (1991). *The historical Jesus: The life of a Mediterranean Jewish peasant*. Edinburgh: T & T Clark; San Francisco: Harper.

Drury, J. (1985). *The parables in the gospels: History and allegory*. London: SPCK.

Farmer, W. R. (1956). *Maccabees, Zealots and Josephus: An enquiry into Jewish nationalism in the Greco-Roman period*. New York: Columbia U. P.

Farmer, W. R. (1982). *Jesus and the gospel*. Philadelphia: Fortress.

Freyne, S. (1988). *Galilee, Jesus and the gospels: Literary approaches and historical investigations*. Philadelphia: Fortress Press.

Funk, R. W. (Revised and trans). (1973 (1961)). *A Greek grammar of the New Testament and other early Christian literature* (5th ed.). Chicago and London: The University of Chicago Press.

Funk, R. W., Scott, B. B., & Butts, J. R. (Eds). (1988). *The parables of Jesus: Red letter edition. A report of the Jesus seminar*. Sonoma, Calif.: Polebridge Press.

Harvey, A. E. (1982). *Jesus and the Constraints of History: The Bampton Lectures, 1980*. London: Duckworth.

Hoover, R. W. (1971). *The harpagmos enigma: A philological solution*. Harvard Theological Review, 64, 95 119.

Horsley, R. A. (1987). *Jesus and the spiral of violence: Popular Jewish resistance in Roman Palestine*. San Francisco: Harper and Row.

Koch, K. (1972 [1970]). *The rediscovery of apocalyptic: A polemical work on a neglected area of biblical studies and its damaging effects on theology and philosophy* (M. Kohl, Trans.). Studies in Biblical Theology, 2.22. London: SCM.

Koester, H. (1990). *Ancient Christian gospels: Their history and development*. London and Philadelphia: SCM; TPI.

Ladd, G. E. (1966). *Jesus and the kingdom: The eschatology of biblical realism*. London: SPCK.

Mack, B. L. (1987). *The kingdom sayings in Mark. Foundations and Facets Forum*, 3(1), 3 47.

Mack, B. L. (1988). *A myth of innocence: Mark and Christian origins*. Philadelphia: Fortress Press.

Meier, J. P. (1991). *A marginal Jew: Rethinking the historical Jesus*: Vol. 1. *The roots of the problem and the person*. New York: Doubleday.

Meyer, B. F. (1979). *The aims of Jesus*. London: SCM Press.

Meyer, B. F. (1992a). *Christus Faber: The master-builder and the house of God*. Princeton Theological Monograph Series, no. 29. Allison Park, Penn.: Pickwick Publications.

Meyer, B. F. (1992b). Jesus Christ. In D. N. Freedman (Ed.), *Anchor Bible Dictionary* (Vol. 3, p. 773-796). New York: Doubleday.

Miller, R. J. (Ed.). (1992). *The complete gospels: Annotated scholars version*. Sonoma, Calif.: Polebridge Press.

Patterson, S. J. (1993). *The Gospel of Thomas and Jesus*. Sonoma, Calif.: Polebridge Press.

Roberts, J. M. (1992 [1976]). *History of the world* (2nd ed.). Oxford: Helicon.

Sanders, E. P. (1985). *Jesus and Judaism*. Philadelphia/London: Fortress Press/SCM Press.

Sanders, E. P. (1992). *Judaism: Practice and belief, 63 BCE — 66 CE*. London: S.C.M. Press.

Sanders, E. P. (1993). *The historical figure of Jesus*. London: Penguin.

Smith, M. (1977 [1956]). Palestinian Judaism in the First Century. In H. Fischel (Ed.), *Essays in Greco-Roman and related Talmudic literature* (p. 183 97). New York: Ktav.

Theissen, G. (1987 [1986]). *The shadow of the Galilean: The quest of the historical Jesus in narrative form* (J. Bowden, Trans.). London: SCM Press.

Tuckett, C. M. (1986). *Nag Hammadi and the gospel tradition: Synoptic tradition in the Nag Hammadi library.* Studies of the New Testament and its World. Edinburgh: T & T Clark.

Tuckett, C. M. (1988). Thomas and the synoptics. *Novum Testamentum, 30,* 132-157.

Vermes, G. (1973). *Jesus the Jew: A historian's reading of the gospels.* London: Collins.

Vermes, G. (1983). *Jesus and the world of Judaism.* London: SCM.

Vermes, G. (1993). *The religion of Jesus the Jew.* London: SCM.

Wansbrough, H. (Ed.). (1991). *Jesus and the oral gospel tradition.* Journal for the Study of the New Testament Supplement Series, 64. Sheffield: Sheffield Academic Press.

Witherington, B. (1990). *The christology of Jesus.* Minneapolis: Fortress.

Wright, N. T. (1991). *The climax of the covenant: Christ and the law in Pauline theology.* Edinburgh: T & T Clark; Minneapolis: Fortress.

Wright, N. T. (1992). *Christian Origins and the Question of God*: Vol. 1. *The New Testament and the people of God.* London: SPCK; Minneapolis: Fortress.

Wright, N. T. (1994). Gospel and theology in Galatians. In *Gospel in Paul: Studies on Corinthians, Galatians and Romans for Richard N. Longenecker* (L. A. Jervis & P. Richardson, Eds) (p. 222-239). Sheffield: Sheffield Academic Press.

Wright, N. T. (1995). *Jesus and the victory of God.* London: SPCK; Minneapolis: Fortress.

# NOTES

1   cf. e.g. Wright 1992b.

2   We may note, for instance, Farmer 1956; Caird 1965; Vermes 1973; 1983; 1993; Meyer 1979; 1992a; 1992b; Harvey 1982; Borg 1984; 1987; Sanders 1985; 1993; Theissen 1987; Horsley 1987; Freyne 1988; Charlesworth 1988; Witherington 1990; Meier 1991, 1994; Crossan 1991; Chilton 1992.

3   Mt. 5.39: cf. *The Five Gospels* 143-5. References hereafter are to this book unless otherwise noted.

4   See, for instance, Funk, Scott and Butts 1988; Miller 1992; and the Seminar's journal, *Foundations and Facets Forum*.

5   Wright 1995, ch. 2.

6   Mk. 1.41 (43). There is a hint here that the transaction between Jesus and the leper was not a healing, but simply Jesus' declaration that he should no longer be treated as an outcast.

7   Mt. 22.12 (234).

8   Lk. 5.20 (283).

9   xiii-xviii; here at xiv.

10   xviii.

11   e.g. Burton Mack, author of *A Myth of Innocence* and other works which have had a profound impact on the work of the Jesus Seminar. Over 200 members are reported to have belonged at one stage or another (34).

12   cf. Sanders 1985, remarkably absent from the bibliography of *The Five Gospels*; cf. too Sanders 1993. Sanders and Davies 1989 is listed in the bibliography of *The Five Gospels* as 'an excellent guide,' though anyone taking it seriously would be forced to reject a good deal of the Jesus Seminar's methods and results. See below.

13   cf. esp. Meyer 1979; 1992a & b.

14   e.g. 34f., whose triumphalism is as breathtaking as it is unwarranted: 'Critical scholars practice their craft by submitting their work to the judgment of peers. Untested work is not highly regarded. The scholarship represented by the Fellows of the Jesus Seminar is the kind that has come to prevail in all the great universities of the world.' Only in the most general terms is the last sentence true; the present essay is a response to the invitation of the previous sentences.

15 e.g. 1: the present book is 'a dramatic exit from windowless studies'; 34: 'we have been intimidated by promotion and tenure committees. . . . It is time for us to quit the library and speak up. . .'; the Seminar's methods have been attacked by 'many elitist academic critics who deplored [its] public face.'

16 There is, for instance, a good deal of important work on Jesus emanating from Latin America; but one would not guess it from reading the Seminar's publications.

17 540, referring to Borg 1987.

18 7f.

19 35.

20 It is interesting to compare the Seminar's work with the comment on the gospels made by a leading secular historian, J. M. Roberts: '[the gospels] need not be rejected; much more inadequate evidence about far more intractable subjects has often to be employed' (Roberts 1992 [1976], 210).

21 In favour: Patterson 1993, noted in the bibliography as being influential in the Seminar. Against: e.g. Tuckett 1986; 1988.

22 e.g. 18, 128.

23 cf. e.g. Koester 1990, on which see Wright 1992a, chs. 13, 14; and, for some comments on Paul's meaning of the term, Wright 1994.

24 The suggestion (500f.) that the gnosticism in Thomas is very much like what we find in John and Paul would be laughable if it did not reveal culpable ignorance of the entire drift of Pauline studies in the last forty years. The brief sketch of how Thomas got its name (20) reveals an astonishing naivety, speaking of the apostle being 'revered in the Syrian church as an apostle,' and giving as evidence for this Matt. 10.3, Mk. 3.18, Lk. 6.15, Ac. 1.13, Jn. 11.16, 20.24, 21.2. The attribution to Thomas, we are told, 'tells us nothing about the author,' but 'may indicate where this gospel was written.' In which of the above texts do we find evidence for Thomas in Syria? If the writers applied the same skepticism to claims about Thomas as they do, on the same page, to claims about the other four (the evidence of Papias, for instance), it would quickly become clear how little evidence there is for an early date, or a Syrian provenance, for the Thomas collection.

25  3. The sayings of Jesus in John are voted almost uniformly black, with 4.43 a solitary pink ('a prophet gets no respect on his own turf'), 12.24f., 13.20 a lonely pair of grays ('unless the kernel of wheat falls to the earth and dies. . .' and 'if they welcome the person I send, they welcome me. . .').

26  Described on 34-7.

27  213.

28  232.

29  cf. too 250, on Mt. 24.32f.: 54% voted either red or pink, but a 35% black vote resulted in a gray compromise (for which, apparently, only the remaining 11% had voted).

30  Emphasis original.

31  Wright 1992a, esp. ch. 4.

32  e.g. 326, on 'daily bread' in the Mt. and Lk. versions of the Lord's Prayer.

33  33.

34  32.

35  The Seminar nevertheless held, we are told, that the judgmental sayings in e.g. Mt. 11.21-4 were uttered by a Christian prophet 'speaking in the spirit and the name of Jesus' (181, cf. 320). We are to assume, it seems, that the prophet in question misunderstood that spirit, and misused that name, quite drastically. 'Jesus. . . would not have told Capernaum to go to Hell after instructing his disciples to love their enemies' (320). This touching naivety is rightly questioned at 214: 'prophetic anger does not entirely contradict the injunction to love one's enemies. It is possible for the two to be combined in one person.'

36  There seems to be an added confusion at this point. According to all the Seminar's literature, the voting was supposed to be on the question of whether Jesus said things, not on whether he was the first to say them. But frequently the votes seem to have reflected the latter point instead: e.g. 106, 168, 176, 240, 298f, 337 and elsewhere. This produces a strange heads-I-win/tails-you-lose situation. The secular, non-Jewish sages who (according to the Seminar) may have influenced Jesus in his early days provide us, we are told, with the model for how he spoke. But if a saying looks as though it came from such common stock, it still does not attract a pink or red vote.

37  Koch 1972 [1970].

38  Any who think this analysis over-suspicious should spend half a day
    reading through the Seminar's journal *Foundations and Facets
    Forum*, and the work of Burton Mack in particular, which was heavily
    influential on the Seminar's decisions at this point. Cf. Mack 1987,
    1988.

39  cf. too 112, where the comment (on Mk. 13.14-20) that 'almost any-
    one could have formulated these warnings' is followed at once by
    the report of near-unanimity among the Fellows that 'Jesus was not
    the author of any of these sayings.' In place of the distinctive Jesus
    of some traditional Christology, who stood out from everyone else
    because of his divinity, we have the distinctive Jesus of the Seminar,
    who was certainly incapable of saying things that almost anyone
    else at the time might have said. This is almost a secular version of
    the Docetic heresy.

40  Wright 1992a, ch. 10.

41  For details, see e.g. (among a great many) Chilton 1984; 1987;
    Beasley-Murray 1986; Barbour 1993; and the discussions in the other
    works about Jesus referred to above.

42  107.

43  246.

44  cf. Wright 1992a, 394f.

45  157.

46  e.g. Thomas 113: the explicit reason given for the vote is that this
    saying provides 'a counterweight to the view that Jesus espoused
    popular apocalypticism' (531). Here, no doubt, is one of the real
    reasons for the Seminar's long-running love-affair with Thomas: the
    collection offers apparent historical grounds for dumping
    apocalpytic.

47  e.g. Ladd 1966; Chilton 1984; 1987; Beasley-Murray 1986; Barbour
    1993; and the many recent discussions of the parables, e.g. Boucher
    1977; Bailey 1983 [1976, 1980]; Drury 1985. The major earlier dis-
    cussions, involving such magisterial figures as Dodd and Jeremias,
    might as well not have happened.

48  34.

49  cf. Sanders 1985; Smith 1977 [1956]. Sanders 1993 has toned this
    right down, perhaps as a result of the further research represented
    by Sanders 1992. For discussion, cf. Wright 1992a, 181-203; on this
    point, 195f.

50   On all of the following, see Wright 1992a, Part III.

51   Compare 362f., where we are blithely told that 'people in the ancient world' (which people? all people? Jews?) 'thought that the sky was held up by mountains that serve as pillars at the edge of the world.' No doubt some people thought that. To offer it as an interpretative grid for a text in the gospels (Lk. 17.6, which is in any case about trees, not mountains) is rather like trying to interpret a Mozart opera by means of nuclear physics.

52   cf. 25-9, discussed below.

53   Even at the level of reporting what is in the text, the Seminar's spokespersons here leave much to be desired. On 210, commenting on Matthew's Transfiguration narrative (17.1-9), they declare that, by contrast with Mt., 'in Mark's version, Jesus says nothing at all,' and say that in this respect Luke has followed Mark. However, in Mk 9.9 we find a saying of Jesus, parallel to that in Mt. 17.9, but simply in indirect speech: 'He instructed them not to describe what they had seen to anyone, until the son of Adam rise from the dead.' Funk, as a grammarian, would surely acknowledge that *oratio obliqua* is still *oratio*.

54   60.

55   62.

56   75.

57   134. Procrustes would have been proud of this one.

58   160.

59   205, cp. 199f.

60   'We' rephrase jokes and witticisms, such as those of Oscar Wilde (27); 'we know' that oral memory 'retains little else' other than sayings and anecdotes that are short, provocative, and memorable (28); 'recent experiments with memory' have reached various conclusions about the capacity of memory, emphasizing that, though people remember the gist of what was said, they do not recall the exact phrases. All of these examples are 100% irrelevant when we are considering a genuinely oral culture, such as still exists in certain parts of the world, not least among peasant communities in the Middle East. On the whole topic cf. Bailey 1991.

61   28.

62   cf. e.g. Wansbrough 1991 (referring to a large amount of earlier work); Bailey 1991. The following discussion depends on these and similar studies, and builds on Wright 1992a, ch. 14.

63   Sometimes the absence of narrative context in the Thomas collection is remarked on (e.g. 122) as though this were of great significance — which it clearly is not, since Thomas never has any such contexts. Waving Thomas around (e.g. 102), as though its detached sayings somehow prove that the saying first circulated independently and only subsequently acquired its synoptic context, constitutes an empty celebration of a circular argument.

64   e.g. 174, where the reference to Micah in Mt. 10.34-6 is given as a reason for inauthenticity. Compare 201, where we are told that 'scholars believe that most, perhaps all, quotations from scripture attributed to Jesus are secondary accretions.' This is quite breathtaking, both in its ignoring of serious and well-known scholarly traditions in which Jesus is seen as a major expositor of scripture, and in the extraordinary nonJewishness of the portrait which emerges.

65   On the worship of Jesus and Jewish monotheism, cf. Wright 1991, Part I; Wright 1992a, 457.

66   Funk 1973 [1961]; Hoover 1971; see Wright 1991, ch. 4.

# Crisis in Christology

# 10

# JESUS AND CHRIST: MULLING OVER A REEMERGING CRISIS

## Durwood Foster

## I

Until recently modern theology, after generations of debate, seemed to have more or less agreed that the historically researchable Jesus and the scriptural Christ of faith are neither identical nor disjoinable, and that a tolerable reciprocity obtains between them. But today the question of their relationship has flared up anew as one of the most pregnant and also disconcerting issues of Christian self-understanding. The following essay reconnoiters some main parameters of the overall problem from the side of historical and systematic theology, in order to call attention to what the current upsurge of Jesus research, especially in the Q-Thomas research paradigm, may portend for Christian faith.[1]

For the Christian mainstream that abjures both fundamentalism and the abandonment of an anchoring historical norm, Jesus as historiographical object and as prime component of the biblical-experiential Christ are categorically different and yet indissolubly linked. As Harvey Cox says in a recent overview of Christianity:

> When asking the question Who was Jesus? we must expect different answers because only part of the response can come from history. The other part comes from the heart of the person answering the question. The query is both historical and personal, so the answers will be both as well.[2]

Or, as J.B. Noss wrote four decades earlier in another summation of Christianity, "There is warrant for saying that every life of Jesus is in some sense a *confessio fidei*."[3] This insight, which has often been ignored, goes far back and requires a more complex parsing than either Cox or Noss attempt to give it. The personal or confessional subjectivity involved in inquiring after Jesus has both a contemporaneous-epistemic and a traditional-textual pole. The contemporaneous pole coincides with the emphasis of Michael Polanyi that all knowledge (including science and thus historiography) is pistically co-determined; and the other, textual pole is salient in Martin Kähler's 1892 insistence that in the New Testament the original facts of Jesus' life are inextricably woven together with believing interpretation. N.R. Hanson's epigram that "all data are theory laden" applies both ways: to a contemporaneous mind assessing its immediate data, or to data in traditional texts. There is a further wrinkle, as Polanyi was aware, in the fact that a contemporaneous mind is always polarized between its ownmost judgment and the communities of interpretation in which it participates. So, as Schleiermacher adumbrated in his hermeneutical lectures of 1827, the interpretation of a text is always an interaction between a more objective and a more subjective consciousness, and indeed at several levels, from the philological, which is more objective without being entirely so, to that of religious experience in both its universality and its historical specificity. Religion is indeed subjective and personal but characteristically, Schleiermacher stresses, it answers as well to communal norms. Consequently the question — Who was Jesus? — being as Cox says "both historical and personal," was highly loaded to become the explosive Pandora's Box it did over the last two hundred years.

In fact of all the problems that spawned modern theology none has been more central or persistent than that of "the Christ of faith and the Jesus of history," to use the caption with which D.F. Strauss in 1865, critiquing Schleiermacher's posthumous *Leben Jesu*, baptized the cluster of issues in view here. Strauss meant the apparent discrepancy found by modern research between the Christ in whom Christians believe and Jesus as he actually was. While this is not an adequately differentiated indication of the problem, it does convey that the ground and norm of Christian faith is directly at stake over against putatively objective knowledge. A parallel problem exists for theism so far as modern cosmology may render untenable belief in God as ground of the world, or for Christian humanology so far as evolutionary biology may explain humanity as no more than a product of chance and necessity. We soberly recall how valiantly modern theology has struggled on sundry such fronts and still does, as witness current efforts to rethink theology in correlation with the natural sciences. But no theatre of operations has been more pivotal for the Christian theological situation since the Enlightenment than the problematic of what might be called "the Jesus of theology" — that is, Jesus as demarcated by the overlap between the concerns of faith and the competence of historiography. It is theology's solemn obligation to indwell the constructive and conflictive intersections occurring between faith and culture. Theology thus always is elliptical. The "Jesus of theology" is the primary ellipse codetermined by biblical faith and *wissenschaftliche* historical research.

# II

A useful way to enter the arena of overlap we are targeting will be to attack Strauss's stark polarity of "the Christ of faith and the Jesus of history." It is fatally misleading, I believe, to cast these two phrases in flat contrast. For the normative Christ of Christian faith integrally bears within itself a Jesus of history: the historical actuality of the original Jesus. In conceptualizing the ground and norm of Christian faith, as that is experienced over the centuries in the ecclesial community, at least three "Christs" must be distinguished — that is, three factors or co-efficients of the unitive Christ who is the ground and norm. These are (i) the original Jesus who lived in Palestine ca. 4 B.C.E.-29 C.E., (ii) the biblical witness to this original Jesus, definitely embracing the antici-patory clues of the Hebrew scriptures, and (iii) the continuing impact in the present of Jesus as the Christ, believed mediated by the Spirit and generally called "the living Christ. "All three of these factors are in prin-ciple co-determinative of the whole Jesus Christ who is ground and norm of faith. Perhaps the credal and artistic and other representations of-fered in church history should count as a fourth co-efficient, and as a fifth, conceivably — if one is a wider ecumenist — the "Christ figures" of all human experience. But for present purposes, focusing as non-con-troversially as possible within Christian theology, I will acquiesce in the common judgment of St. Thomas and Karl Barth and regard such fur-ther factors as subsidiary. As such, of course, they may assist to mediate and clarify the prime factors, as Christian ecumenism now seeks to have happen through the Nicene Creed.

Ideally, one might ask, should not the historical, biblical and living Christs coalesce in an undifferentiated integrity of the one Saviour and

Lord? In that case the original Jesus would be decisive for faith insofar as biblically witnessed, and the biblical Christ would become decisive insofar as manifest to present faith as contemporary and coming Saviour and Lord. But in fact, typically, in the historic experience of the church, the three Christs exist in varying tensions with each other. Peter, standing for memory of the earthly Nazarene, and Paul, standing for authoritative encounter with (only) the Risen Lord, *together* symbolize the unitive diversity for which providence appears to have opted. For eighteen centuries tension among the "Christs" was most conspicuous in collisions between the Word and the Spirit, i. e. the biblical and the living Christ, as seen flagrantly in Montanism and the *Schwärmer.* Nevertheless a restless friction of the historical and biblical co-efficients is also discernible in the struggle to form the canon, in the uncertain interplay of literal and allegorical interpretation, and in the uneasy dialectic of the *theologia crucis* and the *theologia gloriae.* Early on, of course, there was the bitter conflict with Marcion, which resulted in the definitive inclusion for Christological hermeneutics of the Hebrew Bible. After the canon was resolved the first co-efficient, the original Jesus, was perceived as sealed into, though not as ontically reducible to, the second co-efficient, the biblical witness to Christ.

With the rise of modern historiography there developed the whole new ball game in which "enthusiasm" now had an opposing extreme in "historicism." The defiance of the letter for the sake of the Spirit was paralleled by spurning of the faith-witness, and especially of prophetic expectation (as in Second Isaiah), in favor of objectifiable facticity. The historically actual Jesus came unglued from the overarching biblical transparency which had so long mediated him for faith and emerged as an independent object of inquiry. That the inquiry was at first totally dependent on scriptural documents did not dampen its ominous independence. Reimarus forcefully shows how deconstructive analysis of a textual ensemble can undermine the credibility of tradition. One may think today of Crossan who attempts to identify as many as 52 evidentially distinct traces of Jesus from before 60 B.C.E. But even if, as John P. Meier argues, we essentially have just the four canonical Gospels, there is and was — once the demon of historicism was unleashed — that enormous latency for dissecting and recombining critique which continues so busily to engage the army of scholars. Meanwhile the biblical focus, deformed when split from its two co-efficients, became fundamentalism and neo-orthodoxy. Even theologians as exalted as Tillich and Barth seemed to teach that faith could suffice with its scriptural "picture" or *"Sage"* of the Christ and need not worry about a history lying behind that might or might not now be partially recoverable in and of itself. Such was the result — not very convincing, really, or stable — of disconnecting the historical, biblical and living dimensions of the one Christ.

So then, as I see it, the first phrase of Strauss' binary opposition, "Christ of faith," should clearly enunciate that an *historical* co-efficient is already posited within the term. Kähler makes a noble effort to this end when he formulates the antipode to the "so-called historical *(historische)* Jesus" as the "biblical historical *(geschichtliche)* Christ." Unfortunately this move tended to create a semantic bog. Meier currently tries to clarify the discussion of *"historisch"* and *"geschichtlich"* and then proposes to abandon it.[4] I have mixed feelings about this, for I think understanding of the whole issue is enriched by the two German terms, registering the double root of history as (a) what is told and (b) what happens, whereas nevertheless there is much ambiguity in their actual use. In any event Meier is justified in wanting to find an English way of saying what is needed, as I attempt with "historiographical" in place of (not translation of) Kähler's *"historisch."*

# III

If anything, the other pole of Strauss' 1865 couplet, "the Jesus of history," is more objectionable than his "Christ of faith." Strauss means Jesus as the object of scientific research, and the phrase has largely so functioned in ensuing discussion. But can the original Jesus be identified with the figure that is reconstructible by scientific historiography? Absolutely not! Here a pivotal ambiguity in "historical Jesus" must be exposed. The phrase can mean (a) the reality of Jesus as he originally was; this is what I meant above by "the original Jesus." But it can also mean (b) the reality of Jesus as this can be ascertained by historiography. These two meanings would be the same only if (i) historiography possessed data adequate for reconstructing Jesus' life and (ii) the objectifying method of historical science could cope with those aspects of Jesus that are uniquely decisive for faith (e.g., John 1:14: "And the Word became flesh and dwelt among us, full of grace and truth; we have beheld his glory, glory as of the only Son from the Father"). Neither of the conditions clearly obtains; both are very dubious. Therefore the "historical Jesus" of historiographical reonstruction is *not* to be equated with the Jesus of history whom faith affirms as integral to its ground and norm. For this reason I propose speaking of the Jesus who is the object of critical research as "the historiographical Jesus." Strauss, to repeat, misleads in calling this object *"der geschichtliche Jesus"*; and Kähler, who rightly saw the problem with the latter phrase, unfortunately remained mired in the uneliminable ambiguity of *"historisch."*

Nevertheless — and this is equally important to stress — while the Jesus of history whom faith affirms cannot be identified with, he also cannot be separated from, the historiographical Jesus. For the affirmation of Christ's historical reality implies, though it cannot be derived from, the historiographical plausibility of those aspects of the biblical representation of Jesus that may in principle become objects of research. Here I am compelled, not merely semantically, but substantively to part company with Kähler. For he saw the whole *Leben Jesu Bewegung* as a *Holzweg,* and I do not. That impulse and those results of historiographical inquiry after Jesus which have been taken up and augmented by the "new quest" of Robinson and others in the 50s and lately amplified vigorously by such scholars as Schussler-Fiorenza, Crossan, and the leaders of the Jesus Seminar I definitely do not see as a *Holzweg* in principle, either for history or theology. This does not of course endorse *carte blanche* the historiographical results achieved by working with any particular research paradigm. But as detailed New Testament study proceeds the composite image of Christ that pulsates in the mind and heart of faith can by no means be impassive to the results, as shows plainly in the annals of Christology as well as in literature, hymnody and art. Both *dejure* and *defacto* the longing for a fixed portrait of Christ impervious to the fluctuations of critical scholarship is contrary to the radical historicity of the Christian faith. My own esteemed teacher, Tillich, tried increasingly to work beyond his mentor Kähler's position, but was never able, in my judgment, to thematize duly the unavoidable bearing of historiography on faith — in spite of the prodding of such interlocutors as John Knox and C.H. Dodd. Contrary to lowbrow jokes which portray him as indifferent to a real Jesus, the mature Tillich firmly held — as Kahler had too — that such a reality, in the measure faith needs it, is given in, with and through the biblical picture of the Christ. In other words there is an indispensable analogy of the picture *(analogia imaginis)* to its *fundamentum in re.* But Tillich never freely acknowledged that faith must therefore regard historiography, not merely as a discipline which can prune its superstitions, but as a discipline from which it may expect positive clarification as well as threatening obfuscation of its essential concerns.

Where Jesus stood with regard to violence, radical egalitarianism, the status of women, his Jewish heritage, and openness to other worldviews, are not matters of indifference to faith. And they are matters historiography can illuminate. How many such matters are there? An indefinite number are conceivable. Faith's stance toward them at a given time forms something like the belt of subsidiary hypotheses which buffer, as also they exemplify and extend, the "core theory" which Imre Lakatos sees as the heart of a scientific paradigm or research program. The "core theory" here would correspond to that basic dimension of the normative Jesus Christ which faith intrinsically requires to be historical.

Can it be determined precisely what that "dimension" is? Or what its components are, if more than one? How would the determination be made? Presumably it would be the conjoint work of biblical, historical and systematic theology (difficult today with our disciplines so mutually isolated), and would consist in sifting the multifarious data of scripture, including the Hebrew Bible, church history and current ecclesial life to identify a perduring *"Wesen des Christentums"* à la Harnack — or at least a *"Wesen des christlichen Glaubens."* There would be all sorts of disagreement about this, and many would be sure in advance that no such *Wesen* could be found. In any case, the theological labors would have to be assimilated and ratified in appropriate ways by a consensus of the faithful. Do the obvious difficulties render the whole idea of the determination absurd? Surely not, as a regulative ideal! Does not serious theological work go forward all over the earth today, envisaging and anticipating what is Christianly *wesentlich* in an approximative mode, forbearing (hopefully) to claim absoluteness for itself, sensing that consummation can only be approached asymptotically and eschatologically.

I believe the main lines of what is historically requisite in faith in Christ can be approximated by attending to the canonical scriptures, the confessional documents, and the devotional, missional and ethical praxis of the ecumenical church through the ages. Utilizing all feasible biblical leads, the Christo-historical would be inferred from salient thematizations of the Person and Work of Christ, augmented by insights from the soteriological (the freeing and healing) dynamics of Christian experience. From Nicea and Chalcedon would come the dual theme of a decisive enactment of God in a fully human life — implying an actual personal existence as the fundament of the cluster of pericopes comprising the biblical witness. From the worship, proclamation, and moral engagement and loving service of the church, elucidated by the classics like *CurDeusNomo?* and reflected upon theologically in the crucible of current human need, would come cardinal elements of Christ's work: (a) intervention for liberating justice, against the demonic structures, especially for the poor, (b) bearing the cost of human perversity, and (c) personal impartation of healing love. Subsuming the ethos of the Hebraic background (e.g. the telic goodness of creation, the primordiality of love and justice, and redemptive suffering), these distinct forms of Christic work convey, of course, the theories of Irenaeus, Anselm and Abelard. There would remain the question of how to construe the Resurrection. Though particularly awkward for historiography, the Resurrection is undoubtedly the climactic moment in the Christo-historical setting free and making whole of the world. It is an appealing feature of Crossan's inquiry that he takes pains to treat the Resurrection carefully. He succeeds in providing a plausible historical analogy that is not incongruent with the *fundamentum in re* of both the "biblical picture" and Christian experience through the ages.

Let us recapitulate. Through the plethora of detail comprising the tradition there persists an image of the historical Jesus Christ as Lord and Saviour, freeing and healing the world through intervention and suffering believed to be finally victorious, though the end is not yet. Meanwhile we, as his disciples, are called and empowered to carry on his work of siding with the poor, bearing the cost, and imparting love that heals. This persisting image invites comparison with the "virtual image" of optics, which is an "image (as seen in a plane mirror) formed of points from which which divergent rays (as of light) seem to emanate without actually doing so" (Merriam Webster). In the case of faith's Christ image, there would historiographically be little or nothing that unambiguously corresponds to the image, rather only the plethora of traditionary pericopes comparable to the "divergent rays." From an unbelieving perspective the image would for the most part appear to be projected *thither* (cf. Feuerbach) by the collective subjectivity of the Christian movement. In faith, on the other hand, the image has the impact of one projected *hither* to us, to the interiority of our common consciousness as the church, by the agency we name the "Risen Lord," the "Living Christ," and/or the "Holy Spirit." The realistic impact of this experience, mediated wholistically through a medley of pericopes — the Lakatosian belt of subsidiary hypotheses — does not stand or fall with any neatly determinable portion of its media. As with a symbol, the reality symbolized is transcendental to any part or combination of parts of the medium, short of their entirety or an overwhelming proportion thereof. Just where the overwhelming might occur is at best predictable as a quantum probability, and not subject to exact calculation for an individual. This is all the more the case so far as a decisional element is involved in the act of faith.

Bultmann puts one in mind of this overall situation when he says (to the Heidelberger Akademie in 1952) that the "what" of the historical Jesus is not crucial to faith while the "that" is. Here the "what" would be the indefinitely concedable series of outer hypotheses or pericopes, and the "that" the transcendental core which they together specify and mediate. Kierkegaard seems on the same terrain when (in the *Fragments*) he remarks that all faith would need is a brief notation on a page of world history that a person had existed who claimed to be God. Bultmann's proposal is exasperating because one feels a "that" must imply *some* whatness. Kierkegaard settles on a very particular "what" but seems otherwise to scuttle the biblical witness — which would annul the "second co-efficient" of Christ we posited above. Tillich's move at this juncture I find to be right headed. He asserts the necessity for faith only of a point where the split between essence and existence is overcome, which he paraphrases as the appearance of the new being under the conditions of existence. Note that the conceptuality is deliberately transcendental. It is like Parmenides coming up with "being" as the universal ground instead of the "water" or "air" of Thales or Anaximenes. There is no particular segment of finitude — or, in our case, of the tradition — where the *Ding an sich,* the inmost core, is at stake. In discussion Tillich would not even insist that "Jesus" must have existed. The name might have been different, and it might not have been one person alone. Yet an historical taproot is categorically affirmed for the new being in Jesus as the Christ. In contrast, however, to the

Kierkegaard of the *Fragments*[5] Tillich's new being "shines through" Jesus' words, deeds, and sufferings "in a threefold color":

> first and decisively, as the undisrupted unity of the center of his being with God; second, as the serenity and majesty of him who preserves this unity against all attacks coming from estranged existence; and, third, as the self-surrendering love which represents and actualizes the divine love in taking the existential self-destruction upon himself.[6]

Moreover, the Christian norm for Tillich is the new being in Jesus as the Christ as experienced in the encounter of the church with the biblical message. This refers expressly to all three co-efficients explained above (Jesus, as the Christ, encountered in the church.) So, in Tillich's mature thought, the triadic norm, in principle, is in place. If only he had not been so uptight on historiography! For historiography, as its current results show, has compelling input to make to the picture of Christ normative for faith.

In the formation of faith-historical assertions, where the work of the historiographer impinges on matters integral to the biblical Christ, it seems there is a hierarchy from the inmost core, which Tillich expresses as the "new being" or Bultmann as the "that" of the historical Jesus, through successive peripheries where the credibility of detail becomes less and less significant for faith. In other words, the "Lakatosian belt" of subsidiary hypotheses consists of more than one ring. Outmost is the biblical witness to Jesus *in toto,* in its literal sense; whereas close in toward the core itself, if not part of it, are main symbols like the Cross and the Resurrection. Elements of Christ's work as characterized above — intervening for justice, bearing sin's cost, imparting love that heals — or those intended by Tillich in his thematization of the "threefold color" with which the new being "shines through," are middle axioms which lack credal crystallization but prescind from multiple data offered by scripture, tradition and contemporary experience. At comparable radius from the core might be positioned graphic recent emphases such as the radical egalitarianism for women and for all the oppressed of the Jesus Movement (a la Schussler-Fiorenza), the "option for the poor," the "wounded healer" espoused by pastoral care, and Jesus' remarkable openness. Albert Cleage's contention some years ago for Jesus as "black messiah" likewise comes to mind, especially as this was reformulated by James Cone. Many of us would indeed stress that Jesus was literally *not* the Nordic usually depicted in the cinema, and that he *was* symbolically black in the sense expounded by Cone (if not already by Cleage), viz. a person in unreserved solidarity with the disinherited.

Thus different initiatives among the faithful from time to time and place to place (linked to different hurts and joys) reconfigure the Christohistorical image and so reorder the priority of faith-historical assertions. As Tillich says, the norm of the new being concretely reshapes itself from the ongoing encounter between Bible and church. But, as Tillich and his peers did not sufficiently allow, a potent catalyst in the processive concretion of the Christ norm is the ongoing work of critical historiography.

Does this provision contradict the role of faith in receiving the Christ norm? As Augustine classically says, "unless you shall have believed, you shall not understand." But Augustine also is fully conscious of the hermeneutical circle in which faith and understanding are symbiotic. He writes:

> If a man says to me, I would understand in order that I may believe, I answer, Believe, that you may understand. Nevertheless, unless they understand what I am saying, they cannot believe. Hence what he says is in some part true, I would understand in order that I may believe. And I, too, am right when I say, as does the Prophet [Is. vii, 9] Nay, believe that thou mayest understand.[7]

It is completely of a piece with this that St. Anselm, when he does theology *as fides quaerens intellectum,* introduces figures like Boso and Gaunilo who press skeptical questions. When the "age of faith" is at high tide, the 13th Century faculty at Paris is an arena of intense debate between Franciscans, Dominicans, and extreme Aristotelians, out of which comes the profound use of *disputatio* by St. Thomas. The honesty, the authenticity of Christian faith emerges from open-ended testing by the subject matter and by questioning opponents. In its ongoing life till the end of time, faith employs rational endeavor ever afresh to elucidate and sustain itself. This is the case ontologically, cosmologically, morally, and also — since the advent of critical research — historiographically. The present day poses formidable challenges to received faith on various fronts: philosophy, the other religions, the natural and the social sciences, and the vast turbulence of humanity groaning from oppression, anarchic violence, and ecologic peril. But none of these challenges is more pivotal, for the integrity of Christian faith, than the incisive new thrust of historical inquiry into Christian origins and the figure of Jesus.

# IV

There has lately been an exhilarating and also disconcerting boom in Jesus research. Some have seemed peeved about this, since they deem historiographical inquiry into Jesus neither useful nor possible. To the contrary, for reasons already given, I celebrate the challenging new work of Crossan, Schüssler-Fiorenza, Meier, the Jesus Seminar, William Farmer, Raymond Brown, and so many more! One could view the current surge of research as a veritable "third quest" for Jesus, following the 19th Century enterprise (which carried on powerfully, of course, for decades after Schweitzer's classic report) and then the "new quest" heralded — and significantly sparked — by James Robinson in the 1950s and 60s. Or one could see the recent developments as further blossoming of the Robinsonian, post-Bultmann quest. It hardly matters, so long as one takes note of the unprecedented involvement of women, of Catholics, of the disciplines of the secular university, of intercultural insights, and of America as unabashedly a capital site. Moreover,what could be the most dynamic factor is the startling proliferation of putative sources for knowledge of the original Jesus — Q, Thomas and many slighter traces which some claim to antedate 60 C.E.

Some of the things that impress me about Crossan are the ready use of cultural history and anthropology, along with closer up historical study for contextual illumination, the drawing upon psychology and phenomenology of religion for analogies, the rigorous method of layered sources and multiple attestation, the absence of anti-Christian *ressentiment,* along with unswerving commitment to objectivity, the freedom from constrictive "scientistic" dogmas that might have prevented an authentically *historical* approach to themes like Jesus' magical powers and the Resurrection, and in general the boldness to doubt as well as credit by careful argumentation alone. As I was reading Crossan I was trying to digest another important book too: Cone's *Martin and Malcolm.* Some of the concluding passages from the latter resonated intensely with the fresh look at Jesus I was getting from the former.

> Malcolm ... showed us by example and prophetic preaching that one does not have to stay in the mud. We can wake up; we can stand up; and we can take that long walk toward freedom. Freedom is first and foremost an inner recognition of self-respect, a knowledge that one was not put on this earth to be a nobody.... Martin ... was right: "The hour is late" and "the clock of destiny is ticking out." We must declare where we stand on the great issues of our time. Racism is one of them. Poverty is another. Class exploitation another. Imperialism another. We must break the cycle of violence in America and around the world. Human beings are meant for life and not death. They are meant for freedom and not slavery. They were created for each other and not against each other. We must therefore break down the barriers that separate people from one another. For Martin and Malcolm, for America and the world, and for all those who have given their lives in the struggle for justice, let us direct our fight toward one goal the beloved community of humankind.[8]

That much of this rhetoric so rhymed with Crossan's exposition was due not only to Cone's being (deep down) a Christian preacher. I realized I was getting from Crossan a strong fresh sense that the *historical* Jesus had really stood for such things, had started a movement of unrestricted table fellowship and healing, had evinced an amazing openness, had insistently espoused the poor, had died at the hands of the establishment, and yet gone on being present in the breaking of bread. It was inspiring. It nurtures hope, through historiography, that increasing reunion might come about, in the decades ahead, between the "three coefficients" of the whole Christ. Historical and biblical responsibility might join with charismatic buoyancy to follow his path of setting free and making whole. This is the rousing opportunity inherent in today's interface of Christology and historiography.

However, there is another side as well to the current scrutinizing of Christian origins. This is the conspicuously sharpening threat that a controlling slant among historiographers might come to exclude the historical credibility of components vital to the Christ of faith. This would instantiate the situation that Tillich, in 1911, tried to allow for when he pondered the implication for Christian faith should the non-existence of the historical Jesus become historiographically probable. Tillich concluded at that time that such a development would not be theologically fatal, since Christian faith is grounded on the biblical picture of the Christ and not on an historiographically ascertainable Jesus. But there was an ambiguity in this formulation in that it does not tell us whether faith is indifferent merely to the results of historiography regarding Jesus, or also to the putative object of such historiography, the actual Jesus. In 1911 Tillich held the latter view, though subsequently (as brought out *supra*) he came to insist Christianity cannot dispense with its historical foundation.

This later stance was congenial with Bultmann's: the "that" of the Christ event can be affirmed in, through and under the historiographical uncertainties of the "what." It is as though in 1911 Tillich felt a need to allow for the extreme historical negativity of a Bruno Bauer, while later he had to take account only of the theologically permissive historiographical agnosticism of Bultmann, the scholar whom he considered paradigmatic for New Testament research.

Today in any case, along with the heady tide of novel insights into Christian origins, there has arisen within frontal precincts of research an acute radicalization beyond the stance of Bultmann. Not since someone like Bauer has highly credentialed scholarship, in any of its representatives, reached the point of entailing, as it does in the current work of Burton Mack, the *outright untenability* of Christianly central faith historical affirmations, notably those of Jesus' redemptive death and Resurrection. For Mack the whole Christ myth is a fictional concoction with which the earliest traces of the actual Jesus (the primary layers of Q) have nothing in common. It is crucial to notice in this connection the difference between Mack and Crossan, as well as their agreements. Although accepting that Jesus must have been crucified, and aware that his presence continued somehow in the circles of commensality his movement engendered, Crossan denies that the passion and resurrection narratives of the Gospels can be based on eye-witness experience of actual happenings. Thus he impugns the epistemic grounding of the evangelical accounts of Jesus' passion and resurrection without repudiating their analogical viability. Tillich's formula of the "analogy of the picture" is still feasible, even if strained, on Crossan's showing. But it is not on

Mack's. In the latter's hard nosed application of the Q research format, the"nonexistence of Jesus," against which the Tillich of 1911 wanted to fortify faith, once again becomes "historically probable."

By "Jesus" here we mean of course, not just someone with that name, but a figure significantly commensurate with the Jesus of historic Christian faith. For, as John Knox used to say, the Christian question is not whether Jesus *lived,* but whether Jesus (as decisive for faith) lived. Where, then, does this leave us? In spite of his methodological rigor, is Crossan's commitment to the Q-Thomas paradigm compromised by his residual depth of positive Christian feeling? Or, granting Mack's commendable boldness, does his personal alienation from Christianity give his results an aggressive exaggeration — cheered on, to be sure, by those in the audience of general culture who harbor various resentments toward the "Christ myth"?

Amid the gathering storm of issues that mingle here are the following. What really is the cogency of the Q-Thomas research model, and does its espousal as the regulative criterion for earliest Christianity create a slippery slope down which even reluctant friends of the historic Christ of faith must slide? Is there operative any longer a public forum where the claims for and against the Q-Thomas model can be openly debated from all sides? Or has such a forum so eroded that scholars like Raymond Brown and James Robinson, Elizabeth Schussler-Fioraenza, William R. Farmer and Burton Mack are not in mutual communication? What steps might be taken to restore such a forum? Would it be possible to promulgate a contemporary give and take among biblical, historical and systematic theologians, so as to ponder afresh the unity of the Bible and evoke critical witness to the freeing and healing Christ in consistency with scientific honesty and existential openness? The theological community and the church itself must be champing for answers to such questions, even as illuminating and disquieting new results about Christian origins are being rapidly ingested.

## NOTES

1.  An earlier version of this essay was presented at the fall meeting, November, 1993, of the Pacific Coast Theological Society, in Berkeley, California.

2. *Our Religions,* ed. byArvind Sharma (Harper, 1993), p. 366.
3. *Man's Religions* (Macmillan, rev., 1956), p. 556.
4. *A Marginal Jew* (Doubleday, 1991), pp 26-40.
5. In *Training* and *the Edifying Discourses* Kierkegaard's *take* on *the* matter is different; the biblical picture is concretely in view.
6. *Systematic Theology,* II (University of Chicago, 1957), p. 138.
7. Sermon XLIII, Przywara, *An Augustine Synthesis* (Harper, 1958), pp. 53-4.

# 11

# REFLECTIONS UPON 'THE HISTORICAL PERIMETERS FOR UNDERSTANDING THE AIMS OF JESUS'*

## William R. Farmer

As carefully crafted as the title for this essay may be, it remains ambiguous. By the "aims of Jesus" do we mean Ben Meyer's stunning book by that title? If so, we would be obliged to undertake a social historical analysis of Gospel criticism in Germany during the nineteenth century and position Meyer's book within the context of the history of ideas from Reimarus to the present. That is a task worth undertaking, but it is not my present task. Rather, by the "aims of Jesus" I refer not to Meyer's book itself, but the subject of that book, namely the guiding purposes of Jesus, which to understand helps us make the most sense out of as much as possible of all the relevant data bearing on the question of Christian origins.

I think it is fair to say that before Meyer wrote his book, this subject was generally regarded in higher circles of theological scholarship as off limits. One of the basic assumptions of mid-twentieth century critical reflection has been that the self-consciousness of Jesus is beyond recovery. To attempt to penetrate behind the earliest strata of the synoptic tradition as formulated in the primitive Palestinian Christian communities has been to defy the gods of reason and correct academic behavior.

We have yet to take the full measure of Ben Meyer's achievements in his book **The Aims of Jesus**, but for this observer, it already appears that the whole question of what we can know, and/or what we should attempt to understand about Jesus, has been recast in a very constructive way by Meyer's soundly grounded and comprehensive study. The very formulation: "the aims of Jesus," serves to make it clear that what is under inves-

---

* This essay is a shorter version of a paper presented for discussion at a symposium honoring Professor Ben F. Meyer held at McMaster University, December 1989

tigation is not his personality which may be beyond recovery, nor his private life, which in any case belongs to the gossip columns rather than the annals of responsible theological scholarship. What is under investigation is the public career of Jesus. What did he do and say that can make sense out of what emerged from what he did and said? Of course Jesus did not speak and act within a vacuum, and every historical reconstruction must make sense in terms of what we can know about the circumstances of the time — social, historical, political, et al. Jesus did do something. He did say something. And what he did and said stands in some consequential relationship to what happened to his people and what happened to him. And what happened to his people and what happened to Jesus as a consequence of what he did and said stands in some consequential relationship to the Church which from the earliest period has served as the custodian of his oracles, and the perpetuator of his purposes.

We turn now to our topic: "The Historical Perimeters for Understanding the Aims of Jesus."

These historical perimeters include what may be called basic presuppositions, which while they may not be established are regarded by most critics as not only plausible but intrinsically probable.

We may begin with further reference to the common-sense assumption of continuity between Jesus and the community which bears and cherishes his memory. Jesus did do something with his life and did teach or preach something. Is it not reasonable to conclude that this something provided the Church an initial impetus, that is, that authentic Christian life and faith, at one or more decisive points, is commensurate with the original intention of Jesus and the effect he had upon the life and faith of his disciples? Is it not reasonable to think that, however much our understanding of existence may have broadened, deepened, or changed, nothing has happened which sets aside, nullifies or contravenes the significance of the original event.

In addition to this general pre-understanding there are several rather specific presuppositions or material assumptions that are important for this study.

The first is the *historical existence* of Jesus. The fact that some intelligent persons sincerely doubt whether Jesus ever existed as an historical personage, and that theologians have felt constrained to allow for this doubt, reminds us that in the intellectual history of the West this is still an item of unfinished business.

The second is the *sanity* of Jesus. Jesus' sanity is hardly capable of competent definition or diagnosis. But the fact that it has been challenged deserves to be noted. There is no reason in principle why historical studies of Jesus presupposing that he was suffering from one or another mental illness should not be attempted. However, such studies as have been made seem incomplete and their results uncertain.

The third is the *integrity* of Jesus. The point at issue here is primarily this: did Jesus intend to deceive his followers or did he allow them to be deceived? Sensitive pastors are aware of the fact that there are members of their flocks whose faith in their integrity sometimes disposes them to be uncritically naive with regard to the problems pastors experience in maintaining at all times personal integrity in their ministries. Therefore, when the integrity on the part of Jesus is assumed by an historian, this assumption must not be made naively, but should be regarded as a presupposition, for it tends to limit the range of human experience by which the historian judges probabilities and improbabilities in his reconstruction of the past, by leaving out of consideration possibilities which might otherwise be entertained if the suggestion that Jesus may not have been a person of integrity were really taken seriously. To say that Jesus was a person of integrity does not rule out the possibility that he sometimes may have been conscious of failing to adhere to or wholeheartedly affirm what he preached. Such questions are virtually impossible to settle because of the difficulties with which any investigation into the self-consciousness of Jesus is fraught. The materials we have for understanding Jesus do not afford us as much of this kind of knowledge about him as we could wish. The basic question is: did Jesus mean what he said; did he intend others to take his words seriously and did he himself take seriously the understanding of existence to which he gave expression in his teaching? It is an affirmative answer to this question which is presupposed in this essay. The degree to which anyone hesitates to agree that Jesus was in this sense a person of integrity should lead her/him to a corresponding degree of scepticism regarding the possibility of ever knowing with any degree of probability what the aims of Jesus actually were, since any conclusions that may be drawn on this matter presuppose such integrity on Jesus' part.

In the fourth place it is presupposed that within the primitive Church there were those who *remembered* Jesus. That Jesus was remembered in the Church by those who had known him is intrinsically probable from virtually every point of view, but since it has never been demonstrated it needs to be listed as something assumed in any investigation of the "aims of Jesus." In the fifth place it is assumed that all the gospels were written relatively late, i.e. probably a full generation after the events described. The evidence on which such dating is based is admittedly tenuous.

The sixth matter that is presupposed or assumed is closely related to the fourth and fifth. It is that *within the tradition preserved in the gospels, the memory of Jesus is preserved*. The alternative that, in the period between the time when Jesus was remembered in the primitive Church and the time the gospels were written, the memory of Jesus was completely or effectively lost is a real one. And although few would support this alternative, the fact that the contrary is assumed deserves noting.

Finally, we frequently presuppose that it is possible *to distinguish between what was remembered about Jesus and what has been added*. This analysis can be accomplished with the aid of contemporary knowledge of the relevant ancient languages; environmental research into the life situation of Jesus and of the first-century Church; literary and historical criticism (including source, form-critical and redactional analysis); and a reasonably perceptive understanding of human existence, informed by the humanities and social science disciplines. It is not presupposed that *all* the genuine remembrances can be identified, but that *in a significant number and variety of passages* in the gospels it is possible to distinguish between what has been remembered and what has been added. In this connection it can be said that it is to the enduring credit of Professor Joachim Jeremias that he was able to take the form-critical methods of his more sceptical German colleagues and by a careful and judicious application of the principles of form-critical inquiry, demonstrate to the satisfaction of most critics that one could separate the later redactional additions coming from the exegetical tradition of the early church from the earlier parables of Jesus. This triumph of Jeremias, more than his famous "Abba" triumph, accounts for the basic shift that has come over the so-called quest for the historical Jesus. It broke the back of radical scepticism and more than any other single development in German New Testament scholarship in the twentieth century, has served to open up the real possibility of an hermeneutic that can reconcile the demands of the academy with the vital interests of the church.

We turn now to a second category of historical perimeters for understanding the Aims of Jesus. These are facts or conclusions that need not be presupposed. They can all be demonstrated explicitly or inferred from circumstantial evidence.

## Preliminary Methodological Considerations

The chief methodological problem in writing about the aims of Jesus is chronology. Since the turn of the century, critical theology has been aware of the historical uncertainty of the gospel chronologies. This has led to a virtual moratorium on writing "lives of Jesus" according to the nineteenth-century mode. The classic twentieth-century reconstruction by Bultmann in his **Jesus and the Word** is largely restricted to the reconstruction of Jesus' message. Bornkamm's **Jesus of Nazareth** is an improvement on Bultmann, primarily by taking into account the intervening parable research of Dodd (**The Parables of the Kingdom**) and Jeremias (**The Parables of Jesus**).

A peculiar merit of the approach here to be presented is that it goes beyond the simple reconstruction of Jesus' message. Without uncritical dependence upon the gospel chronologies, it attempts to explicate Jesus' teachings within the context of an intrinsic development in his public career. To this extent it serves in a modest way to demonstrate the possibility of a "story of Jesus" acceptable to historians, a story which is not essentially different from the story of Jesus familiar to us from the Gospels.

The gospel tradition originated with Jesus and those who worked with him and experienced his saving influence. It developed in the earliest Christian communities where Jesus was remembered and worshiped as the crucified and resurrected Lord. The tradition's canonical function in the church calls for theological and historical reflection upon the way it developed into the forms given to it in the Gospels and upon the relationship of these Gospels to one another and to Scripture as a whole.

The Gospels embody tradition concerning Jesus. Between Jesus and the Gospels stands the traditioning process, by which the Gospel stories and sayings of Jesus were handed on. These traditions were oral and written and included sayings both of Jesus and of early Christian prophets speaking in the name of Jesus. They also included accounts of eyewitnesses concerning the actions and character of Jesus and later modifications of this tradition made to meet the changing needs of different Christian communities.

This traditioning process has never ceased. It flourished up to and through the period when the Gospels were written and achieved manifold expression during the second and third centuries. It was normed with the adoption of the fourfold Gospel canon, which in turn has enhanced the traditioning process through its influence upon the visual arts, music, literature, and preaching.

The canonical Gospels afford us our best access to the earliest traditions concerning Jesus. From a form-critical study of the Gospels, it is clear that the Jesus tradition was already richly developed by the time the Gospels were written. A study of this developed tradition is rewarding because it helps clarify the character of Jesus and improves our understanding of the evangelists' purpose in writing the Gospels.

The Gospels represent Jesus as he was remembered and worshiped in certain Christian communities a generation after the beginning of the church. This is clear from the traditions concerning Jesus that the evangelists used, which include not only traditions that originated with Jesus himself and his first associates, but also many which reflect the needs of later Christian communities.

Christianity as a religious movement began with Jesus and his disciples in Palestine, a meeting place for diverse cultural influences. This does not mean, however, that no viable distinctions can be made between the environment of Jesus and that of the evangelists. The environment of Jesus of Nazareth was spaceually Palestinian and temporally pre-Pauline. Therefore, whatever he did and said, however distinctive it may have been, would have been accommodated to those who shared this environment. Presumably tradition concerning Jesus' words and actions, which achieved stable form at a very early date, would tend to reflect this environment both conceptually and pictorially.

On the other hand, the environment of the evangelists was extra-Palestinian and post-Pauline. We can assume that what the evangelists wrote was accommodated accordingly. The other New Testament writings make clear that the social and theological forces set in motion by Jesus and his disciples broke out of the original Palestinian environment at an early period. The Acts of the Apostles views this transition in retrospect. More importantly, however, the transition is seen firsthand in the letters of Paul. Thus, Paul's writings are an important control in distinguishing between the environment of Jesus and that of the evangelists.

In his letters it is clear that Paul considered carrying the gospel to the Gentiles his special vocation. This vocation committed him to lengthy journeys among people far removed from Palestine. Therefore Paul himself reflects the transitional situation, not simply because he was a Jew engaged in a mission to gentiles, but also because he knew Jerusalem and met there with those who were apostles before him. He was concerned that these leaders understand that such changes in missionary policy as he had introduced in his efforts to expedite the spread of the gospel did not affect its saving truth. In fact, Paul was prepared to question the integrity of these apostles when they conducted themselves in a manner he perceived as prejudicial to the truth of this gospel.

Basically, then, what is seen in Paul's letters is one way in which it was possible to adapt the gospel so that it was viable for predominantly gentile churches in Asia Minor and points west.

The works of the Jewish historian Josephus serve not only as background material to the letters of Paul and the rest of the New Testament writings, but also provide a basis for observing the contrast between the environments of Jesus and the evangelists. Like Paul, Josephus was basically of the pharisaic persuasion. Unlike Paul and most other New Testament writers, however, Josephus reflects first-century Judaism unchanged by Christian belief. Similarly, the manuscripts from the caves of the Judean desert, Jewish writings from the intertestamental period, and some Mishnaic and other rabbinic materials all afford access to first-century Palestinian Judasim unaffected by Christian belief. These Jewish writings together with the works of Josephus provide a reliable control in determining the nature of the religious, social, economic, and political environment of Jesus. In other words, in the effort to delineate the environment of Jesus, the modern historian is not confined to the limited and selective circle of New Testament writings.

When a tradition concerning Jesus or a saying attributed to him comes alive against the background of his environment as it is known through a study of the topography, geography, and climate of Palestine and the history of Palestinian Judaism prior to A.D. 70, then an element in the tradition is isolated or identified which may be early. If this tradition would be unintelligible outside Palestine or unfamiliar in gentile-oriented circles, then the probabilities increase that such a saying or story belongs to an early stage in the development of the tradition. Material in the Gospels which presupposes the death and resurrection of Jesus and reflects a situation where he is remembered and worshiped as a transcendent being represents tradition which may have originated in some post-Easter Christian community. Such tradition could have developed either early or late, either in Jewish or gentile circles. Paul's letters preserve evidence that mythopoeic tendencies were at work at a very early date in some Christian communities, producing powerful christological statements about Jesus.

There are four major turning points in the development of the tradition leading from Jesus to the Gospels: (1) Jesus' baptism by John followed by the arrest, imprisonment, and death of the Baptist; (2) Jesus' challenge of religious authorities climaxing in his cleansing of the Temple followed by a final institutionalizing meal with his disciples, his arrest, trial, death, and resurrection and the emergence of a post-Easter messianic community; (3) sectarian conflict and division within the Jewish-Christian messianic community over the manner by which Gentiles were to be admitted to full membership; and (4) the inspiring rediscovery and renewal of ecumenical unity in the aftermath of the martyrdom of the chief apostles Peter and Paul in Rome and the outbreak of the catastrophic Roman-Jewish military conflict. From this outline it may be seen that the crucial matter is not where a tradition belongs in some temporal progression conceived chronologically in decades, but in a temporal progression marked off by decisive periods in a developmental sequence. The public career of Jesus falls between the first and second of these decisive periods and took place in Palestine. The Gospels were written during or following the fourth and are extra-Palestinian in provenance. Paul's letters provide us with an indispensable control for understanding how the Jesus tradition developed between the second and fourth turning points by illuminating the third. Paul himself was intimately acquainted with both the Jewish-Palestinian environment of Jesus and with the extra-Palestinian, gentile-oriented environment of the evangelists, and his life and work provide an indispensable bridge between the two.

Because of both the historical uncertainty concerning the gospel chronologies and the mythopoeic character of much of Jesus' "life and ministry," it is best to focus our attention on sayings of Jesus which originated during the period of his earthly ministry if we wish to reflect on the aims of the actual Jesus.

Within the corpus of the tradition which originated during the period of Jesus' earthly ministry, the parables afford the best key for understanding his career and character. However, the following points concerning the parables merit consideration: (1) the parables are not to be interpreted allegorically (Julicher); (2) in his parables Jesus proclaims that the eschatological kingdom of God has already broken into reality (Dodd); (3) form criticism enables the critic to identify the parables of Jesus as belonging to the genre of rabbinic parables, while as a whole presenting theologically distinctive content (Jeremias); and (4) form criticism enables the critic to distinguish the original form of Jesus' parables from the additions that were made by the early church (Jeremias). Once these matters concerning the parables become clear, it is possible to recapture the most adequate image of Jesus' career and character.

To do this it is also necessary to meet minimal chronological requirements. One need only recognize that Jesus' public ministry began with his baptism at the hands of John, whose identity is established by the historian Josephus; that Jesus' ministry ended in crucifixion in response to the fateful decisions of the procurator Pontius Pilate and the high priest Caiaphas, whose identities are also established by Josephus; and that between the beginning and end of Jesus' ministry a two-fold and compound crisis occurred. Central to this crisis was opposition to Jesus by the religious authorities, who felt challenged by his practice of eating with tax collectors and sinners. Recognizing this fact makes it possible to perceive a credible relationship between Jesus' ministry and his death and to develop an intrinsic chronology for his earthly career.

This can be accomplished by arranging the sayings of Jesus and particularly his parables in relationship to this twofold and compound crisis. For example, a parable in which Jesus rebukes the self-righteouness of those who resent God's mercy toward repentant sinners would have been prompted by his decision to defend his action of eating with tax collectors and sinners against the criticism of the Pharisees. This is a decision, however, that could not have come until after a decision by the Pharisees to criticize such conduct, which decision could not have been made before some tax collectors and sinners had decided to accept Jesus' invitation to table fellowship. This decision in turn could not have taken place until after Jesus' decision to invite repentant tax collectors and sinners into the intimacy of his table fellowship. And this decision of Jesus could not have taken place until some of these persons had decided to respond to his gracious call to repentance, which could not have come until after Jesus' decision to leave the sparsely settled regions of the wilderness of Judea where he had been with John and to carry his gracious call to repentance into the more densely populated urban areas of Israel.

With this necessary sequence of decisive moments in Jesus' public career, it is possible to reconstruct in outline form the essential development of his message. The ability to do this rests on the premise that the parables and other sayings of Jesus were not conceived all at once, but like the letters of Paul, were composed in response to particular situations. The essential outlines of this development are as follows:

1. Jesus followed John the Baptist, proclaiming the imminent coming of the kingdom of God.
2. His initial message issued in —
   a. A gracious call to repentance.
   b. A positive response from "tax collectors and sinners."
   c. The acceptance of sinners into table fellowship, which created a new community that existed in anticipation of the coming kingdom.
3. Jesus' ministry was beset by two separate crises, and a third occurred which was compounded by interaction between the other two.
   a. An internal crisis developed among Jesus' followers because of uncertainty concerning the coming of the kingdom.
   b. An external crisis developed because of the Pharisees' resistance to Jesus' message and his table fellowship with sinners. Jesus rebuked the Pharisees and declared that it was better to be a repentant sinner than a self-righteous keeper of the law. The attitude of the Pharisees toward Jesus became increasingly hostile, and they plotted his death. Even in the face of death, Jesus reaffirmed the truth of his message.

c. The external conflict with the Pharisees compounded the internal uncertainty among the faithful, raising the question, Should we really allow sinners in our fellowship? Jesus assured his disciples that God would separate the just from the unjust. God alone, not some ritual, would decide who is justified and who is not.

On the basis of this analysis of Jesus' ministry and message, the image of Jesus is that of one who in the face of God's imminent destruction of the wicked issued God's gracious call to repentance, and with compassion and joy received sinners into his fellowship. Moreover, it is the image of one who defended this action in the face of criticism and rebuked the self-righteous attitude of those authorities who resented God's mercy toward repentant sinners. The significance of this image of Jesus' lifestyle is both theological and existential. There is in the parables of Jesus a theology of grace, a theology which is ethically and morally concerned with the little ones — those who are disadvantaged and victimized by the social and religious structures of their existence. This is a theology out of which comes a call to repentance and a promise of God's salvation to all who respond. In short, Jesus' parables demonstrate beyond reasonable doubt that the one who communicated these parables and their message provides the primal historical and theological context within which to reflect on the meaning of the cross and the resurrection.

When the parables of Jesus preserved in the Gospel of Matthew are analyzed theologically and compared to the parables of Jesus preserved in the Gospel of Luke, in every case the theology of the parables in Matthew can be matched by the theology of one or more of the parables in Luke. Moreover, the theology of Jesus' parables is essentially the same as the theology of Paul. Since we learn from Paul himself that he preached the faith of the church he once persecuted, it follows that Paul preached a pre-Pauline faith. The historian has no alternative but to conclude that the theology common to Paul and to the two streams of parable tradition preserved separately in Matthew and Luke goes back to Jesus. To imagine that these three streams of tradition converge in some unidentified pre-Pauline theologian would be to create an unnecessary set of historical and theological problems.

It is important to clarify one further point. There is solid textual basis for making a fundamental theological distinction between Jesus and John the Baptist. Liberation theologies can be strengthened if they are careful not to blur this distinction and if they do not wrongly conclude that the polarizing effect of John's preaching should be attributed also to Jesus and identified as the cause for Jesus' execution at the hands of the political establishment.

Such a conclusion would be a vast oversimplification of a complex question and would leave important evidence unexplained — evidence both from the parables in Luke and Matthew and from Paul's account of his pre-Christian persecution of the church. This evidence indicates that the religious authorities, who were drawn from the righteous elements within the established world of Jewish piety, were opposed to Jesus' message and conduct. The woes of Jesus (which, to be sure, were added to in the bitterest of terms during the persecution of the church in which Paul the Pharisee took part) and his cleansing of the Temple polarized his relationship with the religious authorities and sealed his fate. Jesus' fate was not in the first instance sealed by direct confrontation with Pilate and his political authority or with Roman military forces stationed in the capital. Thus, while the words of the psalmist "zeal for thy house has consumed me" (Ps. 69:9) have been cited in Scripture in connection with Jesus' cleansing of the Temple (John 2:17), Jesus was categorically more than a zealot or political activist.

There is no one category (like carpenter, king, teacher, or exorcist) that can do justice to the unique career of Jesus. The best way in which to approach an understanding of Jesus as an historical figure is to focus on his role as religious reformer (like Bernard of Clairvaux or Romero of Salvador). He certainly taught his disciples to love their enemies. Any reconstruction that stumbles on that fact will not stand up to criticism. The reconstruction offered here clarifies the relationship between religion and politics in Jesus' environment and focuses attention on what is truly liberating in Christianity.

The theology which comes to expression in the words and actions of Jesus is a theology which works against every form of oppression and exploitation and binds together all persons who love God and thirst after righteousness. It is a theology which calls for resourcement and renewal in the life of the church and for political involvement in the struggle for justice in society — for self-sacrifice and a readiness for martyrdom as exemplified in the lives of Mahatma Gandhi, Martin Luther King, Jr., and Archbishop Oscar Romero. Jesus' prophetic power to unmask hypocrisy and self-righteousness is absolutely central to this theology and very distinctive of it.

Where certain parables of Jesus are interpreted within the context of initial developments in his ministry and specifically within the context of his gracious call for repentance, they enable the historian to make informed suggestions about the intention of Jesus as he responded to the exigencies and difficulties he encountered. How was one to understand the delay in the coming of the kingdom which John had pronounced to be at hand, especially after John's arrest and execution? And if one were to undertake to continue proclaiming the coming of the kingdom, how should he or she perceive this ministry? Was it to be understood as the work of God to be carried out during an extension of the period of grace in the face of the coming judgment? If so, was it not reasonable to expect that in due season, failing the fruits of repentance, this period of grace would come to a sudden and just end (Luke 13:6-9)? As for those who would mistakenly hold back because of their fear that the cost of repentance might be too great, was it not important for their sake to emphasize the joy of the kingdom (Matt. 13:44,45)? Should not those who were delinquent in setting their houses in order be reminded of the inevitability of judgment (Matt. 21:33-41; Luke 20:9-16), the appropriateness of radical action in the face of certain change (Luke 16:1-8b), the folly of not trusting God (Matt. 25:14-30; Luke 19:11-27), and the suddenness and unexpectedness of God's judgment (Matt. 24:45-51; Luke 12:42-46; 13:1-5)?

Certainly parables which dramatically illustrate the folly of postponing repentance (Matt. 22:1-10, 25:1-13; Luke 13:6-9) and which teach the wisdom of living in ready expectation of God's gracious judgment (Luke 12:35-38) most likely would have originated in situations where such expectations would be enlivened and heightened — in the period of Jesus' active ministry after his baptism into the movement of John and his decision to continue proclaiming the imminence of the kingdom following John's arrest and death.

Even within this period it is possible to postulate development. Presumably Jesus would have understood the lesson the authorities intended by John's execution: "A disciple is not above his teacher" (Matt. 10:24). Jesus's decision to carry on would have been realistic only if he understood that he did so at great risk. Although John had been beheaded, a more usual form of execution was crucifixion. For Jesus to say "Take up (your) cross and follow me" (Matt. 16:24) was his way of making clear that he had placed himself outside the discipline and protection of the established world of Jewish piety, and was calling upon others to do the same. This established world of Jewish piety derived its earthly jurisdiction from Rome. Thus, in coming into conflict with the religious authorities, Jesus was risking the ultimate wrath of Roman power. To speak in this way was a determined response to a policy of oppression which had been calculated to discourage dangerous rhetoric associated with messianic activity. But Jesus was not intimidated by what the authorities did to John. He continued to preach. "No one can serve two masters... You cannot serve God and mammon... Repent, and engage in the service of God ... for the kingdom of heaven is at hand" (Matt. 6:24; 3:2).

When Jesus said "Take up (your) cross and follow me" (Matt. 16:24) or "Leave the dead to bury their own dead" (Matt. 8:22), he took upon himself the full measure of God's absolute demand which was entailed in messianic leadership. With such startling statements Jesus challenged others to free themselves from a paralyzing fear of human authorities, both those who sat in Moses' seat and those who represented the emperor. In the former saying, Jesus unobtrusively clarified the all-important question of whether he was naively calling others into a course of action where the sacrifices being risked might be greater than he himself was prepared to bear.

"What will it profit a man, if he gains the whole world and forfeits his life?" (Matt. 16:26). "Whoever would save his life will lose it" (Matt. 16:25). Such brave and bold words staved off the disintegrating effects of temptation to abandon hope for the kindgom's coming, once news of John's arrest and imprisonment was followed by confirmation of his death. Even so, such sayings do not seem to carry one to the heart of Jesus' message. They simply show that Jesus gave expression to qualities that help account for his emergence as a leader in Israel, greater than John.

If we are to trust the earliest and most reliable tradition, Jesus saw himself in prophetic continuity with John in commitment to the call for national repentance in the face of the imminent coming of the kingdom (Matt. 11:7b-19). But Jesus saw himself in radical discontinuity with John regarding the basis for admission into the kingdom (Matt. 21:28-32). John's strictures against the moral laxities of the people were uncompromising, and the ostensible cause for his death was his denunciation of immorality in high places. With Jesus it was otherwise. The misdeeds of the wealthy and powerful did not seem to preoccupy him, though he was not unmindful of the plight of the rich (Matt. 19:23-24; Luke 16:19-31). Jesus came to save sinners, not to condemn them. As children of their Father in heaven, they in turn were counseled to love their enemies even as God loved his (Matt. 5:43-48). They were admonished not to put forgiveness on any calculated basis, but to forgive freely, boldly, unconditionally, and from the heart — not seven times, but seventy times seven (Matt. 18:21-35).

The fellowship of such a community of forgiven and forgiving sinners was poignant and joyful. "There will be more joy in heaven over one sinner who repents than over ninety-nine righteous persons who need no repentance" (Luke 15:7). Therefore, Jesus ate with sinners and celebrated their repentance (Luke 15:1-10). Such radical doctrine and practice was difficult to justify by legal precedent from Jewish scriptures. So revolutionary an attitude on the part of Jesus could only irritate authorities whose social importance rested upon their mastery of the exegetical intricacies of a life-encompassing legal system.

In this respect, the relationship of Jesus to the Pharisees calls for some clarification. Their opposition to his practice of admitting tax collectors and sinners into the intimacy of table fellowship was rooted in two distinguishable legal concerns. First, there were the explicit food laws, called kashrut, which forbade eating pork, a kid seethed in its mother's milk, meat with the blood still in it, and the like. These laws had governed the diet of Jews for centuries and served to keep them from eating with gentiles or other Jews who lived and ate like gentiles. Second, there was the purity code which, when applied to the laity, separated Jew from Jew socially. Such social separation was going on in the time of Jesus when some groups of Jews were applying the priestly purity code to the laity. The Jews who did this, called *haberim* in rabbinic sources, were eventually followed by the rabbis, who attempted to extend the provisions of the purity code to all Israelites.

Since gentiles were present in the Holy Land, righteous Jews were affected in different ways as far as eating was concerned. They sometimes found it helpful to band together to see that the *kashrut* laws were fully observed (and the purity code, too, when that was of concern to them). A common table where proper precautions regarding these laws were observed was in order among righteous Jews who, when away from home, could not depend upon this service being rendered by members of their respective families.

The admission of unrighteous Jews (those lax in their observance of the *kashrut* laws) into the table fellowship of those who were righteous was permitted at the discretion of the leaders of the group. Such admissions were defended on the grounds of *hesed* (covenantal love) and justified as a means of recruiting new members for the fellowship or for the renewal movement, as the case might be.

The Pharisees as righteous Jews, that is, as observants of the Law of Moses, including the *kashrut* laws, had no particular grounds for objecting to this practical way of facilitating the observance of the law within the wider community. To the extent that the Pharisees were looked to by the authorities, that is, the Roman-backed high priestly oligarchy, as the party best able to police the land in terms of observing the law, or to the extent that they were recognized by the people (and so perceived themselves) to be authorized by God to police the land, the Pharisees were nervous about any situation where the righteousness of those observing the law was being dangerously imputed to the unrighteous. (This is precisely what Jesus' acceptance of sinners at table fellowship implied.) Such nervousness could best be allayed by requiring a probationary period during which anyone seeking admission to an eating group could give evidence of a sincere intent to become truly and enduringly observant.

A scandalous feature of Jesus' admitting unrighteous Jews into the intimacy of his table fellowship was the absence of any fixed probationary period. The most liberal of the *haberim* required one month (Tosefta Demai 2:10-12) and the Essenes required two or three years.

Compared to the more established religious groups, then, Jesus' fellowship appeared dangerously subversive of that law upon whose strict observance the Pharisees placed such great importance. In any case, simple prudence dictated that the Pharisees take the precautionary step of warning righteous Jews who were most likely to heed their warnings. (Because of political restraints placed upon them that curtailed their zeal for the law, there was generally little the Pharisees could do against tax collectors and others who lived like gentiles, except to excommunicate them from their table fellowship.)

The Pharisees were certainly not the only righteous Jews in Palestine. The Qumran community constituted a haven for those who wanted to be right with God according to the Law of Moses. Doubtless there were other such righteous communities. But the special status of the Pharisees in the eyes of the people and their role in the power structure of the established world of Jewish piety, attested by Josephus, justify regarding some of the New Testament evidence about them as valid.

First, Paul was a Pharisee, and he was granted police power by Jewish authorities. He was not granted those powers because he was a Pharisee, but since he was a Pharisee he had credentials that stood him in good stead in carrying out his police duties. The local people present at the arrests Paul made, whose cooperation with the arresting authorities was important, knew that Paul was a Pharisee. Therefore they assented to his authority as derived from God, not from Rome. Second, Jesus recognized the Pharisees as righteous and alluded to them when his teaching required the example of a righteous person (for example, the parable of the tax collector and the Pharisee in the Temple). Third, Jesus perceived a difference between the righteousness practiced by the Pharisees and the obedience he taught his disciples to render to God. Fourth, Jesus at times came into conflict with the Pharisees, for example, over Sabbath observance and over his practice of admitting sinners into the intimacy of his table fellowship. This latter opposition possibly arose only in those cases where the sinners were guilty of notorious transgression, as with tax collectors. Finally, Jesus recognized that the Pharisees possessed authority to rule on the interpretation of the Law of Moses. Taken as a legal guild, however, their example discredited their ultimate authority as reliable exponents of God's requirements of his sons and daughters.

Whether Jesus is responsible for the woes against the Pharisees is an historical question affected by the source paradigm that is applied. According to the two-document hypothesis, Matthew 23 can be understood as an expanded Matthean construction representing development of tradition from Q, some of which was also known to Mark. On form-critical grounds, however, even assuming the two-document hypothesis, there is much against this view. The tradition preserved in Matthew 23 reflects the influence of oral tradition, Jewish and Palestinian in provenance. Regarding Matthew as the earliest of the extant Gospels removes all doubt about the Jewish-Christian and Palestinian origin of most if not all of the tradition in Matthew 23.

It is possible on form-critical grounds to reconstruct the more original form of the woes and to separate the tradition that has been added. Paul's own testimony of his attack upon the church fits the historical requirement of a kind of violent persecution which, when inflicted by some Pharisees upon some Christians, would explain these bitter additions. The woes themselves, however, may well be authentic to Jesus. They certainly are profoundly consonant with the best-attested sayings of Jesus.

Thus, it is clear that one can give a credible account of the importance of the Pharisees for understanding the New Testament, especially the importance of their opposition to Jesus' table fellowship with tax collectors and sinners, without settling the question as to the extent the purity code was being applied to all Israelites in the time of Jesus. Depending upon the extent that the purity code was applied and whether the Pharisees had any interest at all in gaining wide acceptance of it among the laity, Jesus' table fellowship with tax collectors and sinners could have been of added concern to the Pharisees. A concern would have been there in any case, based simply on the *kashrut* laws. It would not have been only the Pharisees' concern, but one shared by all righteous Jews, to one degree or another.

It was normative that righteous Jews not eat with sinners. As one who came in the way of righteousness, John had not eaten with sinners. But Jesus did. This marks a profound theological difference between John and Jesus (Matt. 11:16-19).

The objection of scribes and Pharisees to Jesus' practice of eating with tax collectors and sinners led to a major crisis for Jesus. Succumbing to pressure to abandon this practice would possibly have brought Jesus favor; instead, he struck at an important root of the problem--the self-righteousness of a scrupulous religious establishment.

Jesus represented the legal authorities' emphasis on minutiae of the law and their neglect of justice, mercy, and faith as the counsel of "blind guides" (Matt. 23:23-24). This, however, may be a caricature. In any case, Jesus himself came from a religious background so akin to Pharisaism as to command the respect of the Pharisees. Their anxiety over what he was doing may have been rooted in the perception that one of their own kind was endangering the interests of "the righteous." Jesus openly said that he did not come to call the righteous (Matt. 9:9-13). Although he himself was known as a righteous man, in eating with sinners Jesus was breaking down the barriers by which many righteous Jews maintained an inner group strength. This group strength was necessary to withstand external pressures to compromise religious scruples in the interests of achieving an improved economy and a more cosmopolitan society.

Jesus' table fellowship with tax collectors and sinners may not have been in the first instance the nucleus of a new community. Nevertheless, it was based upon the recognition that God is the father of all. Indeed, if a man has a hundred sheep and one goes astray, will he not leave the ninety-nine to search for the one that is lost? And having found it, will he not put it on his shoulder and bring it back rejoicing, and call to his friends, "Rejoice with me, for I have found my sheep which was lost" (Luke 15:3-6; cf. Matt. 18:10-14)? How much more will our heavenly Father rejoice over the return of a lost son (Luke 15:11- 24)? Therefore, how appropriate that we celebrate the repentance of those lost sons of Abraham who, once dead in trespasses, are now alive through God's merciful judgment (Luke 15:25-32, 19:1-10).

By such forceful imagery as this, Jesus defended his practice of table fellowship with tax collectors and sinners. Parables like the one about the lost son and his elder brother (Luke 15:11-32) or the laborers in the vineyard (Matt. 20:1-16) were first created in response to this crisis in Jesus' ministry. They were used to defend the gospel of God's unmerited and unconditional acceptance of the repentant sinner. Similarly, the parable about the great banquet (Matt. 22:1-10; Luke 14: 16-24) served to remind the righteous that they had no ground for complaint over the eschatological acceptance of sinners since they themselves had turned their backs on the kingdom (cf. Matt. 23;13).

These parables in themselves were probably not intended to alienate the scribes and Pharisees, but to forestall their inquisitorial activity among the disciples. Nor is a parable like that of the Pharisee and the tax collector in the Temple (Luke 18-9-14) designed to hurt rather than to heal. The Pharisee in the parable does not represent all Pharisees and certainly not the ideal Pharisee. But to make his point that goodness can become demonic and destructive when it leads good men to isolate themselves from others, Jesus chose a man from one of the most virtuous circles of Jewish society. If such a man, no matter how moral, places his trust in his own righteousness and despises others, he goes from the house of God to his own house in a wrong relationship to God.

However, a sinner who places his or her trust in the mercy of God goes home in a right relationship to God.

The love God has for the sinner shows no lack of love for the righteous. "All that is mine is yours," says the father to his elder son, but "it was fitting to make merry and be glad, for this your brother was dead, and is alive; he was lost, and is found" (Luke 15:31-32). This noble and heartfelt sentiment did not go completely unheeded, but lodged itself within the collective unconscious of the Pharisaic community, there to work its way inexorably against every tendency toward hard-heartedness, within the ranks of the righteous. Subsequently, the elder brother, a strict Pharisee, while persecuting the church, was won over by the powerful reality of God's love. He became a staunch defender of what some regarded as an illicit table fellowship, but which he himself saw as being at the heart of the gospel for which Jesus had died (Gal. 2:11-21).

In spite of the cogency of Jesus' defense of the gospel of God's mercy toward repentant sinners, opposition from the religious establishment stiffened. In this period of opposition by religious authorities responsible for upholding the law in the towns and cities outside Jerusalem, Jesus formulated his woes against the "scribes and Pharisees." These utterances are uncompromising. By this time the issue had become clear; Israel was at the crossroads. The people could either follow those whom Jesus characterized as "blind guides," who hypocritically held in their hands the keys of the kingdom but who neither entered themselves nor allowed others to enter (Matt. 23:13), or they could follow Jesus. Irony turned to bitter sarcasm in the judgment: "Woe to you, scribes and Pharisees, hypocrites! For you build the tombs of prophets and adorn the monuments of the righteous, saying, 'If we had lived in the days of our fathers, we would not have taken part with them in shedding the blood of the prophets'" (Matt. 23:29-30). You hypocrites, Jesus said, because in so speaking you condemn yourselves as among those who murder prophets. For as you disassociate yourselves from those who have done evil and vainly imagine that had you been in their place you would not have committed the sins they committed, you show yourselves to be the very kind of self-righteous persons who will condone the killing of those God sends us as his messengers.

Uncompromising words like these have sealed the fate of Jesus. By their use he unmasked what many in positions of privilege and power could not bear to have unmasked. Jesus penetrated the facade of goodness behind which persons hid their lust for power. He represented them to be like "whitewashed tombs, which outwardly appear beautiful, but within ... are full of dead men's bones" (Matt. 23:27).

After invective like this, the legal authorities were beside themselves to find some charge on which to get rid of Jesus. The compliance of high priestly circles and the rest of the Jerusalem oligarchy was assured once Jesus made it clear that he called for changes not only in men's hearts, but in the institutions of Zion — specifically within the central institution, the Temple itself (Matt. 21:12-13).

With the Pharisees, the high priests, and the elders of the people in concert, the Roman authorities, had they insisted on due process, would have risked a tear in the delicately woven fabric of political collaboration. This collaboration enabled Rome to maintain viable control over a key sector in the defensive perimeter of its frontier with the Parthians, who were an ever-present threat to the stability of the eastern provinces. Ostensibly, in the interest of maintaining Jewish law and Roman order, Jesus was executed. This was done in spite of the fact that Jesus programmatically insisted that he came "not to destroy the law, but to fulfill it" (Matt. 5:17). Moreover, Jesus taught his disciples that unless their righteousness exceeded that of the scribes and Pharisees, they would never enter the Kingdom of Heaven (Matt. 5:20). Yet it can hardly be doubted that in fulfilling the "law and the prophets," Jesus ran afoul of the scribes and Pharisees. This occurred not only when he ate with tax collectors and sinners, but also in regard to other matters as, for example, the Sabbath observance (Matt. 12:1-8; Luke 14:5). Jesus certainly challenged Jewish legal authority and, as for Roman order, it was to be replaced by the Kingdom of Heaven. So the die had been cast well in advance. While Jesus died a righteous man by the standards of the Kingdom of Heaven, he did not go to his cross innocent of breaking the law as it was represented by the mores of the local populace. Nor was he innocent of disturbing the peace as it was preserved in and through imperial order. He was crucified in the end by the Romans as a political criminal. We can imagine the mixed feelings of anguish and relief on the part of responsible Jewish authorities. Yet we are not in a position to know with any degree of certainty the motives of the principals who were involved in his death.

This outline of essential developments between the death of John and the death of Jesus illustrates how tradition originating with Jesus, which is preserved in the Gospels, can be set within the context of his life situation. The tradition can be seen to come alive against the historical background of the Jews in Palestine when Herod Agrippa was Tetrarch of Galilee and Perea, when John the Baptist had been preaching a baptism of repentance in the Jordan valley, and when Pontius Pilate was procurator of Judea.

In retrospect, on the basis of what can be supported by historical inquiry, is it possible to say something about the character of Jesus and about his public ministry? Jesus' character is the mark he left or "engraved" upon his disciples, including the tax collectors and sinners he admitted into the intimacy of his table fellowship. This fellowship heard Jesus gladly and remembered his words and actions. Members of this fellowship took responsibility for formulating and handing on to the earliest churches such authentic sayings of Jesus as in fact have been preserved in the Gospels.

To the degree that the understanding of life expressed in these authentic sayings was actually represented by Jesus in his own life situation, that is, through his words and actions — to this degree it is possible to speak about the character of Jesus. Confining the inquiry to that nucleus of sayings which beyond a reasonable doubt can be accepted as authentic sayings of Jesus, it is possible to conclude the following: in rebuking self-righteousness and chiding those who resented God's mercy toward sinners, Jesus disclosed something about the kind of person he was. He can be seen as a public figure in relationship to other figures. His contemporaries could understand his human concern for others, and many were moved by it. They saw not only his friendship for tax collectors and sinners, but more. They saw a concern for community.

Pretentiousness and self-righteousness on the part of individuals or groups is one of the most serious corrupting influences affecting the health and integrity of communal existence. Individual and collective self-righteousness on the part of authorities, when unchallenged, is like a hard cement by which outmoded and unjust ecclesiastical, economic, political, and social structures are kept defensible in the face of justified opposition from advocates of social or religious reforms. Privileged individuals or castes are secure only so long as it is possible for society to perceive their positions of privilege as clothed with the garments of righteousness. To pull aside these garments and to expose hypocrisy and abuse is a revolutionary act of a most radical nature.

Jesus exposed hypocrisy and abuse. For him to rebuke the prideful self-righteousness of religious authorities was to strike at an important source of contra-redemptive influence in his own life situation and to encourage the continuation of the individual and covenantal renewal that was taking place in response to his preaching. Those whom Jesus had helped to perceive themselves as sinners dependent upon the un- merited grace of God were glad to know that he not only received sin- ners, but defended this action when it was criticized. And insofar as it was possible, they were moved to go and do likewise.

There was in this compassionate but disconcerting stance of Jesus a dynamic source of redemptive power which worked against the at- tempt of the established world of Jewish piety to structure human ex- istence on the exclusive ground of the mosaic covenant. Such a source of power provided the basis for a distinctive style of life wherein Jesus and his disciples worked joyfully for a reconciling mode of human ex- istence open to God's grace and to a future conditioned by (1) sin and the expectation of God's imminent destruction of sinners; (2) the un- bounded sovereign love of God; and (3) a faith which led them to sub- mit to the judgment of God and to trust themselves utterly to the mercy that was intrinsic to and inherent in God's love. This is a style of life grounded in God's sovereign love which results in a new creation (Paul), and being born again (John). Jesus likened this new style of life to "becoming like a child."

This personal structuring and restructuring of their historical exist- ence, this shaping of the realities of their human environment, and the compassion and joy associated with this creative stance sustained and gave theological depth and direction to their fellowship. Clearly there is more to Jesus than this. But this understanding of his public career and character carries the investigator to the very heart of what can be shown as both essential and enduring in Jesus.

# Crisis in Christology

# 12

# THE HISTORICITY OF THE SYNOPTIC GOSPELS

## James D.G. Dunn

Although New Testament scholarship is already well into the second generation beyond Rudolf Bultmann, the study of the Gospels continues to be largely influenced by the tremendous impact of his work — and particularly on the matter under discussion, the historicity of the Gospels. Bultmann's impact is still felt at two points in particular — two points of principle which largely governed his own analyses.

(a) The first can be summed up in the distinction between the Jesus of history and the Christ of faith. That is to say, the conviction that the first Christians were not really concerned with the earthly Jesus; the life and expression of faith focused rather on the exalted Christ. Jesus was not remembered as a teacher of the past (even of the recent past), but as the living Lord of the here and now. Only so can we make sense of the fact that Paul and the other letter writers in the New Testament show no interest whatsoever in the life of Jesus as such, and bother to quote only a minimal handful of sayings spoken by Jesus during his earthly ministry. As has often been observed, if we had to depend on the letters of Paul for our knowledge of Jesus' life and ministry, we could write it all down on the back of a postcard — descended from David, meek and gentle, two sayings about divorce and support for evangelists, the institution of the Lord's Supper, his suffering and atoning death — and that's about it.

(b) The second principle is one of the basic axioms of form-criticism — that the tradition preserved in the Gospels reflects first and foremost the life-setting of the early Church rather than that of Jesus. The literary forms in which the Jesus tradition is now set are the forms used by the early churches in their worship, evangelism, catechetical training and apologetic. So they reflect primarily these concerns, and not those of a merely historical or archival interest in Jesus.

When these two principles are put together, the almost inevitable conclusion is that the Gospels cannot be taken as immediate or direct evidence for the life and teaching of Jesus. Despite appearances, the Gospels do not reflect a desire to remember Jesus as he was and what he said while on earth. The material they contain is testimony first and foremost to the early Christian faith in Christ as crucified, risen and ascended Lord. The traditions they contain have been shaped by that faith and in accordance with the needs of the believing communities. This does not mean that Gospel tradition cannot be traced back to "the historical Jesus." But it does mean that the traditions have almost certainly been shaped and elaborated and added to — Bultmann would say, considerably added to — in the light of the Easter faith and in response to the changing needs of the Christian congregations.

The practical effect of this conclusion can be most simply stated in "burden of proof" terms. According to this logic the burden of proof lies with those who want to maintain that some particular tradition or saying goes back to Jesus. Given the two principles just outlined, it can no longer be simply assumed that a passage in any Gospel is historical until proved otherwise. Rather it must be recognized primarily as an expression of the faith of the early Church. For it to be accepted as evidence of something Jesus said or did, a case has to be argued. The burden of proof lies with those who want to argue for historicity.

This outcome has some unfortunate consequences. For one thing it tends to make a New Testament scholar uneasy when he cites some text as evidence of what Jesus said or did, lest he be thought to handle the text too simplistically or superficially. So in order to justify his use of a text he has to engage in an elaborate analysis and discussion. To the layperson he appears to be devious and embarrassed about something straightforward. This in turn increases the Christian layperson's suspicion of scholarship. It appears to be systematically skeptical and unbelieving. Thus the breach between the lectern and the pew becomes deeper and wider, with the poor occupant of the pulpit often caught uncomfortably in the middle. Such polarization between faith and scholarship benefits no one.

But it need not be so! Insofar as both faith and scholarship are concerned with truth, they should be allies, not enemies. And in fact there need be no such polarization over this issue. Not by rejecting the Bultmann legacy wholesale. That would simply create a new polarization. But by retaining the best insights in the Bultmann legacy while eliminating the over-statements. We can do this most simply be developing two main points — picking up only a few aspects in the time available.

1. The probability that the first Christians were keen to retain and to pass on memories of Jesus' ministry.

    (a) There is a basic plausibility in the assertion that the earliest disciples must have been interested in stories about Jesus and in what he said. Whatever we think of Jesus, it is hardly open to question that he made a profound impact on his immediate followers. We need not become involved in complex christological questions in order to recognize Jesus as the founder of a new religious movement. In terms of human nature as we know it today, it would have been very unusual indeed if the followers of such a leader had not been concerned to preserve memories of the exploits and utterances which first drew them to him and sustained their loyalty to him.

    The claim should not be exaggerated, of course. It is not universally true. We see it borne out to some extent at least in the case of other significant religious or philosophical figures like Jeremiah or Socrates or Diogenes. But it is not true of the mysterious Teacher of Righteousness in the Dead Sea Scrolls about whom we know virtually nothing. On the other hand, there were two factors operative in the case of Jesus, which were not present in regard to the Teacher of Righteousness, and which would go a long way towards quickening the element of "human interest" in Jesus.

    The first is the degree to which Jesus himself featured as part of the earliest Christian proclamation.

Jesus was not remembered merely as one who had provided a system of teaching or a philosophy or a spirituality, which could be preserved and practiced without reference to the original teacher. It is true that the focus of evangelistic preaching centered very strongly on the end events of his life on earth (death and resurrection). Nevertheless, it would be surprising indeed if the disciples had not looked to Jesus' own earlier ministry and pattern of teaching and life-style to provide some kind of guidelines for their own life of faith.

The second is the fact that Christianity from the beginning was an evangelistic faith. It did not withdraw into the desert as a closed sect where all the members would know the facts of its founding and there would be no need to record them. From the first it sought to gain converts, and very soon converts from further afield than Palestine, including Gentiles. Human curiosity being what it is, most of these converts would almost certainly have wanted to hear more about the Jesus in whom they had believed.

In short, on a priori grounds it is more likely than not that the first Christians were concerned to preserve memories of Jesus and to inform their converts of them. Of course, an a priori argument like this does not take us very far unless it is backed up by actual evidence. But in this case there is such evidence.

(b) It is clear that in the earliest Christian communities an important role was filled by teachers and tradition. Luke characterizes the earliest Jerusalem church from Pentecost onwards as devoting themselves to "the teaching of the apostles" (Acts 2.42). And the importance of teachers is strongly attested elsewhere. In the earliest church at Antioch the two most prominent ministries were prophets and teachers (Acts 13.1). In 1 Cor 12.28 Paul takes it for granted that teachers are next in importance in the life of the church to apostles and prophets. And in one of the earliest documents in the New Testament it is already assumed that the teacher must spend so much time on his task that he will have to depend for support on those he teaches (Gal 6.6).

The task of a teacher, almost by definition, would have been to preserve and instruct in the matters regarded as important by the community. It is in very large measure a conserving function. In the case of the Christian congregations, the teaching in question would not simply have been about the Torah. They would be responsible, no doubt, to search the scriptures for prophecies regarding Jesus. But instruction about Jesus, about what he said and did, must have played a prominent part in their teaching. In sociological terms, the teacher in a sect plays an absolutely crucial role in consolidating and preserving the sect's self identity, by recalling the sect to its distinctive character and to the reasons for its separate identity. Unless we wish to argue that Jesus' life prior to his death was undistinctive (but then why was he crucified?), we must accept the probability that the earliest Christian teachers were charged with the task of preserving and retelling the distinctive features of Jesus' ministry which first drew disciples to him.

This is confirmed by the prominence given to *tradition* in the earliest churches. The earliest Christian writer, Paul, speaks on a number of occasions about the traditions he passed on to his churches (1 Cor 11.2; 15.3; Col 2.6; 1 Thes 4.1; 2 Thes 2.15; 3.6). He clearly saw this as an important part of the task of an apostle — to ensure that the congregations he founded were properly informed of the traditions which characterized the Christian churches. These must have included the founding traditions which all Christian communities shared as part of their common heritage and which marked them off from other sects and synagogues. And since Paul was adamant that his understanding of the gospel was received first and foremost from God and not man (Gal 1.11-12), the traditions he refers to cannot simply have been the proclamation of Jesus' death and resurrection itself, but must at least have included stories about and teaching of Jesus.

This is further borne out by Paul's own testimony that three years after his conversion he went up to Jerusalem "to visit Peter' (Gal 1.18). The verb used means more precisely, "to get to know, find out about." Since Peter was best known as the most prominent of Jesus' disciples, and as one of the "inner circle" (Peter, James and John) who evidently had been closest to Jesus, getting to know him must have included learning about his time with Jesus. And since "he stayed with Peter for fifteen days" he would certainly have been able to learn a great deal — including stories of what Jesus did and said when Peter was present. It is scarcely conceivable that such traditions were not included by Paul among the traditions he passed on to the churches he founded.

It would be odd indeed to imagine Christian congregations meeting throughout the eastern Mediterranean, who in their regular gatherings were concerned only with the study of the (Jewish) scriptures, with the message of Jesus' death and resurrection, and with waiting on the risen Lord — and who were quite unconcerned to recall and reflect on the ministry and teaching of Jesus while on earth. On the contrary, it was precisely these memories and traditions which they were most likely to want to share and celebrate together — the founding traditions which gave them their distinctive identity.

(c) All this can be deduced without looking at the Gospels themselves. When we do turn to them, these plausible but still provisional conclusions are confirmed. For the Synoptic Gospels in particular contain just the sort of traditions about Jesus which we would expect the early Christian teachers to take responsibility for preserving and passing on. I refer, first of all, to the nature of the Gospels as *biographies of Jesus*.

Bultmann himself was strongly of the view that the Gospels should not be regarded as biographies. To understand why, we must remember that he was in fact reacting strongly against his own theological education. It was one of the fashions in the heyday of Liberal Protestantism in the latter decades of the 19th century, to write lives of Jesus, with the Gospels treated as sources for a modern biographical study. That is to say, these Lives of Jesus felt free to reconstruct a fairly detailed chronological outline of his life and ministry, to speculate about Jesus' inner life and to discuss the development of his self-consciousness. Bultmann saw this as a complete misunderstanding of the character of the Gospels. They were *not* biographies!

What he meant, or should have said, was that they are not *modern* biographies. Unfortunately this qualification was not recognized and the blanket dictum (the Gospels are not biographies) became a basic axiom in most form-critical studies for the next two generations. It seemed to confirm rather neatly the two-fold assumption outlined at the beginning: the earliest Christians were interested only in the exalted Christ and their own contemporary needs. They had no biographical interest in Jesus as he had been prior to his death and resurrection.

In fact, however, the Synoptic Gospels conform quite closely to the form and function of the *ancient* biography. The nearest parallel in the Greco-Roman world to the genre of Gospel is the *bios* or *vita* ("life"). Whereas modern biography has a central concern with personality development and the chronological framework within which it occurs, ancient biography had a much more static concept of personality and only rarely expressed interest in such development. On the contrary, human personality was thought of as fixed and unchanging. Moreover, a deeply rooted assumption of the ancients was that a person's character was clearly revealed in his actions and words. Consequently it was the principal task of the biographer to portray his subject by relating things he did and said, and thus to depict his character.

But this is very much what we find in the gospels. No particular or at least consistent concern with chronology. And certainly no attempt to describe development in Jesus' character or self-understanding. But a thoroughgoing attempt to portray Jesus by means of what he said and what he did. In terms of the categories of the time, therefore, the Gospels, or the Synoptic Gospels in particular, can be described as biographies. And precisely as such they indicate a considerable concern on the part of the Evangelists to recall and record Jesus as his first disciples remembered him.

(d) Finally, we may reflect a little further on the character of the Synoptic Gospels as *collections of oral memories about Jesus*. This is one of the most positive features of the form-critical approach. It has made us much more conscious of the period of oral tradition which lies *behind* the written Gospels, the tradition as it was being used *before* it was written down. Such an awareness immediately relieves us from over-dependence on arguments about the precise dates of the Gospels. Whatever dates we determine for the Gospels it is hardly to be disputed that the earliest Christian churches were *oral* communities before the Gospels were written. And, as already noted, as with all oral societies then and since, they would inevitably have sought to retain and express their founding traditions, for it was these traditions which justified and explained (to themselves as to others) the reasons for their separate and distinctive existence. And not only to retain these traditions, but to retell them too, to seek and create opportunities to rehearse and celebrate their sacred tradition. So the Jews have celebrated the Passover for millennia. So the Qumran community preserved its Damascus Document. And so the first Christians no doubt recalled and relived the events of the last days of Jesus' life in the memories which now form the passion narratives in particular.

Equally important, the recognition of the oral character of so much at least of the tradition used in the Gospels, frees us from an over-dependence on arguments based solely on literary dependence. Despite the recognition of an oral period of the Jesus tradition, too many Gospel analysts have continued their task as though the relationships between the Gospels could be understood solely in terms of literary sources — of a scissors and paste type of editing. As though the traditions used by Mark, for example, ceased to exist as oral traditions all over the eastern Mediterranean, simply because Mark writing in Rome, say, had written them down! But of course Matthew and Luke, assuming they had copies of Mark to hand, also had access to oral tradition, including oral versions of much of what Mark had recorded. When churches in Syria, for example, received their copies of Mark's Gospel, that was hardly the first time they had heard much or most of what Mark contains.

Being made thus alert to the oral background of the gospel traditions, it becomes fairly easy to spot characteristics which were probably first oral before they were literary, for example, the "pronouncement story," where the episode related builds up to a memorable saying of Jesus as its climax; or the account of some encounter, as between Jesus and the centurion in Matthew 8, where the central focus is clearly the snatch of dialogue between the centurion and Jesus, and the other details are clearly subsidiary to that. Story tellers the world over will recognize the basic rule of thumb of good story telling — to get the punch-line right, whatever else. Another example would be the use of link-words or linking themes: for example, the words "fire" and "salt" which link together the final verses of Mark 9; and or again, the way Matthew uses the theme of "following" to tie together the sayings about discipleship with the account of the disciples being caught in a storm on Galilee -- an effective way of illustrating what "following Jesus" will mean for the would-be disciple.

Mark's Gospel itself has many "oral" features, and may be fairly described as oral tradition written down. Indeed, bearing in mind that Mark would write his Gospel to be read out loud, the Gospel itself can properly be regarded as an extended oral presentation of the traditions of Jesus, little different in character from the many celebrations of the new movement's "founding traditions." I think in particular of Mark 1.21-39, structured on the pattern of "twenty-four hours in the ministry of Jesus;" or 2.1-3.6, a collection of controversy stories, charting the areas of disagreement between Jesus and groups of Pharisees, and building up dramatically to the climax of the complete breach between them; or chapter 4, on the theme of Jesus' parables, illustrating and expounding their rationale; or 4.35- 5.43, a collection of miracle stories on and around the Sea of Galilee, and linked together by the motif of crossing back and forth "to the other side." And not to forget Mark's own characteristic "immediately" — immediately Jesus did this, or immediately he went there — which keeps the tale told by Mark moving along at a brisk pace and never allows the listener's attention to wander.

The point is this. The gospel traditions themselves show that their present form is the outcome of a well established practice of oral use. In other words, they bear witness to a strong and widely prevalent concern among the first Christians to remember Jesus, to celebrate their memories, to retain them in appropriate forms, to structure their traditions for easy recall, but above all to remember.

In short, the idea that the first Christians were *not* interested in the pre-Easter Jesus is little short of ludicrous. On the contrary, they would certainly have been concerned that the memories of "all that Jesus said and did" should be passed on to new converts and re-told in new churches. The "biographical" interest of the Evangelists, in portraying the character of Jesus by recounting his words and deeds, did not begin first with them. In the concern of the new congregations to formulate and celebrate their founding traditions, it was no doubt there from the first. In balance of proof terms, it is this recognition which should be the start-ing point of investigation of the Synoptic traditions of Jesus' ministry.

2. *We can also see HOW the first Christians passed on the traditions about Jesus and gain a clearer perspective on what their concern to remember Jesus meant in terms of historicity.*

In the first chapter of **The Evidence for Jesus** (SCM/ Westminster 1985) I have discussed and documented this topic in some detail and so may be permitted here to treat it more briefly. The point is this. The recognition of the oral character of the Synoptic tradition, also involves recogni-tion of a degree of freedom on the part of the story teller, to shape his material with a view to the needs of his audience. Often and again the story teller or teacher will have been concerned more with themes and high points of the tradi-tion being used, than with details he would regard as sub-sidiary to these themes and high points. He will have grouped his material in order to illustrate a theme rather than to preserve a chronological sequence. He will have told his story in a longer or shorter version depending on time available. He will have slanted his account in detail or tone so that it might better serve the needs of the group to which he ministered.

None of this cuts across what has already been said. The probability that the first Christians were concerned to retain and pass on the memory of what Jesus said and did remains undiminished. What we are now looking at is *how* they did so. We can illustrate the character of these orally recounted memories by simply comparing our own Synoptic Gospels, since, as we have seen, their contents consist in large part of oral traditions written down.

(a) For one thing they grouped the traditions in different ways. As is well know, the material which makes up the Sermon on the Mount in Matthew 5-7 is scattered throughout four or so of Luke's chapters. And for the most part it is clearly the same material. The most likely explanation of this phenomenon is not that Luke broke up and scattered Matthew's Sermon, but that Matthew has constructed the Sermon by grouping together elements of Jesus' teaching which were actually delivered at different points during his ministry. This is simply good teaching technique — to group coherent and complementary material together to make it easier to remember. In fact, Matthew seems to have made some attempt to group almost all of Jesus' teaching into five blocks, probably as a sort of echo of the five books of Moses. If this is indeed the case, the point which bears upon us is that the grouping of this material was determined by teaching technique rather than by historical considerations.

In particular, it is unlikely that Matthew intended his readers to think of the Sermon on the Mount as actually delivered by Jesus on a single occasion. He has simply constructed a framework in which to set these important memories of what Jesus said — a quite understandable and acceptable teaching device which would have misled no one. In short, such an example confirms the earliest Christians' concern, to preserve and pass on the memory of what Jesus had said, by grouping it in easily rememberd form. To insist that the framework be accorded the same historical status as the content of the Sermon, is probably to misconceive the character of the remembering process and to misunderstand the intention of Matthew.

(b) Secondly, we may note examples where the Evangelists preserve the same account but in different lengths or with different emphases. The account of Jesus' disciples plucking ears of grain on the sabbath is a case in point (Mark 2.23-28 pars). Matthew and Mark both have material in their versions which is found in neither of the other Gospels. It is clearly the same incident in each case, but in each case the story teller has either abbreviated a longer tale or expanded a briefer tale. Another example is the story of Jairus' daughter and the woman with the hemorrhage (Mark 5.21-43 pars). Luke's version is twice as long as Matthew's and Mark's nearly three times as long. Again either one has abbreviated a fuller account, or another has lengthened a briefer account. This is the art of story telling — not to reproduce an account always in the same words and with parrot-like precision, but as the needs of occasion and audience may demand.

An example of an episode from Jesus' life retold with different emphasis is the account of the healing of the centurion's servant (Matt 8.5-13/Luke 7.1-10). As already noted, the focus is on the exchange between Jesus and the centurion, but the build up to that central section is rather different in each case. In Matthew's briefer version the centurion meets Jesus and addresses him personally; it would appear from the rest of the account that this is partly because Matthew wants to stress the immediacy of the centurion's faith. Luke, however, in his longer introduction emphasizes the fact that the centurion did not come to Jesus personally but sent others; and it is clear from the details Luke includes that he wants to stress the centurion's humility. It is certainly the same event which is thus related in these two different ways, but the accompanying details were evidently less important than the central exchange and need not be recounted with the same precision. As in all good story telling, the story is lost if the main point is distorted or forgotten, but the subsidiary details can be modified without spoiling the story or misleading the listeners.

Another example would be the account of Peter's denial of Jesus (Mark 14.66-72 pars). What was important was the fact that Peter denied Jesus no less than three times, and that when he heard the cock crow he remembered Jesus' prediction and wept. The details which go to make up that vivid story are less important — who it was who accused Peter, whether the cock crowed once or twice. The accusers are indicated with casual, vague descriptions, which show that it was not part of the story teller's purpose to identify the who and the when with precision — "a maid," "someone else," "the bystanders." To insist that these details can be pressed to yield firm historical facts is to misconceive the purpose of the Evangelists and to distort their emphasis. It is like insisting that symbolical language be understood literally, or a hymn be read as prose.

(c) Thirdly, it is also clear that the words of Jesus could be remembered in different versions. This, of course, would be inevitable to some extent at least, since translation was often involved. Words of Jesus spoken in Aramaic would be translated into Greek, and since no translation can produce a complete set of precise equivalents, in word or idiom, it is inevitable that different Greek renderings of Jesus' words would be in circulation. What was important was the sense of what Jesus had said, not a precision of verbal form. And in order to express that sense, the translation might need to be longer than the original, with some explanatory expansion to make an unfamiliar idiom clear. Anyone familiar with the range of modern translations of the Bible will take the point without difficulty.

We see something of this even with two of the most precious and most used of Jesus' words. As is well known, the Lord's Prayer comes to us in two versions — Matt 6.9-15 and Luke 11.2-4. As the prayer taught by Jesus, to serve as the special prayer and badge of Jesus' disciples, we might have thought great care would have been taken to keep the words the same for all. But Matthew's version has the longer address — "Our Father, who art in heaven" — whereas Luke simply has "Father." And Matthew has two more petitions than Luke, although they seem chiefly to fill out the preceding petitions. Luke's version is generally thought to be closer to the original in length, while Matthew is closer in idiom. What has probably happened is that Luke's translation has not been at pains to reproduce the Aramaic idiom, while Matthew's version has been elaborated in the course of earliest Christian usage — to make it more rounded and easier to say in congregational worship. We see the same thing continuing thereafter with the addition of the now familiar ending at a still later stage — "For thine is the kingdom, and the power, and the glory. Amen." This is just the sort of polishing and refining we would expect in liturgical usage. After all, Jesus had given them a prayer to use, and use it they did. It was intended to serve as their prayer, not just as a memory of something Jesus had said. And in being thus used, its details changed a little, without changing the sense, in order to serve more effectively as their prayer. The process is no different today. In a day when there are three or four English versions of the Matthew 6 prayer, we can understand and appreciate well enough the concerns and priorities of the first bearers of the tradition.

The other example is the words of Jesus at the Last Supper (Mark 14.22-25 pars; 1 Cor 11.24-25). As is well know, here also the tradition comes to us in two main forms — a Matthew/Mark version and a Paul/Luke version. One of the principal differences comes in the word over the cup. According to Matthew and Mark, Jesus says, "This is my blood of the covenant." According to Paul and Luke, Jesus says, "This cup is the new covenant in my blood." The sense is more or less the same, but the emphasis is slightly different. Here too, even in what was probably one of the most precious words of Jesus, there was no attempt to preserve strict conformity. The sense was more important that the form. So too it is probably significant that only Paul's version adds the command, "Do this, as often as you drink it, in remembrance of me." Probably a further example of liturgical polishing — the spelling out explicitly of what was understood to be implied in the shorter formula.

In these cases what we see is tradition not merely being remembered, but tradition used. And tradition valued not simply because it was first given by Jesus, but because it continued to provide a medium of encounter between the divine and the human. Just so, we might say, with the psalms of the Old Testament. They were treasured down through the generations not simply because they were composed by David or Asaph or whoever, but because they continued to serve as an inspired means of worship and of grace.

(d) Finally, this insight probably helps provide an answer to the problem mentioned at the beginning: the fact that the earliest New Testament author (Paul) seems to have been so little concerned to refer his readers to what Jesus said and did. The fact is that there are a good many exhortations in Paul where he is most probably echoing words originally given by Jesus and remembered for that reason. Romans 12-14 and 1 Thessalonians 5 contain a number of examples. The point is that Paul used the Jesus tradition in this way presumably because he saw it as living tradition, valued not merely because it had spoken to them in the past, but because it still spoke to them with the force of inspired authority. Paul spoke it afresh, not because it had been heard as the word of God twenty years earlier, but because he still heard and experienced it as the living word of God there and then.

On this point we can see a parallel with the way the Old Testament scriptures were heard and functioned as authority. Of course there are very many instances where an Old Testament scripture is cited as such, regularly with the formula, "as it was written" or equivalent. However, there are very many more instances where there is not explicit citation as such, but where the scripture has clearly influenced and molded the words and images used. In such cases, we may say, the scripture has exercised its authority in shaping the thought and language of the New Testament author. No doubt in many cases without conscious intention. The scripture has functioned authoritatively, and that authority stems from the original inspiration, but it has been experienced as a living authority and not as a casual echo of a dead past.

So with the memory of what Jesus said and did. We have already noted how probable it is that the material contained in the Synoptic Gospels was fairly widely known in the earliest Christian congregations. The fact that Paul makes so little explicit reference to it almost certainly means that he could take knowledge of it for granted. Now we may add that he could also make allusion to the Jesus tradition, just as he often made allusion to Old Testament scripture, and for the same reason. The words of Jesus were not merely remembered but experienced afresh as words of the Lord. This sense of a living tradition is crucial for our understanding of the earliest handing on and use of the corporate memories of Jesus. For the first Christians the words of Jesus were not like some dead corpse, with limbs stiffened and fixed by rigor mortis, to be conveyed from place to place like some revered relics, but a living voice which was heard again and again speaking with ever new force and effect in a variety of fresh situations.

In all these areas illustrated above, there are many other and often more complex cases. But hopefully sufficient has been said to give a clear enough flavor of the character of the earliest Christian remembering of Jesus in his life and ministry.

*To sum up*. It is clear from all this that the earliest Christians were concerned to remember Jesus and to pass on these memories to new converts and churches. But again and again it is equally clear that they were more concerned with the substance and meaning of what Jesus had said and done than with a meticulous level of verbal precision or with a pedantic level of historical detail. It is important to recognize the force of both points. To underestimate the former is to cut Christianity off from its historical foundation and fountainhead. But to misplace the emphasis in the latter stands in equal danger of distorting the concerns of the first Christians. The Synoptic tradition as history — Yes, indeed! — but the Gospels also as the living tradition of the earliest churches — that too.

We therefore can make the strong and confident affirmation that the Synoptic Gospels are a source of historical information about Jesus; the Evangelists were concerned with the historicity of what they remembered; in burden of proof terms we can start from the assumption that the Synoptic tradition is a good witness to the historical Jesus unless proved otherwise. But we must be careful not to overstate our case. To claim that the Evangelists had the same level of historical concern in every phrase and sentence they used, runs counter to the evidence and almost certainly misunderstands their intention. Equally serious, such a claim *undermines* the case for the historicity of the Gospels, since it makes that case depend on a series of implausible harmonizations. Properly to recognize the Evangelists' concern for historicity in their own terms, means recognizing also their other concerns and above all the character of that earliest remembering as a living word.

# 13

# JESUS, THE MESSIAH OF ISRAEL
## The Debate about the
## "Messianic Mission" of Jesus

### Martin Hengel
### (Translated by Paul A. Cathey)

## 1. Χριστός in Paul

Paul, the earliest Christian author, gives Jesus the name "Christos" 270 times. A few texts may retain, at most, a glimmer of its titular use in the sense of Messiah, "The Anointed One," but as a rule the compound name Ἰησοῦς Χριστός has completely absorbed the title ὁ χριστός — there is only one Χριστός, this very Jesus who was crucified. The title has become fully a part of the name.

In Paul's bible, the LXX, the situation is very different. There the verbal adjective χριστός, translates מָשִׁיחַ, the Anointed One, some 37 times — the Anointed of God, i.e., either the king or the priest.

For a Greek, however, χριστός would not have been used with reference to persons. The neutral χριστόν meant "rubbing ointment," and νεόχριστος "newly plastered."[1] The new name Χριστός was so unusual that non-Jews confused it with the common slave name Χρῆστος.[2]

This Χριστός as a personal name for Jesus was already in use long before the letters of Paul, e.g., in Rome, and above all in Antioch, where barely 10 years after the death of Jesus the Christians were described as Χριστιανοί. This means that they changed the title "The Anointed One" into a name within an astonishingly brief period, and thereby usurped it exclusively for their Lord, Jesus of Nazareth.

Accordingly, we find several times in Paul the formula, "Christ died for us."[3] We can still discern in this formula traces of the originally titular meaning, for at the center of the new message was this: it was the sinless *Messiah*, the eschatological emissary and saviour — not merely a suffering righteous man or prophet — who sacrificed his life "for the many." Thus Paul speaks of "[the] Christ crucified" as the content of his preaching. The bipartite form of the name, the familiar Ἰησοῦς Χριστός, as well as the Χριστὸς Ἰησοῦς preferred by Paul, were originally formulaic confessions. Ἰησοῦς Χριστός derives from ישׁוע משׁיחא, Jesus the Messiah, whereas Χριστὸς Ἰησοῦς originally was probably used analogously to the cry of acclamation κύριος Ἰησοῦς.

That Paul was perfectly acquainted with the Old Testament-Jewish conceptions bound up with the *messianic name* Ἰησοῦς Χριστός can be seen from any number of texts. Thus, the reference to Jesus' descent "from the seed of David" (Rom. 1:3f). Son of David was an epithet for the Messiah. To be numbered here as well is the rehearsal of the salvation-historical privileges of Israel (Rom. 9:3-5): "... my kinsmen by race ... are Israelites, and to them belong the sonship, the glory, the covenants ... the worship, and the promises ..., the patriarchs, **and of their race, according to the flesh, is [the] Christ.**"

The descent of Christ from Israel forms a climax to this series. For Paul Christ is the Messiah promised to Israel — to be sure his salvific work has universal significance. At the end of Romans (15:7ff) he treats this question: Jews and Gentiles in Rome, ought to welcome one another "as Christ has welcomed you, for the glory of God. For I tell you that **Christ became a servant to the circumcised** to show God's truthfulness, in order to confirm the promises given to the patriarchs ...."

With this "Christ became a servant to the circumcision," Paul refers to the "messianic ministry" of the earthly Jesus to his own people, through which the truth of God's promises to the patriarchs (and later to the prophets) becomes manifest: God has promised nothing in the messianic prophecy of Scripture that he does not keep (cf. Rom. 11:28f). On the other hand, the "Gentiles'" access to salvation in Christ results from his free mercy, and for this reason they ought to give God the glory.

An adoptionist christology, first valid via the resurrection, was an impossible idea for Paul. This can be seen not only in Paul's pre-existence and "mission" christology, but also in that the earthly Jesus, i.e., the Crucified, is already the Kyrios;[4] it is also apparent in the account of the institution of the Lord's Supper (1 Cor. 11:23ff): Jesus dedicates the fruits of his death to his disciples; i.e., already before his death, as Kyrios, he promises them full salvation. Paul holds in common with all the gospels the certainty that Jesus was the Messiah of Israel promised in Scripture. Even in John Jesus acquires his first disciples because they recognize and confess him to be the Messiah of Israel.

Here the question necessarily arises: "Does this confession of Jesus as Messiah of Israel have anything to do with the real person of Jesus, his ministry and death, or is it confined merely to its 'later influence' [Wirkungsgeschichte] in the post-Easter communities'"?

## 2. The Pre-Pauline Tradition and the Resurrection of Jesus

The transition of the title "Messiah" into a name, and its fusion with the person of Jesus, happened already early on in the crossover of the Gospel from the Aramaic into the Greek language sphere. The description of the Antiochene followers of Jesus as "Christianoi" (Acts 11:26) presupposes this as long since accomplished. Presumably, the confession formula "Jesus is the Messiah," by virtue of constant use, gave rise of itself, so to speak, to a permanent name both among Christians, who thereby emphasized that only **one** could bear this name, and their Gentile auditors, who were not particularly conversant with the language of Jewish piety.

This also means however that this confession was fundamental to the earliest community in Jerusalem. The persecution of the early church in Jerusalem stems from this very confession of Jesus of Nazareth as the crucified Messiah whom God had raised from the dead.

The connection is inseparable between the appearances of Jesus, which established the new messianic community of disciples, and the proclamation of the crucified Messiah by the messengers whom he himself authorized, the "apostles of the Messiah, Jesus."[5] However, there is no proof whatever for the current supposition[6] that in the beginning the confession "God raised Jesus from the dead" stood alone — the appearances of Jesus being understood merely as the beginning of the general resurrection — and only after a secondary level of reflection, was the Resurrected One proclaimed as the Messiah. How are we to suppose this to have happened? After waiting vainly for the general resurrection, did someone perhaps suddenly "discover" the messiahship of Jesus' as the solution to the dilemma? Were the beginnings of early Christianity based on a twofold self-deception?

No, the certainty that Jesus' resurrection also meant his exaltation as Messiah-Son of Man to the right hand of God was rather a direct consequence of the appearances; for the commissioning of the disciples as messengers of the Messiah was connected with these.[7] Their task was to proclaim Jesus as the Messiah of Israel, and to offer the people a final opportunity for repentance. The ancient confession, "God raised Jesus from the dead," only became a meaningful part of the proclamation because it originally stood beside the confession "Jesus is the Messiah." The mere revivification of a person or, as the case may be, his translation into the heavenly realm, established neither messianic majesty nor eschatological mission, nor could it, of itself, supply the content of a message of salvation.

Here it is popular to refer to two "adoptionist" statements, Rom. 1:3f and Acts 2:36. However Rom. 1:4 does not say that the Son possessed no messianic claim prior to the resurrection; rather, this is referring to the enthronement of the Son of God in his **full** eschatological majesty and power. This is valid for Acts 2:36. This text — formulated by Luke — expresses not an adoptionist christology, but a radical volte-face of the "powers that be": God made him who had been crucified on the accursed tree to be "Lord and Anointed"; i.e., he installed him in his eschatological office as the Lord and Judge. That an adoptionist christology in the fullest sense — i.e., in which Jesus is not regarded as the Messiah until his Passion, this first being established through the resurrection — ever existed in early Christianity seems to me more than doubtful.

Jewish **Religionseschichte** presents an additional problem. To be sure, we have accounts of the translation of certain righteous men, and we hear also of isolated instances of resurrection. But that a righteous man via resurrection from the dead was appointed as Messiah, is absolutely without analogy. Neither resurrection nor translation have anything to do with messiahship. Indeed, the suffering righteous man attains a place of honor in Paradise, but there is never any question of messianic majesty and the transfer of eschatological functions in this connection.

If Jesus never possessed a messianic consciousness of divine mission, nor spoke of the coming, or present, "Son of Man," nor was executed as a messianic pretender — as is maintained by radical criticism untroubled by historical arguments — then the emergence of christology, indeed, the entire early history of primitive Christianity, is incomprehensible. But this is not all — all four gospels, and above all the Passion narrative as their most ancient component, would be a curious product of the imagination very difficult to explain, for the Messiah question is at the center of them all. When all is said and done: if the eleven disciples with Peter at their head, on the basis of the appearances of the resurrected Jesus so difficult for us to comprehend, and completely unprompted, reached the view that Jesus was the Son of Man exalted to God, knowing that in reality he had been merely a proclaimer of the kingdom of God, a rabbi and a prophet, knowing nothing of eschatological offices, did they not then completely falsify the pure (and so unmythologically modern sounding) intention of their master? Is it not the case that not only Judas, but also the disciples, wallowing in messianic mythology against their master's will, were — viewed historically — at bottom betrayers of Jesus, since they misunderstood his cause as thoroughly as it could possibly be misunderstood?

On the other hand, since human beings also had memories then, why do we nowhere find a protest against this "messianic" falsification of Jesus? A pious veneration of a suffering righteous Jesus, who now (as with all the righteous) resided with God, would have given less offence among their own compatriots, and the impending separation from Judaism could have been avoided (removing all the contemporary difficulties of Jewish-Christian dialogue). But such a protest in favor of **the true, unmessianic intention of Jesus is nowhere attested.**

## 3. The Problem in the History of Research

William Wrede first set the unmessianic Jesus in motion with his 1901 study **Das Messiasgeheimnis in den Evangelien [The Messianic Secret in the Gospels]**, with the sub-title **Being a Contribution Toward Understanding the Gospel of Mark.**[8] He regarded the messianic secret in the Gospel of Mark as an apologetic construction of the Evangelist based partly in the community's tradition. He classifies various material under the term "messianic secret": not only Jesus' prohibition of the disciples speaking about his messiahship, but also the commands of silence to those who had been healed, to the demons who knew his true identity, also the unbelief or incomprehension of the disciples in various situations, and finally, the parable theory that Jesus only spoke in parables in order that the hearts of the people might be hardened. To be sure, later investigations have shown that this entire complex cannot be traced back to the single motive of masking the unmessianic character of Jesus' ministry, and reading post-Easter christology into his history. Rather, this is seen as a paradoxical style device intended to allow the hidden "glory" of the Messiah, who goes to the cross, to shine even brighter.

Leading New Testament scholars of the day more or less rejected Wrede's hypothesis. Their criticism focused above all on three points: first, Wrede's denial of the historicity of Peter's confession at Caesarea Philippi, second, his unsatisfactory treatment of the Passion narrative, where in the trial before Pilate the Messiah question stands at the center, and brings Jesus to the cross, and third, his disregard of the religion-historical problem and the question connected with it concerning how, through the Easter visions alone, the disciples suddenly could have made the unmessianic Jesus into the heavenly Son of Man and Messiah. To this list one might add Wrede's failure to recognize the importance of the Galilean-Jewish origin of Jesus and his first hearers and disciples. These queries remain unresolved to this day.

It must be said that these liberal theologians were not particularly interested in Jesus' messiahship. For their enlightened humanistic picture of Jesus it was rather an embarrassment. W. Bousset referred to this problem:

> Inadequate as the conceptions "kingdom of God" and "judgement," were ... in the light of Jesus' preaching, so inadequate ... also was the title "Messiah" as an expression of his innermost being.[9]

Here one might raise the objection, "Why then did Jesus make use of these messianic hopes at all, so alien to his innermost being — why did he not reject this conception"? Bousset answers:

> Because ... it was absolutely necessary to him. As the conceptions "kingdom of God" and "judgement" were indispensable for making himself intelligible to his people, so also was the idea "Messiah" indispensable for understanding himself... Jesus wanted to be more than one in a series ... of the Prophets... But

according to the popular conception, this [could only be] the Messiah ... He felt himself to be standing in a nearness to God such as no one before him ... He spoke with confidence the final, decisive, word, was convinced that he was the perfecter — after him none other would come.[10]

Although Bousset's language here has been influenced by Carlyle's[11] model of heroic personality veneration, he is no less the expert for Jewish apocalyptic and messianic expectations, and grasped the actual historical basis for the messianic secret in Mark better than his friend, Wrede. On the other hand, it must be admitted that the liberal literature at the turn of the century frequently shows a deep aversion against the Jewish messianic hope. It is therefore understandable that the new discovery of the unmessianic Jesus also found an enthusiastic reception. The Heidelberg scholar, Adalbert Merx concluded:

... that Yeshua never claimed to be the Messiah, that his prohibiting his disciples to declare him as Messiah was not only temporary but absolute, and that consequently Yeshua's true being will remain misunderstood as long as Christians do not resolve to erase this characteristic from his intellectual make-up just as [all other] apocalyptic fanaticism.[12]

Willy Staerck closed a study on Jesus' attitude towards the Jewish Messiah concept with a challenge:

Now let us also finally be done with speaking of the messiahship of Jesus, pulling him down into **the atmosphere** of ethnic religiosity ... Jesus [is] not the Messiah, but ... the Saviour of the world, through the liberation of religion from its bonds of materialism, whether legal, cultic or chauvinistic — **in hoc signo vincemus!**[13]

This false pathos is alien to us today at the close of a century that weighs particularly heavily on us Germans. But the rejection of Jesus' messianic claim has remained, although the reasoning has changed. H. Conzelmann's seminal article, "Jesus Christus," in the third edition of the RGG, is one example among many. Conzelmann emphasizes that, "the question concerning Jesus' **self consciousness**" is too quickly attached to the concept "messianic consciousness" and is "not [exhausted] in the problem of whether and how J[esus] applied the Jewish christological title to himself."[14] This is certainly correct. However, in the investigation of the titles he concludes that they all derive from "community theology," so "that Jesus' self-understanding is not accessible via the titles.[15] Nor can the words in which Jesus speaks of his sending and coming "be formulated from a retrospect on his completed ministry." However, he admits that, "the conceptions of the prophets and rabbis [typify] only partial aspects(!), yet nothing of the center. Jesus understands himself as **the final herald** ('der letzte Rufer') ... for after him no one else 'comes' but God himself.[16]

Yet by his own interpretation — contra the statements of the primitive Christian texts — grave difficulties must ensue. The **final herald**, after whom "no one else 'comes' but God himself," is not Jesus, but John the Baptist. If Jesus were the "final cryer" what then would distinguish him from the Baptist? The synoptic accounts give a clear answer: For example, in Q:

> The law and the prophets were until John; since then the good news of the kingdom of God is preached ... (Lk. 16:16). [From that time] the kingdom of heaven has been coming violently and men of violence take it by force (Mt. 11:12 ).

However, where the kingdom of God is breaking through, "**God is already coming** ", i.e., in Jesus' activity itself . The treasure in the field, the pearl of great price, will be discovered now or not at all, and appropriated by means of a "violent" decision! Jesus says nothing of a **merely future** "coming" of God. The plea for the coming of the kingdom of God in the Lord's Prayer refers to present **and** future, just as all the other pleas. The future reserves only the revelation of the Son of Man, whatever Jesus may have meant by this, and will make manifest the decision which is consummated now regarding Jesus' message. In contrast to the Baptist, the final and greatest prophet, Jesus brings the eschatological **fulfillment** of the promise:

> Blessed are the eyes which see what you see, and the ears which hear what you hear! For I tell you that many prophets and kings

desired to see what you see, and did not see it, and to hear what you hear, and did not hear it (Mt. 13:16f; Lk. 10:23 ).

Is it not rather the "Fulfiller" who speaks thus, the "Bringer of the Kingdom of God" than the "final cryer," and is it not so, given the prophetic promise of the Old Covenant, in which Jesus lives, that (in E. Kasemann's words), "the only category which does justice to his claim ... is that in which his disciples ... placed him — namely, that of the Messiah"? If this is so, then is not the construction which has ruled German Protestant research of the past 90 years, the completely unmessianic Jesus, a fundamental error?

## 4. The Religion-Historical Problem

Earlier research assumed almost as a matter of course the existence of an established, traditional, Jewish "Messiah dogmatic." Under this rubric aspects of Christian teaching from a much later period were read into ancient Judaism. A "firmly established 'Messiah' concept," such as Wrede presupposes[17] and uses to account for an originally unmessianic Jesus, never existed. Instead there were different Messiah pictures with numerous descriptions, often expressing not so much titles as functions. We would do better therefore to speak of a — relatively broad and variable — "Messiah Haggada."

Our knowledge here has been greatly increased by the Qumran texts. But already the material assembled by Billerbeck, shows that Judaism had no unified, predominantly **political**, Messiah picture, but rather that the views here were extremely diverse. The messianically interpreted Old Testament texts were already extraordinarily variable. Thus, e.g., the contrast between an earthly, political, "Messiah' and a "heavenly, transcendent," Son of Man is questionable, for the "Son of Man" coming from Heaven in Dan. 7 is also victorious against the godless "world powers," and in Ps.Sol. 17 functions in an even greater capacity as judge. On the other hand, the Messiah cannot attain his God-given rule without God's help: slaying the army of nations gathered against Jerusalem "with the rod of his mouth and the breath of his lips" (Is. 11:4), is no less a miracle than flying along with the clouds. The earthly and heavenly world formed **one** continuum, were bound together and continually influenced one another.

The timing of the eschaton is also variable. In the zoomorphic apocalypse of 1 Enoch the Messiah is not born until after God himself has destroyed the power of the nations and passed judgement. Might not this order sometimes have been reversed? Ps.Sol. 17 already attests that the Messiah will be the Spirit-filled teacher and judge of his people. This refutes the alleged contradiction, emphasized chiefly by Vielhauer, between Messiah and rule by God. God sets up his through the king from David's house who, taught by God and armed with the gifts of the Spirit mentioned in Is. 11:2ff, will lead and judge his people in righteousness.[18] In Test. Jud. 24 we find a non-warlike Messiah from Judah with an ethical orientation. Alongside this, Test. Lev. 18 speaks of the messianic high priest as saviour. The circumstances of place and time of the Messiah's appearance, his concealment before his public ministry, the forms of his legitimation through God himself, through a prophet like Elijah, or **coram publico**, and his coming in humility or glory, remain astonishingly variable in the later Messiah Haggada. Even the pre-existent Messiah, hidden by God, or the suffering and dying Messiah, are not absent.

The thesis that there is no reference whatever to a pre-Christian suffering Messiah appears questionable in light of the messianic features of the LXX translation of Is. 53, and an Aramaic text from Cave 4 concerning an atoning revelator.[19] In fact, we have only very few **pre-Christian** messianic texts, which nonetheless already show an astonishing variety; Qumran has significantly increased these. We now know of the two Anointed figures, the pre-eminent priestly, and the Davidic. To this may be added the eschatological role of Michael as heavenly saviour. With such a **widely arrayed** background, it may be presumed that the messianic spectrum was even much broader.

The word מָשִׁיחַ refers already in the Old Testament to God's activity. He is the actor in the "anointing" carried out in his name. Thus, מָשִׁיחַ - χριστός is not simply a "title of majesty," which one can adopt, but presupposes God's acting. But the concept need not possess, **a priori**, a greater theocratic-political content, than the metaphor "kingdom of God." Is. 61:1f is especially fitting as an eschatological text here: "The Spirit of the Lord God is upon me, because the Lord has anointed me to bring good tidings to the afflicted."

I know no other Old Testament text that better describes the ministry of Jesus in Galilee. Luke, with excellent historical-theological flair, puts this word on Jesus' lips in his sermon at the outset of his public ministry in Nazareth (Lk. 4:17-19). The importance of this text for Jesus himself can be seen from his answer to the Baptist's question, and the Beatitudes. The same motif, however, appears in one of the most influential texts of those referring to the "kingly" Messiah, Is. 11:1ff: "And the Spirit of the Lord shall rest upon him ..."

We know from the Qumran texts that the messianic prophet of Deut. 18 plays a role, not only in the Samaritan Eschatology (where there could be no royal Davidic Messiah), and in Christian texts, but also in Jewish texts. Moreover, there the Old Testament prophets are sometimes described as "Anointed," above all, "of the Holy Spirit" (CD 2:12; cf. 6:1). Moses appears once as "God's Anointed."[20] In another text the "Shoot of David" is the "Anointed of Righteousness."[21] David was not only the prototype of the kingly Messiah, but, next to Isaiah, the most important prophet as well.[22] What was true for the prophets of Israel was certainly valid for a figure bringing eschatological salvation, as is seen by the appearance of such a one in 11Q Melch. There the messenger of good tidings from Is. 52:7, with an allusion to Is. 61:1, is interpreted as the one "Anointed with the Spirit" משיח הרוח who "[preaches] good news, proclaims [salvation], of whom it is written, [when] it says, 'to comfort [all who mourn in Zion], and to teach them in truth ..."[23] The variability of the משיח manifest in the Qumran texts accords with the possibility of describing the "Son of Man" as Messiah since the Similitudes of Enoch.

If, then, a prophetic teacher figure with the authority of God's Spirit appeared with the outrageous claim that with his activity God's eternal reign became reality, if he applied the apocalyptic cipher "(Son of) Man" to himself, and also to the future heavenly Judge, if he also came from a family of the lineage of David, then does it not appear probable, that he was invested with the title "Anointed," and took a position with regard to the title, and under the charge of being the long-awaited "Messiah" and "King of the Jews" was executed on the cross as a political criminal?

## 5. The Crucified Messiah

H.J. Holtzmann said of Jesus' death on the cross that it was "of all things, the most certain."[24] On this single point, even in research today, there is still a consensus. But here the consensus ends. The workbook by Conzelmann and Lindemann, following R. Bultmann, manages to admit that it must have been "a political accusation that was leveled against Jesus" and "that a trial before the representative of the Roman government actually did take place,"[25] which led to crucifixion; all else is alleged to be redactional, secondarily "spun from" Old Testament material, or simply legend. All that remains of the Markan Passion narrative is what we can otherwise derive from the Pauline statement that Jesus was executed by crucifixion.

On the other hand, it seems that scholarship is widely agreed that, as Bultmann emphasizes, Mark "had already before him a Passion story that was a continuous narrative,"[26] indeed the earliest of all the early Church's connected narratives about Jesus. To be sure, there is much disagreement about the date and extent of this pre-Markan "Passion story." Paul provides a hint in 1 Cor. 11, where he refers to Jesus' last meal. This account may already have existed at the end of the Thirties when Paul was preaching in Syria. Can then the account of Jesus' suffering be very much later? If the oldest narrative account about Jesus, the Passion story, represents a mere conglomerate of "dogmatic" and legendary community formulations, as radical criticism postulates, can anything at all of the Jesus tradition be trustworthy? The disciples must have been much more interested in Jesus' Passion --which formed the basis for the beginning of the Church and the Kerygma--than in individual logia and parables. Wellhausen, the great sceptical historian, comments: "the reminiscences of him are one-sided and sketchy; only the last days of his life remained etched in memory."[27] The early Jerusalem church, under the leadership of Peter and James, the Lord's brother, was for the next three decades the primary church that could gather information about that unique event. If they were not interested in this, but instead, contrary to all memory, freely constructed and historized, than neither can we expect them to have had any interest in sayings of Jesus. But no one is prepared to accept this consequence. Bultmann wrote a classic study on Jesus, and Conzelmann is able to tell us a good deal about Jesus in his article, "Jesus Christus."

With good reason. For how can the disciples have forgotten the most convulsive day of their lives. If, however, we take the view that the disciples, Peter at their head, held this day in memory, and attempted to supplement their knowledge of their Master's death through additional information from Simon of Cyrene, the women, Joseph of Arimathea, and others, then we cannot ignore that **the Messiah question runs through the Passion story of all the gospels like a red thread.**

N.A. Dahl has already pointed out the line of connection between the Pauline message of "Christ crucified," and the statement of the gospels that Jesus was executed as **King of the Jews.** This was the decisive charge against Jesus, that brought him to the cross; for "the formulation 'King of the Jews' derives neither from a prophetic proof nor from the Church's christology."[28] It is improbable that the early Church, with no reference to historical reality, introduced of itself the politically prejudicial expression, "King of the Jews," since this would have justified the Roman proceedings against Jesus as a rebel. All those who even stretched their hand towards the crown, from the last of the Hasmoneans, Antigonus, to the pseudo-messiah, Bar Cochba, were rebels against Rome and suffered a violent death. Had the earliest Church applied the title, "King of the Jews," to Jesus, it would itself have been responsible for arraying him with the worst of all possible company, defaming both him and itself. But it was unnecessary to invent this charge: it was, in fact, brought by the hierarchs against Jesus before Pilate as the most certain means of bringing this seducer of the people to the cross.

With good reason, Dahl refers here to the **causa poena** on the cross (Mk. 15:26): King of the Jews. This informed everyone in Jerusalem of the charge against Jesus. Conzelmann and Lindemann, however, see even in this item, which disadvantaged Christians in the eyes of their opponents, "a christological [motive] without historical background"; for, "there is no evidence for affixing such inscriptions ... as a Roman custom."[29] But this argument is misleading. For it must be recognized that antiquity has supplied us with very few real descriptions of crucifixion at all.[30] The gospels are by far the most extensive accounts of execution on the cross. Ancient authors generally considered it far too unsavory a subject. For **this reason** we find hardly any details. The **practice** of publicizing a **causa poena** on a placard for general deterrence at an execution is attested in several texts. These were hung around the delinquent's neck, or carried before him when he was led to the place of execution.[31] With crucifixion however the suffering of the condemned man before his death could last for days; to increase the deterrent effect, the placard will have been affixed to the cross. There is no basis then for dismissing as "dogmatic invention" the reference to the **causa poenae**, likely to be understood by ancient readers as a defamation. The **titulus** on the cross is just as historical as the ensuing account that Jesus was crucified between two "robbers," i.e., presumably two political insurrectionists. The same is true of the mocking of Jesus by the anti-Jewish soldier rabble, who deride him in a parody of royal homage as a king wearing a purple mantle and crown of thorns.[32]

Further, I find improbable the view that Pilate's question, "Are you the King of the Jews?," and Jesus' positive answer, was secondarily interpolated into the original unity of 15:1 and 3. For it is incredible that the original account of Jesus' delivery to Pilate should have been no more specific than the banal, "And the chief priests accused him of many things," of 15:3. Is the earliest Church supposed to have believed that Jesus was executed on such unspecific grounds? In fact, v.3 underscores only the one point of the charge, to which Jesus confesses in v.2, and in which all four gospels agree. Jesus' confirming answer to Pilate seals his fate: **confessus pro iudicato est**.

Here, one thing leads to the next. Jesus was delivered to Pilate with the capital charge, "King of the Jews." But how did the hierarchs arrive at **this** charge, graver than any other? Through the previously narrated interrogation at night before the highest Jewish office, the High Priest and the court over which he presided. In favor of the Markan account is the curious note concerning the alleged Temple saying of Jesus. The erection of the new eschatological sanctuary was a messianic task. Thus the provocative question of the High Priest concerning Jesus' messianic dignity. Is it not plausible that Jesus answered this question with a word of judgement which, in its turn, provoked the Sanhedrin, confirmed his God-given authority, and at once referred the hierarchs to the coming Son of Man with whom he was inextricably bound? This would explain their indignant reaction, and the abuse he suffered as a false prophet. The precautions taken at Jesus' arrest, and the speed with which he was delivered to Pilate, show that his influence with the people was feared, making it necessary to avoid public proceedings. It was his messianic claim that finally led to their making short work of him.

The Messiah question, according to Mark, was predominant during the final, tense days in Jerusalem. He dramatically prepares the way for it with the healing of blind Bartimaeus in Jericho; this healing falls outside the topics of the customary miracle stories. The address, "Son of David," marks Jesus as a messianic pretender. Jesus' entry into Jerusalem, riding down from the Mount of Olives into the Holy City — as in

Zech. 9:9 — accompanied by the acclamation of his fellow pilgrims, brings the Messiah question distinctly to the fore. Why should not the crowd of accompanying pilgrims, who knew only too well a prophetic word such as Zech. 9:9, have seen in Jesus the messianic Prophet, and have harbored the hope that he would be "the one to redeem Israel"? And Jesus himself--why should he not have acted out a — messianic — symbolism, with the Holy City and its Temple in view?

The Cleansing of the Temple also presupposes a scriptural reference from Zechariah — the last word in the book: "And there shall no longer be a trader in the house of the Lord of hosts on that day" (14:21b). With this second symbolic action, Jesus cleanses the Temple for the kingdom of God in a paradigmatic act in his full authority as Messiah designatus. It is no wonder that the hierarchs question him concerning his authority (11:27-32). A messianic background is evident in other episodes as well. The Parable of the Wicked Husbandmen, showing a familiarity with Palestinian conditions, threatens the hierarchs with the judgement of God for rejecting his messengers. Other anecdotes demonstrate his authority as a charismatic teacher, "not as the scribes." If Mark has invented all this material — historically authentic to an incredible degree--then he has done it with ingenious empathy, intuition, and understanding. But in the opinion of many critics he was a simple Gentile Christian![33] How is this supposed to have come about?

With these all too brief reflections I have intended no more than to point out that the Passion narrative **can** (and in my opinion must) be viewed very differently than the widespread historical scepticism in contemporary criticism allows. **Absolute proof** for the historicity of the individual episodes in the Markan passion is not the issue here. This can hardly be obtained, given the limited source basis — as is frequently the case in Ancient History. Whoever radically strikes the Messiah question from the Passion story makes the account not only incomprehensible, and a banal torso, but is also unable to explain the Easter events and the origin of post-Easter christology. This is a high price — much too high a price — to pay for the postulate of an unmessianic Jesus.

## 6. The Titles "Messiah" and "Son of Man"

Might one not object here that in all four gospels Jesus never applies the appellation "Christ," Anointed, to himself, but, on the contrary, this title is always applied to him by others. However Jesus never rejects the title — neither in the trial before the High Priest, nor before Peter and the disciples. During the trial before Pilate he might yet have denied this charge, and explained that he was only a rabbi and prophet declaring the will of God. But even as he refused a hasty flight the night before to avoid arrest, so also he refuses this option. In Mk. 8:24ff he merely forbids Peter and the disciples to betray the secret. The ensuing repudiation of Peter as "Satan" (is this also a product of the earliest Church?) results from Peter's reaction to the revelation that Jesus "must suffer many things." We do not know whether, or how, these accounts originally belonged together.

I would put the question the other way round: Is it not an indication of the relative trustworthiness of the gospel tradition that the alleged great creativity of the "community" never produced an unambiguous scene in which Jesus announces his claim **coram publico** with a clear "I am the Messiah, the Son of God"? Could this not be the result of the "community" knowing that Jesus never proclaimed himself to be the Messiah in this manner, or even that it was simply impossible thus to proclaim oneself Messiah, e.g., because this word could unleash dangerous political reactions, or still more, because the revelation of God's Anointed in his majesty could only be accomplished by God himself? The messianic secret then would stem **in nuce** from the — eschatological — secret of Jesus himself, and his conduct.

This is shown by his use of the disputed cipher, "the man," for himself and the coming Judge. This expression, incomprehensible in Greek as which with one exception (Acts 7:56) occurs only on the lips of Jesus, and always in the four gospels, is among those imitations of Jesus' speech found in the gospels such as "the kingdom of God," "**amen** I say to you," the prayer address, "**Abba**, Father," and "this generation." I am simply unable to believe that the so-called earliest community (i.e., in reality, his closest disciples) made him the resurrected Son of Man after the appearances, and then very quickly suppressed this cipher because it was unsuitable for mission proclamation, while at the same time being extremely careful to insure that in the gospel tradition only Jesus speaks of the Son of Man, never his disciples, just as the Messiah title was strictly held at a distance from him in the production of the dominical sayings. Radical exegetes seem to me to be too "trusting" here.

Since in the following section I want to treat Jesus' "messianic" conduct and teaching, and no longer the titles, here I address this supremely disputed problem, whose secret we can no longer fully unveil, only briefly. It sometimes seems as if New Testament scholarship has little new to say about this problem. But there is no cause for complete scepticism. It is in any case wrong to construct a thoroughgoing antithesis between the "(Son of) Man," and the "Messiah." Already the (few) Jewish sources referring to the "(Son of) Man" of Dan. 7:13 forbid this. Jesus employs " ( Son of) Man," an expression characterized both by Dan.7:13, and ordinary, everyday use, because it is a cipher, and not explicitly messianic. It becomes then, paradoxically, the expression for the mystery connected with his mission and passion. Mark appears already to have understood it in this way, and thus for him it is not included in the messianic secret. We meet the expression 81 times in the gospels. That **all** these texts were secondarily inserted by the Community, I hold to be impossible. In the interest of space, I restrict myself to what seems to me to be the most plausible solution. The earthly and suffering Son of Man are a cipher with which Jesus, in certain situations, expresses both his authority (indeed, we may say as "**Messias designatus**"), and his humility and tribulation, which ultimately lead him to suffering and death. Regarding the coming Son of Man, who appears as a mysterious heavenly figure, I refer to the seminal study by Carsten Colpe: "The apocalyptic Son of Man is a symbol for Jesus' certainty of perfection."[34] Just as the Son of Man may not be set in opposition to Jesus, neither may he be set over against the kingdom of God. On the other hand, a precipitous identification in the contemporary ministry of Jesus was impossible . A text such as Lk. 12:8f emphasizes the inextricable connection between Jesus and the coming Son of Man, but does not remove the dialectical tension between the earthly preacher and the coming judge.

This means, however, that Jesus himself, in obedience to his God-given task of announcing the eschatological fulfillment of the promise, and thereby introducing it, **expounds, through his conduct and his way, just what was really fitting for God's chosen "Anointed."** It was not a given Jewish "messianology" that determined his service, but rather his service established the standards for what was, in the truest sense, legitimately "messianic." His God-given task, the fulfillment of His will, stood before, and above, the titles. To this messianic ministry to his own people we now turn our attention.

## 7. The Messianic Ministry of Jesus

Despite the widespread aversion to attributing to Jesus a "messianic consciousness," there is broad consensus that Jesus' ministry and conduct can hardly be explained as that of a mere rabbi and prophet: "And they were astonished at his teaching, for he taught them as one who had authority, and **not** as the scribes (Mk. 1:22). For Mark, this is the teaching authority of the perfect Spirit-bearer (1:10;13), which brings the radically New. This same authority shows itself in Jesus' behavior and conduct. He promises to sinful men the forgiveness of their sin, that which is the prerogative of God alone; the scandalous fellowship with tax-collectors and sinners has a similar intention. He justifies it with the saying: "I came not to call the righteous, but sinners" (Mk. 2:17b). The Pauline justification of the sinner derives from Jesus' messianic activity.

His dismissive answer concerning the Pharisees and the Baptist's disciples, "Can the wedding guests fast while the bridegroom is with them?," rests on this mission-consciousness which exceeds the bounds of the prophetic. This saying, even as Jesus' behavior with the tax-collectors and sinners, is only comprehensible if the promise is already **present** in Jesus' ministry, if the kingdom of God comes **with him**. Because the promises are now being fulfilled, those who witness with eye and ear are counted blessed; thus the cry of acclamation that the eschatological revelation of the Heavenly Father's salvation for the poor and dis-enfranchised is come (Lk. 10:21 = Mt. 11:25); thus also healings and exorcisms, the deeds of him in whom the fulfillment of the promises becomes reality. "But if it is by the finger of God that I cast out demons, then the kingdom of God has come upon you."

The kingdom of God, overcoming the old aeon and the kingdom of Evil, is not only near, it is present in Jesus' ministry. When Jesus speaks of the earthly Son of Man on the one hand, and the coming Son of Man on the other, the tension between the two corresponds to that between the presence of the kingdom in his ministry — which undergoes testing and trial — and his coming in power. Jesus' answer to the charge of being in league with the Devil tends in this direction: "... how can one enter a strong man's house and plunder his goods, unless he first binds the strong man? Then indeed he may plunder his house (Mt. 12:29). Jesus is he who brings "liberty to the captives" (Is. 61). As the victor in this battle he can also call out to his disciples as they return full of joy from their exorcisms: "I saw Satan fall like lightning from heaven" (Lk. 10:18). What follows this is no less astonishing:

"Behold I have given you authority to tread upon serpents and scorpions, and over all the power of the enemy; and nothing shall hurt you. Nevertheless do not rejoice in this ... but rejoice that your names are written in heaven" (Lk. 10:19f).

Who utters such an outrage is not only certain, in his high-flying, idealistic enthusiasm, that the power of the "Enemy" is broken here and now, but he also dares to anticipate the judgement of God. Thus also, in three blessings (following Is. 61:1), he can promise the poor, the hungry, and the grieving, unconditional participation in the kingdom of God. As he already now promises salvation with absolute certainty, so also he can anticipate the word of the last judgement; thus, we find the woes pronounced against Chorazin and Bethsaida, where he had done such "mighty works," and even more sharply, against the center of his activity: "And you, Capernaum, will you be exalted to heaven? You shall be brought down to Hades" (Mt. 11:20-24 = Lk. 10:12-15 [Q]).

We meet the same "messianic" self-consciousness in the answer to the Baptist to his question whether he was "he who is to come." Jesus refers to his healing and salvific ministry in which the promises of Isaiah are fulfilled, as well as his liberating good news to the poor. He emphasizes his eschatological authority and majesty with the concluding, "blessed is he who takes no offense at me" (Lk. 7:23; Mt. 11:6).

For this very reason, then, one cannot demand a sign of him — as from a prophet. Rather, Gentiles will rise up as witnesses against this generation of Jesus' contemporaries: the Queen of the South, who came to hear the wisdom of Solomon, the wisest of the wise, and the Ninevites, who repented at the preaching of Jonah, the most successful of the prophets; for "behold, a greater than Solomon is here," and "behold, a greater than Jonah is here" (Mt. 12:42; Lk. 11:32). How are we to understand this "behold, a greater is here" if not in the sense of the end of the old "salvation history," and the dawning of the kingdom of God in the work of Jesus himself? Because he is "more than a prophet" he does not begin his authoritative words with the Old Testament's "Thus says the Lord," but with the unique "Amen, I say to you."

In my judgement, the real Jesus was more enthusiastic, more ecstatic, more passionate, and that means also, more alien to us, than we enlightened Central Europeans care to admit today. We all tend to shape him theologically "in our own image." The enthusiastic, messianic Jesus is further from us than the "rabbi and prophet" who has become dear to us, or even the "herald before the end."

Jesus' "ethical" preaching, as well, stands under his "messianic authority," which can anticipate God's judgement: whoever judges, will himself be judged, only he who hears and obeys his word builds upon the rock, whoever is anxious makes mammon his idol. This very saying, "Do not be anxious," contradicting all wisdom and experience, presupposes that limitless care of God, which is part of his kingdom. With the seeking of the kingdom of God as a present power, anxiety and fear fall by the wayside. This command, "Do not be anxious," is just as much a part of his divine "messianic" certainty as the saying about faith that moves mountains, and the certainty of answer to prayer. That he reveals the kingdom of God in parables shows that he — alone — knows its present **and** future secret.[36]

The trial of Jesus, which ends with his execution as messianic pretender, and the unique authority, which determines his preaching, his ministry, and his conduct, illuminate each other. Therefore, it seems to me also probable that he goes to Jerusalem in this very authority, with his death before his eyes as the way that the Father has determined for him. The double saying, "I came to cast fire upon the earth; and would that it were already kindled! I have a baptism to be baptized with; and how I am constrained until it is accomplished!" (Lk. 12:49f), indicates that he is going to his death for the sake of his mission. This is also true of the question by the sons of Zebedee, the debated ransom saying (Mk. 10:5), and above all, the words spoken at the Last Supper. Jesus goes to his death for the sake of his messianic ministry to Israel.

That he intended to address not only the Galilean population, but all Israel, is seen by his call and appointment of the Twelve and his sending them out among the people. He calls them to follow him as God once called the prophets, and commissions them with his message.

Just as the Son of Man and the Messiah cannot be fundamentally separated, neither may one **a priori** completely tear the "prophetic" from the "kingly" Messiah. Each is "Spirit-bearer" in a unique way, and this connects the two. Also, the "kingly," and the "prophetic," Messiah can be teacher and proclaimer of God's will, and even more so, judge. At first, the motif of the political Messiah can recede into the background:

the overcoming of the worldly powers at enmity with God, not only the ruling political kingdoms, but above all in Satan as their lord, was accomplished "**in power**" by God's miracle. One cannot deny all political consequence to Jesus' efficacy, but this was of a very different kind than that of the various "messianic" pretenders of his time.

About Jesus, one may say that he made his appearance in Galilee as "Anointed of the Spirit," in the manner of Is. 61, and was executed in Jerusalem as "King of the Jews." That his family was reported to be descended from David, that he addressed the entire "twelve tribes" with the fulfillment of promise and the dawning kingdom, that he not only entered Jerusalem accompanied by a crowd greeting him as a messianic figure, but entered with eschatological authority, all may have played a role here. With regard to the charges at his trial, he did not renounce the messianic claim.

How he himself viewed the eschatological **accomplishment** of his work, we may only **presume** by examining such texts as Mk.14:25, 10:37, or 14:62. In our lack of knowledge, however, we should not forget that Jesus' disciples knew infinitely more about Jesus than we today, and that this knowledge also flowed into the earliest christology which began directly with, and after, the Easter appearances. How could this have been otherwise! Easter did not alter the direct **remembrance** of Jesus. This was burned into the hearts of the disciples.

With our extant sources, we **today** can sketch only a very fragmentary "picture" of Jesus' ministry. To be sure, this is true of many great figures from antiquity. I am reminded of the debate over the "historical Socrates." Many features remain obscure. However, we ought not therefore to make of necessity a virtue, and, with radical critical scepticism, reject **a limine** information which is plausible. That Jesus neither intended to be a mere "rabbi and prophet," nor **one** "eschatological prophet" among many, ought no longer to be disputed. Just as one-sided is the picture, so popular today, of the supertemporal, benevolent teacher of brotherly love and humane principles, who died in the end as a martyr for his good cause. Here, aspects appealing to the modern mind are emphasized in a one-sided manner. With his messianic claim, Jesus the Jew may appear alien, indeed vexing, since his "mythical" characteristics obscure our ethically determined, demythologized picture of him. But the real Jesus was very different. He lived in the language and imagery of the Old Testament and its Jewish-Galilean environment, and he conducted himself with the — in the truest sense of the word — "apocalyptic" (the word comes from "to reveal") right to usher in God's reign over Israel (and all nations), and, as the "Anointed of God," to fulfill the promises made to the fathers and the prophets. His death — which he consciously affirmed — placed the seal of confirmation on this right.

That Jesus conducted himself in this manner, I hold to be provable by the methods of historical-critical research. From this flow consequences for theological reflection as well; for, as the messianic bringer of salvation, he is the fundament of our faith, who fulfilled the Old Covenant, and breathed the breath of life into the New. His person and work charge us with the task of a "whole" biblical theology that realizes its Jewish heritage (and the present Israel), a biblical theology that does not eradicate the lines between the Old and New, but properly defines them, and, remembering a long and checkered history, considers them afresh. I could also express this in the words of Paul with which I began (Rom. 15:8): The Jew, Jesus of Nazareth, became the Messiah of Israel in order to fulfill the promises made to the fathers, and he became for us, the Gentiles, "the author of our salvation," because we experience in him what the love of God is, that we might, for the sake of such grace, praise as **our** Father, the God of Israel and Father of Jesus Christ.

# NOTES

1. Liddell/Scott/Jones, 1170.
2. Suetonius, **Claudius**, 25:4; cf. Tacitus, **Annals** 15:4: "**Chrestiani**" .
3. Rom. 5:8, cf. 5:6; 14:9,15; 1 Cor. 8:11, 15:3; 2 Cor. 5:15;1 Thess. 5:10; Gal. 2:21; 1 Pet. 3:18).
4. 1 Cor. 7:10; 9:1; cf. 1 Thess. 4:5.
5. 1 Cor. 1:1; cf. 2 Cor. 1:1; 11:13; Eph. 2:1; Col. 1:1.
6. See, e.g., J. Becker, **Auferstehung der Toten im Urchristentum**, SBS 82 (Stuttgart 1976), 14f; 28.
7. 1 Cor. 9:1; 15:-8; Gal. 1:15f; Acts 1:8; Mt. 28:19f; John 20:21.
8. Third edition (Gottingen 1963).
9. W. Bousset, **Jesus, RV 1**. Ser. 2/3 (1904), 86.
10. Ibid 87.

11. For Bousset and Carlyle see A.F. Verheule, **Wilhelm Bousset. Leben und Werk** (Amsterdam 1973), 733-375. Cf. the critique by J. Weiss, **Die Predigt Jesu vom Reiche Gottes** (Gottingen 1964), 56.

12. Ibid., **Bd. II/2**, 481. See also bid., **Bd. II/3, Das Evangelium des Johannes**, (1911), 557, index, s.v. "Ablehnung des Messiastitels." Cf. H.J. Holtzmann's critique, **Messiasbewutsein**, 9f.

13. W. Staerck, "Jesu Stellung zum judischen Messiasbegriff," **PrM** (1902), 309.

14. H. Conzelmann, "Jesus Christus," **RGG3** (1959), 619-653.

15. Ibid , 631.

16. Ibid., 633 (italics, Conzelmann).

17. Wrede, **Messiasgeheimnis**, 220.

18. Ps.Sol. 17:3f; 21;36f; 43.

19. Cf. M. Hengel, **The Atonement** (London 1981), 58. (4Q 541)

20. בפי מושה משיחו = SL 12:2x5 (4Q 377, 2-5: as yet unpublished).

21. 4Q Patr 3 (4Q 456, 2-6) משיח הצדק צמח דויד .

22. J.A. Sanders, **The Psalm Scroll of Qumran, Cave 11**, DJDJ IV (1965), 96 = Col. XXVII, 9-11.

23. Cf. P.J. Kobelski, "Melchizedek and Melchiresha," **CBQ Mon.ser.**, 10 (1981), 6 (1n. 18) .

24. **GGA** (1901) 959

25. H. Conzelmann and A. Lindemann, **Interpreting the New Testament: An Introduction to the Principles and Methods of N.T. Exegesis**, transl. from the 8th rev. German ed. by S. Schatzmann (Peabody, Mass.: Hendrickson Publishers, 1988) [**Arbeitsbuch zum Neuen Testament 9. Aufl.** (1988), 53-60,000 copies printed], 333; -331.

26. R. Bultmann, **The History of the Synoptic Tradition**, rev.ed., transl. by John Marsh (New York [et al.]: Harper & Row, 1963), 275. [**Geschichte der Synoptischen Tradition** (FRLANT, 29), ²1931)]. Close to the ancient kerygma of the "Passion and Death of Jesus, as the analysis has shown, was a short narrative of historical reminiscence about the Arrest, Condemnation and Execution of Jesus" (ibid.; cf. 279; cf., ibim, **Die Erforschung der synoptischen Evangelien**, 1966, 45).

27. J Wellhausen, **Israelitisch-jüdische Geschichte**, 8. Aufl. (1921), 367.

28. N.A. Dahl, "Der gekreuzigte Messias," in H. Ristow/ K.Matthiae (Hrsg.), **Der historische Jesus und der kerymatische Christus** (Berlin, 1961), 159.

29. Conzelmann and Lindemann, **Interpreting the New Testament**, 333.
30. See M. Hengel, **Crucifixion** (London 1977).
31. Suetonius, **Caligula**, 32:2; ibid., **Domitian**, 10:1; Cassius Dio, 54:3,7; Eusebius, **Church History**, 5:1,44.
32. Mk. 15:16-20; cf. Philo, **Flacc.** 36-42.
33. Conzelmann and Lindemann, **Interpreting the New Testament**, 218: "The only thing we can state is that the author of Mk is a Gentile Christian with whom we are not otherwise acquainted." Cf., ibid.: "Mk has quite obviously not been written by a Jew."
34. Colpe, TDNT 8:.

# 14

# THE INFLUENCE OF ISAIAH ON CHRISTOLOGY IN MATTHEW AND LUKE

## Adrian M. Leske

The influence of Isaiah on the gospel message is readily acknowledged. From the hopes expressed during the exile by Deutero-Isaiah came the gospel motifs of the restoration of the Kingdom of God, pardon for sin, good news for the afflicted, being a light to the nations and many others. These restoration hopes were carried forward by a prophetic minority after the return as is evident in Trito-Isaiah and later, to varying degrees, in Malachi, Zechariah 9-14, Daniel, Wisdom of Solomon and the Similitudes of Enoch. Because Jesus came announcing the Kingdom, preaching the good news, and pronouncing the forgiveness of sins, the message especially of Isaiah 40-66 is important for the understanding of christology. Both Matthew and Luke quote from this source to illustrate Jesus' mission and purpose. Because of this many have traditionally held that Jesus defined his messiahship in terms of the Suffering Servant, that on the basis of Isaiah 53 Jesus saw as a major purpose of his mission to give his life as a sin-offering for Israel and the nations. Oscar Cullmann, for instance, argued that with the title *ebed Yahweh* we come straight to the heart of New Testament christology.[1]

However, the Servant motif was generally too narrowly defined, often limited to the so-called Servant songs (Isa 42:1-4; 49:1-6; 50:4-9; 52:13-53:12), the Servant being seen as an individual messianic figure. For many scholars this traditional view was successfully overthrown by, among others, Morna Hooker's work, *Jesus and the Servant: The Influence of the Servant Concept of Deutero-Isaiah in the New Testament.*[2] Although she acknowledged the influence of Deutero-Isaiah on the Gospels she claimed there were no certain references in them which in any way suggested that Jesus was identified with a messianic interpretation of the Servant.[3]

While a full re-examination of this whole question is not possible in the scope of this paper, I shall attempt to open up some of the issues by approaching the question from a different standpoint. In recognition that our conclusions are often formed by our presuppositions, I shall survey briefly first the christology of the infancy narratives in Matthew and Luke on the assumption that both writers were consciously setting down there their christological tenets for their readers. I will then explore some of the major quotations and allusions to Isaiah in Matthew's Gospel comparing them to Luke's where applicable. Then I will look at the importance of the Lucan quotations and allusions for that Gospel. On the basis of this I shall draw conclusions regarding the possible dependence of Luke on Matthew and suggest some implications of the study for other christological titles.

## The Christology of Matthew's Infancy Narrative

Matthew's christology is stated quite emphatically at the very beginning (1:1). Jesus is introduced as "Jesus Christ, son of David, son of Abraham." Here "Jesus Christ" appears to be a title familiar to Matthew's readers. It is used again in v.18, although a number of MSS omit "Jesus." Matthew never uses this combination in the rest of his Gospel. Elsewhere in the infancy narrative he speaks of "the Christ" (or "the Anointed One," Mt 1:17; 2:4) or "Jesus who is called Christ" (1:16). In 2:4, Herod inquires where the Christ is to be born. The meaning here is obviously "the royal Messiah," since the chief priests and scribes answer with the quotation from Micah 5:1/2 Sam 5:2, and the magi's inquiry was for him "who has been born king of the Jews"(2:2). One must assume that the same is true, then, of the reference to "the Christ" at the end of the genealogy (1:17), particularly since the genealogy emphasizes Davidic sonship, and also of "Jesus who is called Christ" in 1:16 (Pilate uses this same phrase in Mt 27:17,22).

The genealogy, arranged in its symbolic pattern of three sections of fourteen, emphasizes four focal points — Abraham, David, the Babylonian exile, and the Christ. All four are significant christologically. First of all, Jesus is a descendant of Abraham and as such is not only a true member of Judah but also the one who will fulfil the promise to Abraham that through his seed all the nations will bless themselves (Gen 22:18; cf Mt 8:11). Thus it is appropriate that Jesus' genealogy should start with him. Secondly, he is the son of David, the promised royal messiah expected by the Jews. Thirdly, the Babylonian exile is significant because this is the turning point and the time of the promised restoration of the Kingdom which will be inaugurated by the Anointed One, the Christ. This, and the patterning of the genealogy into three sections of fourteen, probably to make a subtle reference to David,[4] is part of Matthew's strong apologetic to the Jews that Jesus is the long awaited royal Messiah, the son of David.[5] This is also the reason why David is mentioned before Abraham in 1:1.

However, it must be kept in mind that from the time of the Babylonian exile, ὁ Χριστός ("the Anointed One") had taken on a different meaning for the prophetic minority. According to Isaiah 55:3-5 the eternal covenant made with David that he and his descendants would be Yahweh's son and servant forever (2 Sam 7:13-16) was actually transferred to the people. They were now to be witnesses to Yahweh's power (Isa 43:10,12; 44:8) in place of David (55:4). Because of this, Trito-Isaiah could speak in the role of Servant Israel as the one "anointed" by God to bring good news to the afflicted (61:1), reaffirm the everlasting covenant (61:8), call the people a "crown of beauty" and a "royal diadem" in the hand of Yahweh who reigns (62:3), the "shoot" (נצר) of God's planting (60:21; cf 11:1), the "sprout" of righteousness and praise (61:11 — the righteous branch of Jer 23:5; 33:16). In this case "the Christ" means Servant-Israel *anointed* by God to be a people-covenant and a light to the nations (Isa 42:6; 49:6,8) as they witness to the reign of God.

Matthew may very well have been conscious of this second meaning, but he wished to emphasize here that Jesus fulfils *all* the hopes of the Jewish people and so claims royal messiahship for Jesus. He is the son of David by a legality — Joseph, son of David (1:20), becomes his father legally in marrying Mary the mother of Jesus.[6] His conception was "from the Holy Spirit," brought about by divine power. In the birth narrative (1:18-25), Matthew makes one further christological point: his name shall be called "Jesus (Savior) for he will save his people from their sins"(1:21). This is paralleled with a citation from Isaiah 7:14 in which the virgin's son "shall be called Emmanuel (God with us)" to emphasize the point that God is working through this Jesus to bring about deliverance. Deliverance from the guilt of sin is a concept deriving from Deutero-Isaiah who saw deliverance from exile and the restoration of the Kingdom as a setting free from the punishment for breaking the covenant (cf Isa 40:2; 42:24; 43:24,25; 44:22; 45:17; 46:12,13; 47:6; etc). In Matthew, the forgiveness of sins is, therefore, always a sign of the Kingdom (Mt 6:12,14,15; 9:2,5,6;12:31;18:15-35; 26:28).

In Mt 2 the christological emphasis changes somewhat. Matthew's combined quotation of Micah 5:1-2 and 2 Sam 5:2 in response to the magi still affirms Jesus coming as the royal son of David, but the emphasis now shifts to implications of Jesus' purpose. It is the magi, representing the nations, who recognize the coming of the Messiah and give the new-born king homage (2:1-11). The promise to Abraham is already being fulfilled. This mission to the nations is further implied by their gifts (2:11), a clearer allusion to Isaiah 60:6 than to Psalm 72:10-11. While the star is mentioned, Matthew makes no reference to Num 24:17. This is probably because the emphasis in 2:1-12 is on Israel's witness to the nations, particularly as that is set out so clearly in Isaiah 40-66. However, it is Israel's mission, and this is why, in 2:13-23, Matthew wants to show that Jesus represents Israel. In this brief sketch of the child's flight to Egypt and return and consequent withdrawal to the district of Galilee, he relives the whole history of Israel in miniature. The mentioning of the strategic places, Bethlehem, Egypt, Ramah and Galilee, covers messiahship, the Exodus, Exile and mission to the gentiles (2:22; cf 4:1416) — what Krister Stendahl called "christological geography."[7] There are certainly Mosaic allusions here (2:13, cf Exod 2:15; 2:20, cf Exod 4:19,20) but the Jer 31:15 citation connects the Exile with the Exodus in a way as to suggest the coming restoration of the Kingdom as a new exodus similar to the Exodus typology of Deutero-Isaiah.[8]

The other citations are also important christologically. The Hos 11:1 quotation ("Out of Egypt have I called my son") not only emphasizes Jesus' status as representative Israel but anticipates the baptism and temptation of Jesus (3:17-4:11) in which Jesus once again relives Israel's history of testing in the wilderness as God's son (cf Exod 4:22-23 and Deut). The other citation, "He shall be called a Nazarene" (Ναζωραῖος) spoken "by the prophets"(2:23) most likely alludes to the "shoot" or "branch"(נצר)of Isa 11:1, transferred to the people in Isa 60:21 who will grow up into "oaks of righteousness" in 61:3. Similar terminology was used in Isa 63:2 ("like a young plant, like a root out of dry ground"). That נצר and its related terminology were used in this way of the faithful of Israel collectively is clear from the Qumran psalms (1QH 6:15; 7:19; 8:5-10).[9] Thus, once again, Jesus is depicted as the representative of faithful Israel in terms of Isaiah 40-66.

## The Christology of Luke's Infancy Narrative

By drawing parallels between the annunciations and births of John the Baptist and Jesus, Luke's main point of concern in the infancy narrative appears to be to show that John was great but Jesus is greater. His christology is set in this context.

Mary is told that she is to have a child whom she will call Jesus. The angel then tells her that her son will be called "son of the Most High." Calling God "the Most High" is a Lucan characteristic. Here Jesus is called "son of the Most High" (1:32, as also in 8:28) just as John the Baptist will be called "prophet of the Most High" (1:76) and the Holy Spirit is referred to as the "power of the Most High"(1:35).[10] Being given this title and receiving the throne of "his father David," simply emphasizes that Jesus is the royal Messiah. Raymond Brown has rightly pointed out that 1:32-33 is a free interpretation of 2 Sam 7:8-16.[11] The promise to David is thus fulfilled in Jesus. The parallel statement in 1:35: "will be called holy, the son of God" also recalls 2 Sam 7:14 with its echoes in Pss 2:7 and 89:26-29. Jesus is clearly identified with the Davidic Messiah. That is further alluded to in the hymn of Zechariah (1:68-70) who praises God that he has *"redeemed* his people," "raised up a horn of salvation ... in the house of his servant David," and made explicit in the birth announcement to the shepherds (2:11).

In the Magnificat (1:46-55) Mary praises God that "he has helped his *servant* Israel in remembrance of his mercy, as he spoke to our fathers, to Abraham and to his seed forever" (vv 54,55). The reference here to "servant Israel" is reminiscent of Deutero-Isaiah where Israel's purpose is to be "a light to the nations" (42:6; 49:6), and is mentioned here in relation to the promise to Abraham and his seed (Gen 22:17; cf Isa 41:8). This is developed further in Zechariah's hymn in which the salvation through the house of "servant David" will lead them "to perform the mercy promised to our fathers, and to remember his holy covenant, the oath which he swore to our father Abraham" (1:72,73). What we have here is very similar to what we found in Matthew. Jesus' christology is presented as Davidic messiahship through which he will fulfil the promises of blessing to the nations through Abraham's seed in terms of the Isaianic servant Israel. As Brown has pointed out, it is scarcely accidental that David and Abraham are mentioned in these verses in the same order as in Mt 1:1.[12] The final verse of this hymn (1:79: "to give light to those who sit in darkness and in the shadow of death") clearly alludes to Isa 9:1-2 (cf Mt 4:15,16) and 42:6-7 and the many ensuing references to light in Isaiah 40-66.

The combination of Davidic messiahship with the role of the Servant is also found in the birth announcement and in the angelic song of praise (Lk 2:11,14). The announcement is of a "Savior who is χριστὸς κύριος. "Savior" is not found in Matthew or Mark, and in Luke only here and in 1:47 where it refers to God. However, Matthew had made the point that the child was to be called Jesus, "for he will *save* his people from their sins (1:21). Jesus is the means by which God saves. As the bringer of the good news of the Kingdom of God, Jesus is the one who "publishes salvation" (Isa 52:7; cf 61:1), and through whom salvation comes (Isa 49:6,8; 52:10; 62:11). In the light of this, the unique title, χριστὸς κύριος probably should be translated as "anointed Lord," leaving it with double meaning to refer both to Davidic Messiah and the anointed one who brings good news in Isa 61:1 (cf 40:9; 52:7). Brown sees Isaiah passages behind the whole Lucan account of the birth and angelic announcement: Isa 1:3 behind the manger motif, 9:5(6) behind the angelic message to the shepherds, and 52:7 for the mention of good news in Lk 2:10.[13] To cap it all off, the heavenly host in 2:14 uses the word εὐδοκία which in Isaiah 40-66 has the special meaning of the blessing bestowed by God in the restoration (see especially Isa 61:2; 49:6,8; 60:10. The verbal form is in Isa 42:1).

The Isaianic motif is brought out more explicitly in the depiction of Simeon (2:25-35). He is described as one waiting for the "consolation" of Israel. "Consolation" is the "comfort" to those who mourn promised so frequently in Isaiah 40-66 (40:1; 49:13; 51:3,12; 52:9; 57:18; 60:20; 61:1-2; 66:7-11,13).[14] Similar is the phrase used of Anna who speaks concerning Jesus "to all who were waiting for the 'redemption of Jerusalem'" (2:38). This is an Isaianic parallel to the "consolation of Israel" as illustrated most clearly in Isa 52:9: "Break forth together into singing, you waste places of Jerusalem; for Yahweh has *comforted* his people, he has *redeemed* Jerusalem." Similar also is the phrase regarding Joseph of Arimathea (Lk 23:51) who was one "waiting for the Kingdom of God." All three phrases probably give evidence of a group among the people who were looking for the coming Kingdom specifically in terms of the Isaianic promises, and who may have been one of Luke's special sources. Consequently, Simeon's conviction that he would not see death before he has seen "the Anointed of the Lord" (2:26) would likely have reference to Isa 61:1. Simeon's response to the child Jesus (vv 29-33) is loaded with Isaianic allusions. It is really a composite of Isa 40:5 (LXX); 52:10; 42:6; 49:6; 46:13.[15]

Clearly, the Lucan christology in the infancy narrative is for all intents and purposes the same as Matthew's. Jesus is the royal Messiah, the son of David, who carries out his mission in terms of the Servant of Yahweh in Isaiah 40-66. Luke's references to Jesus as that Servant are less subtle than Matthew's, do not bring out the representative nature of the Servant as Israel, and rely primarily on hymns for the traditional terminology. Also, in regard to Jesus as the son of David, Luke appears to come across less apologetic than Matthew.

One final comment regarding Luke's christology in reference to his use of the term κύριος Luke uses the word 27 times in chs 1-2, 25 times for God and twice for Jesus (1:43; 2:11). In the rest of his Gospel, he uses the word 76 times: 13 for God, 27 times as a general term for "master," and 15 times (incl. Lk 24:3 not found in some MSS) it is used by Luke in his narrative to refer to Jesus. In comparison, Matthew uses κύριος only 6 times in his infancy narrative and always for God. In the rest of his Gospel, it is found in discourse sometimes for God (14 times), mostly for "master" generally (36 times) or when Jesus is addressed as such (22 times). Matthew never uses it of Jesus in his narrative. In the light of this we cannot read too much into Luke's use of χριστὸς κύριος in 2:11, nor into Elizabeth's greeting Mary as the mother "of my lord" (1:43). In the latter case Luke's theological concern, as Brown points out, is to indicate the superiority of Jesus over John the Baptist.[16] But it does echo, with Luke's general use of the term, its more developed devotional use in regard to Jesus in the early church than is found in the Gospel of Matthew.

## Servant Christology in Matthew and the Lucan Parallels

The body of Matthew's Gospel begins with John's baptism (3:1-6) as a fulfillment of Isa 40:3 — as do also the Gospels of Mark and Luke. This is the indication that the promises contained in Isaiah 40-66 are about to be accomplished. As the voice calling for people to prepare for the coming of the Kingdom, John calls on them to repent and to undergo a rite of purification in the Jordan. Luke speaks of John as "preaching a baptism of repentance for the forgiveness of sins," thus reading back into John's baptism the early church's practice of announcing the forgiveness of sins to those baptized into Christ (Acts 2:38). For Matthew, Jesus as the inaugurator of the Kingdom is the one who brings the forgiveness of sins (cf Mt 9:2-6; 26:28). To the quotation of Isa 40:3, Luke adds a couple more verses in abbreviated fashion in order to end the quote with "and all flesh shall see the salvation of God" for his gentile readers (3:1-6). However, that only tends to put salvation as part of John's task. He further blurs the function of John with that of Jesus by suggesting that with his warnings of coming judgment (Lk 3:15-17), John "preached good news to the people" (3:18). In Matthew, forgiveness of sins, salvation, preaching good news all belong to Jesus.

## Mt 3:13-17/Lk 3:21-22

Matthew's account of the baptism of Jesus (3:13-17) begins with Jesus' insistence on undergoing it "to fulfil all righteousness" (3:15). A variety of different interpretations have been given of this phrase.[17] What must be taken into account is that these are Jesus' first words in Matthew's Gospel, and they are words that speak about his mission which the Baptist has been calling people to prepare for. This is not simply fulfilling some righteousness demanded by the Baptist. The meaning is in the references constantly made about righteousness in Isaiah, where the promises of God and the fulfillment of Israel's purpose are described as both divine and human righteousness. Yahweh will graciously act according to his own righteousness (Isa 59:16,17) to vindicate his people, so that in the restoration they will all be righteous, the shoot of his planting (Isa 60:17,21). Thus through them God will cause righteousness to spring forth before all the nations (61:11). Thus the Righteous One, Yahweh's servant, will cause many to be accounted righteous (53:11).[18] Thus, in undergoing baptism to "fulfil all righteousness," Jesus inaugurates the whole plan of the action of God's righteousness, his people's righteous response, and their consequent witness to all nations. In other words, Jesus thus begins the process of proclaiming God's deliverance and at the same time responds in righteousness as representing faithful Israel. Luke omits this saying as he does all references to righteousness (except the one quoted in Zechariah's speech, 1:75) likely because it would be meaningless to his gentile audience.

In Mt 3:16, Jesus is baptized, the heavens are opened, and he sees the Spirit of God descending upon him like a dove. Some see this as an allusion to Ezek 1:1.[19] But in the present context, this must recall the cry of the returned exiles in Isa 63:15-64:8, still waiting for the promised restoration: "Look down from heaven and see" (63:15), "O that you would rend the heavens and come down" (64:1[H 63:19])[20] These utterances come after recalling how God had delivered his people at the time of the Exodus, regarded them as his "sons" (63:8), put his Holy Spirit in their midst (63:11,14), as well as in the midst of the repeated cry to God of the faithful: "You are our Father" (63:16 twice; 64:8). The "Spirit of God coming down like a dove" not only recalls this context but also the promises of the Spirit in Isa 42:1; 44:3; 48:16; 57:16; 59:21; 61:1. Luke's reference to the Holy Spirit coming down as a dove "in bodily form" (Lk 3:22) is certainly secondary, possibly misunderstanding Matthew's "in comparison to" to mean "in the form of." With this background in Isaiah, the "voice from heaven" (Mt 3:17/Lk 3:22/ Mk 1:11) is God's response to the faithful who address him as "Father." In Isaiah 40-66, this calling God "Father" has come as the result of faithful Israel being called Yahweh's servant whom he has created and formed (43:1), his faithful sons and daughters called by his name (43:6,7), formed from the womb (44:1,21), borne by God from birth, carried from the womb (46:3). Israel had responded: "Yahweh called me from the womb, from the body of my mother he named my name" (49:1) "to be his servant" (49:3,5).

In the light of this, it would be natural for the words of the Father to say: "This is my son, the beloved, with whom I am well pleased," thus combining many of the descriptions of the Servant of Yahweh into one summary title, using Isa 42:1 as the basic quotation. This is typical of Matthew's use of quotations.

"The Beloved," summarizes a theme often expressed in Deutero-Isaiah regarding the Servant. In 41:8, "Israel, my servant" is also called "my beloved." Again, in 43:1-4 Yahweh addresses Israel: "Fear not, for I have redeemed you; I have called you by name, you are mine ... because you are precious in my eyes, and honored, and I love you." The same is expressed in 48:4. We can also add to this the LXX's translation of "Jeshurun," an endearing term for Israel in 44:2, as "the beloved Israel." Thus there is no need to see in these words a reference to Exod 4:22-23 or Gen 22:2,12,16 which play no part elsewhere in the Gospels[21] nor to the Targum of Ps 2:7.[22]

To have "my son" instead of "my servant" should not be regarded as unusual. In the OT and ancient near East "son" and "servant" were interchangeable as designations of a vassal in a covenant relationship.[23] Interchange between the two in regard to Isa 42:1 can already be seen in the allusions to the Servant of Yahweh in the Wisdom of Solomon (particularly in chs 1-5). There the Servant is referred to as "the righteous one" who "professes to have knowledge of God and calls himself a servant of the Lord" (παῖς κυρίου, 2:12,13; cf Isa 53:11). This servant boasts that God is his father (2:16; cf Isa 63:16; 64:8) and is referred to as "son of God" (2:18).[24] Further evidence of interchange is seen in the Johannine account of Jesus' baptism where "this is the son of God" (1:34) was originally, according to some of the earliest MSS, "this is the Chosen One of God (cf Isa 42:1).[25]

So Matthew's "This is my son" should be taken as a reference exclusively to Isa 42:1[26] Some recent commentators now agree that any reference to Ps 2:7 is secondary, since elsewhere in the NT that text is only applied after the resurrection to the risen Christ (Acts 13:33; Heb 1:5; 5:5),[27] and that "at some time in the history of the tradition a quotation of Isa 42:1 was altered in order to gain an allusion to Ps 2:7."[28] If we do not presuppose Marcan priority that "time in the history of tradition" becomes obvious. Luke saw in Jesus' baptism and the divine proclamation not only a recognition of Jesus as Servant but also his being anointed as the royal Messiah in terms of Psalm 2 (cf Acts 4:25-27; 10:38) and changed "this is" to "you are" to conform to Ps 2:7. Mark then simply followed Luke.

In Matthew, therefore, the christology expressed in Jesus' baptism is Servant christology. Jesus is acknowledged as representative of true Israel, the Servant of Yahweh, and as such he then successfully undergoes temptation in the wilderness as God's son (Mt 4:1-11; cf Wisd 3:5), just as Israel was tempted in the wilderness as God's son (Hos 11:1; Mt - 2:15). That is why Jesus fasts for forty days and forty nights as did Moses when receiving the Sinai covenant (Exod 34:28; Deut 9:9) and why he answers each temptation with quotations coming from the account of the testing of Israel in the wilderness (Deut 8:3; 6:16; 6:13). Similarly, in Wisdom of Solomon 1-5, the Servant of Isaiah 40-55 is individualized in the account of the "righteous poor man" who is depicted as both "servant" and "son of God" and is tested. Where Israel of the past failed, Jesus as Servant Israel succeeds. He is now ready to begin his Servant mission of proclaiming the good news of the Kingdom (Mt 4:23). Luke's later christology is evident not only in his changing the words "This is my son" of the baptism to "You are my son" to allude to Ps 2:7, but also in his following this with Jesus' genealogy to trace his sonship to God back through Adam (3:23-38) before continuing with the story of the temptation (Lk 4:1-13).

## Mt 8:17/Lk 4:40-41

For the sake of brevity we must pass over the many allusions to Isaiah 40-66 in the Sermon on the Mount (Mt 5-7) to look at Matthew's explicit quotation from Isa 53:4 in Mt 8:17. This comes at the end of the first cycle of three healing miracles: healing of the leper, the centurion's paralytic servant, and Peter's mother-in-law of a fever. Then, after saying that Jesus "cast out spirits with a word and healed all who were sick," Matthew has: "This was to fulfil what was spoken by the prophet Isaiah, 'He took our sicknesses and bore our diseases.'" In Isa 53:4, it was the kings and nations speaking, acknowledging their part in afflicting Israel which led to their exile and death as a nation. But they say this in wonder as they witness the restoration of Israel by Yahweh. Matthew quotes this passage here not only to recapture the wonder at these healings as signs of the restoration of the Kingdom, but also to identify Jesus christologically as the Servant of Yahweh who is the bearer of God's restoration in word and deed. In this sense it is closely related to the answer to John's disciples in Mt 11:2-6. Matthew's mention (v 16) that Jesus cast out the spirits "with a word" does help bind together Jesus' teaching and healing ministry[29] as a kind of interim statement between the *inclusio* verses of 4:23 and 9:35, but it goes further. It ties in with the centurion's affirmation of faith in 8:8: "Only say the word, and my servant will be healed," and also with 8:26-27 where Jesus stills the storm with his word so that the people marvel. All seems to be an affirmation of Deutero-Isaiah's final statement that God's word would accomplish that which he purposes (Isa 55:11). The point of this quotation, therefore, is not to illustrate Jesus' "humiliation," as Gerhard Barth and others have argued,[30] but rather to highlight that Jesus is the Servant who brings healing and restoration to all.

In the parallel (Lk 4:40-41), Luke omits the Isaiah 53 quotation and inserts a christological statement of his own by having the demons who were cast out crying: "You are the son of God" — probably borrowed from Mt 8:29 (healing of the Gadarene demoniacs) — and follows that with a command to silence "because they knew that he was the Anointed One." In this case his use of "the Anointed One" must recall his use of Isa 61:1 earlier in the chapter (4:16-30). Luke's dependence on Mt 8:16-17 in this chapter may be indicated in his reference in 4:33 to a man "who had the spirit of an unclean demon." This may be reminiscent of Matthew's "he cast out the spirits" (v 16) where parallels in Mark and Luke have simply "demons." The people's exclamation, "What is this word?" on witnessing the exorcism (Lk 4:36) is a possible allusion to Matthew's casting out spirits "with a word" (v 16). Luke may also have omitted the quotation because he had a narrower understanding of the meaning of Isaiah 53, referring it only to the suffering and death of Jesus and not to the healing. This seems to be affirmed by the Lucan quotations and allusions to it (cf Lk 22:37; 23:34,42,47; 24:26,27; Acts 3:13,14; 7:52; 8:28-33).

## Mt 11:2-6/Lk 7:18-23

According to Matthew, John in prison had heard of "the works of the Anointed One." This is the first time, apart from the infancy narrative, that the term χριστός is used in Matthew's Gospel, so it is important to understand how it is used here in context. John's disciples have been sent to ask Jesus whether he is "the Coming One," that is, the returning Elijah of Mal 4:1-6 (cf Mt 3:11-12). Jesus' response (Mt 11:4-5) is to refer back to his "works" of proclaiming the good news and healing as signs of the restoration of the Kingdom promised in Isa 25:8; 26:19; 29:18-19; 35:5-6; 42:7; 43:8; 61:1-3. All these works described so far in Matthew's Gospel have illustrated what Jesus summarizes in his response to John (11:4-6). Matthew's use of χριστός in this context must then point to the "anointed one" of Isa 61:1. He may have spoken of the "works" of the anointed one with Isa 60:21 in mind: "Your people shall all be righteous ... the shoot of my planting, the *works* of my hands that I might be glorified." Isa 61:1-3 follows that verse as an expression of those works, the acts of faithful Israel exemplifying the restoration of the Kingdom. So the use of χριστός here is related not to royal messiahship as it is in Mt 1-2, but to Jesus' role as the Servant of Yahweh.

In Luke's parallel account, which is often regarded as secondary,[31] he uses the later christological title saying that John sent his disciples "to the Lord" (although some MSS have "Jesus" for "Lord"). Besides, Luke has placed this pericope into a context in which to demonstrate that Jesus is Elijah and not John.[32] His retention of the quotation from Mal 3:1/Exod 23:20 (Lk 7:27) which in Matthew sets the scene for Jesus' saying that John is Elijah (11:14) is evidence of Luke's dependence on Matthew. Moreover, by changing Matthew's ἀκούετε καὶ βλέπετε ("hear and see," 11:4) to εἴδετε καὶ ἠκούσατε ("have seen and heard," 7:22) he has lost the real significance of Matthew's phrase. In Matthew the phrase conveys a subtle reminder to John truly to see and hear what is going on and not be afflicted with spiritual blindness and deafness, an Isaianic theme (6:9-10; 29:18; 30:20-21; 32:3; 35:5; 41:20; 42:6-8,18-20; 43:8; 44:18; 48:6-8; 50:4-5; 52:8,10,15; 55:3; cf Mt 13:13-17). Luke misses the subtlety and refers it to the healings John's disciples have just witnessed. In this way Luke has failed to build on the Servant christology he had established in 4:16-21.

## Mt 11:25-30/Lk 10:21-22

After the answer to John's disciples (Mt 11:2-6) and the ensuing discussion on John (Mt 11:7-19), Jesus upbraids the Galilean cities for their lack of belief and warns of coming judgment (Mt 11:20-24). It is in this context and in the light of the Servant christology so far evident in Matthew's Gospel that we need to examine 11:25-30. Much has been written on these verses expressing a variety of theories from theosophical mysticism as a protest against Hellenistic gnosis (Norden), the celebration of the Mysteries (Arvedsen) to Jesus as a new Moses (Allison).[33] However, the saying is thoroughly semitic and has its origins in the discussion of Israel's purpose as expressed particularly in Isaiah 40-66. The crucial word in this whole section is ἐπιγινώσκει ("know") which translates the Hebrew ירצ. Particularly in the prophetic literature, this word conveys the meaning of "being in a relationship." This is most evident in Hos 2:20[H 2:22] where "knowing" Yahweh expresses the intimacy of a marriage relationship (cf also Hos 4:1,6; 5:4; 6:3,6; 11:12[H 12:1]). This is so also in the Isaiah tradition. The "spirit of knowledge and the fear of Yahweh" which the shoot of Jesse would generate and spread (11:2,9) is a faithful covenant relationship with God. When the leaders in Jerusalem proved to be just the opposite, the prophet despaired: "Whom will he teach knowledge ... Those who are weaned from the milk, those taken from the breast?" (28:9). Hence the "babes" in Mt 11:27. Such knowledge of God leads to peace and security: "This is rest, give rest to the weary, and this is repose; yet they would not listen" (Isa 28:12). Hence the "I will give you rest" in Mt 11:28. Because they would not listen, Yahweh condemns their superficial religion (in words later quoted by Jesus in Mt 15:8) and warns: "The wisdom of their wise shall perish and the discernment of their discerning men shall be hid" (Isa 29:13,14). Hence the "you have hidden these things from the wise and understanding" in Mt 11:25. Deutero-Isaiah in Exile called the people to *know* God who is the creator of heaven and earth (Isa 40:21-23,28; 42:5; hence Mt 11:25 — "Lord of heaven and earth") so that through their witness to God's power evident in their restoration they might cause the nations to know the only true God (Isa 41:26-29; 42:1-7; 43:10; 44:18; 48:1-8; 49:1-6). Thus, "by his knowledge shall the righteous one, my servant, make many to be accounted righteous" (Isa 53:11).

In this logion Jesus recalls this motif in response to the rejection of his good news encountered not only from the Galilean cities (11:20-24) but also from "this generation" (11:16-19) and even from John questioning his role (11:2-6). Jesus here acknowledges that his role is that of the Son/Servant of Isa 42:1-6; 49:1-6; 61:1-3. The εὐδοκία ("good pleasure, gracious will") in Mt 11:26 recalls the εὐδόκησεν ("well pleased") of Isa 42:1 in Mt 12:18 and the pronouncements at Jesus' baptism and transfiguration. In those pronouncements the Father had acknowledged his relationship with the Son, and it is only through the Son that others can come into that relationship with God (cf Isa 45:14). Jesus' invitation in 11:28-30 is the call of Servant Israel, the herald of good news, calling to the faint and weary of Isa 40:28-31. His saying that he is "afflicted and lowly in heart" (πραῢς καὶ τπεινὸς τῇ καρδίᾳ) is a statement of his solidarity with faithful Israel using terms often used to refer to Israel in Isaiah (cf 29:19; 41:17; 49:13; 51:21; 53:4,7; 54:11; 61:1), and used by Jesus himself in Mt 5:3,5.[34] The fact that this invitation seems to echo the invitation of wisdom in Sir 24:19-34; 51:23-30 is deliberate to show that true wisdom is justified by her works (Mt 11:19).[35]

Lk 10:21-22 is almost identical with Mt 11:25-27 but omits the invitation. Luke places the warning of judgment to the Galilean cities into the context of sending out the Seventy (Lk 10:1-16) and then, as a joyful response to this, our pericope (Lk 10:21-22). Thus, Luke has changed what was a response to rejection in Mt 11:25-27 to a response of rejoicing over the reception of the good news among the gentiles. Luke has also changed Matthew's "know" (ἐπιγνώσκει) to "know who is" (γινώσκει τίς ἐστιν) which changes the meaning from the Semitic "relationship to" to the Hellenistic "knowledge of."[36] Luke may not have understood the subtleties of the Semitic or may simply have accommodated to his gentile audience. Nevertheless, these changes do show the secondary nature of Luke's version. However, in introducing the saying with "he *rejoiced* in the Holy Spirit" and urging the Seventy to "rejoice that their names are written in heaven" (10:20), he seems to have had in mind Isa 29:18,19 (LXX) which states that "the deaf shall hear the words of a book" and "the afflicted shall *rejoice* because of the Lord with gladness."

## Mt 12:15-21

After 11:25-30 Matthew then follows with two examples of the different approaches to the Sabbath — that of the compassionate Servant and that of the so-called "wise and understanding." It is significant in this context that Jesus again quotes from Hos 6:6 which reads in full: "I desire steadfast love and not sacrifice, the *knowledge* of God, rather than burnt offering." This then leads on to Matthew's quotation of Isa 42:1-4. As Matthew's longest quotation at a point where Jesus' mission is being brought into question, Isaiah 42 is portrayed here as pivotal for understanding who Jesus is and what he sees as his mission. As such it not only relates to the conflict with the Pharisees over the Sabbath (12:114) and Jesus' decision to withdraw with the request to those healed not to make him known (12:15,16), but to the whole of chapter 12 and with implications for what follows.[37]

In this quotation Mt follows neither the MT nor LXX but makes slight changes to emphasize certain aspects of Jesus' mission as the Servant.[38] He retains the word "servant" here although "son" was used in the Baptism and Transfiguration accounts. But, as Lamar Cope has pointed out,[39] the interchangeability of these two terms is also indicated in Jesus' response to his family: "Whoever does the will of my Father in heaven is my brother and sister and mother" (Mt 12:46-50). The intimacy of that relationship between Father and Servant/Son is again emphasized with the inclusion of "my beloved" as found in the accounts of the Baptism and

Transfiguration. "I will put my Spirit upon him" is picked up in the ensuing discussion with the Pharisees (12:22-32) to further clarify Jesus' mission. "He shall proclaim justice to the nations" is part of the Servant's role as a "light to the nations" implied in the sign of Jonah (12:38-42). The Greek κρίσις as a natural rendition of the Hebrew מֹשֶׁפֹט, is really more than "justice" or "judgment" as we generally understand those terms and involves God's whole plan and purpose. "He will not wrangle or cry out" (v 19), a slight change from the MT's "he will not cry out or lift up his voice," alludes to Jesus not wishing to get into debate with those who reject his message, as with the Pharisees in Mt 12:14-15 (cf Mt 7:6; 10:14). That "he will not break a bruised reed or quench a burning wick till he brings forth justice successfully" (v 20), has not only been exemplified in Jesus' actions summarized in Mt 11:2-6 and his associating with tax collectors and sinners, but also in his announcement that judgment comes at the end of the harvest, not at the beginning (cf Mt 13:24-30,36-43).

In Isaiah 42 the description of Servant Israel's purpose continues — it is to be a people-covenant, a light to the nations, to "open the eyes that are blind" (Isa 42:6,7; cf 43:8-10). Matthew picks that up in v 22 with Jesus healing the blind and dumb demoniac. In his previous reference (Mt 9:32-34), the demoniac had only been dumb, and it is this version which Luke follows (Lk 11:14-16). The people who witness this utter in amazement: "Can this be the son of David?" The Pharisees respond by saying that it is by Beelzebul that Jesus casts out demons. In the following discussion there is no further reference to "son of David." Rather, Jesus picks up on Isa 42:1 — he casts our demons by the Spirit of God (Mt 12:28). It is worth noting that in the body of Matthew's Gospel, Jesus is called "son of David" in only five instances — by two blind men (9:27 and again in 20:30,31), by the Canaanite woman (15:22), by the crowd entering Jerusalem and their children (21:9,15), and the people here (12:23). In fact, this story of the "blind and dumb demoniac" seems to merge the two stories of the two blind men in Mt 9:27-31 and of the dumb demoniac in 9:32-34. The healing of the two blind men in Mt 20:29-34 seems to be an expansion of 9:27-31 to illustrate that the two sons of Zebedee (Mt 20:20-28) also need to have their eyes opened. This would reduce the number of actual incidences in which Jesus is referred to as "son of David" in Matthew. Mark (10:47,48) and Luke (18:38,39) only have a parallel to Mt 20:29-34.

The disciples never use the term "son of David" and Jesus never responds to it until he raises the question concerning the sonship of the Anointed One with the Pharisees (Mt 22:42-46/Mk 12:35-37/Lk 20:41-44). When the Pharisees respond, "son of David," Jesus questions the accuracy of that response on the basis of Psalm 110. The implication there appears to be that their concept of the messiah is incorrect, that the traditional royal Davidic role has been superseded by another, that of the Servant who is God's son (3:17).40 That seems to be implied here also in the way Jesus is seen referring his power to heal to the Spirit of God according to Isa 42:1 and 61:1. That emphasis is further indicated in Mt 12:29. This is an obvious allusion to Isa 49:24-25 which pictures the nations bringing the scattered children of Israel back to the restored Kingdom. The question is raised in this context whether the mighty nations will let them go, and Yahweh's response is: "Even the captives of the mighty shall be taken and the prey of the tyrant be rescued, for I will contend with those who contend with you and I will save your children." The point of the allusion is that any attempt on the part of the Pharisees to prevent Jesus from gathering the lost sheep of the house of Israel will come to nought, for God's Kingdom *will* come. Part of the Servant's purpose was "to bring Jacob back to him, and that Israel might be gathered to him" (Isa 49:5). Jesus saw his role as doing just that, so that having gathered a faithful nucleus into the Kingdom they might be a light to the nations. This is why, at this stage, he has sent his disciples only to the lost sheep of the house of Israel (10:5; cf 15:24). Making disciples of all nations will come later (28:19-20). While Jesus here is aligning himself with Servant Israel, the Pharisees are aligning themselves with the nations that oppress.[41] So Jesus continues in Mt 12:30: "He who is not with me is against me, and he who does not gather with me scatters." Not to participate in the gathering of Israel is to work against the Spirit, and that is the blasphemy against the Spirit which will not be forgiven (vv 31-32). The title "Son of man" is clearly subsumed under the concept of Servant Israel.

The sign of Jonah (Mt 12:38-42) relates to this also. The whole point of the Book of Jonah is that Israel had failed to be a light to the nations, and when Jonah finally went to Nineveh at God's insistence, the wicked city repented. The point is that Israel's purpose to the nations is to be carried out, and anyone who hinders that will be judged and condemned by those nations. Verse 40 is really an intrusion into the meaning of the sign and is likely an interpolation of the early church.[42] It should be noted also that the repetition of "no sign shall be given ... except the sign of Jonah" (Mt 16:4) comes after the healing of the Canaanite woman's daughter (Mt 15:21-28), the healings on the mountain alluding to Isa 29:18-19 (Mt 15:29-31), the feeding of the four thousand (gentiles) with its allusions to Isa 49:10-13, the Exodus feedings, and celebration of God's reign in Isa 55:1-3 (Mt 15:32-39). The Servant's mission to the nations will not be deterred, not even by the leaven of the Pharisees and Sadducees which is not bread (Mt 16:5-12).

Luke, of course, does not have the quotation of Isa 42:1-4. The various pericopes, which in Mt 12:22-50 belong together as part of the whole, Luke has as separate sayings or incorporates them into different contexts. His account of the Beelzebul controversy diminishes the christological content as found in Matthew. He has also rewritten the "strong man" passage to emphasize Jesus' power over Beelzebul. Mt 12:3132 is reduced to one verse (Lk 12:10) and placed into a different context of collected sayings about the Son of man and the Holy Spirit. The saying on the sign of Jonah also loses some of its impact in Luke's version (Lk 11:16, 29-32). There is some evidence that Luke has been dependent on Matthew[43] and has not always understood the significance of the sayings in his source.

## Mt 16:13-23/Lk 9:18-22/(Mk 8:27-33)

This pericope is included here not because it has any explicit allusion to Isaiah 40-66 but because it is generally regarded as the most important christologically. Without entering into debate with the vast literature on this section, I wish only to make some tentative suggestions for an alternative reading of these events. If we can accept that Matthew's christology so far illustrates the Isaian influence on Jesus' teaching and Matthew's own understanding of Jesus' mission, then we need to examine this pericope in that light.

First of all, there seems to be a purpose in the almost cumbersome Matthean version of the question to the disciples: "Who do the *men* say that the *son of man* is?" It may be to emphasize the representational nature of the Son of man, which is also that of the Servant in Isaiah. But it may also be to check out how the disciples understand a term Jesus may have associated with himself. Their answer to the first question is that the Son of man is thought of by the people as some kind of prophet. The people do not see him as a royal messianic figure. The figure of the Son of man familiar to the people may be that of the Similitudes of Enoch, which give evidence of having been influenced by the Isaian traditions.[44] That Son of man in Enoch is also referred to by various Servant titles such as "the Chosen One," "Righteous One" (38:2; 53:6) and "Anointed One" (48:10; 52:4), and is seen as gathering the chosen, righteous ones and pronouncing God's judgment on the unrighteous.

Secondly, Peter's answer to the second question: "You are the Anointed One, the Son of the living God," may be a combination of Isa 61:1 with the concept of the Son of man in the Similitudes. "Son of the living God" is not necessarily a royal title, since it is not used of kings in the OT. However, it is used of the faithful of Israel in Hos 1:10 who are to be called "sons of the living God." Thus the representative nature of Jesus' mission would be emphasized. Thirdly, Jesus' saying in Mt 16:17 that it is his Father in heaven who has revealed this to Peter probably relates to what Jesus had said in Mt 11:25-27. Peter/rock may allude to Isa 51:1-2 and the reference to "build my church" draws on the idea of building the restored Kingdom in Isa 58:12 and 61:4. The "gates of Hades" recall Isa 28:15-19 and 38:10. The "keys of the kingdom" uses the image of responsibility pictured in Isa 22:15-25. The "binding and loosing" has to do with "opening the prison to those who are bound" and "loosing the bonds of wickedness (Isa 42:7; 49:9; 58:6; 61:1), but also deals with binding those without a wedding garment (Mt 22:11-14; cf Isa 61:10). How this is done is referred to in Mt 18:15-18 where this responsibility is given to all the disciples. Mt 16:20: "Then he strictly charged the disciples to tell no one that he is the Anointed One" relates also to Mt 11:25-27 as well as the concept, found in the Similitudes of Enoch (48:7; 62:7; 69:27), that the Son of man would only be revealed to the faithful.

Now that Jesus' purpose and mission has been more fully revealed to the disciples, he can now reveal the shadow side of the Servant role. This is the significance of Matthew's "From that time" (16:21). Jesus can now speak about his impending suffering, death and resurrection. In the Exile Israel had suffered and died but had never really fulfilled the resurrection of Isaiah 53. Just as Jesus had succeeded where Israel failed in the wilderness temptation (4:1-11), so he would succeed in the resurrection. That part of the Servant role Peter did not understand. This then leads Jesus to explain the relation of the disciples to him as Servant/Son of man (16:24-28).

Luke's account of this (Lk 9:18-22) is abbreviated. He simplifies Jesus' first question to "Who do *the people* say that I am?" and makes no mention of the Son of man until the passion prediction which follows (v 22). Peter's answer is shortened to "the Anointed One of God," which probably alludes to Isa 61:1. He omits Matthew's account of Jesus' answer to Peter (Mt 16:17-19) but does mention in different contexts both the "keys" of the Kingdom (Lk 11:52) and "binding and loosing" (Lk 13:15,16). This may show that Luke was familiar with these concepts either from Matthew or the tradition. He may have regarded the Isaian images of Mt 16:17-19 too much for his gentile audience. In the passion prediction Luke's account is the same as Matthew's except for the addition of "Son of man" and "and be rejected." The latter may have been with Isa 53:3 in mind, or Luke was thinking of the stone which the builders rejected mentioned in Ps 118:22. Because that stone is understood to allude to Jesus (Mt 21:42/Lk 20:17/Mk 12:10) may be the reason why Luke omits any reference to Peter being a rock. He also omits any reference to Peter's rebuke (Mt 16:22-23). One further note on Lk 9:22: when he added "and be rejected" he probably should have changed Matthew's ἀπ,' "from" to ὑπ,' "by." Mark accepted Luke's additions but thought it more appropriate to change the ἀπό to ὑπ.'

## Mt 17:5/Lk 9:36

Matthew's account of the voice at the Transfiguration is exactly the same as his account of the voice at Jesus' baptism, but with the addition of "listen to him" from Deut 18:15. As such, it is a reaffirmation of Jesus' Servant role superseding that of Moses and Elijah. In this case, Luke follows Matthew but omits "with whom I am well pleased" and changes "my beloved" to "my Chosen One," recognizing that it recalls Isa 42:1, not Ps 2:7. For this reason, he also retains Matthew's "*This is* my son." Jesus' command in Matthew: "Tell no one the vision until the Son of man is raised from the dead" (Mt 17:9) is also omitted by Luke. But in Matthew the relation between the titles, Son of man and Servant, has been established: Jesus will carry out his Servant role in terms of the Son of man who will finally be revealed as the Vindicator and Judge.

## Mt 20:28/Lk 22:27/(Mk 10:46)

Part of the context of this statement in Matthew is Jesus' response to the sons of Zebedee: "Are you able to drink the cup that I am to drink?" That this is the cup of suffering is quite clear from Mt 26:39. In the history of Israel the time of the Exile was the "cup of God's wrath" (Jer 25:15-31; 49:12; Ezek 23:31-33), and near the end of the Exile Deutero-Isaiah announced that Yahweh would now take the cup of his wrath from the exiles and put it into the hand of their tormentors (51:17-20). But Jesus now sees that like the Servant of Isaiah 53, he must still drink that cup in order to bring Servant Israel's role to completion (Mark, who follows Matthew's version closely, thinks the cup refers to the Eucharist and so adds a reference to Baptism, Mk 10:38,39). With this in mind the allusion to Isa 53:10-12 in Mt 20:28 becomes clear. Both "his soul" and "many" are used three times in that passage in a context of suffering and death. But λύτρον, "ransom," is not really a translation of the Hebrew אָשָׁם, "guilt offering." In Isa 53:10 the latter implies that Israel as a nation gave her life in exile as a guilt offering for her own sin. The "ransom" here implies that Jesus gave his life to bring about Israel's redemption and through her witness also that of the nations. The Greek verb λυτρόω is often used to translate the Hebrew גָּאַל, "redeem." This word is used 22 times in Isaiah 40-66. It means to pay the ransom price to buy back a relative from slavery. Yahweh is that relative (referred to variously in the role of father/mother or husband to Israel/Jerusalem) who will redeem Israel from exile and restore his Kingdom. According to Matthew, then, Jesus is saying that his purpose is to give his life to bring about this redemption for many. Thus the two Isaian concepts — that of the servant who becomes a guilt offering in death and is raised up to live in righteousness and to declare many righteous, and the redemption which God brings about — have been merged. As he lives out his representative role as Servant Israel/Son of man, Jesus sees this as his supreme act in bringing about the Kingdom (Cf Mt 3:15).

Luke's account (22:24-27) is considerably diminished and generalized, so that Luke has Jesus as not the one who sits at table, but as the one who serves. The account lacks any allusion to Isaiah 40-66. However, the verbal form λυτρόω is used in the story of the men on the way to Emmaus who say of Jesus: "We had hoped that he was the one to *redeem* Israel (Lk 24:21).

## Mt 26:28/Lk 22:20/(Mk 14:23,24)

In the light of Mt 20:28 it is easy to see the image of the Isaianic Servant in what Matthew records Jesus as saying in the Last Supper. This saying draws on a number of images — the sealing of the covenant by sprinkling blood in Exod 24:8, the reaffirmation of Isa 42:6-7; 49:9; 61:1-3 against the background of the covenant renewal ceremony and the pouring out of the sacrificial blood during the Feast of Booths in Zech 9:11-12. However, the words, "which is poured out for many for the forgiveness of sins" must recall Isa 53:12: "He poured out his soul to death ... yet he bore the sin of many." Only Matthew has "for the forgiveness of sins." Some see this as a gloss which detracts from the main point of the saying.[45] But, as stated earlier, in Isaiah 40-66 the forgiveness of sins is the basis for the restoration of the Kingdom, and in Isaiah 53 the Servant's suffering is seen as the means for extending that forgiveness to the nations. So it is really essential here. In the next verse (Mt 26:29), Jesus' statement that he will not drink wine again until he drinks it new with the disciples in the Father's Kingdom refers to Isa 55:1-5, where it speaks of sharing in the blessings of the restored Kingdom in an everlasting covenant with God.

While Mark's rendering of this saying is fairly close to Matthew's (he omits "for the forgiveness of sins" with Luke), Luke's account is shorter, tones down the allusions to Isa 53:12, omits the allusion to Isa 55:1-5, and has more in common with the Pauline version in 1 Cor 11:25.

There are other Isaian allusions in Matthew. In 21:5, Matthew combines a quotation from Isa 62:11 with Zech 9:9. This is omitted by Luke, but he does retain the quotation from Isa 56:7 (Lk 19:46; Mt 21:13), probably because of the importance of prayer in his Gospel. Matthew's allusions to Isa 34:4 and 13:10 in Mt 24:29 is diminished in Lk 21:25-26. The parable of the Last Judgment (Mt 25:31-46) with its allusion to Isa 58:7 is not in Luke. Matthew's allusions to Isa 53:7 ("he opened not his mouth") in 26:63 and 27:12,14 are not in Luke. Luke omits the "spitting" (Isa - 50:6) of Mt 26:67 but he has included it in the third passion prediction (18:32), while Matthew does not (20:19). Luke's accounts of the passion predictions are essentially the same as Matthew's but with a strong emphasis on the disciples' lack of understanding (Lk 9:45;18:34).

## SERVANT CHRISTOLOGY UNIQUE TO LUKE

Luke's frequent allusions to Isaiah have often been emphasized.[46] But as we have seen, most of the Lucan references to the Isaian tradition have also been found in Matthew's Gospel. There are, however, three quotations or allusions which are unique to Luke's Gospel (4:16-30; 22:37; 23:35).

The Sermon at Nazareth for Luke (4:16-30) is the inauguration of Jesus' ministry in which, by means of a quotation combining Isa 61:1-2 and 58:6, Jesus defines his mission. Matthew's general reference to Jesus preaching in the Nazareth synagogue comes after there has already been growing resistance to his teaching (Mt 13:53-68). Luke's placing of this Sermon here to illustrate who Jesus is appears to be a substitute for Matthew's Sermon on the Mount which he found too complex for that purpose. Fitzmyer rightly makes the point that Luke has put this story here "to encapsulate the entire ministry of Jesus and the reaction to it." This whole section thus stresses the success of his Spirit-guided teaching as well as his rejection by his own people, leading to the mission to the gentiles.[47]

Certainly, this section identifies a number of christological issues for Luke. The opening verse of the quotation, "The Spirit of the Lord is upon me," picks up the Spirit descending upon Jesus at the baptism (3:22), his being "full of the Holy Spirit" and "led by the Spirit" in the temptation story (4:1), and his returning to Galilee "in the power of the Spirit"(4:14). Thus, in this Sermon Jesus is announcing publicly that he has been anointed with the Holy Spirit, which Luke sees as having taken place at his baptism (cf Acts 10:38). But in what way does Luke understand this anointing? Bock argues that because of the connection with the baptism, Jesus was here announcing that he is the Anointed One not merely as Isaian Servant or Herald but more so as the royal Messiah. He argues that "the larger Lucan context is regal and messianic, not prophetic" and that points to a messianic understanding of this passage.[48] However, the whole quotation has nothing to do with any Davidic or royal function, and Jesus' comment that "no prophet is acceptable in his own country" (4:24) emphasizes Jesus' prophetic nature as the Anointed One in spite of the allusions to Ps 2:7 in the baptism. What we found in Matthew is also true of Luke: in the body of their Gospels the term "the

Christ" is not normally used of a royal messiah, except in the mouth of Jesus' accusers (as in Lk 23:2). Luke's version of Peter's confession is simply "The Anointed One of God" (9:20). His rendition of Jesus' question to the Pharisees is: "How can you say that the Anointed One is David's son?" (20:41). In Matthew (22:42) the question is more ambivalent. Otherwise Luke's use of the term is associated with Jesus' saving activity and his suffering — both strong Servant motifs in Luke. Even the rulers at the cross scoff at Jesus calling on him to save himself "if he is the Anointed One of God, his Chosen One" (Lk 23:35; cf 23:39) — an obvious allusion to Isa 42:1 and 61:1. If Luke is summarizing Mt 27:40-43 here he has understood Matthew's reference to "son of God" in terms of Isa 42:1 (cf Lk 9:35). The two references to the Anointed One in the post-resurrection accounts both emphasize the necessity of his suffering (Lk 24:26,46; cf Isa 53). It should be noted that Luke connects Isa 61:1 to Jesus being called "the Anointed One" later on in chapter 4 (v 41), as well as to the terms "the holy one of God" (v 35) and "son of God" (v 41). That Luke sees Jesus' mission in terms of Isa 61:1 is clear from Jesus' final statement in this chapter: "I must preach the good news of the kingdom of God to the other cities also; for I was sent for this purpose" (4:43). Luke depicts Jesus here as taking on a prophetic role in terms of the Isaianic Servant. As such, he will be greater than the great prophets of the past, Elijah and Elisha (cf Lk 7:16,39; 13:33; 24:19).

Luke's other unique quotation is from Isa 53:12 (Lk 22:37). Jesus tells his disciples: "That which is written must be fulfilled in me, 'And he was reckoned with the lawless.'" This clearly identifies Jesus as the Servant of Yahweh, and the necessity of his suffering as such in terms of Isaiah 53 is set out by Jesus after the resurrection (Lk 24:26,27,44-47). Luke sees this as the fulfillment of all the OT scriptures. As has often been noted, there is no explicit reference in Luke's use of Isaiah 53 to a vicarious atonement, just as there was not in Mt 8:17. Yet Luke's use of Isa 53:12 indicates that this was an underlying concept in his understanding of Jesus' mission. It is intriguing that both Matthew and Luke fail to be more explicit about the idea of vicarious atonement in Isaiah 53. For Matthew the reason appears to be two-fold: he wanted to portray Jesus as fulfilling the whole role of Servant Israel and did not want to isolate the idea of sacrifice. The idea of sacrifice was generally played down in the prophetic movement as is also indicated in Jesus' quotation of Hos 6:6 twice in Matthew's Gospel. Luke did not want to get any more explicit than Matthew, perhaps because he would rather simply imply the idea of atonement for his gentile readers. For Luke the two focal points of Jesus' ministry in terms of the Servant are to be the bearer of the good news to the afflicted and to go the way of suffering and rejection in order that repentance and forgiveness, the good news of the Kingdom, might then be preached in his name to all the nations (24:27).

## Conclusions

1. In the infancy narrative Matthew has set down emphatically that Jesus is the son of David, a royal messiah, and then eased into a description of Jesus as representative Israel. Yet the references to the "son of David" in relation to Jesus in the body of his Gospel are ambivalent at best. This would indicate that royal messiahship was not a focal point of Jesus' ministry, but that Matthew wished to defend the post-resurrection conviction that the Anointed One had fulfilled all the hopes of Israel in his proclaiming the Kingdom.

2. Luke's infancy narrative followed the same approach, but it lacks the apologetic tone of Matthew which had been necessary for the earlier Palestinian situation. Luke also moves from portraying Jesus as the royal messiah to describing him as the Servant Israel by making use of a number of hymns and sayings in the tradition attributed to various people. It seems that for Luke, the Matthean depiction of Jesus as representing true Israel in Mt 2, while obvious to those of Jewish background, would not be clear to his gentile audience. So he used different sources that would make it more explicit.

3. In the body of both Gospels Jesus is portrayed as fulfilling the role of the Servant of Yahweh depicted in Isaiah 40-66. Christological terms such as "son of God" and "Christ" are subsumed under the concept of the Servant. The use of the term "Christ" is understood primarily in terms of the Anointed One of Isa 61:1. The concept of the Son of man is merged with that of the Servant.

4. In the survey of the various quotations and allusions to Isaiah 40-66, we have noticed a tendency for Luke to lessen the impact of or omit the allusion, either because he did not fully comprehend its implications or wished to make the saying more meaningful for his gentile audience. Luke was always conscious of the need to make this Jewish story relevant to the nations for whom Jesus was also Good

News. All this would suggest that Luke was dependent on Matthew or his tradition.

5. While both Gospels focus on Jesus as the Servant, the Chosen One, Matthew's Gospel shows a more wholistic understanding of the content and meaning of Isaiah 40-66 and of the role of the Servant. Luke's Gospel focuses more on the Servant as the One Anointed to preach good news (Isa 61) and on his role in suffering and dying (Isa 53).

6. Looking at the Gospels from a different perspective changes the scene. The Two Gospel Hypothesis offers opportunity for a fresh approach and new insights into christological problems which, from the perspective of the Two Document Hypothesis, have often seemed insoluble.

## Notes:

1 Oscar Cullmann, *The Christology of the New Testament* (Revised edition; Philadelphia: Westminster, 1963), 51.

2 (London: SPCK, 1959).

3 Hooker, 149.

4 Since the numerical value of the consonants in the name "David" add up to 14.

5 Many of these points are made by Raymond E. Brown, *The Birth of the Messiah: A Commentary on the Infancy Narratives in Matthew and Luke* (Garden City, N.Y.: Doubleday, 1977), 59-81.

6 Cf Brown, 139.

7 Krister Stendahl, "Quis et Unde? An Analysis of Matthew 1-2," in *The Interpretation of Matthew* (Graham Stanton, ed.; Philadelphia Fortress Press, 1983), 59. See also Brown, 217.

8 See Bernhard W. Anderson, "Exodus Typology in Second Isaiah," *Israel's Prophetic Heritage: Essays in Honor of James Muilenburg* (Bernhard W. Anderson and Walter Harrelson, eds; New York: Harper, 1962),177-195. Anderson isolates 10 Exodus allusions: Isa 40:3-5; 41:17-20; 42:14-16; 43:1-3, 14-21; 48:20-21; 49:8-12; 51:9-10; 52:11-12; 55:12-13.

9 See Brown, 212-213. However, Brown prefers to see Isa 4:3 and Jud 16:17 as the background for this citation, 223-225. The name of the town, "Nazareth," itself may have derived from נצר (see D. C. Pellett, "Nazareth," *IDB* III, 524) in which case it may have been a settle-

ment established by those who regarded themselves as the "shoots" of God's planting (Isa 60:21). If that were so, it would have given Joseph and Mary good reason for going there.

10   Note also that where Mt 5:9 has "shall be called sons of God," Lk (6:35) has "sons of the Most High."

11   Brown, 310.

12   Brown, 383. However, Brown traces both back to a pre-Gospel tradition. For other similarities between Mt's and Lk's infancy narratives suggesting Lucan dependence, see John Drury, *Tradition and Design in Luke's Gospel* (Atlanta: John Knox, 1976),122-128.

13   Brown, 425. \

14   See my comments on Mt 5:4 in "The Beatitudes, Salt and Light in Matthew and Luke," *SBL 1991 Seminar Papers* (Atlanta: Scholars Press, 1991), 826-828.

15   Cf Brown, 458. Also Darrell Bock, *Proclamation from Prophecy and Pattern: Lucan Old Testament Christology* (Sheffield: JSOT Press, 1987), 86-88.

16   Brown, 341, 342.

17   See, for instance, W.D. Davies and Dale C. Allison, *A Critical and Exegetical Commentary on the Gospel According to Saint Matthew* (ICC; Edinburgh: T&T Clark, 1988), I, 325-327.

18   See further my discussion on righteousness in Mt 5:6 in "The Beatitudes," 830-831.

19   Davies and Allison, I, 329; R.H. Gundry, *The Use of the Old Testament in Matthew's Gospel* (Leiden: Brill, 1967), 28.

20   Mt and Lk both use the passive of "to open." The active form is used by the LXX (Isa 63:19) to translate the Hebrew "to tear, rend" reflected in Mk's σχιζόμενος. See Gundry, 28-29.

21   Against Paul Bretscher, "Exodus 4:22-23 and the Voice from Heaven," *JBL* 87 (1968), 301-311; and C.H. Turner, "Ο ΥΙΟΣ ΜΟΥ Ο ΑΓΑΠΗΤΟΣ" *JTS* 27(1926), 113-129. Cf also Bock, 99-105; Davies and Allison, I, 340-341; Joseph Fitzmyer, *The Gospel According to Luke I-IX* (Anchor; Garden City, N.Y.: Doubleday, 1981), 485-486.

22   Against Gundry, 30-31.

23   Cf the interplay in 2 Sam 7 and Ahaz's submission to Tiglath-Pilesar: "I am your servant and your son," 2 Kgs 16:7. See Roland de Vaux, *The Bible and the Ancient Near East* (London: Longman and Todd, 1966), 154-158.

24  See the interchange of "servants" and "sons" in Wisd 9:4 & 7; 12:7, 20 & 19, 21. See also J. Jeremias, "Παῖς Θεοῦ," *TDNT*, V, 678. Also, compare the uses of terminology in the story of the centurion's servant/son in Mt 8:5-13/Lk 7:1-10/Jn 4:46-54.

25  See Jeremias, *TDNT*, V, 689. However, there is no need to argue that an original "my servant" was later changed by the early church. See also Jeremias' *New Testament Theology: The Proclamation of Jesus. Vol I* (New York: Scribners, Macmillan, 1971), 53-55.

26  So Jeremias, New *Testament Theology,* 53-55; Cullmann, 66.

27  E.g. Fitzmyer, 485.

28  Davies and Allison, I, 338.

29  Davies and Allison, II, 37.

30  Gerhard Barth in *Tradition and Interpretation in Matthew* trans. P. Scott (Philadelphia: Westminster, 1963),128-129; also Davies and Allison, II, 38.

31  Fitzmyer, 663, says: "The shorter form found in Matt 11:2-4 is generally regarded as representing the more original 'Q' form." Davies and Allison, II, 240,242, think that Mt has just abbreviated.

32  Following his references to Jesus as a prophet like Elijah and Elisha (4:24-27), Luke has used the story of the healing of the centurion's servant in Lk 7:1-10 to parallel Elisha's healing in 2 Kgs 5:1-14 and the story of the raising of a dead son (Lk 7:11-17) to parallel the story of Elijah raising a widow's son (1 Kgs 17:17-24). Other parallels to Elijah are: Lk 9:51(2 Kgs 2:9,11); Lk 9:54 and 12:49 (1 Kgs 18:36-38; 2 Kgs 1:9-14; 2 Kgs 2:9-15); Lk 9:61-62 (1 Kgs 19:9-21); Lk 24:51-53 and Acts 1:9-11 (Mal 4:5-6).

33  See the bibliographies on this pericope in Davies and Allison, II, 297-302; and on Lk in Fitzmyer, *The Gospel According to Luke X-XXIV* (New York: Doubleday, 1985), 875-876. Also Graham Stanton, *A Gospel for a New People: Studies in Matthew* (Edinburgh: T&T Clark, 1992), 340-342, 364-377.

34  The Greek word praÁj usually translates the Hebrew עָנִי, עָנָו, "afflicted," commonly used in Deutero-Isaiah for the exiles and in Trito-Isaiah for the faithful of Israel. It is closely related to terms such as "the broken-hearted" (Isa 61:1), "the crushed and lowly in spirit" (Isa 57:15; 66:2; cf Ps 34:18). This has little to do with our idea of "meekness." See my discussion of Mt 5:3,5 in "The Beatitudes," 825826,828-829.

35  Against M. Jack Suggs, *Wisdom, Christology, and Law in Matthew's Gospel* (Cambridge, Mass.: Harvard University Press, 1970), 106-107.

36  In disagreement with Fitzmyer, *Luke X-XXIV,* 874, who reads into Lk's account "the intimate relationship of Father and Son" from Mt's version.

37  In agreement with Lamar Cope *Matthew: A Scribe Trained for the Kingdom of Heaven* (CBQ Monograph Series 5; Washington D.C., 1976), 32-52; and Jerome H. Neyrey, "The Thematic Use of Isaiah 42:1-4 in Matthew 12," Biblica 63 (1982), 457-473.

38  For a thorough examination of Mt's text, see Krister Stendahl, *The School of St. Matthew and its Use of the Old Testament* (Philadelphia: Fortress, 1968), 107-115; Gundry, 110-116.

39  Cope, 45-46.

40  The early church understood this not as an "either or" but as a "both and" situation. Cf Acts 2:34-36. In Mt and parallels, the statement is left ambiguous because of Matthew's concern to emphasize that Jesus is also the Davidic Messiah. Cf Joseph A. Fitzmyer, *Essays on the Semitic Background of the New Testament* (Missoula: Scholars Press, 1974), 113-126. Also Brown, 505-512.

41  Against Hooker, 73.

42  In agreement with Stendahl, *The School of St. Matthew,* 132-133, and Cope, 40-41.

43  See H. Benedict Green, "Matthew 12.22-50 and Parallels: An Alternative to Matthean *Conflation, "Synoptic Studies: The Ampleworth Conferences of 1982 and 1983* (C.M. Tuckett, ed. Sheffield: JSOT Press, 1984), 157-171.

44  See especially George W.E. Nickelsburg, "Salvation without and with a Messiah: Developing Beliefs in Writings Ascribed to Enoch," in *Judaisms and Their Messiahs at the Turn of the Christian Era,* ed. by Jacob Neusner, *et al* (Cambridge: University Press, 1987), 49-68.

45  Eg, Hooker, 82.

46  Eg, David Secombe, "Luke and Isaiah," NTS 27 (1981), 252-259; - James A. Sanders, "Isaiah in Luke," in *Interpreting the Prophets* (James L Mays and Paul Achtemeier, eds; Philadelphia: fortress, 1987),75-85.

47  Fitzmyer, *Luke I-IX,* 529.

48  Bock, 109-110.

# Crisis in Christology

# 15

# JESUS OF NAZARETH - THE CHRIST OF OUR FAITH

## Peter Stuhlmacher

Anyone today who takes up the question of who Jesus was and who the Christ is in whom Christians believe must be prepared to take a position on a complex of problems which has developed out of more than one hundred years of theological and ecclesiastical discussion. Although both of our questions are acutely relevant,[1] they are by no means new. They have engaged the interest of Christians and non-Christians for a long time. In the year of 1892, Martin Kaehler, who was then teaching at Halle, held a lecture with the seemingly strange title, "The So-Called Historical Jesus and the Historic, Biblical Christ." Kaehler protests in this lecture against the attempt by critical scholars with learned methods to "squeeze out"[2] of the four biblical Gospels an alleged historically dependable picture of Jesus and then to raise this to the standard for faith in Jesus Christ. The Christ of our faith from which the Church has proceeded from its beginnings and from which it must proceed in the future is, according to Kaehler, the biblical Christ of whom the Gospels tell and in whom the other authors of the New Testament confess their faith. The picture which the evangelists paint of Jesus is based on the impressions which the disciples had gathered of Jesus during his period of earthly activity together with them. This picture does not conflict with faith in Jesus Christ but strengthens such faith, and the church can and indeed should be satisfied with this situation in its proclamation of the faith.

Adolf Schlatter (1852-1932), who from 1898 on was Professor of Dogmatics and New Testament at Tuebingen, agreed with Kaehler's position but was, at the same time, able to decisively define this position. Schlatter stood for the view that the Christ of faith is none other than the historical Jesus, and he considered Jesus' status as the messianic Son of God[3] to be the prime test case for this identification. According to Schlatter, Jesus of Nazareth came forward in the same way that this is reported by the Gospels, i.e., with the claim to be the Son of God and the Messiah of Israel. The apostles then confessed for this very reason Jesus to be the Son of God and the Messiah. A deep-seated difference between the historical Jesus and the Christ of faith can, in Schlatter's opinion, only arise when one neither can nor wants to conceive of the earthly Jesus coming forward as the Messiah. Only a few scholars such as Julius Schniewind,[4] Joachim Jeremias[5] and Leonhard Goppelt[6] have followed (Kaehler and) Schlatter in this; most exegetes of the New Testament in Germany and elsewhere did not. They have ignored Schlatter's warning and have promptly become entangled in those contradictions which Schlatter had predicted. The unity of the biblical picture of Jesus is shattered for them,[7] the result being that some of them make a clear distinction between the historical Jesus on the one hand and Christ on the other who was not preached and believed upon until after Easter. Rudolph Bultmann, for example, considers the preaching of the Jewish Rabbi and prophet Jesus to be one of the prerequisites for a New Testament theology, but not an integral part of the development of the New Testament tradition of faith.[8]

The programmatic retrospective look at the person and work of the earthly Jesus, promulgated by Ernst Kaesemann,[9] Guenther Bornkamm[10] and Ernst Fuchs[11] in the 1950's, also proved unable to produce a sound solution. Indeed, up to the present an allegedly historical view of Jesus as an end-time prophet contrasts with that of Jesus as the Christ of our faith who only after Easter is proclaimed to be the Son of God. Both views are often combined in such a way that one can speak of an indirect messianic claim by Jesus before Easter and a direct confession to Jesus as the Messiah in the post-resurrection preaching.[12] Although this way of putting it is a compromise which in view of the biblical sources is at least to a certain degree tolerable, it cannot (in my opinion) permanently solve the problem indicated by Kaehler and Schlatter. The question as to whether early Christianity subsequently stylized Jesus into the saving Christ is of great soteriological interest. Whether this was the case or not must in the interest of the truth and of the Christian faith be clarified as exactly as possible.[13]

The usual solution is even less of a help when the Jewish-Christian dialogue (which has fortunately been reinitiated!) uses a reductionist view of Jesus as a common point of orientation. The Jewish side discovers (and rightly so!) a Jesus in the Gospels who lived, acted and suffered as a Jew, and it is ready and willing to recognize Jesus as "one of the prophets" (Mk 8,2), or perhaps even "more than" a prophet, and as a teacher of wisdom who is "more than Solomon" (Mt 12:41-42).[14] Whether the earthly Jesus was (and is) the Messiah of Israel is, understandably, either left unanswered or denied.[15] The Jewish participants in the discussion, however, do not need to accept this, because the Christian participants accommodate them with their critical view of Jesus, date the confession to Jesus as the Messiah and the Son of God to a post-resurrection period and deny any direct messianic claim of the earthly Jesus.[16] The earlier position which Schlatter took appears in the course of this dialogue to be either antiquated or (what is worse) tainted with anti-Semitism and thus an evil to be avoided.

The fact is, however, — and in this historical judgement I agree with my friends and colleagues in Tuebingen, Otto Betz[17] and Martin Hengel[18] — that Schlatter was right. Even though we have a much more discriminating view of the Gospels and other books of the New Testament with regard to historical details than Schlatter had considered necessary,[19] his main point deserves our agreement: Without seeing and recognizing that the earthly Jesus had already claimed to be the messianic "Son of Man" whom God had sent to Israel, there is no way to historically understand either Jesus' work or the passion story. The apostles did not simply attach to Jesus certain characteristics and ways of behaviour subsequent to Easter which he never had on earth (nor claimed to have); on the contrary, the post-resurrection confession of the Christian Church in Jesus as Son of God and Messiah confirms and recognizes who Jesus historically wanted to be and who he was and remains for faith. God's history in and with Jesus, the Christ of God, is the basis for the Christian faith from the beginning.[19] This history bears and determines this faith; faith does not initially create this history.[20]

## Problem and Task

In view of that which has been presented so far, some will ask whether this whole debate is anything more than a typical quarrel among (university) theologians, having no meaning for church practice. One can indeed see the situation in this way, but one should be careful not to oversimplify things. This is because the question as to what justification

Christians have for confessing Jesus to be Christ and Son of God is of importance to every Christian (and to every non-Christian as well, inasmuch as he claims the right to reject the Christian confession of faith or to consider it unimportant).

We recognize easily that we are confronted with true questions of faith when we try to bring together two post-resurrection confessions of faith in Jesus as Christ and Son of God with the Jesus tradition of the Gospels and when we consider that the Gospels themselves do not tell of Jesus and his suffering each in the same way but differently. It becomes evident in both of these cases that considerable intellectual effort is required to really achieve a biblical view of Jesus which is convincing on its own merits.

## Two Post-Resurrection Confessions of Faith in Christ

The three articles which form the Apostles' Creed, the dominating Creed in our churches today, want to be a summary of the testimonial statements of the Holy Scriptures which are essential to the Christian faith. The second article of the Creed models itself primarily upon those early church dogmas and confessions of faith in Jesus as Son of God and Messiah which had already been formulated in the Bible. Let us take a look at two such confessions of faith. The first one is cited by Paul in 1 Cor 15, and he indicates that it is a confession characteristic of all apostles; the second is to be found in 1 Timothy and is representative of the Church in the post- apostolic period.

Paulus writes in 1 Cor 15:3-8 to the church in Corinth:

"For I handed on to you first of all what I myself received (as teaching), that Christ died for our sins in accordance with the Scriptures;(4) that he was buried and, in accordance with the Scriptures, rose on the third day;(5) that he was seen by Cephas (= Peter), then by the Twelve.(6) After that he was seen by five hundred brothers at once, most of whom are still alive (Incidentally: 1 Corinthians was written by Paulus in Ephesus around 54/55 A.D.), although some have fallen asleep.(7) Next he was seen by James; then by all the apostles(8) Last of all he was seen by me, as one born out of the normal course."

In verses 3-5, we have before us a brief, didactic formulation of the "gospel" (cf.Cor 15:1) which originated in the first few years after Jesus' death and resurrection. The core of the gospel is the death of "the Christ" for our sins, his burial, his resurrection by God on the third day and his appearance before Peter, the twelve and the other apostles. The death and resurrection of Jesus occurred, as the text expressly states, "according to the Scriptures," i.e. according to the will of God as it is recorded and vouched for in the Old Testament. According to 1 Cor 15:3-5, the core of the gospel of Christ is the death of Jesus for our sins and his resurrection by God. Similar but somewhat different in its perspective is the confessional text 1 Tim 2:5-6:

"...'God is one. One also is the Mediator between God and men, the man Christ Jesus,(6) who gave himself as a ransom for all.' This truth was attested at the fitting time . "

According to this text, Jesus is chosen by God to be the one mediator between God and man who fulfilled his divine mission through the laying down of his life and who established the testimony of the gospel at the time determined by God (cf. v.6 with 2 Tim 1:8 and Gal 4:4). This is the gospel which Paul and the leaders of the church(es) who follow him are to preach.

The two formulations of the gospel from 1 Cor 15 and 1 Tim 2 look back upon Jesus from a post-Easter perspective and see in his suffering and death the decisive climax of his mission as Messiah and (Son of) Man which leads to salvation for those who believe. The focus on the passion tradition is obvious in both texts and can only be questioned through artificial argumentation (which is, however, on occasion still the case.[21]) .

It is exactly this concentrated look upon the passion which causes great difficulties, even among interested Christians. The narrative of the sacrificial death of Christ, a death willed by God, appears from the perspective of our modern thought conventions to be not only hard to understand but offensive as well. Why is the sacrifice of the Son of God on the cross necessary in order to achieve forgiveness for our sins? A God who allows his own son to be executed on the cross and who only through this can then forgive sinners appears cruel and strange, like a Molech (cf. Lev 18:21; Isa 30:33) and not like the God of love. Whether this offense can be overcome is one of the most important questions which present themselves in our context. The early Christian confession of faith in Jesus as the Christ of God (and thus the whole Christian faith) must remain foreign to all who cannot understand the passion of Jesus. We are faced therefore with a true problem of faith.

## The Diversity of the Testimonies of the Gospels and the Necessity of Critique

All of the four biblical Gospels coincide with the early Christian confessions of faith in Jesus as the Christ of God and as the mediator between God and Man in the great emphasis which they place upon the passion of Jesus in their narratives. As Martin Kaehler appropriately has said: "One can, somewhat provocatively, call the Gospels passion stories with detailed introductions."[22] Without an understanding of the passion story there is no understanding of the Gospels. But it is precisely the passion story which is by no means told in the same way by each of our Gospels. The biggest difference exists between the Gospel of John as compared to the first three Gospels (although the [pre-] Lucan passion narrative already differs from that of Mark and Matthew and is similar to that of John). It is the differences in dates and in accentuation which exegetes since early church times have noticed and with which they have had trouble dealing. According to the Gospel of John, Jesus dies on the cross in the very hour that the paschal lambs are being slaughtered in the temple prior to their being prepared for the evening Passover meal. While according to the reports of Mark, Matthew and Luke, Jesus was celebrating the Passover meal with his twelve disciples on that evening, he had already died according to John. We seek, therefore, without success in the fourth Gospel for a report of the last supper like that given by the first three Gospels and also by Paul (in 1 Cor 11 :23ff.). At the same time, one notes that, except for a few allusions (cf. 13:21; 19:28), all of the statements concerning Jesus' lowliness, with which we are familiar from the passion narratives in the other Gospels, are corrected in John: Jesus' trembling and sorrow in Gethsemane (cf. Mk 14:32-42 par.) is almost turned into the opposite in Jn 12:27-33 and 18:2-11. The moving scene of Jesus collapsing while carrying the cross, which he had to drag out to Golgotha, so that the soldiers forced Simon from Cyrene to carry the cross for him (cf. Mk 15:20f.), is replaced in

Jn 19:17 with the pointed remark: Jesus carried "the cross for himself," i.e. under his own power. Instead of the cry in prayer "My God, my God, why have you forsaken me?" from Ps 22:1 (Mk 15:34 and Mt 27:46), Jesus' last words on the cross in John are: "It is finished" (Jn 19:30). In view of these weighty shifts in accentuation by John in comparison with the first three Gospels, we have no other choice than to read the four Gospels critically and not attempt to simply get around the differences in the narratives by harmonizing.

There are also differences, however, between the three synoptic Gospels which need to be considered and explained: Why, for example, does the Gospel of Mark begin with the report of the appearance of John the Baptist and the baptism of Jesus, whereas Matthew and Luke present their famous preparatory narratives (among them the Christmas story in Lk 2)? How is it to be explained that we find the Sermon on the Mount in Mt 5-7 and in Luke only the short so-called "Sermon on the Plain"(Lk 6:17-49); at the same time we read other sayings of Jesus which Matthew had placed in the Sermon on the Mount dispersed throughout the Gospel of Luke. Mark does not tell of a Sermon on the Mount or of a Sermon on the Plain at all. Nor does he hand down the Lord's Prayer which Matthew offers in ch.6:9-13 and Luke in ch. 11:2-4. Conversely, in no other Gospel except Mark can one find the comment to the effect that Jesus' family left Nazareth to come and take charge of Jesus, because they think "he is out of his mind" (Mk 3:20f.). We must therefore extend our resolution to read the passion narrative critically to cover the Gospels as a whole if we really want to obtain a fairly accurate picture of Jesus.

A critical reading of this sort does not by the way do injustice to the Bible! First of all already at the end of 1 Thess Paul called upon the church not to show contempt for prophetic testimonies but to test everything and to hold on (only) to the good (1 Thes 5:20f.; cf. similarly Rom 12:2) and in the second place 1 Pet calls upon the Christians to "always be prepared to give an answer to everyone who asks you to give the reason for the hope that you have" (1 Pet 3:15). But to give an answer is in our context and in the current discussion only possible when it becomes very clear to us just how the preaching of Jesus and faith in him relate to one another and what we are to make of the testimony of the Bible as a whole. If one wants to do justice to 1 Pet 3:15 in view of the current state of the discussion - a discussion which is characterized by a true chaos of opinion both within and outside the church then critical historical work with the the Holy Scriptures is indispensable.

# From the Preaching of Jesus to Faith in Jesus Christ

Tracing the way from the preaching of Jesus to faith in Jesus Christ as it is exemplarily expressed in the creeds which have been mentioned requires risking a critical reconstruction which takes into consideration the problems and differences in the biblical sources which we have touched upon. Every reconstruction must follow certain methodological guidelines which are just as open to discussion as that which is reconstructed. So that my argument can be critically followed I will first identify the principles of reconstruction which guide me and only then will I proceed to present the actual reconstruction itself.

## The Principles of Reconstruction

In the process of determining the relationship between the four Gospels I proceed from the assumption (an assumption which is largely accepted but which is not valid beyond all question) that the oldest Gospel is the Gospel of Mark which was edited for the final time by John Mark probably in Rome (cf. in him Acts 12:12; 13:5.13; 15:37-39; Phlm 24; Col 4:10; 2 Tim 4:11 and 1 Pet 5:13) before the destruction of Jerusalem by Roman troops in the year 70 CE. It is based on Petrine traditions and on other apostolic narrative and kerygmatic traditions.[23] The Gospels of Mathew and Luke used Mark's Gospel as a source and model. However they have drawn from additional material from a "sayings and discourse source" which was used by Christian teachers and prophetic missionaries in Palestine and Syria as a handbook for their preaching activity. This source — usually just called Q for the German word Quelle (=source) — contained for example most of the traditional material of the Sermon on the Mount (and the Lucan Sermon on the Plain). If we take both the Q material and Mark together we obtain a reasonably dependable picture of the words and work of Jesus. This can be supplemented by narrative material which is only offered by Mark, Matthew or Luke respectively the so-called "special material" of the Gospels. This picture is dependable because the traditional narratives and sayings in

Mark, the logia-source and the "special material" are all based on the memories of Peter and of those women and men who had accompanied Jesus during his earthly ministry and who then after Easter were called by the resurrected Christ to become his apostles and formed the core of the primitive church. The continuity in the circle of disciples from the pre-resurrection to the post-resurrection period secured a continuity in the Jesus tradition.[24]

The Gospel of John represents a new stage of tradition differing from that of the first three Gospels. It assumes (above all) the Petrine tradition just mentioned, critically carries on this tradition and adds to it a new spiritual dimension. The Fourth Gospel, based on the figure and witness of the "disciple whom Jesus loved" (cf. John 13:23; 19:26; 20:2; 21:7.20), attempts to present the mission and work of Jesus in light of the insight (provided by the Holy Spirit only after Easter) into the truth of the revelation (cf. Jn 14:16f.26; 15:26; 16:7-14). It is for this reason that even the early Church already regarded the Gospel of John as the chief spiritual Gospel. Its testimony to the truth seemed to include the other three Gospels and bring them to completion.

Alongside this determination of the historical relationship of the four Gospels stands a further principle of reconstruction which will guide me. This consists in the insight — an insight supported by all the different stages of the tradition of faith and by the history of the Christian Bible — that a New Testament separated or separable from the Old Testament never existed in the Christian Church (the exception being the Bible of the "Reformer" Marcion who was excluded from the Roman church in 144 CE) and that this could therefore only be an artificial creation. Jesus and his disciples as well as Paul, who was called later, were Jews by birth. They grew up with the faith of Israel and read the Law, Prophets and Psalms (Lk 24:44) as Holy Scripture, memorizing it (as was the custom at that time) in part. It was through Jesus and the disciples that these "Holy Scriptures" of the Old Testament became the Bible of those congregations putting their faith in Jesus. The first Christian congregations were reading the Old Testament (in Hebrew and Greek) as Scripture and interpreting it in light of Christ even before the first New Testament writing ever existed. Seen from the Christian perspective the New Testament supplements the Old and provides the decisive key to its interpretation, but it cannot nor does it want to take the place of the Old Testament. This all means that the way from the preaching of Jesus to faith in Jesus Christ can only be reconstructed when one begins with a critical look at the New Testament sources collectively and proceeds to view Jesus simultaneously in light of the Old Testament witness from God's singularity, its promises for Israel and its annunciation of the coming messianic saviour. To word it even more precisely: The revelatory witness of the Old Testament indicates the deciding direction in which we must look in order to understand both biblically and historically the way from Jesus' preaching to faith in Jesus Christ.[25] Whoever refuses to consider this perspective cannot adequately answer the question which is before us.

## Jesus' Message concerning God, Repentance and Faith

As especially the Lucan infancy narrative shows and as is confirmed by many other texts in the Gospels, Jesus was well versed in the Old Testament and in the Jewish faith from the very beginning (cf. only Lk 2:41-51 and Jn 7:15-17). Through the conversion message of John the Baptist (his cousin), Jesus, then around thirty years old, allowed himself to be called to the Jordan and to be baptized. Jesus' baptism in the Jordan was not, as it was for the other candidates for John's baptism, simply the confirmation of his conversion to a new life, pleasing to God, in expectation of the impending final judgement but represented the act of breaking all family ties and the initiation of his public, messianic ministry. The experience with the Spirit which Jesus had during his baptism made it clear to him that the hour had now come for his public ministry. To minister in public meant to call in his own authority to repentance and to faith in the message of the kingdom of God which was near at hand. According to Mk 1:15, Jesus' public ministry began with the words: "The time has come, the kingdom of God is near. Repent and believe the gospel!"

The ideas which Jesus and his Jewish contemporaries had about the identity of God and the kingdom of God, were a product of the Old Testament and Jewish piety at that time. Let us just consider the first commandment and its preamble: "I am the Lord your God, who brought you out of Egypt, out of the land of slavery. You shall have no other gods before me" (Ex 20:2-3). Every pious Jew prayed (and prays) daily the confessional prayer formed out of Deut 6:4f. and other scripture verses

(= Deut 11:13-21; Num 15:37-41): "Hear, O Israel! The Lord our God, the Lord is one. Therefore love the Lord your God with all your heart and with all your soul and with all your strength..." The present kingdom of God is mentioned in the Psalms (in an exemplary way in Ps 145) or in Daniel (4:3; 4:34) and we hear of the impending kingdom of God in (so-called Second) Isaiah (52:7) and in the Jewish prayer tradition. In addition to the "Hear, O Israel!," pious Jews since the time of Jesus have daily prayed (and pray) the so-called "Eighteen Benedictions." The 11th benediction states: "Restore our judges as at the first, and our counsellors as at the beginning; and reign over us, you alone. Praise be to you, O Lord, who loves that which is right." Jesus announces the impending dawning of the reign of the one God to which the Old Testament testifies. This is done in such a way that Jesus' listeners feel compelled to prepare themselves completely and undividedly for the coming of the one God as judge and saviour of his chosen people. Though for Jews unusual, Jesus characteristically speaks directly to the one and coming God as "Father" (cf. Lk 10:21 Par.; Mk 14:36 Par.) and even allows his disciples in the Lord's Prayer to participate in this relationship to God. It is precisely through this novel way of addressing God as Father that Jesus shows himself to be the Son of God.

Jesus himself teaches to recognize anew and to take to heart that which God gives to those persuaded by Jesus to listen as well as to do that which God requires of them. In his (well-disposed) dialogue with the scribes concerning the question as to which was the most important of the 613 directives (= 248 commandments and 365 prohibitions) which the Law according to rabbinic count included, he answers, in a way not at all characteristic of Palestinian Judaism but of fundamental importance to Jesus, with the combination of two commandments:

> "This is the first (commandment): 'Hear, O Israel! The Lord our God is Lord alone! Therefore you shall love the Lord your God with all your heart, with all your soul, with all your mind, and with all your strength.' This is the second (commandment): 'You shall love your neighbor as yourself.' There is no other commandment greater than these" (Mk 12:29-31).

According to Jesus, the dual commandment of love to God and neighbor defines the will of God completely. When Jesus emphasizes the commandment to love so centrally, he is proceeding from the idea that the one God, his Father, is a God of love, and that he has more pleasure in the repentance and life of the poor, god-forsaken and sinners than in their destruction.

One obtains a clear picture of how the repentance of the sinner accomplished through Jesus actually occurred in the well-known narrative of Jesus' visit with the (chief) tax collector, Zacchaeus in Jericho (Lk 19:1-10). Jesus angers many people in the town when he invites himself to visit just the tax collector - who was considered godless and unjust - and is heartily received. The encounter compels Zacchaeus to give up half of his possessions to the poor and to pay back four times the amount to those whom he had cheated. Jesus accepts this promise with favour and speaks of him as son of Abraham who has been won back into the community of God. This whole occurrence illustrates that "the Son of Man has come to seek and to save what was lost "(Lk 19:10).

Repentance in Jesus' sense means therefore two things. It is first a turning away from the present life in unrighteousness and in distance from God (a turning away which grows out of the contact with Jesus) and a turning towards the one God and Father to whom Jesus also belongs. Second, it means to live according to the will of God through acts of love and righteousness.

Just how important acts of love and righteousness were and are for Jesus is exemplified in detail in the Sermon on the Mount and emphasized in the famous parable of the Great Judgement of the Nations in Mt 25:31-46.[26] To do deeds of love and righteousness means to feed the hungry, to give the thirsty something to drink, to take in the stranger, to clothe the naked, to look after the sick and to visit those in prison. This is to be done wherever and whenever it becomes necessary (cf. Isa 58:6f). Jesus identifies himself so much with those who suffer that he considers a good work done for one of them to be a work also done for himself.

Jesus' invitation and call to repentance, however, has naturally another side to it as well; it must not be rejected. Whoever refuses to hear the call to repentance will remain separated from God and must himself bear the consequences of his refusal. Jesus' view that these consequences will inexorably catch up with those who are unrepentant, at the latest on the day of judgement, is taught for example in his cries of woe over the two Galilean cities of Korazin and Bethsaida which had rejected him (Mt 11:20-24f/Lk 10:12-15). Jesus' call to repentance corresponds with the expectation of the coming last judgement.

The degree to which the one God, whom Jesus serves and preaches, wants mercy and forgiveness of sins rather than judgement and punishment, is made clear by Jesus through his message and through his own behaviour. The three parables bundled together in Luke 15 of the lost sheep, the lost son and the lost coin all document beautifully that, in Jesus' view, there will be more rejoicing in heaven (i.e. by God) over the repentance of one sinner than over ninety-nine righteous persons who do not need to repent (Lk 15:7). Jesus shows just how welcome precisely the sinners and the lost are in the community of God by way of his table fellowship with them before God (cf. Mk 2:15f.; Lk 15:2).

The healing miracles, too, should be seen in this connection. Much to the anger of some scribes, Jesus, with the power (of the Spirit) which filled him, not only healed the sick but dared even to forgive them their sins. The story of the healing of a paralytic in Capernaum from Mk 2:1-12 documents this:

"He came back to Capernaum after a lapse of several days and word got around that he was (again) at (the) home (of Peter). At that they began to gather in great numbers. There was no longer any room for them, even around the door. While he was delivering God's word to them, some people arrived bringing a paralyzed man to him. The four who carried him were unable to bring him to Jesus because of the crowd, so they began to open up the roof over the spot where Jesus was. When they had made a hole, they let down the mat on which the paralytic was lying. When Jesus saw their faith, he said to the paralyzed man, 'Child (of God), your sins are forgiven.' Now some of the scribes were sitting there asking themselves. 'Why does the man talk in that way? He commits blasphemy! Who can forgive sins except God alone?' Jesus was immediately aware of their reasoning, though they kept it to themselves, and he said to them: 'Why do you harbor these thoughts? Which is easier, to say to the paralytic,'Your sins are forgiven,' or to say 'Stand up, pick up your mat and walk again'? That you may know that the Son of Man has authority on earth to forgive sins' (he said to the paralyzed man), 'I command you: Stand up! Pick up your mat and go home.' The man stood and picked up his mat and went outside in the sight of everyone. They were awe struck; all gave praise to God saying, 'We have never seen anything like this!'"

This story, the settings of which can still be located in Capernaum, contains nothing unbelievable. We see how Jesus, who calls himself Son of Man, answers the trust - the text speaks of "faith" - which the four men who carried the sick man have in him with the word of forgiveness and with the healing through the word. This was unheard of mainly because Jesus here encroached upon rights reserved (according to the Jewish view) for God alone. When seen from this perspective, the narrative indicates the following: Through the spoken word of Jesus, God takes possession of the sick man and restores the health of his body and soul. Jesus makes that which we read in Ps 103:2-3 become a reality: "Bless the Lord, O my soul,... who pardons all your iniquities, he heals all your ills...".[27]

This incident in Capernaum is not a one-time event but is characteristic of Jesus' ministry. A second example from the Gospel of Mark (Mark 9:14-29) demonstrates this fact; it tells of the healing of an epileptic boy and of the following discussion between Jesus and his disciples about this healing. At some time when Jesus was not present, a father had brought his son, who was plagued with epileptic seizures, to the disciples. They had tried without success to help the boy. When Jesus returns, they inform him about the difficult case. He then approaches the father and asks him:

"...'How long has this been happening to him?' 'From childhood,' the father replied. 'Often it (= the evil illness-demon) throws him into fire and into water. You would think it would kill him. If out of the kindness of your heart you can do anything to help us, please do!' Jesus said, 'If you can? Everything is possible to a man who trusts.' The boy's father immediately exclaimed, 'I do believe! Help my lack of trust!' Jesus, on seeing a crowd rapidly gathering, reprimanded the unclean spirit by saying to him, 'Mute and deaf spirit, I command you: Get out of him and never enter him again!' Shouting, and throwing the boy into convulsions, it came out of him; the boy became like a corpse, which caused many to say, 'He is dead.' But Jesus took him by the hand

and helped him to his feet. When Jesus arrived at the house his disciples began to ask him privately, 'Why is it that we could not expel it?' He told them, 'This kind (of spirit) you can drive out only by prayer.'"

This very vividly told story does not, as some exegetes hold, say anything about the faith of Jesus. In the four Gospels, Jesus' special relationship with God is never described with the word "faith."[28] We see, rather, how Jesus stands at God's side. He calls upon the father to believe in the God with whom, in the words of Jesus, all things are possible (cf. Mk 14:36). When the father then confesses his faith and asks that Jesus help him overcome his unbelief, Jesus turns his attention in God's name to the sick boy and heals him through his word. Since epilepsy was considered in classical antiquity to be incurable, that which is accomplished through Jesus' word and actions is the deed of the God who really can do all things. The disciples in a similar situation can only petition God in prayer that this deed might be done; it does not lie within their own authority to do it. In the context of our story, faith means to ask the almighty God to do something through Jesus for the petitioner.

The Gospel of Matthew adds a logion from the sayings source to the discussion at the end which Jesus has with his disciples: "I assure you, if you had faith the size of a mustard seed, you would be able to say to this mountain, 'Move from here to there,' and it will move. Nothing would be impossible for you" (Mt 17:20). This word about mountain-moving faith appears in Mark in another context. During his last stay in Jerusalem, Jesus admonishes his disciples who are amazed at the cursing and withering of the fig tree:

"...put your trust in God. I solemnly assure you, whoever says to this mountain, 'Be lifted up and thrown into the sea,' and has no inner doubts but believes that what he says will happen, shall have it done for him. I give you my word, if you are ready to believe that you will receive whatever you ask for in prayer, it shall be done for you (Mk 11:22-24)."

Since, according to the Old Testament, only God, the creator and judge, has the power to form (cf. Ps 65:6) and move (Job 9:5; Jer 51:25) mountains, and his creative word and word of judgement work that which

God commands (Ps 33:9; 148:5; Jes 55:11), it is clear what Jesus means to say: When the disciples pray with all their heart, then God will stand by them so that spirits and worlds are literally divided through their works. The logion is interested in the power entrusted to the disciples to bind and loosen (cf. Mt 18:18) and is mentioned by Paul in this same way in 1 Cor 13:2 where it is considered to be in need of supplementation through love.

The Gospel of Luke presents a parallel saying in 17:6. Jesus says to his disciples who have asked him to provide them with faith:

"If you had faith the size of a mustard seed, you could say to this sycamore, 'Be uprooted and transplanted into the sea,' and it would obey you."

Again, the meaning is similar. The roots of the sycamore tree go especially deep. The uprooting of a tree is an Old Testament image for the execution of judgement (cf. Jer 1:10 and the Greek translation of Dan 4:14). A Jewish teacher who knew how to dispute cleverly was called a "mover of mountains." So the meaning is again that faith can work judgement and salvation in the authority of God and thereby accomplish that which is impossible with man.

Whoever wants to understand the way from the preaching of Jesus to faith in Jesus Christ must know these verses from the Gospels which were just mentioned. When one compares them with the faith traditions of the Old Testament and of the Jews as a whole, one discovers quickly that no Jewish prophet or teacher since the prophet Isaiah in the 8th century BCE (Isa 7:9; 28:16; 30:15) had spoken about faith as Jesus does here. Jesus introduced into the faith tradition of Israel a new way of speaking and thinking about faith! The believer is able to participate in the activity of the almighty God when he turns to God in prayer and God acts for him.[29] In the time of Jesus, every Jew knew from the Old Testament what it means for God to act, and he is - and this is of decisive importance - reminded anew of this knowledge by Jesus' words and deeds. In these stories of healing, which we have reflected upon, Jesus acts as the mediator of the almighty and gracious God for those in need. He establishes God's saving righteousness by passing judgement on the illness (-demon).

With this we have answered at least in part the question as to how the preaching of Jesus proceeds on to faith in Jesus Christ but have yet to reach our goal. Jesus himself laid the foundation for the faith in him by being God's mediator. "Faith" still clearly means in Jesus' preaching, however, "faith (mediated through Jesus) in God" (cf. Mk 11:22). Only in the story of the healing of the paralytic do we hear by way of intimation that the men who bring the paralytic "believe in" or trust Jesus and his power to heal (Mk 2:5). When Jesus in other stories of healing dismisses the healed person, for example the woman in Capernaum who was subject to bleeding, with the words: "Daughter (which as we learn in Lk 13:16 means 'Daughter of Abraham'), it is your faith that has cured you. Go in peace and be freed of this illness" (Mk 5:34; cf. with 10:52 and Lk 7:50), then faith is understood in a similar vein. We are not yet dealing here with a conscious faith in Jesus Christ in the manner of the post-resurrection confessions of faith.

How did it, then, come to the belief that Jesus is the Christ (1 Cor 15:3) or the (Son of) man, the mediator between the one God and those in need of salvation (1 Tim 2:5)? Without taking a still more intense look at how Jesus' contemporaries thought of him and — above all — how he saw himself, we cannot give a binding answer to this question.

## Jesus' Self-Designation as "Son of Man" and "Messiah"

John the Baptist pointed in his preaching of repentance to the coming "stronger" one who would come after him and who would baptize the repentant not only with water but with the Holy Spirit and fire (cf. Mk 1:7 and Mt 3:11/Lk 3:16). The "stronger" one refers to Old Testament-Jewish expectation of the judge of the universe who would bring judgement and new creation and thus the definitive kingdom of God. He who was to establish the kingdom of God was sometimes called by the Old Testament the Messiah from the house of David (cf. e.g. Isa 11:1-9); sometimes, however, it is the "Son of Man" from heaven who will bring about a reign of peace for Israel, the people of God, who are tormented and oppressed by their enemies (cf. Dan 7:13-27). Messiah and Son of Man are identified with each other in the post-Old Testament writings to such a degree that the baptizer with the Spirit and fire, in whose presence John the Baptist considers himself unworthy to perform even the lowly slave's job of taking off and putting on his sandals (Mk 1:7), can only be the "messianic Son of Man" or the "Son of Man - Messiah" (cf. 1 En 48:2-10).[20] Jesus, then, was confronted through John the Baptist's message of repentance with the pronouncement of the messianic Son of Man who is coming for judgement and new creation. The experience with the Spirit which Jesus had at his baptism gave him through God's confirming words ("You are my beloved Son in whom I am well pleased" Mk 1:11) the certainty that he himself was to accomplish publically the work of the Son of Man — Messiah the coming of whom had been pronounced by John the Baptist.[31] In the so-called "temptation" (Mk 1:12f. par.), Jesus acknowledges this mission. He wrests from himself in this "decision at the beginning"[32] the willingness to go in the way of the messianic Son of Man and to do this only in the strict "obedience of the Son" (A. Schlatter) to God's will. He is true to this decision even in Gethsemane, the "decision at the end."[33] Jesus' complete public ministry, from the temptation to the end of the passion, bears the stamp of this resolution: Jesus goes, and only wants to go, in the way of the Son of Man — Messiah and of the Son who is obedient only to God. The three titles of Jesus which appear with regularity in the Gospels: "Son of God," "Son of Man" and "Messiah" do not represent in their biblical sense alternatives but designate all together, in a typically Jewish way,[34] Jesus as the mediator through whom God desires to accomplish his salvation-work, the definitive establishment of his reign for Israel and for the whole world.

In recent critical scholarship, the opinion surfaces with regularity that Jesus did not use the known Jewish messianic titles, "Son of God," "Messiah" or "Son of Man," to describe himself. They were, so it is said, onlyu applied to him later by the post-resurrection Church. Before Easter, Jesus was no more, and did not claim to be more, than the last prophetic messenger of God before the judgement of the world. No matter how often this view is repeated up to the present time,[35] it remains an abstraction which conflicts with the texts as well as with historical probability. Our attempt to trace the development of faith in Christ can be significantly advanced by following the transmitted texts closely and being aware of the fact that, in view of Jesus' striking deeds and his astonishing words among his contemporaries, the question must have arisen: Who is this man? What authority — or also: what demon (cf. Mk 3:22.30) — does he have? The assumption that Jesus never answered nor had anything to say to this question (an assumption which modern critical scholarship has to make) is very unlikely and makes Jesus into a walking historical riddle. The texts, in any case, depict him in another (historically believable) way.

At the beginning of his last journey to Jerusalem, Jesus withdrew with his disciples to the area around Caesarea Philippi. On the way he asked them who the people thought he was. He received the answer that some considered him to be John the Baptist (having been beheaded by Herod Agrippa only to receive a new form in Jesus and his message); others considered him to be Elijah, whom God, according to Mal 4 :5f,, was to send before the great and terrible "day of the Lord" that he might "turn the hearts of the fathers to their children, and the ears of the children to their fathers" (i.e. exhort them to renewed study in the will of God in the form of the law) thus saving them in judgement; still others, according to this report from the disciples, consider Jesus to be merely "one of the prophets" (cf. Deut 18:18). All of these designations indicate that one cannot eliminate from Jesus' preaching the call to repentance in obedience to God's will. In response to the disciples' replies, Jesus inquires further:

> "And you," he went on to ask, "Who do you say that I am?" Peter answered him,"You are the Messiah!" Then he gave them strict orders not to tell anyone about him. He began to teach them that the Son of Man had to suffer much, be rejected by the Elders, the chief priests, and the scribes, be put to death, and risen three days later. He said these things quite openly (Mk 3:28-32)."

According to this report (which is taken up by Matthew and Luke), Jesus spoke with his disciples in their seclusion about the purpose of his mission. The dawning recognition among the disciples that he was the Messiah is implicitly confirmed by Jesus; as he stood before the Sanhedrin and chief priests and before Pilate, he explicitly acknowledges that he is the messianic Son of God (cf. Mk 14:62; 15:2) Jesus, however, enjoins his disciples to refrain from making this insight public. The reason for this is probably that the open proclamation, "Jesus is the Messiah," threatened to determine Jesus' way and mission too much according to the very lively expectation of the people then that the Messiah from the house of David would free Israel from Roman tyranny, purify Jerusalem from the godless Gentiles and bring about an era of righteousness (cf. PssSol 17:21-46). Jesus did not want to submit to this scheme. Only as the events in Jerusalem had come to their decisive climax, did Jesus openly acknowledge his messianic mission before his Jewish judges and before the Roman prefect; he again, however, insists on seeing this mission from the perspective of the"Son of Man" who serves God (cf. Mk 14:61f. par.).

According to Dan 7, the Enoch tradition (= 1 En 40; 45-49; 53; 61-62; 71) and 4 Esra 13, the Son of Man is a messianic figure. As is the case with the Davidic Messiah, he is expected to be sent by God to perform the final judgement, to establish the kingdom of God for the good of Israel and to gather up the end-time, righteous people of God. The national-political flavour which characterizes the expectation of the Davidic Messiah is much less evident in the texts concerning the Son of Man. Jesus took over the mysterious title Son of Man, seldom found in the Jewish tradition, from the preaching of John the Baptist, and in the course of his ministry he impressed his own unique stamp upon it.[36] During his earthly life, Jesus wanted to unite anew his Father with Israel by way of the unconditional ministry to the "poor" (cf. Isa. 61:1f.), the serving love (Lk 19:10; Mk 10: 42-45; John 13:2-17) and substitutionary suffering. Only after this earthly life of service did Jesus expect to be exalted to a place at the right hand of the Father and to be installed into the office of eschatalogical judge (Mk 14:61f. par.; Lk 12:8f. par.). It was for this reason that he modified Peter's expectations regarding the Messiah (and those of all the disciples) by emphasizing that precisely his mission as messianic Son of Man called for him to enter into suffering first and only through suffering to experience the glory of the resurrection and power (Mk 8:27-33 par.)

Since we have no texts in the early Jewish tradition, except for Zech 12:10; 13:7 (cf. with Mt 24:30; Mk 14:27 par.) which refer to a suffering Messiah, and since none of the Old Testament-Jewish texts mention a Son of Man who must suffer, Jesus' response to Peter's confession of Jesus to be the Messiah is totally unheard of. We are confronted here with a revolutionary new interpretation of all Jewish expectations regarding the Son of Man and the Messiah — a new interpretation born from Jesus' nearness to God and his obedience as Son! If Jesus' designation of himself as "Son of Man" was puzzling then this new version of the title Son of Man is a real mystery. Jesus' response to Peter's confession, then, meets with incomprehension and resistance. In Mk 8:32-33 we read:

> "Peter then took him (=Jesus) aside and began to remonstrate with him. At this he turned around and, eyeing the disciples, reprimanded Peter: 'Get behind me, Satan! You are not judging by God's standards but by man's!'"

In this unusually sharp saying (for which reason it cannot possibly be a post-resurrection creation) of Jesus, Peter is strongly commanded to take his place behind Jesus as an imitator of him because with his resistance to Jesus' preparedness to suffer he confronts his Lord as a tempter.

Jesus' ministry on earth as the messianic Son of Man was therefore even for the disciples enshrouded in mystery. The so-called "messianic secret"[37] which frequently appears in the Gospel of Mark (especially clear in 9:9f.) is not simply a post-resurrection theological construction and it has nothing to do with an attempt to obscure the fact that Jesus' life was not in reality a messianic one and was placed in a messianic light only after Easter. On the contrary it is a basic characteristic of Jesus' own ministry! His message in parables and in symbolic actions could only (and were only intended to) be understood by those who were really open to involving themselves in his message; their meaning remained hidden from the outsider and was sometimes a source of irritation (cf. Mk 4:33). It is by no means an accident that Jesus' offer of rest to the weary in Mt 11 begins with the words: "Father, Lord of heaven and earth, to you I offer praise; for what you have hidden (i.e. that which I preach) from the learned and the clever you have revealed to the merest children. Father it is true. You have graciously willed it so..." (11:25f.). Jesus' way as Son of the Father was continuously a riddle even for his closest companions; they always seemed to expect Jesus to act in a different way than he then actually did (cf. only Mk 1:36-38; 8:32f.; 10:35ff.; Lk. 9:54-56; 24:21). Only after Christ appeared in new divine life to the disciples who had all deserted him in the night of betrayal (Mk 14:50 par.) and only after they learned in the power of the Spirit to bear witness to Jesus' resurrection and his exaltation to the right hand of the Father, did they really know who the earthly Lord was whom they had followed (cf. Jn 14:16.26; 15:26; 16:12-14).

But let us now return to our main topic and summarize the extent to which the report in Mk 8:27- 33 par. is helpful to us in our line of questioning. We find in this text the two titles, "Christ" or "Messiah" (cf. with 1 Cor 15:3) and "Son of Man" which were fundamental for the early post-resurrection confessions (We will see how the Son of Man title is behind the "man" in 1 Tim 2:5.). The fact that Jesus himself openly acknowledged his messianic mission before the Jewish tribunal and before Pilate is documented in Mk 14:62 par.; 15:2 par. and in the inscription, "The King of the Jews" (Mk 1:26), which the Romans (and not the Christians!) attached to the cross. We have thus discovered traces of the titles of Jesus which were taken over in the Easter confession of the Christians. They apparently originate in the pre-resurrection Jesus tradition and were used and affirmed by Jesus himself. To first attribute these predications to the post-resurrection insight and faith of the Church would mean to render Jesus' way and thus his passion histori-cally inexplicable.

## Towards an Understanding of Jesus' Passion

We must more closely investigate the significance of this passion for three reasons. We have, first of all, already noticed the peculiarity of Jesus' predictions of his suffering. Second, we have already established that Jesus' messianic call to repentance has another side to it: the unre-pentant is threatened with judgement. Third, both of the confessions to Christ which we have taken as examples refer thematically precisely to Jesus' substitutionary suffering. The question, then, is unavoidable: Why was it necessary and why was it Jesus' will that he take the path of suf-fering as the Son of Man - Messiah sent by God?

In order to penetrate the mystery of Jesus' passion, one must join the perspectives supplied by history with the attempt to "re-think" the thoughts of Jesus upon which his willingness to suffer are based.

## The Historical Necessity of the Passion[38]

When one takes a look at the path which Jesus took on his way from Galilee to Jerusalem as recorded by the first three Gospels one quickly notices that his path was marked by confrontations of increasing severity with representatives of all the important Jewish factions of the time. Although Jesus' disciples followed him almost without condition, placing all of their hopes in him, and although the poor and downtrodden were constantly surrounding him, his call to repentance and his message of the kingdom of God in parables, his discussions and his messianic symbolic actions (i.e. table fellowship with the poor and outcast and the miracles of healing) became an increasingly intolerable provocation for not a few of the Pharisees, Zealots and rich Jews. The most powerful of Jesus' enemies, however, emerged from the faction which wielded the most influence in Jerusalem, that of the chief priests and the Sadducean nobility. They controlled and administered the temple affairs, and it was precisely this group which Jesus had provoked exceedingly through the demonstrative act of the cleansing of the temple during the last days of his ministry.

The cleansing of the temple was in all probability a messianic symbolic act of Jesus.[39] Israel expected with the advent of the kingdom of God the raising of "the mountain of the Lord's temple," i.e. Zion, that it be established as "chief among the mountains" (Mi 4:1ff., Jes 2:1-5). Various early Jewish texts speak of the glorification and the rebuilding of the temple in those last days.[40] The Essenes from Qumran expected the Messiah from the house of David to erect anew the sanctuary (4QFlor I 1ff); the early Pharisaic Psalms of Solomon state concerning this same Davidic Messiah that "he will glorify the Lord in a place which towers above the whole earth. And he will purge Jerusalem and make it holy as it was in the beginning (PssSol 17:30; cf. with Micah 4:1ff.); the fifth book of the so-called Sibylline Oracles (414-433) tells of how "a blessed man from the ends of heaven," i.e. surely the messianic Son of Man, will renew the city of God and the temple in glory; and in the Targum (i.e. the Aramaic interpretive paraphrase) to Isa 53, which originated in post-New Testament times, we read that the Messiah will build the temple again which had been defiled and destroyed (in 70 CE). Jesus' actions against the moneychangers and the sellers of sacrificial animals as briefly depicted in Mk 11:15-17, put him squarely on line with the messianic expectations of the time. If — as is very probable — he spoke, in the context of this action, of the destruction and the raising up of the temple through himself (cf. John 2:19), then the significance of this symbolic act becomes clear: Jesus presses for a decision between the traditional cultic practices and the nearness to God which he himself, the messianic Son of Man, preached and mediated.[41] Only through this nearness can the temple again become a house of prayer for all peoples (cf. Isa 56:7). It was to be expected that the Sadducees would consider this action to be a threat to the institution of the temple and that they would respond accordingly, but Jesus was prepared to accept the consequences in advance. This is indicated by the Parable of the Tenants (Mk 12:1-12 par.) which Jesus told shortly after the cleansing of the temple and which is also tailored to fit the Sadducees.

If one puts all of the various people who took offense at Jesus' appearance together, then there arises an overwhelming front of opposition to which Jesus in the end fell victim. Historically speaking, it was to a certain extent inevitable that the conflict between Jesus and his enemies finally came to a head and that they brought him to trial in Jerusalem as a false messianic prophet and as a seducer to false belief, who had violated the faith and cultic order of Israel (cf. Dtn 13:2-7; 17:1-7 and 18:20).[42]

It is astonishing that, rather than seeking to evade this conflict by fleeing, Jesus clearly acknowledged his mission before the Jewish tribunal and boldly added that his present earthly judges would have to answer to him as the Son of Man and judge of the world who sits in God's judgement seat and comes on the clouds of heaven. In response to the question of the high priest: "Are you the Messiah, the Son of the Blessed One?," Jesus said: "I am, and you will see the Son of Man sitting at the right hand of the Mighty One and coming on the clouds of heaven." (Mk 14:61-62 par.).[43] To declare oneself to be the Messiah was not in itself blasphemy, but to proclaim oneself to be the judge of the world sitting at the right hand of God and to pronounce judgement for the leading judges of Israel as well, was indeed to claim divine authority and thus blasphemy which according to Jewish law was punishable by death (cf. Ex 22:27; Lev 24:15f.; Jn 19:7).[44]

Consequently, Jesus was convicted of messianic agitation and of making claims to divine authority. Although the Jewish tribunal in the time of Jesus could not carry out the death penalty (cf. John 19:31), the Sadducean enemies of Jesus were able on the following morning to bring him to Pilate and denounce him as being a messianic agitator, thus forcing the Roman prefect to take action against the suspicious man. Jesus continued in his appearance before Pilate to acknowlege himself to be the Messiah, and he did not try to defend himself

(Mk 15:1-5). His acknowiegement led to the scourging and the death on the cross. Jesus therefore chose clear-sightedly and consciously the way leading to his death.

## Jesus' Willingness to Sacrifice Himself

The apparent reason for Jesus not running from the doom which he was facing is that his whole ministry, up to the cleansing of the temple and his acknowlegement before the tribunal, was in accordance with his divine mission as the Son of Man — Messiah which he received at his baptism, and that Jesus wanted to confront the people of God which had come together for the passover feast one last and deciding time with his message.[45] The protection of his own person was less important for Jesus than his mission to personify the consolation as well as the demands of the near and one God, whom he called "Father." The fulfilment of his mission was not something which came easily, as the temptation at the beginning of his ministry and the struggle in prayer at Gethsemane at the end show. Although Jesus stood at God's side, he was still a man of flesh and blood, and only at the price of prayer, fasting, sweat and tears was he able to fight through to complete obedience by going in the way that he had to go (cf. Heb 5:7-10).

The classic texts illustrating Jesus' willingness to sacrifice himself are found first in the saying referring to ransom in Mk 10:45 which Jesus spoke as he and his disciples began the last journey to Jerusalem and then in the introductory words to the Lord's Supper in Mk 14:22-25 par. Both times Jesus relates traditions from the atonement and about the suffering servant of God (Jes 53) to himself and to his way.

The saying referring to ransom,[46] as can be easily shown by comparing the two texts, is adopted in the confessional formula in 1 Tim 2:5-6 which has already been mentioned. The congregation, in a confessional act, repeats that which they heard about Jesus. Jesus' own logion states:

"...the Son of Man has not come to be served, but to serve — to give his life in ransom for the many" (Mk 10:45 and Mt 20:28).

This saying, which is informed by the Old Testament both in its concept and wording, represents Jesus' interpretation of his own mission. As the Son of Man, he is not there to require and receive attendance and homage while he is still on earth which according to Dan 7:13-14 the heavenly Son of Man should properly receive from the angels of God and the nations of the world. It is, rather, the other way around. He is sent and is there for the purpose of serving, in the name of and on behalf of God, "the many," the lives of whom are lost before God because of sin and guilt, and he is to serve even to the point of giving his body and life as a ransom for all. The background of this saying of Jesus is formed by the pronouncements of the (so-called Second) Isaiah in Isa 43:3-4 and 53:11-12. According to the former, it is the will of God, the saviour of Israel, to pay himself the ransom which redeems his people out of love for his people bound up in guilt; this he does through "men" whom he gives in exchange for Israel's salvation.[47] We hear in Isa 53:11-12:

> "...my Servant shall justify many, and their guilt shall he bear. Therefore, I will give him his portion among the great, and he shall divide the spoils with the mighty, because he surrendered himself to death and was counted among the wicked; And he shall take away the sins of many, and win pardon for their offenses."

Isa 53 points us to the two statements of Jesus spoken at the last meal with his disciples. Jesus, in his vicarious existence (i.e. his life for others), openly spoke these words to the twelve and to all of those represented by the circle of the twelve: "This is my body" and "This is my blood of the covenant, which is poured out for many" (Mk 14:22.24).[48] With these two statements Jesus allows his companions at the table to share in the fruits of his substitutionary death and makes them participants in the new covenant and future partakers of the messianic table fellowship in God's perfected kingdom (cf. Mk 14:25 with Jes 25:6ff.). As strange as the events to which the aforementioned texts point may appear to us with our modern criteria of thought, that which the texts state is clear: Jesus wanted to go in his earthly way as the Son of Man and was in the end able to remain steadfast in this way only because he knew himself to be the Servant of God and the person chosen to be a "ransom" thus serving as a representative for Israel's existence and for all who are lost. Put in a modern way: Jesus lived and suffered as the enbodiment of the loving will of God to forgive sins; or more succinctly:

Jesus lived and suffered as the reconciler of God with the sinners from Israel and the whole world.

## The Easter Experience Leading to the Confession of Faith in Jesus Christ

Judging from 1 Cor 15:3-5 and 1 Tim 2:5f., the early Christian confessions of faith in Jesus as the Christ and God's mediator are confessions which look back upon the completed mission and passion of Jesus from a post-Easter perspective and praise him as "Lord" who was resurrected and exalted by God. Despite the preaching of Jesus, these confessions would have never come into existence without the events of Easter. These events are constitutive for these confessions and indeed for any Christian confession to Jesus Christ for the simple reason that it was the experience of Easter which first gave the disciples of Jesus the certainty that Jesus' way which led to death was not in vain. We must now, in concluding, make this clear.

On that Good Friday as night fell upon Jesus, who had died on the cross of ridicule and was quickly laid by his friends in a tomb cut out of rock, every Jew who had been against Jesus could and must at that point have said in concordance with Dtn 21:22-23: This man executed on the cross has suffered the deserved penalty; he has died as one "accursed by God"! The disciples, full of fear and doubt, were not able to prevail against this logical and terrible interpretation of Jesus' death on the cross (cf. John 19:31; Acts 5:30; 10:39; Justin, Dial. 89:2; 90:1) until the crucified Jesus appeared to them in divine vitality at various times after Easter morning, and until they had been able to confirm for themselves the reports of several women near to Jesus that Jesus' place of burial on the outskirts of town had been opened on Easter morning and found to be empty. When the very Lord whom the disciples had left one by one in the night of the betrayal (cf. Mk 14:50) appeared to them in Galilee and Jerusalem in new divine vitality and greeted them with the blessing: "Peace be with you!" (cf. Lk 24:36; John 20:19.21.26), Peter and the other disciples who were present experienced and recognized that God had not rejected their Lord, but that he had justified him. It is he, the living Son of God, who through his greeting of peace establishes once again his communion with them which they had broken as they flew in fear for their lives. They receive forgiveness for their failure and their flight.

A few years later, Paul, the persecutor of Christians, would go through the same experience.

This is not the place for a detailed analysis of the New Testament narratives and short reports of Jesus' appearances to Peter, the Twelve, to Maria Magdalene and the disciples from Emmaus or of the narratives about the discovery of the empty tomb which frame these texts. It should be expressly pointed out, however, that the core of neither the appearance stories nor of the reports surrounding the empty tomb can be circumvented by simply labeling them apologetic legends. The appearance stories reflect genuine religious experiences, fundamental in nature, of the new, and at the same time renewed, encounter with the glorified Jesus after Good Friday. To dispute this — as Ferdinand Christian Baur[49] already recognized — is to render inexplicable primitive Christianity along with its missionary activity. The reports of the empty tomb, as well, appear to be apologetic legends only when viewed later from our Gentile persective. Originally, such reports did not make it easier to preach the saving death of Jesus and his justification by God among the Jews (of Jerusalem), and it is this fact which proves them to be old traditions. In the time of Jesus prophetic martyrs were seen to be living intercessors in heaven and were thus prayed to, though their mortal remains rested (in an incorruptible state) in their graves till the last judgement.[50] The stories about the discovery of the empty tomb show that the Christians could not apply this scheme of Jewish religiosity to Jesus; they were not able to see and preach Jesus as simply a prophetic martyr as modern scholarship would have it. The Son of Man who was resurrected by God is not to be found among the dead (Lk 24:5); he has already been bodily exalted to the the right hand of God. The eschatological resurrection of the dead through God has already become a reality of promise through him and in him (cf 1 Cor. 15:4.20ff.; Rom 1:4). Jesus'cross is not just a gruesome instrument of martyrdom. The significance of Golgotha is, rather, the path made open to all sinners by Jesus, namely the "coming to God by passing through the sentence of death,"[51] i.e. the live-giving atonement and the promissory defeat of that death which came over the world with the banishment of Adam from paradise.

# Result

Jesus, who took up in his own way the Baptist's call to repentance, was the first to exhort to faith in the gospel which he preached of the coming kingdom of God (Mk 1:15), and he spoke in a completely new manner of "faith in God" (Mk 11:22). Jesus' gospel and the faith in God which he taught were taken up by the Easter witnesses and incorporated into the gospel of Jesus Christ which they proclaim as the message of salvation for Jews and Gentiles.[52] From this point on "faith" in the missionary preaching means faith in the God who realized his promised work of salvation for Israel and the world through the mission, the atoning death and the resurrection of Jesus (Rom 4:24f.). This Jesus, the Lord and Messiah, who was crucified (cf. Acts 2:36), raised from the dead and exalted to the right hand of God, vouches for salvation in the coming last judgement for those who confess him to be Lord and reconciler. For this very reason can Paul, assimilating here a Christian confessional tradition, formulate as follows: "...if you confess with your lips: 'Jesus is Lord' and believe in your heart, 'God has raised him from the dead,' you will be saved" (Rom 10:9). While Jesus exhorted to faith in the one God who can do all things, a faith which he himself mediated, it is because of his passion and resurrection that faith in Jesus Christ was made possible. Through him did the almighty God allow righteousness to befall his chosen people Israel and the world of Gentiles, the righteousness which they need to live with and before God. The believers in the ancient world who were called "Christians" (Acts 11:26) were recognized as such by their testimony to this faith and by their relationship to Christ, and they remain identifiable as such in the present. In summary, Jesus of Nazareth appears indeed to be the Christ of Faith as Schlatter has said. The deciding impulse for faith and confession in him as the Messiah (Christ) and Son of Man proceed from his earthly work and words, from Easter and from the testimony of the Old Testament tradition through which Jesus' ministry and God's salvatory act first become really understandable. Even before Easter, Jesus was a man of controversy who had many enemies; he remains controversial also from the (post-)Easter perspective. Jesus can and will be understood only by those who become purposefully involved with Jesus' message (cf. John 7:16-17) and whose faith has been initiated by God through Jesus' word.

# Notes

1.  This is indicated by the continuing stream of new publications related to this subject. For the Anglo-Saxon discussion see Ed Parish Sanders, **Jesus and Judaism**, (1985) 1986; James D.G. Dunn, **The Evidence for Jesus**, 1985, and James H. Charlesworth, **Research on the Historical Jesus Today: Jesus and the Pseudepigrapha, the Dead Sea Scrolls, the Nag Hammadi Codices, Josephus, and Archaeology**, The Princeton Seminary Bulletin, N.S. VI, 1985, 98-115. The liveliness of the German discussion can be seen in Hans-Friedrich Weiss, **Kerygma und Geschichte. Erwaegungen zur Frage nach Jesus im Rahmen der Theologie des Neuen Testaments**, 1983; Gerd Theissen, **Der Schatten des Galilaeers. Historische Jesusforschung in erzaehlender Form**, 1986; Otto Betz, **Jesus. Der Messias Israels, Gesammelte Aufsaetze I, 1987**, and Eduard Schweizer, **Jesus Christ: The Man from Nazareth and the Exalted Lord**, Macon, Georgia (Mercer University Press), 1987; id., Jesus als Gleichnis Gottes, in: **Dialog aus der Mitte christlicher Theologie**, edited by Andreas Bsteh, Beitraege zur Religionstheologie 5, 1987, 85-103.

2.  Martin Kaehler, **Der sogenannte historische Jesus und der geschichtliche, biblische Christus**, reedited by Ernst Wolf, ThB 2, 1956², 49.

3.  Adolf Schlatter, **Der Zweifel an der Messianitaet Jesu**, (1907) now in: A. Schlatter, **Zur Theologie des Neuen Testaments und zur Dogmatik**, edited by Ulrich Luck, ThB 41, 1969, 151-202.

4.  Cf. for example his commentary "**Das Evangelium nach Markus,**" 1963¹⁰.

5.  **Neutestamentliche Theologie, Erster Teil: Die Verkuendigung Jesu**, 1973², 239-284.

6.  **Theologie des Neuen Testaments**. Erster Teil: Jesu Wirken in seiner theologischen Bedeutung, edited by Juergen Roloff, 1975, 210-253.

7.  Schlatter writes loc.cit. (see n.3), 154: "...If we take away from Jesus' his messianic thoughts and only allow his companions and messengers to pronounce him to be the Christ, then there arises...a cleft, the bridging of which will hardly be achieved by the skill of historians."

8. Rudolf Bultmann, **Theologie des Neuen Testaments**, 1965⁵, 1f: "The preaching of Jesus belongs to the prerequisites of New Testament theology and is not itself part of it. The reason is that New Testament theology consists in the devolopment of those thoughts with which the Christian faith assures itself of its subject, its foundation and its consequences. The Christian faith, however, first came into existence with the Christian kerygma, i.e. a kerygma which proclaims Jesus Christ as the eschatological saving act of God, meaning Jesus Christ who was crucified and rose from the dead."

9. Cf. Ernst Kaesemann, **Das Problem des historischen Jesus**, (1954) in: id., Exegetische Versuche und Besinnungen I, 1960. 187-214.

10. Guenther Bornkamm, **Jesus von Nazareth**, (1956) 1968⁸.

11. Ernst Fuchs, **Zur lrage nach dem historischen Jesus**, Gesammelte Aufsaetze I,1960 .

12. Kaesemann writes loc. cit. (see n. 9), 206: Jesus "was indeed a Jew and presupposes the contemporary Jewish piety, but at the same time he breaks through the boundaries of this sphere with his claims. The only category which does justice to his claims is (and this totally apart from whether or not he used it or demanded it himself) the one which his disciples actually applied to him, namely that of the Messiah." Somewhat more open in its wording is Eduard Schweizer's comment, **Jesus Christus im vielfaltigen Zeugnis des Neuen Testaments**, 1968, 26: "In God's work" performed on Jesus "the aims have been accomplished which the Old Testament had hoped to come from the Messiah, from the Son of God and from the servant of God. Jesus leaves things open however; he does not use titles which necessarily fix and conclude and which allow God's sovereign work to become the object of human thought to such a degree that it comes to be at the disposal of such thought. It is precisely through his avoidance of current labels that Jesus keeps the heart of each person whom he encounters open. Jesus wants that he himself, in the complete reality of his words and deeds, should come into this heart and not an image which is already formed before he has a chance to encounter this person." In his latest publications on this subject (see n.1) Schweizer varies this position slightly and suggests we understand "Jesus as the similitude of God."; this suggestion is in its substance an excellent one.

13. Accurate and to the point is Schlatter's comment, **Das Christliche Dogma**, 1977³, 122: "A Christology in which we confer divinity upon Jesus through our faith or a doctrine of righteousness in which we declare ourselves to be righteous through the creative-power of our faith are superstitions." Cf. for the context of this statement my article: Adolf Schlatter als Bibelausleger, in **Versoehnung, Gesetz und Gerechtigkeit**, 1981, (271-301) 285ff.

14. Cf. David Flusser, **Jesus in Selbstzeugnissen und Bilddokumenten**, 1968; Schalom Ben Chorin, **Bruder Jesus. Der Nazarener in juedischer Sicht**, ( 1977) 1987¹⁰; Pinchas Lapide -Ulrich Luz, **Der Jude Jesus**, 1979.

15. David Flusser, loc. cit. (see n. 14), 96ff. is of the opinion that Jesus in the end identified himself with the Jewish messianic conception of the Son of Man; Schalom Ben Chorin, loc. cit. (see n. 14), 108 states (in agreement with Rudolf Bultmann), "that Jesus did not consider himself to be the Messiah"; Pinchas Lapide, **Der Jude Jesus** (see n.14), 58 cites Juergen Moltmann in agreeing with him: "Jesus became the saviour of the Gentiles through his crucifixion. Through his return he will show himself to be the Messiah of Israel as well." He formulates this more pointedly in his contribution: **Der Messias Israels?** in: Bertold Klappert und Helmut Starck (eds.), **Umkehr und Erneuerung**, 1980, (236-246) 242: "Jesus was **not** the Messiah of Israel, but he still became the saviour of the Gentiles" (cursive by Lapide).

16. Classic examples for this are citations from such critical New Testament scholars as Rudolf Bultmann, Eduard Schweizer, Hans Conzelmann, Ernst Kaesemann, Guenther Bornkamm, Guenther Klein, Eduard Lohse and others in the publications of Pinchas Lapide. Cf. e.g. "Der Jude Jesus" (see n.14), 29f.34f.46, or **"Wer war schuld an Jesu Tod?,"** 1987, 59.61f.66.77 etc. Donald A. Hagner reports on the same procedure in the Anglo-Saxon discussion in: **The Jewish Reclamation of Jesus**, Grand Rapids 1984, 242-271.

17. Cf. Otto Betz, **Die Frage nach dem messianischen Bewusstsein Jesus**, in: id., **Jesus. Der Messias Israels** (see n. 1), 140-168; id., **What Do We Know About Jesus?**, 1968, 92ff .

18. Martin Hengel, **Nachfolge und Charisma**, 1968, 41-46.74--79; id., **Der Sohn Gottes**, 1975, 95f.; id., **Jesus als messianischer Lehrer der Weisheit und die Anfaenge der Christologie**, Sagesse et Reli-

gion (Colloque de Strasbourg), 1979, (147-188) 175.180ff.; id., Zur matthaeischen Bergpredigt und ihrem juedischen Hintergrund, ThR 52, 1987, (327-400) 377; id., **The Atonement,** London 1981, 71-73. Also Howard Marshall, **The Origins of New Testament Christology,** 1985, 55-90, and Petr Pokorny, **Die Entstehung der Christologie,** 1985, 35-51, proceed carefully from the assumption that the historical origins of New Testament Christology are already to be found in Jesus' own messianic claims.

19. Schlatter writes in his autobiographical **"Rueckblick auf meine Lebensarbeit,"** 1977[2], 233f.: My attempt to give my theology a form which was clear for the church was grounded in the fact that I saw the story of Jesus before me as a unity. I did not have a synoptic Christ alongside a Johannine one, a prophet who preached the Sermon on the Mount alongside a Christ who carried the cross, nor did I divide his consciousness into different "circles" which overlapped one another in his consciousness, producing a multiple gospel. I saw him before me with one goal and one mission which produced the whole wealth of his words and works, and this unity which stood before me was not the core of any harmonizing which veiled the precision of the individual words and events but was the result of the most concrete apprehension possible of their historical nature. It appeared to me that I had the right to try to show him to others in this way. - I also saw no cleft between Jesus' work and that of his messengers, between the calling of Israel to repentance and the founding of the Christian church, between the work of Peter in Jerusalem and that of Paul among the Greeks, but had a unified New Testament. This was, again, not because it had been given a unity through my skill and apologetics, but because after Jesus' departure a solidly integrated history (which was produced in its entirety by the same forces) brought forth the Church - gathered together by the disciples - and the documents of that Church. That is why I place my description of the New Testament church alongside those which are lacerated with thousands of contradictions" (cursive by Schlatter). Although Schlatter's basic thoughts are correct, he underestimates the sharp confrontations which took place in the early church over the correct understanding of Jesus and the way of faith. We must therefore make a more exact distinction between historical and biblical-dogmatic evaluation of texts than he did then.

20. Cf. Ernst Kaesemann, loc. cit. (see n. 9), 203: "The faith of Easter established the Christian kerygma, but its contents is neither first nor totally produced by this faith. This faith, rather, perceived that God acted before we became believers, and it bears witness to this belief by including Jesus' preaching in the accounts of his earthly life. For a similar judgement see Guenther Bornkamm, loc. cit. (see n. 10) 11-23 and Hans-Friedrich Weiss, loc. cit. (see n.1), 102-105. This perspective of Kaesemann needs in my opinion to be worked out to its full conclusion by gospel scholarship.

21. This is the case for example when doubt is expressed as to whether Paulus had any knowledge at all of the (synoptic) tradition of the passion. If one takes this view then one can also dispute that 1 Cor 15:3-5 refers in any way to the last supper and burial traditions. Joachim Gnilka for example thinks that the tradition in Mk 16:1-8 came into being through an author who "referred back to the structure of faith in 1 Cor 15:3-5 and illustrates the message of the resurrection with the help of the empty grave," and a bit further on he points to the "invinceable argument" (!) of the "absence of any mention of the empty grave in the old confessional formula of 1 Cor 15:3-5" (**Das Evangelium nach Markus** II 1979, 339.346) .

22. Loc. cit. (see n. 2), 60.

23. For the formation of the Gospel of Mark before 70 CE and Marcan traditions cf. Martin Hengel, **Studies in the Gospel of Mark**, London, 1985.

24. This continuity is rightly emphasized by Birger Gehardsson, **Die Anfaenge der Evangelientraditionen**, 1977 and Rainer Riesner, **Jesus als Lehrer**, 1984[2] which is summarized in id., **Der Ursprung der Jesus-Ueberlieferung**, ThZ 38, 1982, 493-513.

25. Already classically fromulated by Martin Kaehler, loc. cit. (see n.2), 66: "...(it) will always remain the case that one cannot assess Christianity without the Old Testament. It is wrong to think and to say that the relationship is such that only Christ throws light upon the Old Testament. Just as Jesus obviously could not come forth as the Messiah anywhere else than among the Jews, so could we never be able to assess Jesus without the Old Testament's teaching"; and a bit further on, 67: "...it will always remain the case that this Jesus is indeed the Messiah whose spirit spoke through the prophets (1 Pet

1:11); and one will not be able to describe the historical Christ without using the Old Testament to identify him or without paying attention to the Old Testament background and the Old Testament coloring of the life which he leads before his Father and in his power."

26. For the Jesuanic roots of this parable and the Jewish traditions which have gone into it cf. Johannes Friedrich, **Gott im Bruder?**, 1977.

27. Cf. Otto Betz, **Jesu Lieblingspsalm**, in:id., **Jesus. Der Messias Israels** (see n. 1), (185-201) 198f.

28. Only the letter to the Hebrews calls Jesus in 12:2 "the author and perfecter of our faith," following here, however, - as ch. 11 shows - early Jewish patterns of faith .

29. Cf. for this Adolf Schlatter, **Der Glaube im Neuen Testament**, 1982[6], 94-176; Gerhard Ebeling, **Jesus und Glaube**, in: id., **Wort und Glaube**, Gesammlte Aufsaetze I, 1967, 203-254; Hans-Juergen Hermisson - Eduard Lohse, Glauben, 1978, 89-102 .

30. So in agreement with Friedrich Lang, **Erwaegungen zur eschatologischen Verkundigung Johannes des Taufers**, in: **Jesus Christus in Historie und Theologie,** Neutestamentliche Festschrift fuer Hans Conzelmann zum 60. Geburtstag, edited by G. Strecker, 1975, (459- 473) 470f.

31. Joachim Jeremias, loc. cit. (see n. 5), 62 connects Mk 1:9-11 par. with Mk 11:27-33 par. and concludes from this that Jesus considered his messianic authority to be grounded in his call and in the reception of the Spirit both of which occurred at his baptism.

32. Cf. Fritz Neugebauer, **Jesu Versuchung. Wegentscheidung am Anfang**, 1986.

33. For the story of Gethsemane and its historical basis cf. Reinhard Feldmeier, **Die Krisis des Gottessohnes**, 1987.

34. Julius Schniewind writes loc. cit. (see n. 4), 193 (on Mk 14:62): Everybody could understand Jesus: "Messiah, Son of God, Son of Man, the judge of nations who sits enthroned with God, these had already been identified with one another in the Jewish tradition. But Jesus said: I am he. Precisely in his death is he the coming judge of all nations; this coincides with the promise of Jes 52:13; 53:10ff." Schniewind's view is corroborated by the equation of different messianic and similar titles for the mediator of salvation in 4QpsDan A[a] (=4Q243), 11QMelch, En1 48 + 49; 61+62; 4 Ezra 13 etc.

35. Rudolf Bultmann notes loc. cit. (see n. 8), 33: "The fact that the life of Jesus was an unmessianic one soon became incomprehensible - at least in the hellenistic-Christian circles where the synoptics were formed. It appeared to them self-evident that Jesus Christ, the Son of God, had proven himself to be so in his earthly work, and as a result the gospel report on his work was placed in the light of the messianic faith. The conflict of this view with the traditional material comes to expression in the theory of the messianic secret which gives the Gospel of Mark its unique Character..." Ernst Kaesemann asserts loc. cit. (see n. 9), 211: " I consider any text which contains a messianic title to be church kerygma." Guenther Bornkamm, loc. c:it. (see n. 10), 206-210 says exactly the same and Hans-Friedrich Weiss in loc. cit. (see n. 1), 74 has recently affirmed this view once more: "...all ...messianic and similar such titles are already interpretive elements, and with their help the post-Easter Church...expressed the eschatalogical significance of Jesus." Finally, Siegfried Schulz writes in **Neutestamentliche Ethik**, 1987, 32: Jesus "was the last prophet, and his appearance and work are unique because after him nothing is to come except God and his kingship alone."

36. Cf. Werner Georg Kuemmel, **Jesus - der Menschensohn?** SbWGF 20,3, 1984, 179: "...Jesus took up the Jewish-apocalyptic expectation of the eschatological "man" who was to be judge and ruler but relates it to his person and his work in the present in a way unprecedented in the Jewish realm of ideas." While Kuemmel considers the idea of substitutionary atonement to be "incompatible with Jesus' message of salvation" (loc. cit., 178), Traugott Holtz, **Jesus of Nazareth**, 1979, 93 asserts on the basis of the same texts and with good reasons the exact opposite: "Jesus (understood) himself in such a way that his path to becoming the eschatological Son of Man had to lead through suffering."

37. William Wrede in **Das Messiasgeheimnis in den Evangelien**, (1901) 1963[3] interpreted the messianic secret to be a Christian theory which already existed in the tradition which Mark the Evangelist presupposed. Rudolf Bultmann saw in it loc. cit. (see n.9), 33 an attempt to veil the unmessianic life of Jesus. But Heikki Raisanen, **Das "Messiasgeheimnis" im Markusevangelium**, Helsinki 1976, has shown that the evangelist Mark works with a multi-layered

tradition and not one (with Wrede) which can be interpreted in just one direction. The Markan "theory" has its roots in the time before Easter.

38. Cf. to pp. 32-36 my paper **"Warum musste Jesus sterben?"** in: Peter Stuhlmacher, **Jesus von Nazareth - Christus des Glaubens**, 1988, 47-64.

39. Petr Pokorny has put it very well loc. cit. (see n.18), 41f.: "Some of Jesus' works are to be interpreted as symbolic actions." They differ from the symbolic actions in the Old Testament in "that they express the eschatological fulfilment. One such action is the so-called cleansing of the temple (Mk 11:15f.) ... Jesus pronounces with this symbolic action the fulfilment of the promise concerning the pilgrimage of the nations to Zion (e.g. Jes 56,7) which he perhaps interpreted in the light of the expectation of a new eschatological temple... He probably, either at this time or on a similar occasion, gave a vaticinium concerning the destruction of the temple in the form of a prophetic threat which the evangelist later modified ex eventu (Mk 13:2). This was also apparently the immediate motive for the charge against Jesus before the Sanhedrin." In my opinion one needs to emphasize the messianic motives of Jesus' actions in the temple to a greater degree than Pokorny does.

40. The relevant texts are given and critically discussed by Ed Parish Sanders, loc. cit. (see n. 1), 77-90.

41. For a similar view see Helmut Merklein, **Jesu Botschaft von der Gottesherrschaft**, 1983, 135f.: "The problem for Jesus does not seem to have been the cult as a God-given institution but - similar to the situation in the discussion about the Torah - the way in which **Israel** claimed this cult for itself. If the whole of Israel is a single collective of the lost whose only possibility for salvation lies in the acceptance of the eschatological elective act of God represented by Jesus, then it cannot lay claim to the cult as a possibility to achieve atonement **against** the elective act of God which takes away sin, nor can it by appealing to the possibility of achieving salvation through the cult exempt itself from making a descision for the elective act which is there to be taken hold of now. It was probably this decision which led Jesus to say and do such provocative things in the temple" (cursive from M.). Also informative on the cleansing of the temple is Ben F. Meyer, **The Aims of Jesus**, London 1979, 197-202.

42. Cf. Martin Hengel, **Nachfolge und Charisma** (see n.18), 44ff.; August Strobel, **Die Stunde der Wahrheit. Untersuchungen zum Strafverfahren gegen Jesus**, 1980, 81ff.; Otto Betz, **Probleme des Prozesses Jesu**, 1982, ANRW II 25,1 (565-647) 577ff.638f. - Pinchas Lapide's critique of the gospel reports dealing with the Jewish trial of Jesus in his book **Wer war schuld an Jesu Tod?** (see n. 16) proceeds from historical perspectives and hypotheses which have long been corrected and rejected by the authors named here.

43. In every new edition (up to now) of the **Arbeitsbuch zum Neuen Testament** from Hans Conzelmann and Andreas Lindemann, the assertion has been made concerning Mk 14:61f. "that the scene does not contain a historical core because the narration is fully determined by Christology ... It is very apparent that Mk 14:61f. has been conceived as compendium of church Christology; it means to show that all the titles of Jesus - Messiah, Son of God, Son of Man -are equal." (1983[7],379f.) This judgement not only ignores the cumulative use of such titles in early Jewish texts (see n. 34), but also the linguistic similarities with 4QPsDan A[a] (=4Q 246) which indicate old tradition and the novel analysis of the trial of Jesus presented by August Strobel. Strobel has a different view of Mk 14,61f. He writes: "We are confronted...with a tradition, original in its core, which contains — probably very accurately — Jesus' own expectations of being exalted spoken in front of the highest court of the Jewish people at the time of Passover. We are dealing here...with the historical core of the expectations and mission of Jesus."

44. Cf. August Strobel, loc. cit. (see n. 42), 92ff., Otto Betz, loc. cit. (see n. 42), 636ff. and Otfried Hofius, "blasphemia," EWNT I, (527- 532) 530.

45. "First of all we can assume that the intention of Jesus' journey to Jerusalem was to confront the people in the holy city with the message of the kingdom of God and to call on them to make a decision in the last hour." Guenther Bornkamm, loc. cit. (see n. 10), 142f.

46. Cf my article: Existenzstellvertretung fuer die Vielen: Mk 10:45 (Mt 20:28), in: Peter Stuhlmacher, **Versoehnung, Gesetz und Gerechtigkeit**, 1981, 27-42; see there also for the substantiation of the following arguments.

47. While the Masoretic text of Isa 43:4a states that God wills to give 'adám (= man (or men)) in return for Israel, the Isaiah Scroll

A from cave I at Qumran, 1QIsa, speaks of ha-'adam. Grammatically speaking this is surely an article for defining generic character (cf. Wilhelm Gesenius - Ernst Kautzsch, **Hebraeische Grammatik**, 1902[27], §126,1), but one can of course also read: "the man" (in general) and then interpret this to refer to the Son of Man.

48. For more on the sacramental words see my article: "Das neutestamentliche Zeugnis vom Herrenmahl" in Peter Stuhlmacher, **Jesus von Nazareth – Christus des Glaubens**, 1988, 65-105.
49. Cf. Klaus Scholder, **Ferdinand Christian Bauer als Historiker**, EvTh 21, 1961, (435-458) 455f.
50. Cf. Joachim Jeremias, **Heiligengraeber in Jesu Umwelt**, 1958, 126ff.
51. Hartmut Gese, The Atonement in: id., **Essays on Biblical Theology**, 1981, (93-116) 114.
52. On the continuity of the preaching of the gospel see my article: "Evangelium," EKL I[2], 1217-1221.

# Crisis in Christology

# 16

# APPOINTED DEED, APPOINTED DOER: JESUS AND THE SCRIPTURES

## Ben F. Meyer

Of the many indices to Jesus' consciousness of his mission to Israel, three kinds are especially revealing: his identification of himself and his disciples as eschatological antitypes of Israel, her kings and prophets; his allusions to divinely appointed eschatological "measures" (of time, of evil, of revelation) being filled to the brim: and his pointing, as to signs of the time, to the enacment, in his own activities, of God's promises of salvation for the end-time. We begin our effort of reflection with the observation that these three facets of the consciousness of Jesus exhibit a point of convergence: a full awareness of being charged with the climactic and final mission to Israel as promised and previewed in the scriptures.

Second, we shall *independently* (i.e., without dependence on the foregoing) establish this same conclusion by a cumulative and convergent argument drawing on five data in the gospel narratives, the historicity of which has won almost universal agreement. These are: Jesus' proclamation that the reign of God was at hand; the fact that Jesus spoke and acted "with authority"; that he was widely known as and was a wonderworker; that he "cleansed" — or mounted a demonstration at — the Jerusalem temple; and that he died crucified, condemned by the Romans as "the king of the Jews." From these as yet disparate and unelucidated data I propose to argue to the main currents of the gospels' christology. All the themes belonging to these main currents, according to the argument, derived from Jesus and reflected his grasp of the scriptures as bearing on his own mission.

The form of the argument is as follows: the above-mentioned data, of which the historicity is all but universally accepted, establish Jesus' consciousness of being charged with God's "climactic and definitive" mission to Israel in view of the imminent consummation of history, or the reign of God. *But to speak of a "climactic and definitive mission" in the context of the imminent consummation of history is to imply the imminent consummation or fulfillment of the whole of eschatological promise and prophecy.* It follows that we ought positively to expect to find on Jesus'part not only an eschatological consciousness, but one marked by *the awareness of present fulfillment*, a phenomenon without parallel in ancient Israel.[1]

Crucial to the argument is the ascertainment that, like his contemporaries, Jesus understood the great soteriological themes of the scriptures as prophetic, that is, as awaiting fulfillment from the moment at which the end-time would break out. This is why we should positively expect the bearer of God's climactic and definitive mission *to focus on and to coordinate these themes.*

The sheer sweep and power of the argument — from the consciousness of an eschatological mission, through the necessity of all the scriptures to come to fulfillment, to the main currents of the messianology or christology of the gospels — invite us to press it for its validity, i.e., to test the sufficiency of its premises and the cogency of its logic. Do the gospels in fact exhibit the requisite data? Do they confirm that Jesus, like others who looked for the eschatological consummation, read the scriptures as prophecy awaiting its moment of convergent fulfillment? Is there any plausible escape from the argument?

Finally, this argument evokes an antecedent expectation that the profusion, the positive explosion, of christological speech following on "the Easter experience of the disciples" will have been rooted in Jesus' own self-understanding. We shall accordingly conclude by entertaining the question of whether this expectation is confirmed.

## THREE SORTS OF INDICES TO JESUS' CONSCIOUSNESS OF HIS MISSION

Three words — the temple riddle (Mark 14:58=Matt 26:61=John 2:19; cf. Mark 15:29=Matt 27:40; Acts 6:14), the response to Antipas (Luke 13:32), and the Jonah saying in response to the demand for a sign (Matt 12:39=Luke 11:29; cf. Mark 8:12; Matt. 16:4) — share a set of sharply profiled traits that reflect the Jesus of history: first, a context of clash with authoritative or elite forces in Israel; second, the "three-days" motif, which evokes (in consciously enigmatic fashion) the divine governance of the life and fate of Jesus;[2] third, a consequent and ummistakable note of perfect confidence. Jesus clearly regarded the looming crisis (or eschatolosical ordeal) in the light of its subjection to God's royal sovereignty.

Two of these sayings present "types" of salvation: the sanctuary (*naos*/Heb.: *hekal*/Aram.: *hekela'*) of the temple is presented as a type of the messianic community of salvation, transfigured in the reign of God.[3] Jonah, saved from the sea-monster, is presented as a type of one raised from the dead, returning (at the great consummation, the day of "the [son of] Man") to confound those who pressed Jesus for a "sign." There would be no sign but that one![4] Both sayings thus belong to the series of words presenting Jesus and his disciples as eschatological antitypes of familiar biblical figures: Moses (Matt 5:17, 21-48; cf. John 6:14; 7:40), David (Mark 12:35-37=Matt. 22:41-46=Luke 20:41-44; Mark 2:25-26=Matt. 12:3-4=Luke 6:3-4); Solomon (Matt. 12:42=Luke 11:31), Elisha (Mark 6:35-44=Matt. 14:15-21=Luke 9:12-17), Isaiah (Mark 4:12=Matt 13:13; Luke 8:10), the Servant of the Lord (Mark 10: 45=Matt 20:28; Mark 14:24c=Matt. 26:28b; Luke 22:20c; John 6:51), the one like a [son of] man and the tribes and prophets of Israel (Mark 3:13-14=Matt 10:1-2=Luke 6:13; Matt.:12=Luke 6:23). The typological interpretation of the early Church was not an independent development; it was grounded historically ln Jesus' own use of typology. The two typological texts adduced here (the riddle of the new sanctuary and the sign of Jonah) are, in particular, words of Jesus;[5] nor is the eschatological character of the antitypes open to reasonable doubt.

Second, we meet the motif of divinely appointed measure of all things and its specific application to the eschaton in the Markan form of the public proclamation: *peplerotai ho kairos*/ the time is fulfilled — or filled full. Though the verb is used variously of time, the probable image here is a great vase that with the years has been slowly filled until at last it is full to the brim.[6] As Paul Jouon pointed out long ago,[6] the parallelism of *peplerotai* and *eggiken* suggests that the latter (substratum: *qerabat*) means "has arrived." The whole is aligned closely with the "today" and "fulfilled" motifs in Luke 6:21 ("Today this scripture has been fulfilled [*peplerotai*] in your hearing").

Elsewhere Jesus applied the same filling-up-to-the-appointed -measure motif to "evil" and to revelation." "This evil generation" (of unbelievers and killers of God's envoys) will find itself overwhelmed by the rapidly approaching ordeal/tribulation, when God will exact from it the blood-debt for all the murders recorded in the scriptures from first to last (i.e., from Cain's fratricide in Gen 4 to the stoning of Zechariah in 2 Chron 24:20-25; Matt 23:34-36=Luke 11:49-51). Fill up, then, the measure of your fathers!( Matt 23:32), spoken to men already set on the death of Jesus (Matt 21:45-46), is a bitterly ironic summons to bring to completion with this prospective crime the last wave of evil allotted to history.

By contrast, the final measure of revelation allotted to Israel is bestowed, now at last, through the agency of Jesus. "Do not think that I have come to annul the Law [or the prophets]; I have come, not to annul but to complete (Matt 5:11).[8] This motif of the eschatological completion of God's revelation is carried through in the following antitheses (Matt 5:21-22,33-34,38-39,43-44) as well as in the accounts of Jesus' teaching in general, e.g.,in the move, from Moses's provisional legislation on divorce (Deut 24) to the eschatological restoration of the ideal of paradise (Gen 2:24), enacted anew for the already inaugurated restoration of Israel (Matt 19:3-9=Mark 10:2-10). In short, Jesus here presents himself as the prophet like Moses, bringing to Israel the final measure of revealed truth.

Third and last, when John in prison sent the question to Jesus, "Are you he who is to come [Ps 118:26], or shall we look for another?" Jesus allowed his actions to speak for him; in the urgent staccato of two-beat rhythm, he answered: Go and tell John what you hear and see:

blind men see,
cripples walk,
lepers are cleansed,
deaf men hear,
dead men are raised,
and good news is broken to the poor! (Matt 11:5=Luke 7:22-23).

Jesus is saying that his own public activity in Israel must be read as the superabundant fulfillment of eschatological promises (Isa 35:5-6; 29:18-19; 61:1).[9] He had come as the messianic consolation of Israel (Isa 40:1; Tg Isa 33:20). Like the answer to the high-priest in the Sanhedrin trial (Matt 26:64a; cf. Luke 22:70d), Jesus' response is averse to claims (in manner), while entirely affirmative (in substance).

It seems to me that these three phenomena — self-identification as eschatological antitype, the claim that in him and his mission the divine measures assigned to the eschaton were being brought to completion, and, finally, the specific invitation to interpret his public activity as the fulfillment of eschatological promise and prophecy — are inexplicable except as attesting a unique consciousness: that of mediating God's last, climactic visitation of his people. (We are looking back from two millennia later; this should not distract us into supposing that the Jesus of the public ministry envisioned a long history still to come.)[10] The historicity of the texts is solidly probable and their central meaning appears to be perfectly clear. Let him who has ears hear. But since the music of these texts apparently falls outside the auditory range of many professional listeners, I shall propose a distinct and independent consideration of texts equally intelligible and still more widely acknowledged to be historical, namely, the five data listed in the introduction to this essay.

## DID JESUS ANNOUNCE THE IMMINENT END OF HISTORY?

We take it that scholarship has copiously established the historicity of the proclamation of Jesus. The one relevant issue that has not found universal agreement bears on its eschatological character. When Jesus spoke of the imminence of the reign of God (*basileia tou theou/malkuta' de'laha'*), was this meant to signify the imminence of the end of history? Starting a hundred years ago with Johannes Weiss, this question has periodically appeared to have been settled in the affirmative — only to be upset by some new effort of revisionist scholarship.

In 1935 C.H. Dodd offered a brilliant reconstruction of Jesus' scenario of the future, which included an affirmation of the imminent end of history.[11] But Dodd followed his reconstruction with a historico-hermeneutical account of what it finally meant. The account, under the name "realized eschatology," left nothing still to be expected in the future, whether by Jesus or by the believer today. (In this Dodd was followed by T. F. Glasson[12] and J.A.T. Robinson,[13] who worked out this view with such consistency that its latent defects became patent.)

Meantime, in an article little noticed (it appeared during the Second World War in a journal that ceased publication before the war was over), Joachim Jeremias offered a positive appreciation of Dodd's historical reconstruction, adding a number of corrections and refinements, and dropping Dodd's unhelpful attempt to free Jesus from the liability of a mythical view of the future.[14]

In the post-War period, existentialist kerygma theology also had its say. Ernst Käsemann attempted, like Dodd, to save Jesus from the luggage of apocalyptic expectations, but forgoing Dodd's laborious indirection. Without flinching at the necessary literary and historical surgery on the gospels, Käsemann directly attributed to the historical Jesus an exclusively realized eschatology.[15]

Yet another rescue attempt was mounted by George B. Caird.[16] Caird did not contest that Jesus spoke the language of apocalyptic eschatology. The issue was whether he meant this language literally or metaphorically. According to Caird, Jesus expected a metaphorical end of the world. On the literal plane this corresponded to the end of the current era in human history. (Disciples of Caird today include Marcus Borg and N.T. Wright.)[17]

Several of these efforts to interpret the proclamation of Jesus came under critical review in 1985 by Dale C. Allison, Jr., in a monograph based on an earlier doctoral dissertation.[18] Allison conclusively showed that many of them (those especially of Glasson, Robinson, and Caird) were unsalvageable. His account (though he was apparently unaware of this) was largely a reprise of Joachim Jeremias's 1941 reconstruction of Jesus' scenario for the end-time. Indeed, Jeremias's brief presentation was in certain details more exact,[19] though Allison's monograph provided a fullness of treatment — in the framing of the question, the survey of the gospel sources, and the repertory of relevant intertestamental and other Jewish literature — that far surpassed the reach of Jeremias's short review-article.

Having recently taken up anew the question of Jesus' future scenario,[20] I shall not review the entire question here. Let it suffice to say that Johannes Weiss was right at least about Jesus' expectation of the imminent end of the world. Just prior to Jesus, the Baptist proclaimed the imminence of the last judgment. Just after Jesus, Paul repeatedly indicated his hope and expectation of the imminent parousia of the Lord. In the interim between the Baptist and Paul, Jesus affirmed that the last judgment, for which the men of Nineveh and the Queen of the South were to be raised from the dead, was on the brink.[21]

What Weiss and Schweitzer missed, and what Dodd caught, was the present realization in Jesus' own time of at least part of Israel's heritage of eschatological promise and prophecy. To this should be added the nascent Christian community's unambiguous affirmation of the era of fulfillment as having *already arrived*. Both in Jesus himself and in the Easter community of his followers there were two facets of the eschatological consciousness: first, a consciousness of eschatological promise/prophecy "already fulfilled"; second, the complementary consciousness of promise/prophecy "still to be fulfilled." Together these facets of eschatological consciousness commend, as the most useful terminological rubric both for the views of Jesus and for those of the post-Easter church, "eschatology inaugurated and in process of realization."

## FOUR MORE DATA ACNOWLEDGED
## TO BE CERTAINLY HISTORICAL

No one doubts the historicity of Jesus' proclamation of the reign of God. Similarly, the historicity of the following data is secure: (1) Jesus impressed his contemporaries of one who spoke and acted "as having authority" (*hos exousian echon/kesalita*,' Mark1:22=Matt 7:29=Luke 4:22; Mark 1:27=Luke 4:26). What sort of authority? Not, emphatically, the authority of the professionally trained theologian (Mark 11:28=Matt 21:23=Luke 20:2); rather that of a charismatic wielding supernatural power over demons, a power that he could and did sovereignly transmit to his disciples (Mark 3:15=Matt 10:1; Mark 6:7=Luke 9:1). More, Jesus acted as one bearing the authority to remit sins (Mark 2:10=Matt 9:5=Luke 5:24) — in short, like the plenipotentiary of a new economy of salvation.[22]

(2) Once, when some Pharisees delivered a threat against Jesus' life, allegedly from Antipas, Jesus coolly responded with a memorable word on his invulnerability until the moment of God's choosing, when he would indeed be subject to the onslaught of Satan:

"Behold, I drive out demons
and perform cures
today and tomorrow,
and on the third day I complete my course" (Luke 13:32).

Since the three-days motif connotes God's sovereignly appointed plan, the sense of the text is: "(Tell that fox that) I cannot be touched until the divinely appointed time." Quite incidentally, however, the saying defines the public career of Jesus under the rubric of exorcisms and cures, thus significantly adding to the sum of testimonies to Jesus' career as a wonderworker.

Central to these testimonies is a series of sayings: (a) the double *masal* on Beelzebul and the advent of the reign of God (Matt 12:27-28=Luke 11:18-20); (b) the *masal* on dynasties and households divided against themselves (Mark 3:24-26=Matt 12:25-26=Luke 11:17-18); (c) the *masal* on the binding of the strong man (Mark 3:27=Matt 12:29=Luke 11:21); (d) the inference that, if (in the context established by Jesus' proclamation) it was by God's power that he drove out demons, *the reign of God had already* (virtually)[23] *come* (Matt 12:28=Luke 11:20). This last motif epitomizes at least one of the many facets of Jesus' wonderworking.

(3) The historic drama of the cleansing of the temple, as I have recently argued elsewhere,[24] has been underplayed both by the gospels themselves and by recent historical-Jesus research. The historicity of the event is not in doubt. The meaning of the event is clearly many-faceted.[25] In the present context, however, the critical point is that in all its aspects the cleansing is peculiarly charged with an implicit claim to plenary authority over the destiny, the definitive restoration, of Israel. A secondary matter is the provenance, in the public life of Jesus, of the riddle on the new sanctuary. It seems to me to belong, with mid-range probability, to the follow-up on the cleansing of the temple. This follow-up was hardly the question of *exousia/resut* (Mark 11:27-33=Matt 21:23-27=Luke 20:1-8); it must rather have been the demand for a sign, as John presents it (John 2:18-19). But whatever the precise source of this word, it is clear that in Jesus' riddling answer (something like: "Destroy this sanctuary and after three days I will build it"; cf. John 2:19 and Mark 14:58), the "authority" was that of the son of David/son of God (2 Sam 7:12; 1 Chron 17:12-13; Ps 2:7; 110:3; 4QFlor 11) commissioned to build God's house (2 Sam 7:13-14; 1 Chron 17:12-13; Hag 1:1-2;2: 20-23; Zech 6:12-13). Inasmuch as "God's house" in texts such as these was open to signifying God's eschatologically restored people (*ekklesia/edta'*), and since this is precisely the sense of the new sanctuary in Jesus' word, the cleansing itself as well as this word (which, in the present hypothesis, immediately followed on the cleansing) showed that Jesus understood the restoration of Israel to belong to his mission — indeed, as its central task.[26]

(4) In the light of the above ascertainments, the titulus on the cross, "the king of the Jews," makes excellent historical sense. In the passion story the key religious question (as shown by Mark 14:61=Matt 26:63; cf. Luke 22:67) had been whether Jesus would acknowledge his claim, up till now exclusively implicit in the public forum, to be the appointed agent (the Messiah) of the appointed eschatological act (the restoration of Israel). When the Sanhedrists presented this question to Pilate, they gave it a political twist. The *titulus*, doubtless a product of Pilate's own malicious irony, is a solid index to the crime of which Jesus was accused: pretention to royal dominion. The *titulus*, besides being well attested (Mark 15:26= Matt 27:37= Luke 23:39=John 19:19), interlocks easily with the other data on the Sanhedrin's effort to bring about the suppression of Jesus.

Our purpose is not to deal on its own merits with each of the five data adduced here; it is rather to point to the fact that, taken collectively, they converge on Jesus' consciousness of being the bearer of a divinely appointed, climactic and definitive, mission to Israel. Once again, consider these data cumulatively: (a) He proclaims the imminence of the divine saving act celebrated in the prophets as the eschatological restoration of God's people. (b) But he does not just announce it. His public performance, including teaching and wonderworking, strikes his contemporaries as maximally authoritative, the authority deriving directly from God. (c) When threatened by Antipas--just as when questioned by the Baptist--his response points to his career as wonderworker: it accords with the divine plan and proceeds under its protection (Luke 13:32) and it fulfills the promises of the scriptures (Matt11:5=Luke 7:22-23). (d) When "reign of God" is taken in the sense that Jesus intended, namely, as God's definitive act of salvation,[27] its correlates include new covenant, new sanctuary, new cult. The thrust of the symbolic action at the temple accordingly appears to intend the end of the old (Mosaic) dispensation and to intimate some new, implicitly messianic, dispensation. (e) The last wisp of remaining ambiguity is dissipated by the *titulus* on the cross. The conclusion that we find imposed on us (again, not from these five data taken singly but from the five taken cumulatively and collectively) is that Jesus did indeed think of himself as called to a climactic and definitive mission to Israel.

## THE SCRIPTURES MUST BE FULFILLED

Many years ago John Downing, in an article on Jesus and martyrdom,[29] offered an apparently irrefutable observation: Jesus, by his proclamation of the imminent coming of the reign of God, implicitly defined himself as God's last voice, the last prophetic envoy to Israel. "He was the last prophet," argued Downing, "for men's reactions to him and to his preaching determined their eschatological destiny (Luke xii.8 and par.)."[30] Or, in the expression of Amos Wilder, Jesus' role was "that of mediator of God's final controversy with his people."[31]

Keeping in mind this motif of "last envoy, last prophet" (which Jesus himself made thematic and emphatic by his warnings to the crowds that time was running out, that the great judgment was on the brink), we should perhaps bring it into relation with the biblical conception of God's word and of his fidelity to his word.

YHWH could be counted on. Thus, when Joshua's work was done, the narrator of his story writes:

> So YHWH gave unto Israel all the land
> that he swore to give unto their fathers,
> and they possessed it and inhabited it;
> and YHWH gave them rest round about
> according to all that he swore unto their fathers;
> and there stood not one of their enemies against them;
> YHWH delivered all their enemies into their hand.
> There failed not aught of all the good things
> that YHWH had spoken unto the house of Israel.
> All came to pass (Josh 21:42-43; English versions: 21:42-45).

The key word is "all." YHWH gave Israel *all* the land he had promised, and he gave them rest according to *all* he had sworn. Of *all* their enemies not one withstood them; YHWH delivered them *all* into their hands. Of *all* the good things that he had said, not one failed. In a word, *hakkol ba': all* came to pass.

This passage is not only repeated again and again in fragmentary fashion in the texts that follow in the book of Joshua; it also epitomizes the biblical theme of YHWH's *sedaqah/righteousness* and his *emunah/ fidelity*, motifs endlessly recurrent in the scriptures. We are moreover in the presence of a massive index to the way in which Israel would come to understand promise and prophecy for the end-time. The whole of it, all without exception, would come to pass. That specifically included the salvation of the nations by assimilation to eschatologically restored Israel.

The background to new developments in the reading of the scriptures might be sketched in a few strokes. The traumatic events of the sixth century — the loss of king and aristocracy in 597, the far more violent and severe losses in the capture of Jerusalem in 587, another deportation in 582; return followed by disillusionment; rifts and factions in the Judean restoration — are diversely reflected in the new foundations laid by prophecy (Trito-Isaiah and Deutero-Zechariah) and by the reforms of Ezra and Nehemiah. The true restoration of Israel became a leading theme and an ongoing, contentious issue. The transcendent terms into which Trito-Isaiah and Deutero-Zechariah transposed the restoration theme opened the era of proto-apocalyptic, remotely preparing the scene for new forms of faith-literature.

The Macedonian conquest of the East similarly instigated new developments in the way indentured Israel envisaged the salvation of the nation. The probable influx from the eastern diaspora of mantic wise men (not the representatives of proverbial wisdom such as we find in Ben Sira) may well explain the origins and salient features of the book of Daniel.[32]

In Qumran we find a systematic way of reading the scriptures, one facet of which is the specification of "the (prophetic) meaning" (*peser*), which focuses on the community, its origins, status, and destiny. The biblical books partly retain their original sense, but by the time of Jesus they (the prophets in particular) were read as pointing toward definitive fulfillment at the outbreak of the end-time. Qumran furnishes the fullest data on this;[33] but we find it also in intertestamental literature,[34] in the targums,[35] and in John the Baptist (e.g., John 1:23 on Isa 40:3; cf. Mark 1:3=Matt 3:4=Luke 3:4).

Paul, looking back, would say, "Whatever promises God has made, their Yes is in him" (2 Cor 1:2b). Similarly, Jesus himself, repudiating the charge of annulling the scriptures, claimed rather to bring them to completion and fulfillment (Matt 5:17=Luke 16:17;Matt 11:5=Luke 7:22).

In the introduction to this essay we sketched an argument according to which a consciousness like that of Jesus, i.e., of one charged with a climactic and definitive mission to God's people, should lead us to expect to find in him a phenomenon otherwise unexampled in ancient Israel: the conviction that God's promises for the end-time *were already being fulfilled*. Now we may be more specific. We should expect to find that, as time passed and the fulfillment of the whole-to-be-fulfilled was inaugurated and underway, Jesus should somehow indicate (a) that some of this whole-to-be-fulfilled had now, already, found fulfillment; (b) that some of it was now finding fulfillment (i.e., during his public career);(c) that some of it was about to find fulfillment; and (d) that, since the prominent, perhaps dominant, end-time scenario (e.g., Dan 12:1-2) posits a distinction between the great affliction and its cessation (e.g., with the resurrection of the dead), all the rest, i.e., whatever of prophecy remains still outstanding (including the very resolution of the ordeal) would find fulfillment when the mission of Jesus would be crowned by the advent of God's "reign."

In point of fact, we find among the data of the gospel story the full confirmation of this multiple expectation. (a) After Antipas's execution of the Baptist, we learn that in Jesus' view God had already fulfilled the Elijah promise/prophecy (Mal 3:23-24; English versions: 4:5-6; Ben Sira 48:10) in the mission of John. (b) Earlier, by way of answer to the Baptist's query, Jesus pointed to his own career of wonderworking and proclaiming as bringing prophetic oracles of salvation to fulfillment here and now. (c) Again, he instructed the inner circle of his disciples that he was destined by prophetic necessity to be repudiated and killed (in accord with the role of the Servant of the Lord who, to be sure, was equally destined to be vindicated and glorified; see Mark 9:1 and its many parallels);[36] moreover, the disciples were to share in this suffering, which would signal the outbreak of the eschatological ordeal. (d) Finally, once the tribulation or ordeal had run its fierce but brief course, he would complete his work as the Davidic master-builder of the new sanctuary (i.e., of the people of the new covenant) (Mark 14:58=Matt 26:61=John 2:19; cf.Acts 6:14), a saying that, once more, inescapably implied the total reversal of his personal fate. This would be the moment at which the gentile world would be judged and saved (Matt 8:11=Luke 13:29).[37]

These data of fulfillment — not exhaustive, but merely representative of the full picture offered by the gospels — are telling. They meet our expectation that, given the kind of consciousness of mission that we can with assurance affirm of Jesus, and given the ancient Judaic view of the scriptures as having the aspect of prophecy to be fulfilled in the eschaton, we should expect to find in him the conviction that *in this last, climactic mission to Israel, and therefore in the bearer of this last, climactic mission, the scriptures — all the scriptures without remainder — had, of divine or prophetic necessity, to come to fulfillment.*

## JESUS: PROXIMATE SOURCE OF THE MESSIANOLOGY OF THE GOSPELS

If the scriptures had prophetically spoken, as Jesus was fully persuaded that they had, of God's decisive saving act, namely, the restoration of Israel, of the *mebasser* or herald who was to announce it (Isa 52), of the prophet like Moses who was to reveal its demands (Deut 18:15,18), of the Davidic Messiah anointed to accomplish it (2 Sam 7; cf. 4QFlor), of the Servant who would extend it to the ends of the earth (Isa 49:6), of the one like a (son of) man whose triumph would seal it (Dan 7), it follows that we are faced immediately with prophecies and promises which, precisely at that last moment, called inescapably for fulfillment.

How might we form an idea of what, in the scriptures, Jesus took to be soteriologically significant, to call for fulfillment? The clues must be sought in the gospel texts. After an initial period of public activity as the ally of the Baptist until the latter's arrest (John 3:22-26),[38] Jesus inaugurated his own independent public career in Galilee (Mark 1:14=Matt 4:12=Luke4:14) with the public proclamation, made especially in synagogues but also out-of-doors: "The reign of God is at hand/has arrived!" (*eggiken he basileia tou theou/qerabat malkuta' de'laha'*). To many who heard it, these words surely recalled the *Qaddis* prayer ("may he allow his reign to reign...") recited weekly in the Synagogue and just as surely evoked the news of salvation epitomized in the cry *malak 'elohaik*, "your God reigns" (Isa 52:7). This accordingly suggests that Jesus spoke in the voice of the Isaian *mebasser/euaggelizomenos* — a figure interpreted at Qumran in "messianic" terms: "one anointed with the Spirit" (11Q Melch 18).[39] In Isaiah, then, Jesus found both his career as proclaimer of salvation and the essential burden of his proclamation.

Though, as it happens, we have no confirmatory textual index, it is highly probable that, like his contemporaries, Jesus took the promise of a prophet like Moses (Deut 15:15,18) to await its fulfillment in the end-time — and concretely to find this fulfillment in his own act of bringing to completion the last measure, the fullness, of revealed truth (Matt 5:17).

It is quite out of the question that Jesus should not have been aware of the many strands of biblical tradition promising a new David or son of David appointed to mediate God's act of restoring his people. Let it suffice to refer to the riddle of the new sanctuary (Mark 14:58=Matt 26:61=John 2:19) with its biblical antecedents on the one appointed to build God's house (2 Sam 7:12-13; cf. 1 Chron 12:13-14; Hag 2:20-23; Zech 6:12-13). There are, of course, many other texts that show Jesus' hold on motifs of royal messianism (e.g., the Caesarea Philippi scene;[40] the royal entry into Jerusalem;[41] repeated use of shepherd imagery).[42]

So far as the Isaian Servant passages are concerned, we find at least two pieces of evidence for Jesus' awareness especially of the last, great passage as soteriologically significant prophecy. These two crucial texts are Mark 10:45=Matt 20:28 (the ransom word, which specifies the beneficiaries of the ransom as "many" [cf. Isa 52:14-15; 53:11-12], and for which Peter Stuhlmacher has provided both a striking exegesis and a persuasive argument in favor of historicity),[43] and Mark 14:24=Matt 26:28 (the word over the cup, which brings together two motifs of Isa 53: the "pouring out" of the Servant's life [Isa 53:12] and, again, the many).

The two most significant indices to Jesus' keen awareness of the great apocalyptic scene of Daniel 7 are, first, his references to the thrones for the court of judgment (Dan 7:9-10) in Matt 19:28=Luke 22:29 and, second, the "little flock" saying in Luke 12:32, where the motif of transferring to the disciples a share in royal dominion is derived from Dan 7:27.[44] We might add that the Lukan form of Jesus' words in the Sanhedrin scene (Luke 22:69), which takes nothing from Dan 7 except the term Son of man, is probably prior to the parallels in Mark and Matthew and probably authentic.[45]

Our conclusion is that Jesus, in the consciousness of election to a climactic and definitive mission to Israel, sought and found in the scriptures the specifications of God's eschatological deed and the specifications of his own role as the chosen instrumental doer of that deed. By ineluctable logic these scriptures could not, in Jesus' view, fail to find fulfillment in the drama of his own mission and in its swiftly approaching climax — the ordeal and its resolution. All the scriptures must find fulfillment, whether in the now of his mission or in the rapidly approaching ordeal and final triumph. If the Baptist had fulfilled the EliJah role, Jesus with his disciples was to fulfill the roles of servant of the Lord and Davidic builder of the house of God. Moreover, though Jesus never simply relaxed that altereity which typified his words on the Son of man,[46] picturing him, for example, as witnessing for or against men in accord with how they had stood vis-a-vis Jesus (Mark 8:38; Matt 10:33=Luke 12:9), it is ultimately inescapable that he understood himself as destined to perform the triumphant role of the Son of man. It is an attractive hypothesis that, adopting a deliberately ambiguous use of *bar enasa'*/Son of man, he applied it both to man in general and to himself (in his prediction of the passion, in Mark 9:31 parr.).[47] If Luke 22:69 is an authentic word, we are given a hint of Jesus' focus on Ps 110; this in turn grounds the hypothesis that he provided at least a hint (e.g., Mark 12:35-37a=Matt 22:41-46= Luke 20:41-44) that he himself, now the lowly son of David, but soon to be transcendently enthroned — David's "lord" — at the right hand of God.[48] This, of course, correlates and converges with the role of the Son of man on the "Day when the Son of man will be revealed" (Luke 17:30; cf. 17:24,31). Nevertheless, for the disciples only the Easter experience would definitively break down the altereity that somehow differentiated between Jesus and "the (Son of) man." (In the light of that breakdown, it is amazing that the original form of the sayings, which exhibit it, should have been so well preserved in the tradition.)

The procedure of the above argument, one that puts a premium on the value of heuristic anticipations, has been consciously and inevitably schematic. First, we acknowledged evidence for Jesus' firm personal conviction of election. He was a man with a mission; the mission bore on, belonged to, the climactic and definitive saving act of God. Jesus accordingly found himself called to function as God's (intimately instrumental) agent with respect to what the scriptures defined as the final restoration of Israel, comprehending (by assimilation to Israel) the salvation of the nations. Second, to this we added the observation that Jesus could not have failed to expect that the sum total of scriptural promise and prophecy was bound by divine necessity to come to fulfillment in connection with his own mission. Third, we consequently found ourselves in the position of being able to articulate a set of significant anticipations: that the accounts of Jesus should yield evidence (a) of eschatology inaugurated and in process of realization; (b) of eschatology in accord with the schema of crisis to be followed by resolution Dan 12:1-2; cf. Isa 53) and hence of some elements of fulfillment postponed until the moment of resolution; (c) on Jesus' part, of some reflection on and correlation of such soteriological themes (interpreted as prophecy) as the herald of salvation, the awaited prophet, the royal Messiah, the Servant of the Lord, and the one like a man in Dan 7; (d) on the disciples' part, of the probably fragmentary, only partly thematic, and gradually developing knowledge or realization of the eschatological roles of Jesus. Fourth, we found that these anticipations were solidly met by the data of the gospels. Fifth, we concluded that Jesus himself had been the principal source of the earliest post-Easter messianology/christology.

We should add that in this reconstruction Jesus is seen as intent on listening to the scriptures for the orientation of his life and mission. We do not, however, find in him one constantly and restlessly engaged in adjustments, revisions, changes of heart and mind. The paucity of messianic self-revelation accorded on the part of Jesus neither with simple ignorance nor with any supposed sense of personal ordinariness, but with an economy of revelation that withheld the secret of his person and destiny out of realism and wisdom respecting his listeners. Hence the special importance that accrues to the esoteric traditions in the gospels. It should be added that the disciples were neither swift nor deft in construing the intentions and paradoxical self-disclosures of Jesus. The conditions of the possibility of accurate comprehension were not given except with the so-called Easter experience. But what this experience generated in the disciples was not the celebration of new, previously unknown messianic and soteriological themes. *All* had been repeatedly adumbrated, if not made thematic, by Jesus.

## CONCLUSION

We have offered the reader an experiment, a mode of investigation (moving from heuristic anticipations to the interpretation of data) hitherto little used in biblical criticism,[49] though it has been successfully brought to bear on other fields.[50] Its principal advantage is that the orientation of the investigation, made explicit from the start, derives less from the undiscussed preferences of the investigator (which in some measure are always present, albeit most variously in how, from scholar to scholar, they relate to the purity of the desire to know) but from a grasp of procedures spontaneously operative in ancient Judaism. The orientation in question here derives from the manner in which Jesus and his contemporaries typically read the scriptures.

We moved (a) from the evidence of Jesus' conviction of personal election to a mission bearing on God's climactic saving act (b) through the scriptures, read as prophecy reserved for eschatological fulfillment, (c) to the anticipation, *and its satisfaction*, of a many-sided, scripturally prophesied role and destiny. To the chosen one the scriptures revealed in advance the saving mission and its bearer — deed and doer alike in all their variety.

Among the limits of this procedure two are noteworthy: its schematic character and its essential incompleteness vis-a-vis the reality of Jesus and his mission. (Where do we find in the scriptures so much as a hint of Jesus' initiatives toward notorious sinners? Where do they foretell his heavy accent on forgiveness and the rejection of resentment and vengeance?) Its two main strengths are also noteworthy: the orienting principle of the inquiry is a set of verifiable observations about antiquity which markedly diminish that ever widening gap between ourselves and the suppositions operative in ancient Judaism but not among us. Of these we tend to be oblivious or amnesiac, or at least we systematically minimize them. The result is to find that data — unambiguous in context — tend, without that context, to grow dim and almost to vanish before our eyes in a cloud of ambiguity.

Those who suppose that scholarship consists in a leisurely cultivation of ambiguity and in recoil from "closure," including the closure intrinsic to framing arguments and drawing conclusions, are likely to repudiate the procedure either with cool disdain or the vehemence of offended ideology.[51] Those, on the other hand, who think that historical inquiry should devise new ways of heading for historical conclusions may well find some merit in the procedure.

## NOTES

1.  On whether the realized element in the eschatology of Jesus and of earliest Christianity has any true parallel in ancient Judaism, see Dale C. Allison, Jr., **The End of the Ages Has Come** (Philadelphia: Fortress, 1985) 91f. Here Allison significantly nuances the account

of "realized eschatology" in David Aune, **The Cultic Setting of Realized Eschatology in Early Christianity** (Leiden: Brill, 1967). But despite his clarity on the main issues, Allison himself has been led to suppose that *T. Job* 39:9-40:6 might offer a true parallel to the realized eschatology of the resurrection of Jesus. In presenting the "resurrection" of Job's children, however, the writer of the testament never steps out of the narrative world of Job into that shared by writer and reader. This does not hold for NT texts on the resurrection of Jesus, as 1 Cor 15:3-8 unequivocally shows by its accent on available living witnesses to whom the risen Christ had appeared. Moreover, this difference grounds another: the impact attributed to Jesus' resurrection vs. the total lack of impact of the "resurrection" of Job's children.

2. Joachim Jeremias, "Die Drei-Tage-Worte der Evangelien," in **Tradition und Glaube** [K. G. Kuhn Festschrift], eds. Gert Jeremias, H.-W. Kuhn, H. Stegemann (Gottingen: Vandenhoeck Ruprecht, 1971) 221-229, at 227.

3. J. Jeremias, "Die Drei-Tage-Worte"; B. F. Meyer, "The 'Inside' of the Jesus Event," in Meyer, **Critical Realism and the New Testament** (Allison Park, PA: Pickwick, 1989) 157-172.

4. Joachim Jeremias, *"Ionas,"* in eds. Kittel and Friedrich, **Theological Dictionary of the New Testament** III, 406-410.

5. Respecting Jesus' use of typology, a detailed special study is still lacking; meantime, see R. T. France, **Jesus and the Old Testament** (Grand Rapids: Baker, 1982 [lst ed., 1971]) 38-82.

6. Franziskus Zorell, **Lexicon Graecum Novi Testamenti** (Paris: Lethielleux, 1931) *"pleroma,"* 1079; see also *"pleroo,"* 1076. For Mark 1:15 it follows that kairos here is not punctiliar but equivalent to *chronos.* Among recent treatments, see Joel Marcus, 'The Time Has Been Fulfilled!' (Mark 1.15), in **Apocalyptic and the New Testament** [J.L. Martyn Festschrift], eds. J. Marcus and M.L. Soards (Sheffield: JSOT, 1989) 49-68. On the theme of eschatological measure: R. Stuhlmann, **Das eschatologische Mass im Neuen Testament** (Gottingen: Vandenhoeck & Ruprecht, 1983).

7. Paul Jouon, "Notes philologiques sur les Evangiles," *Recherches de science religieuse* 17 (1927) 537-540, at 538.

8. Joachim Jeremias, **New Testament Theology. I. The Proclamation of Jesus** (New York: Scribner, 1971) 82-85.

9. "Superabundant," especially inasmuch as the Isaian texts on which Jesus drew do not include reference to raising the dead.

10. B. F. Meyer, **The Aims of Jesus** (London: SCM, 1979) 202-208.

11. C. H. Dodd, **The Parables of the Kingdom** (London: Nisbet, 1935; repr. London-Glasgow: Collins [Fontana] 1961) ch. 2 and 3.

12. T.F. Glasson, **The Second Advent** (London: Epworth, 3rd ed., 1963).

13. J.A.T. Robinson, **Jesus and His Coming** (Philadelphia: Westminster, 2nd ed., 1979).

14. Joachim Jeremias, "Eine neue Schau der Zukunftsaussagen Jesu," *Theoloogische Blatter* 20 (1941) 216-222.

15. Ernst Kasemann, "The Beginnings of Christian Theology" in Kasemann, **New Testament Questions of Today** (London: SCM, 1969) 82-107; "On the Subject of Primitive Christian Apocalyptic," *Questions*, 108-137; "Sentences of Holy Law in the New Testament" *Questions*, 66-81.

16. George B. Caird, **Jesus and the Jewish Nation** (London: Athlone, 1965); **The Language and Imagery of the Bible** (Philadelphia: Westminster, 1980).

17. Marcus J. Bors, **Conflict, Holiness and Politics in the Teaching of Jesus** (New York and Toronto: Mellen, 1984); **Jesus A New Vision** (San Francisco: Harper, 1987). N. T. Wright, **New Testament and the People of God** (Minneapolis: Fortress, 1992) 332-334.

18. See above, note 1.

19. In his numerous historical-Jesus studies Jeremias repeatedly affirmed that Jesus understood his coming suffering to inaugurate the eschatological ordeal. The metaphor Jeremias used in *Neutestamentliche Theologie I. Die Verkundigung* Jesu (Gottingen: Vandenhoeck & Ruprecht, 1971, 2nd ed. 1973) 231, was that his suffering would constitute *der Auftakt* (the first syllable, first beat, opening phase, prelude) of the eschatological ordeal. The choice of the term "prelude" in the English translation, however, led Allison, 118, (a) to suppose that in Jeremias's reconstruction Jesus took his own suffering to precede, but not to belong to, the ordeal; and (b) to find fault with Jeremias's failure to prove the view thus mistakenly attributed to him. (For his own part, Allison took the tribulation to be already underway during Jesus' ministry [117-128]). See how some of the most relevant texts (e.g., Matt 26:18; Luke 12:49; 13:33; John

12:19; 16:16a) are read in Jeremias, "Drei-Tage-Worte" and **New Testament Theology,** 127-141.

20. Meyer, "Jesus' Scenario of the Future," *Downside Review 109* (1991) 1-15.

21. See, e.g., Allison, **End of the Ages,** 111, note 40.

22. A point made cogently by N. T. Wright in a text (as yet unpublished) delivered at a McMaster University seminar, December 14, 1989, on hermeneutics and the historical Jesus.

23. The scholastics, building on the Aristotelian distinction of potency and act, differentiated within "act" between what was formally and what virtually actual--a distinction often appropriate to the advance presence of God's reign.

24. B.F. Meyer, "The Expiation Motif in the Eucharistic Words: A Key to the History of Jesus?" *Gregorianum* 69 (1988) 461-487, at 481-484.

25. Among these facets was one that, recently and independently, J. Neusner and I inferred from the negative stance toward the cult implicit in Jesus' demonstration at the temple, namely, that the counterpart of the temple cleansing must be--the last supper. See J. Neusner, "Money-Changers in the Temple: The Mishnah's Explanation" *New Testament Studies* 35 (1989) 287-290; Meyer, "Expiation Motif," 482-484.

26. Hence the thesis that "to predicate 'Messiah' of Jesus in the sense he himself intended is to grasp the 'inside' of the Jesus event as the single task of re-creating Israel--and the nations by assimilation to Israel--in fulfillment of the scriptures." Meyer,"The 'Inside' of the Jesus Event," in **Critical Realism** (see above,note 3) 157-172, at 169.

27. The case was made by Gustaf Dalman, **The Words of Jesus** (Edinburgh: Clark, 1902) 96-101, who differentiated this from other senses of the phrase in ancient Judaism.

28. See Johannes Behm, *"diatheke,"* in eds. Kittel and Friedrich, **Theological Dictionary of the New Testament** II, 124-134, esp.128, 132-133; Jeremias, **Die Abendmahlsworte Jesu** (Gottingen: Vandenhoeck & Ruprecht, 3rd ed., 1960) 217f.: the (new) covenant is "Korrelatbegriff zu *basileia ton ouranon.*" ET. **The Eucharistic Words of Jesus** (London: SCM, 1966) 226. But what holds for new covenant holds for new sanctuary and new cult. On the new temple/ sanctuary see E.P. Sanders, **Jesus and Judaism** (London: SCM, 1985) 77-90.

29. John Downing, "Jesus and Martyrdom," *Journal of Theological Studies* 14 (1963) 279-293.

30. Downing, "Martyrdom," 286f.

31. Amos N. Wilder, "Eschatology and the Speech-Modes of the Gospel," *Zeit und Geschichte* [R. Bultmann Festschrift] (Tubingen: Mohr-Siebeck, 1964) 19-30, at 29.

32. John J. Collins, **The Apocalyptic Vision of the Book of Daniel** (Missoula: Scholars, 1977) 56f.

33. Though there are numerous good general expositions, e.g., Otto Betz, **Offenbarung und Schriftforschun** (Tubingen: Mohr-Siebeck, 1960); M.P. Horgan, Pesharim: **Qumran Interpretations of Biblical Books** (Washington: BBA, 1979), to understand concretely the Essenes' style of interpreting, special studies of individual texts, e.g., William H. Brownlee, **The Midrash Pesher of Habakkuk** (Missoula: Scholars, 1979), are indispensable.

34. See John Barton, **Oracles of God** (Oxford: Oxford University Press, 1986); Christopher Rowland, *"The Inter-Testamental Literature"* in eds. J. Rogerson, C. Rowland, B. Lindars, **The History of Christian Theology II. The Use of the Bible** (Grand Rapids: Eerdmans, 1988) 153-225.

35. In the present context, see especially Bruce Chilton, **A Galilean Rabbi and His Bible** (Wilmington: Glazier, 1984) and Bruce Chilton, **The Isaiah Targum** (Wilmington: Glazier, 1987) .

36. Jeremias, **New Testament Theology** on Mark 9:31 and its many parallels, 281-286 .

37 . Still valuable: Bengt Sundkler, "Jesus et les paiens," *Revue d'Histoire et de Philosophie religieuses* 16 (1936) 462-499; J. Jeremias, **Jesus' Promise to the Nations** (London: SCM, 1958); Jacques Gupont, "'Beaucoup viendront du levant et du couchant...' (Matthieu 8, 11-12 Luc 13,28-29," *Sciences Ecclesiastiques* 9 (1967) 153-167.

38. On Jesus as "baptizer," Meyer, **Aims**, 122-124.

39. Joseph A. Fitzmyer, *"Further Light on Melchizedek from Qumran Cave 11,"* in Fitzmyer, **Essays on the Semitic Background of the New Testament**. (Missoula: Acholars, 1974) 245-267.

40. Meyer, **Aims**, 185-197.

41. Meyer, **Aims**, 168-170, 199.

42. Messianic shepherd imagery: Ezek 34:23-24; 37:24; Zech 13:7-9; cf. 12:10; 13:1-6. On imagery in gospels: Gustaf Dalman, "Arbeit und

Sitte in Palästina vi," *Beiträge zur Forderung christlicher Theologie*, series 2, 41 (1939) 249-250, 253-255.

43. Peter Stuhlmacher, "Vicariously Giving His Life for Many, Mark 10:45 (Matt. 20:28)," in Stuhlmacher, **Reconciliation, Law, and Righteousness** (Philadelphia: Fortress, 1986) 16-29. Also Volker Hampel, **Menschensohn und historischer Jesus** (Neukirchen-Vluyn: Neukirchener Verlag, 1990) 302-342.

44. Otto Betz, **Jesus und das Danielbuch. II. Die Menschensohnworte Jesu and die Zukunftserwartung des Paulus (Daniel 7,13-14)** (Frankfurt: Lang, 1985). On the two texts adduced, see Jeremias, **New Testament Theology**, 205, note 4; and 265.

45. B. F. Meyer, "How Jesus Charged Language with Meaning: A Study in Rhetoric," *Studies in Religion/Sciences Religieuses* 19 (1990) 273-285, at 285, with note 32.

46. Jeremias, **New Testament Theology** 265f. and, still more relevantly and incisively, 275f.

47. See above, note 36.

48. On the sense of the pericope on David's son and David's lord, see Jeremias, **New Testament Theology** 259, 276.

49. An exception (though perhaps not an altogether successful one) is the collaboration of Wilhelm Thüsing and Karl Rahner, **A New Christology** (New York: Seabury, 1980).

50. An example is the argument from human problem to the heuristic specification of the divine solution in Bernard Lonergan, **Insight** (New York: Longmans, Green, 1958) 687-730.

51. The recoil from the closure proper to judgments of credibility and to beliefs pervades Northrop Frye's transactions with the Bible in **The Great Code** (New York-London: Harcourt Brace Jovanovich, 1982). If ideology is the rationalization of alienation, this is ideological, transparently alienated as it is from belief, which Frye conceives single- and narrow-mindedly as headed for religious war. See my essay, "A Tricky Business: Ascribing New Meaning to Old Texts," *Gregorianum* 71 (1990) 745-761.

# 17

# TOWARD A CONTEMPORARY CHRISTOLOGY

## Roch Kereszty
### edited by Jonathan Leach

This essay is written from the perspective of a Catholic systematic theologian trying to deepen his understanding of the mystery of Christ. In doing so, he also hopes to help his fellow searchers, wherever they find themselves in their journey. Given the limitations of space, however, I shall attempt only to explain why systematic christology is a worthwhile enterprise; to locate christology's sources and to outline its method; and finally, to apply that method to a single christological theme, the sacrifice of Christ.[1]

## I. Why A Christology?

Why should anyone who is not a professional historian concern himself with the story of an itinerant Jewish rabbi who lived two thousand years ago, spent most of his life in an obscure province of the Roman Empire, wrote not a single line of poetry or prose, and was condemned and executed as a criminal by the highest religious and political authorities of his country? Why this fascination with the person of Jesus of Nazareth, a fascination which has endured throughout the centuries in his followers and foes, experts and laymen alike? In trying to answer this question, we may begin by analyzing an apparently universal human experience. In every human life, there are situations in which one experiences at least a glimpse of genuine goodness, some sort of true love. Such love may be that of a parent, friend, marriage partner or of a caring community. Experiencing this love, one becomes aware of his own worth, while discovering the worth of another (or others); one begins to surmise, as well, that ultimate value and ultimate reality may be Goodness and Love.

Typically, however, this experience is followed by disappointment. The child discovers the limits of his parent's goodness and love; the friend is revealed to have certain repugnant traits; the marriage partners encounter the "dark side" of each other. If, then, our words are to do justice to the whole of human experience, we must speak of both genuine goodness and genuine evil in the human being. We must affirm that human goodness is real, but also that it is limited, elusive, and mixed with evil. Furthermore, if we seek not just to describe this state of affairs, but to explain it, we must be attentive to what the various religions and religious philosophies offer for an answer.

Virtually every form of religion conceives of human goodness and love as being, in some way or another, identical with divine reality or grounded in divine reality (or divine realities).[2] Another remarkable convergence appears in the various religions' attempts to express a basic law of morality (however restrictive its interpretation might be), the Golden Rule: Do not do to others what you do not wish to be done to yourself.

These converging features in most religions provide both a context for, and a sharp contrast to, the unique phenomenon of Christianity. The first of these shared intuitions — namely, that goodness is, in some sense, the principal trait of Ultimate Reality — confirms the Christian claim: "We have come to know and to believe in the love God has for us" (1Jn 4:16 ). At the same time, Christian revelation differs from all other religions in apprehending the mystery of God as the mystery of an infinitely holy, personal and free love. The one God is in himself a loving communion of three persons, Father, Son and Holy Spirit. The eternal Son (infinitely different from and yet the archetype of God's creation) has truly become man; he has shared a full human destiny, to the extent of taking upon himself the burden of all our sins, so that mankind may share in the Trinitarian communion of divine life. In other words, only Christianity proclaims that God has manifested his love for humankind to the utmost, going infinitely beyond what any other religion has expected: out of love He became man and died the death of a sinner, so that we might share in his life. In Christianity, then, we see the emergence of a revelation of divine love, the greater than which no one can think or imagine.[3] This divine love is not only the object of Christian faith, but also the ideal for Christian action, and the power which enables the

Christian to approach the ideal. Thus, the Golden Rule familiar to all religions is taken up in, but also transcended by, Christian morality.

Additionally, Christian revelation perceives the gradual manifestation of God's love in a sequence of historical events in a Salvation History whose significance extends across all human history, and indeed the history of the whole universe. These events, particularly as they culminate in the history of Jesus of Nazareth, are attested to by reliable witnesses and can be verified with sufficient historical certainty or by a convergence of historical probabilities.[4]

At the end of such existential, philosophical and historical considerations, Christian faith should appear not as a system of truths that can be rationally "proved," but rather as the self-revelation of Truth, philosophically plausible, historically anchored, and existentially inviting. It confronts the searcher with an inescapable choice between acceptance and rejection. After embracing the Christian faith, the believer discovers that his quest for the truth (the reality) of goodness entailed, from the start, something more than his own effort. For the searcher's initial suspicion that ultimate Truth and Reality are goodness and love was itself inspired by the gracious initiative of this Ultimate Goodness.

Such is the nature of the faith presupposed in the following discussion on christology's method, its sources, and its central theme. These reflections presume a *fides quaerens intellectum*, a faith which seeks a deeper understanding of its object.

## II. Sources And Method

### 1. The Apostolic Church and the Bible

Our knowing anything, today, about the people of past ages requires that those people have made an enduring impact on history: the effects of their existence and activity must remain accessible to the present-day researcher. So it is with Jesus of Nazareth. The effects of his existence and activity endure today, not simply in a book, the New Testament, but in the living community or communities of the Church.[5]

But there is a major difference between other communities and the Church of Jesus Christ. When death deprives a community of its founder, its members typically continue to venerate him, even as they drift progressively farther from his direction and ideas. The believer, on the other hand, knows that Christ's presence in the community of his disciples did not end with his death. Rather, after his resurrection, Christ himself continued the founding of his church by sending his witnesses into the whole world and endowing them with his Holy Spirit.

Integral to this laying down of the Church's foundations was the production of a variety of written documents under the providential guidance of Christ's Holy Spirit. These documents (letters, gospels and the prophetic book of Revelation) all center on the teachings of Christ and the saving events of his life, death, and resurrection, as witnessed by the first disciples, applied to the changing circumstances of the Church, and put into writing by first-, second-, and possibly some third-generation Christians. When in the second century, spurious documents about Christ and his apostles began to circulate, all claiming an apostolic origin, the Church began the gradual process of defining her New Testament canon, the list of books in which she recognized an authentic apostolic witness to Christ. These books were deemed to be the inspired word of God insofar as they presented a written record — its reliability guaranteed by the Holy Spirit himself — of what Christ taught, did, and suffered.

At the same time, the Church defined her canon of the Old Testament books as part of God's written word. Here again, the criterion for including these sacred books of the Jews was ultimately christological: in the Church's judgment, these books, in one way or another, all pointed to Christ. They were identified as being prophetic, in a broad sense of that term.[6]

So the Bible, comprising the books of the Old and New Testaments, is part of a God-given foundation for his church; it is his Word, presented as a written record of Salvation History that culminated in Christ. As God's Word, it contains God's truth. In the New Testament, we encounter Christ's saving history and teachings, from the perspective of God and without error or distortion.

But we cannot forget that the Bible, and the New Testament in particular, is a collection of human documents. When he entered human history and became man, God must also have consented to be remembered and written about by human authors, whose humanity was in no way stripped from them as a precondition to their engaging in such work. The biblical writer retained all the limitations of any other finite human being who lives in a particular culture and writes for a specific audience. God did not miraculously transform the literary genre adhered to by a given author, nor did he hold in check the "historical forgetfulness" by which the details of a remembered event are transposed, omitted, or reshaped in the course of their transmission. Nevertheless, the Holy Spirit has ensured that the New Testament has achieved its God-given purpose: even where their interpretations are incomplete, requiring the complementary perspective of other biblical documents, the sacred writers have correctly interpreted the meaning of a particular event or teaching of Jesus within the overall context of God's plan of salvation.

## 2. The Later Church and the Bible

Christ's assisting his Church through the Holy Spirit did not end with the close of the first "constitutive period," the stage in which the Church established its basic structures. What changed was the **mode** of this assistance. Having laid down the apostolic foundation of the Church — a substantial building block of which was the Scriptures — the Spirit of Christ has remained active in the Church. He has assisted her in — among other things — the interpretation of those same Scriptures which he himself inspired.

Thus, to attempt a contemporary interpretation of the New Testament (or of the Old, without which the New cannot be understood), while ignoring or opposing earlier, official ecclesial interpretations, would be both historically and theologically mistaken. It would be a historical mistake, since the New Testament was written by members of the Church, for the Church; we cannot eradicate the writings' essential nature as the reflection and extension of the Church's oral preaching during its foundational stage. It would be theologically false, since only the Church (and her members only insofar as they remain within the Church) is promised the assistance of the Spirit who inspired her Scriptures.

The result is that the meaning of the Scriptures, their witness to Christ, can adequately be understood only within and by the Church. To proceed otherwise, seeking an interpretation which isolates the New Testament from either its original or subsequent ecclesial context, leads to the kind of violent misreading so amply documented in the liberal "Quest for the Jesus of History": in a Jesus made after the image of the researcher himself.[7] For the christologist's own interpretive bias (his

**Vorverständnis**, pre-understanding) must inevitably occupy the void created as soon as he attempts to uproot the New Testament from its own congenial interpretive context.

Let us, instead, be fully cognizant of the dialectical relationship, in christology, between Bible and Church. On the one hand, the whole of a christology must be biblical; it must be an interpretation of the manifold biblical witness to Christ. On the other hand, all christology begins and ends with the faith of the Church; its attempts to recover biblical meaning — like all human enterprises, partial and imperfect attempts — necessarily rely on the historical unfolding of this meaning within the Church. Any christological synthesis will therefore draw heavily upon the documents of the Church's Magisterium, as well as the christological systems of her theologians.[8]

Finally, no christology is intelligible which fails to take into account the concepts, the images, indeed the philosophies of the age to which it speaks. Yet no merely human image, concept, or philosophy can ever be adequate to the task of expressing the mysteries of God. Thus, these communicative "tools" must in every age be corrected and transformed, made suitable for their purpose under the impact of the christological mystery.[9]

Having considered these criteria for a christological method, let us now apply such a method to a central theme in christology, the sacrifice of Christ.

## III. THE SACRIFICE OF CHRIST

### 1. The Starting Point: The Kerygma of the Saving Death and Resurrection of Christ

The conventional starting point for a christology is to identify "the Jesus of history" as distinguished from or even opposed to "the Christ of faith."[10] While in my view no opposition between the two has ever been proven, the attempt to establish such a distinction is a legitimate task of New Testament exegesis, however difficult the enterprise might prove. As regards a systematic christology, however, this search for a dividing line can only draw us into a labyrinth of never-ending discussions about historical details, even as we neglect the central historical and theological issues.

I propose, instead, to adopt the perspective of the Gospels themselves. Let us examine the history of the earthly Jesus from the vantage point of its denouement: we begin with the New Testament's most primitive kerygma, the summary proclamation of his death and resurrection. Here we find ourselves on firm historical footing, as no historian can deny either the fact or the primitive character of this kerygma. This analysis, in turn, enables us to establish the historical and philosophical credibility of Jesus' resurrection, and hence to understand the origins of the Easter faith of the disciples. We would then have a better grasp of the process at the end of which Jesus' own contemporaries proclaim that this itinerant rabbi from Galilee is the Messiah, Lord, Son of God, and God himself.[11]

In the light of Easter, the whole earthly life of Jesus shines forth with a new intelligibility: it appears as part of a coherent divine plan, a drama of divine and human freedoms whose overarching theme is God's unfathomable love. This same light exposes the "opposition" between Jesus' preaching of his Kingdom and the apostolic kerygma of his saving death and resurrection; what exegetes for two centuries have cultivated as a contradiction is revealed to be an artificial construct, without historical foundations. Real and present in our human world, though "like a seed" and therefore hidden from view, the Kingdom of God attains its transcendent dynamism precisely in and through the death and resurrection of Jesus. We find that the hidden presence of the Kingdom in our midst is nothing less than the presence of the crucified and risen Christ who, through his Spirit, continues to extend his presence throughout history. At the same time, we come to understand the history of the earthly Jesus, his preaching of the Kingdom and performing its signs, as a gradual embracing of the cross: that through which God's Kingdom came to be established, definitively if inchoately, in this present world. In what follows, I shall pursue further this connection between Jesus' message of the Kingdom and the Apostolic Church's kerygma about Jesus' redemptive work.

## 2. The Kingdom of God and the Sacrifice of Jesus

What price forgiveness? Those who see a conflict between Jesus' message and that of the Apostolic Church point out that Jesus' message offers free forgiveness to sinners, whereas the Apostolic Church speaks about the "price" Jesus paid, and the sacrifice he offered for the forgiveness of sins. But to reflect on Jesus' words and actions is to recognize the falsity of this contradiction.

Jesus indeed proclaims that God forgives all sinners, out of generous love alone, without demanding "payment" in return. Yet the proclaimer himself actively seeks out sinners: he gets close to them, allows himself to be touched and kissed by the penitent woman, stays in the chief tax collector's house, and is surrounded by sinners at Levi's banquet. Far from being a royal decree, uttered from on high, Jesus' good news of gratuitous forgiveness is embodied in his ministry, from whose very beginning he starts to pay the "price," and to offer himself as a sacrifice. He is compassionate towards the shepherd-less crowds; he heals their diseases, thereby taking upon himself their infirmities (Mt 8:17); he carries, like the lost sheep on his shoulders (Lk 15:5), the burden of our sins. To put it briefly, Jesus carries out his ministry of healing, forgiving, and giving life by identifying himself from the start with sick, dying, and sinful human beings.

And in contrast to those sick and sinful ones, who admit their infirmities, and with whom his expressions of solidarity might seem relatively undemanding, there are the self-righteous, who respond to his compassionate love for sinners by accusing and rejecting him. Their hostility becomes active hatred and persecution, which in turn results in his violent death.

Thus, we may say that Jesus indeed offers free forgiveness for all sins, but precisely in doing so, he begins to pay a price, and to offer himself as a sacrifice. The price is his compassion, through which he identifies with all human misery; the sacrifice comprises everything he does in obedience to his Father's will. He thereby offers to God the only acceptable sacrifice, the free gift of his own self. So to claim to see a contradiction between these acts and words of Jesus, on the one hand, and the apostolic preaching, on the other, is to overlook the connection between the existential language of the first and the cultic-legal language of the second. For what now becomes apparent is that the Apostolic Church's themes of sacrifice and paying a price express, in cultic-legal terms, the existential reality of Jesus' free gift of self. This connection, of course, is the same connection already made explicit by Jesus at the Last Supper, and extensively developed in the various theologies of the New Testament.[12]

## 3. *The Last Supper and the Sacrifice of Jesus*

The Last Supper concentrates, in a single event, the sacrificial character of Jesus' entire life, particularly his public ministry, and it anticipates the consummation, at Calvary, of his sacrifice. From the beginning of his earthly life, Jesus sought to give himself to us as food: through his words and fleshly gestures, his compassionate, forgiving love attempts to enter and transform us. This gradual gift of self to us was at the same time an expression of his consistent, step-by-step obedience to the Father's will. Conversely, whenever he was praising and thanking his Father, he did so in solidarity with us sinners, freely taking upon himself the consequences of our sins. Now, at the Last Supper, all this comes together, a prophecy realized in acts. His giving thanks to God and his giving up his body for us announce and anticipate the infallible fulfillment of his complete gift of self on the cross.

Fully to appreciate this gift, we should consider the meaning of sacrifice, particularly as it was practiced in Israel. Throughout the history of religion, the sacrifice of precious objects to the Divine expressed (or distorted) man's vague awareness that the only true gift he can offer God is his own obedience, his own self. Animals and the first fruits of the land acknowledged, symbolically, man's dependence on God and his readiness to place himself in God's hands.

But even as he approached God with these gifts, man could not help being aware of his guilt: he felt that, in truth, he had lost his right to live, let alone to communicate with God. Such guilt warranted his own death. Hence the elaborate rituals of killing the sacrificial animal or human being: in the immolation of the gift, each member of the community vicariously acknowledged that it was he himself who deserved death. By offering something precious to God in lieu of his own life, he could appropriately ask for God's forgiveness.[13]

This dual nature of sacrifice — obedient act and acknowledgment of sin — appears clearly in the Suffering Servant prophecies of Isaiah. Like Jesus, the Servant begins his ministry not as a cultic priest, but as a prophet, proclaiming God's word. In sacrifice to God, the Servant offers, not an object, but his own life: he endures the torture and death inflicted upon him by sinners. And this giving of himself as a sin-offering is done freely. The Servant takes upon himself the punishment that we deserve for our sins.

Yet not even the Suffering Servant prophecies fully convey the mystery of Christ's sacrifice. True, the Servant is innocent, and offers his life voluntarily for the sinners who torture him. As profound as his sacrifice is, however, we must not forget that the Servant is only a human being. What the Resurrection makes clear is that, in Jesus, God the Son has offered his own divine self, through his humanity, to God the Father.

In Jesus, the Father receives a uniquely congenial gift, the only gift worthy of his infinite goodness, the Son himself. Only the Son can and does love, praise, and thank the Father as the Father deserves to be loved, praised, and thanked. The Son's eternal sonship, his eternal self-giving to his Father within the eternal Trinity, is in Jesus' sacrifice "translated" into the language of fallen human existence. So to the extent that we are united to the man Jesus, we, too, are drawn into the intra-trinitarian life of the Son; in a way proper to our fallen humanity, we share in the Son's eternal giving of himself in love and praise.

To believe that the man Jesus is God himself is to understand why Jesus' sacrifice is the most perfect — rather, the only acceptable — sin-offering. God himself, bearing infinite and divine love within his human heart, identifies with the sinner; God feels the misery which the sinner has brought upon himself through his sins. If Jesus the man is God himself, then we realize why Jesus alone can understand the full gravity of our offense against God the Father. Since only the Son fully comprehends the Father's love, only the Son knows the evil in the human sin of rejecting God precisely as Father.[14] Likewise, only the Son can and does offer a love to counterbalance — indeed, to overwhelm — the offense of all possible sins, with the result that sin and evil shall not be victorious in this universe. On the contrary, we now see that our sins were allowed only because they brought to light the ultimate depth of God's love in the man Jesus.

## 4. The Sacrifice of Jesus and the Cross

The question still remains why Jesus' sacrifice should culminate in his death on the cross. Part of the answer lies, again, in the history of sacrifice. In most religions, an essential aspect of sacrificial offerings is their destruction: the burning of the grain, the first fruits, or the incense; the killing of the sacrificial animal or person. Destruction does not simply signify the object's being removed from human use. It also symbolizes another "translation," this time from the worldly to the sacred realm: to be *sacrificed*, made sacred, the gift must necessarily be transferred into the transcendent realm, made forever a possession of the Sacred.

Jesus' voluntary and violent death offers both similarities and contrasts to this understanding of sacrificial killing. From the instant of his conception, Jesus is *to hagion*, "the holy thing" or Holy One of God. Yet as he obediently offers himself to God in the daily routine of his public and private life, this self-giving must by its very nature remain limited. It requires only a piecemeal renunciation of the self: only a part of Jesus' possessions, time, and energy are given away. Such giving does not entail the giving up of his existence in this world. He remains in possession of himself, and indeed this continuing self-possession is what enables him to continue offering himself in his daily work of preaching, comforting, and healing.

By contrast, when Jesus voluntarily accepts death, he freely renounces life in this world. Placing his life unconditionally in his Father's hands, he renounces, not just something of himself, some piece or part, but the totality of his existence in this world. He abandons all claim to that specific mode of being that characterizes human existence, self-possession through self-awareness and through free acts, a self-possession which is expressed and thereby perfected in the human body. Freely accepting the disintegration of his human existence, Jesus entrusts himself to his Father alone and, in doing so, anticipates his passing from this world into the transcendent realm of the Father. It is in this pass-over that he consecrates himself in a new way, becoming the eternal and living sacrifice, the Lamb slain yet alive forever in the Father's presence.[15]

At this point, one may object that Jesus' death lacked the uncertainty that makes the Christian martyr's death so difficult. As the Son of God (the argument goes), Jesus must have had some "unfair advantage": if not the beatific vision asserted by Church tradition, at least some intuition of eternal life and of his own resurrection. We have no grounds for denying this; on the contrary, there are many reasons for maintaining that Jesus indeed had such an intuition. But would it have made Jesus' giving of himself any easier?

Two considerations should be borne in mind here. Jesus' human sensitivity has not been dulled by sin, original or personal. As his parables and similes abundantly demonstrate, Jesus perceived everywhere the goodness and beauty of his Father's creation; he loved and appreciated, with a keen sensitivity, all that was good in his own life and in the world at large. Our perceptions, by contrast, have been numbed by the bitter taste of all our sins, a condition which — to the extent we crave holiness — has stirred in us the desire to leave behind this world of temptations, to get past our half-hearted striving for good. For Jesus, who knew no sin, how much harder it must have been to forfeit earthly life, a life whose savor was entirely good and which presented not a single regrettable, sinful moment.[16]

The second consideration evolves from Simone Weil's intuition that, in murder, only the victim knows the evil in the heart of his murderer. To be able to commit an evil act, yet live with his guilt afterwards, every sinner must to some degree suppress his own awareness of the evil; it is therefore the innocent victim alone who experiences, through the pain inflicted on his body, the full evil of his torturer's act.[17] In that case the suffering of Jesus stands alone in its intensity. As the Son, Jesus would have understood better than any other human being the outrage of the sins committed against him. He would have known, in mind and body, the workings of the Satanic intention to eliminate the heir, to kill God himself.[18] So in the sins of those responsible for his death, he experienced the evil of all human sins. To have loved the sinner with an infinite compassion, yet to see with supreme clarity the evil of his sins: this must have caused Jesus a suffering beyond our comprehension.

Beyond comprehension, yet not without an analogy: we have the example of the saints. They, too, endured the sting of loving the sinner while seeing his evil. They could sustain this tension only because of their faith in God's love for the sinner, and because their hope of eternal life gave them a firm anchor of peace and tranquillity. Without these, they could not have avoided the temptation of despair when confronted with the bottomless pit of human wickedness.[19]

We can surmise, then, that only through awareness of the Father's infinite love, and of God's complete victory over evil, could Jesus have assumed full solidarity with sinners, indeed have loved them beyond measure as they focused all their hatred of God upon him. The experience of the saints directs our attention to the correlation between one's knowledge of sin, one's suffering of its evils, and one's knowledge and love of God. We can conclude that the Son alone — who had already tasted, in his earthly life, the full measure of God's holiness, goodness, and mercy -- that he alone could see and suffer the evil of sin to its fullest. The atoning sacrifice of Jesus makes sense only if he is truly the Son, and is aware of being the Son.[20]

Jesus countered all sins with a love for his Father, and for sinners, infinitely more powerful than any sin. This is not to neglect the dreadfulness of the fight: *mors et vita duello conflixere mirando*.[21] Yet, ultimately, the same love that made possible his willing death, that manifested itself in that heart violated by the soldier's lance, conquered all sin. To the Father, the Son offered a love which was infinitely more pleasing to the Father than any sin could be offensive to him.

Hence the cross. Only there could the perfect atoning sacrifice, the perfect offering for sin, occur. Only on the cross, in the voluntary acceptance of a violent death, could the Son made man express to the fullest his interceding, forgiving love. For only there was the evil of our sins, in all its brutality, unmasked. Only there, in response, could Jesus offer his Father a gift of unsurpassable value.[22]

### 5. The Anthropological Significance of the Sacrifice of Jesus: Overcoming Human Alienation

Every deliberate, sinful act can be understood as a false affirmation of self: in sin, man asserts his absoluteness, deciding what is good and evil for himself in opposition to the will of the true God. The result is that he is estranged from God, on the one hand, and from his true self on the other, since he opposes his own conscience, the inmost "center of man" and the point of his contact with God. Moreover, if man considers himself absolute, he places himself in opposition to other human beings: he must either use them for his ends, or, if they dare to oppose his ends, overcome them. So to the extent that he is a sinner, no one can associate with his neighbor on a basis of mutual respect and love.

And sin carries in itself its own punishment. Far from being a penalty prescribed in some heavenly penal code, applied by a divine judge, but only extrinsically related to the wrong itself, the punishment of sin is the very three-fold alienation which man freely chooses when he sins. At death, this alienation reaches its climax. The dying man has a last chance to acknowledge where his sin has led him, and to seek a reversal of this process. That he is estranged from God, the fullness of life: when would man comprehend this fact more clearly than at his dying? That he himself is not absolute, but that an essential component of his nature, his body, is about to become mere dust: how but in dying could he be so brutally forced to see this? As to his fellow creatures: when are other people less able to identify with him than in his dying? Yet even as the dying person experiences more sharply than ever the pain of alienation, he is helpless to reverse it. Just here, then, is where we grasp the importance for every human being of the sacrifice of Christ.

In his dying, Christ teaches us to accept the lesson of our own dying. He places his life and his future unconditionally in the Father's hands and teaches us to do likewise: not to try and keep ourselves to ourselves, not to cling to our existence in this world, but to entrust all that we are to God. Only in this way can we accept the truth of our being creatures, of having and being God's gifts in every moment of our lives.

And only in entrusting ourselves to God can we overcome the alienation that afflicts us all. Offering our whole being to God as a gift, we in effect say to him, "I accept the 'falling apart' of this, my self, and trust that you will re-make it into a new creation." We abandon our false self-affirmation and, returning to God, restore our own true identity. Uniting ourselves with the self-giving of Christ on the cross, we become one, as well, with those of our fellow human beings who already have joined in the self-giving of Christ. Thus, to the extent that we are united with the sacrifice, we overcome the three-fold alienation that is the wages of sin.

Once we accept this perspective on human existence, we also begin to see the central role of the Eucharist for our lives. Through this sacramental realization of the crucified and risen Christ, we may unite our own efforts at self-giving to his perfect offering of self, the permanent state of the Lamb who is slain and lives forever. We may, in the Eucharist, "practice" daily our dying with him, and indeed anticipate, in this earthly realm, his risen life.

## Conclusion

The secret of our human fulfillment, then, consists in giving up our obsession with ourselves and in turning towards God. It requires that we learn from the example of the Son, God made man, both to accept our creaturely dependence upon God and to return ourselves unconditionally to Him. The Son can do this for us because he is the transcendent archetype of man, in whose image man has been created. Nevertheless, to attain such fulfillment, we need the Holy Spirit of Christ, who enables us to make our own the creaturely relationship Christ holds with God. Moreover, through the same Spirit, we participate in the intra-trinitarian life of the Son: we can give thanks and praise to the Father for making us not only his creatures — servants, but for raising us to the status of his own sons and daughters, in union with his only Son.

And once we see that God has taken the two worst manifestations of evil, sin and death, and used them to demonstrate to us his love which surpasses all understanding, we find that our initial longing for the final victory of goodness has been vindicated. We can then recognize and respect, in everyday human experiences and in non-Christian religions, signs of divine love and goodness: signs that, purified of distortions, point to the historical climax of the revelation of divine love in Christ.

## NOTES

1. Of course, my approach is only one among many, and not everyone may find it helpful in his own quest. In its second and third parts, this article tries to highlight and develop further what has been treated more extensively in my book, **Jesus Christ. Fundamentals of Christology** (New York: Alba House, 1991). For a more complete bibliography, consult the appropriate chapters of that work.

2. We do not have the space here to go into a detailed analysis, but the grounding of goodness and love in a transcendent source is true about the heavenly gods of primitive religions, even about some of the gods in the decadent pantheons of Greco-Roman, Teutonic or Indian gods; it is true about Brahman, the universal Buddha nature, Tao, "Heaven" in traditional Chinese religion, the ineffable Reality experienced in Zen Buddhism, Yahweh, and Allah; all, in some way or another, may be defined as a or the source of goodness.

3. See H. U. von Balthasar, **Love Alone** (New York: Herder & Herder, 1969).

4.  Judaism and Islam also claim that divine revelation has constituted a sacred history, a history that partially coincides with what Christians call Salvation History. Yet, both lack a culmination in the revelation of divine love in a historical person. Other religions, however, locate the encounter between the Divine and man either in the re-enactment of a mythical event or in the privacy of individual religious experience.

5.  At this point "church" is a broadly used term that applies, in varying degrees, to the many Christian churches.

6.  The great events and personalities in the Old Testament all receive their final intelligibility from the fact that they prepare and prefigure Christ. On the formation of the canon, see W.R. Farmer & D.M. Farkasfalvy, **The Formation of the New Testament Canon** (New York: Paulist 1983); D. Farkasfalvy, **"Prophets and Apostles": The Conjunction of the Two Terms Before Irenaeus," Texts and Testaments** (San Antonio: Trinity University Press, 1980) 109-134).

7.  Even though the so called "New Quest for the Historical Jesus" which began in 1953 resulted in more objective portraits of Jesus, these portraits still remained fragmentary and inadequate. See **Jesus Christ**, pp. 5-20.

8.  See more on this in my "The 'Bible and Christology' Document of the Biblical Commission" Communio 13 (1986) 342-367.

9.  In this article, however, I avoided the use of any properly philosophical term except for some well known existentialist notions.

10. A most helpful article on this distinction is J. P. Meier, "The Historical Jesus: Rethinking Some Concepts" Theological Studies 51 (1990), 3-24.

11. I received the first incentive to develop this method from a conversation with D. Farkasfalvy.

12. On the Last Supper, see B.F. Meier, "The Expiation Motif in the Eucharistic Words: A Key to the History of Jesus", *Gregorianum* 69 (1988) 461-487. A. Feuillet shows that the priestly and sacrificial character of Jesus' work does not restrict itself to the Letter to the Hebrews but is also a leit-motif of the Fourth Gospel [**The Priesthood of Chist and His Ministers** (Garden City: Doubleday, 1975)], Cf. also M. Hengel, **The Atonement. The Origins of the Doctrine in the New Testament** (Philadelphia: Fortress, 1981).

13. Cf. D. Farkasfalvy, & R. Kereszty, **Basics of Catholic Faith** (Dallas: for the private use of the Cistercian Prep School, 1990), pp. 71-72.

14. Catholic faith teaches that by sinning we go not only against the will of the Creator, but we also reject God's grace. The latter part of this statement means that we reject God's love which intends to transform us into his very children. Thus we offend God precisely in his fatherly love.

15. Cf. Jn 17:19; Rev 5:6.12.

16. Cf. St. Thomas, S.T. III Q 46 a 6, esp. the response to the fourth objection.

17. Cf. **The Simone Weil Reader**. ed. G. Panichas (New York: D. McKay, 1977), p. 383.

18. Cf. Mk 12:7; Jn 13:2.

19. Again, S. Weil's intuition is very helpful here: "In order to be merciful, one must have a point of impassibility in one's soul." **The Simone Weil Reader**, p. 432.

20. The history of christology bears witness to this connection. Wherever the true divine sonship of Jesus is lost, so is his atoning sacrifice.

21. From the Sequence of the Easter Mass: *Victimae paschali* : "death and life fought in a most amazing fight."

22. Here we see that the traditional themes of redemption (by way of merit, satisfaction, and buying back) can all be unified into the notion of sacrifice as explained above.

# Crisis in Christology

# INDEX

## A

Albright, W.F., 31
Allison, Jr., Gale C., 316
Anselm, 169
*Apologia Pro Vita Sua*, 27
Aquinas, Thomas, 1, 105, 112, 120
Aristotle, 108
Athanasius, 120
Augstein, Rudolf, 99, 100
Augustine, 169
Avigad, 32

## B

Baillie, D.M., 58
Balthasar, Hans Urs Von, 112
Barth, Gerhard, 251
Barth, Karl, 13, 16, 107, 120, 161,
Baur, Ferdinand Christian, 298
Beard, Charles A., 84
Becker, Carl, 83
Berkhof, H., 15, 17, 18, 20, 22
Bernard of Clairvaux, 186
Bernheim, E., 85
Betz, Otto, 273
Billerbeck, 275
Bloch, Ernst, 102, 104
Borg, Marcus, 118, 119, 316
Bornkamm, G., 51, 179, 272
Boso, 169
Bousset, W., 222, 223
Brentano, Clemens, 102
*Brideshead Revisited*, 111
Brown, Raymond, 170, 173
Buddha, Gautama, 111

Bultmann, Rudolf, 14, 84, 85, 86,
104, 105, 106, 167, 168, 179,
201, 228, 272
Buren, Paul Van, 14
Butler, B.C., 75

## C

Caird, George C., 316
Cameron, Ron, 118
Calvin, John, 1
Carlyle, Thomas, 223
Carmichael, Joel, 100
Chilton, Bruce, 118
*Christ Without Myth*, xii
Christian Faith, 17, 20
Church Dogmatics, 13
Cleage, Albert, 168
Commager, H.S., 83
Cone, James, 169
Confucius, 111
Conzelmann, H., 223, 228
*Cosmos, Bios, Theos*, xi
Cox, Harvey, 159
Crossan, Dominic, 118, 162, 164,
170, 171, 172
Cullmann, Oscar, 86, 241
Cupitt, Don, 2

## D

Dahl, N.A., 229
Dante, 8
Darwin, Charles, 26
*Das Prinizip Hoffnung*, 103
Davis, Jefferson, 84

# BIOGRAPHICAL INFORMATION ON THE CONTRIBUTORS

**William R. Farmer:**
Emeritus Professor of New Testament, Southern Methodist University; Bollingen Fellow; Guggenheim Fellow; Research Scholar, University of Dallas. Series Editor of **New Synoptic Studies: Monograph Series**, Mercer University Press. Author of: **The Maccabees, Zealots and Josephus**: Columbia University Press (1956); **The Synoptic Problem**: Macmillan (1964); **The Synopticon**: Cambridge University Press (1969); **The Last Twelve Verses of Mark**: Cambridge University Press (1975); **Jesus and the Gospel**: Fortress (1983); **The Gospel of Jesus**: Westminster/John Knox (1984). Editor and co-editor of eleven volumes of scholarly essays; author of numerous articles in learned journals. At the time of publication of this anthology Professor Farmer is under appointment as Visiting Fellow of Fitzwilliam College, Cambridge University for the Easter Term, 1995. He has served since 1991 as the Editor of the **International Catholic Bible Commentary**, an ecumenical work which is scheduled for publication in Spanish, English and French.

**Brian Hebblethwaite:**
Fellow of Queens' College, Cambridge University. Books include **The Problem of Theology; The Incarnation; The Ocean of Truth**. Contributor to **The Truth of God Incarnate** and **Incarnation and Mythology**.

**Klaas Runia:**
Professor Emeritus of Practical Theology, Reformed Theological University, Kamper, The Netherlands. Books include **The Present Day Christological Debate**.

**Paul Johnson:**
Historian. Books include **A History of Christianity, A History of the Jews** and **Modern Times: A History of the Modern World from 1917 to the 1980's**.

**David Martin:**

Emeritus Professor of Sociology, London School of Economics and Political Science. Ph.D., London University. Books include **The Religious and the Secular, A General Theory of Secularization, Dilemmas of Contemporary Religion, Tongues of Fire**. President, International Conference of Sociology of Religion, 1975-1981.

**Charles F. D. Moule:**

Emeritus Professor of Divinity, Cambridge University. Books include **The Birth of the New Testament, The Phenomenon of the New Testament, The Origin of Christology, Essays in New Testament Interpretation.**

**R. T. France:**

Principal, Wycliffe Hall, Oxford. Books include: **Jesus and the Old Testament; Matthew** (Tyndale Commentary); **The Evidence for Jesus; Jesus the Radical; Matthew - Evangelist and Teacher; Divine Government.** Co-editor of **Gospel Perspectives** I-III.

**E. Earle Ellis**

Research Professor of Theology, Southwestern Baptist Theological Seminary. Author of over 600 articles and papers in scholarly journals. Books include: **Paul and His Recent Interpreters** (1961); **The World of St. John** (1965); **The Gospel of Luke** (1966); **Prophecy and Hermeneutic in Early Christianity** (1978); **Pauline Theology: Ministry and Society** (1989); **The Old Testament in Early Christianity** (1992);

**Nikolaus Lobkowicz:**

President, Catholic University of Eichstaett. Past President of the University of Munich. Member of the Pontifical Council for Culture. Books include **Theory and Practice from Aristotle to Marx, Marx and the Western World** and **Handbook of World Communism.**

**N.T. Wright:**

N.T. Wright is currently Dean of Lichfield, England. He was formerly Fellow, Tutor and Chaplain of Worcester College, Oxford, and Lecturer in New Testament studies in Oxford University. He has also taught at McGill University, Montreal, and Cambridge University. He is the author of several books, monographs and articles on the

New Testament and related topics. New Testament books include **The Climax of the Covenant** and **The New Testament and the People of God**.

**Durwood Foster:**
Professor of Christian Theology Emeritus, and formerly Dean, Pacific School of Religion. Previously taught at Union Theological Seminary and Duke University Divinity School.

**James D.G. Dunn:**
Lightfoot Professor of Divinity, University of Durham. Books include **Jesus and the Spirit, Unity and Diversity in the New Testament, Christology in the Making: A New Testament Inquiry into the Origins of the Doctrine of the Incarnation, The Partings of the Ways Between Christianity and Judaism**; commentaries on **Romans** (Word) and **Galatians** (Black/Hendrickson).

**Martin Hengel:**
Professor Emeritus, Institut fur Antikes Judentum, University of Tubingen. Books include **Judaism and Hellenism: Studies in Their Encounter in Palestine During the Early Hellenistic Period; The Zealots; Between Jesus and Paul: Studies in the Earliest History of Christianity; The Son of God: The Johnanine Question; The Prechristian Paul**.

**Adrian M. Leske:**
Professor and Chair of Religious Studies, Concordia College, Edmonton, Alberta, Canada.

**Peter Stuhlmacher:**
Professor of New Testament Theology, University of Tubingen. Books include **Gerechtigkeit Gottes bei Paulus; Historical Criticism and Theological Interpretation of Scripture; Jesus von Nazareth-Christus des Glaubens; How to Do Biblical Theology**. Editor **The Gospels and the Gospel**.

**Ben F. Meyer:**
Professor Emeritus of Greco-Roman Judaism and Christianity, McMaster University. Books include **The Aims of Jesus; Christus Faber; Reality and Illusion in New Testament Scholarship**.

**Roch Kereszty:**
Adjunct Professor of Theology, University of Dallas. STD, Pontifical University of St. Anselm. Books include **God Seekers for a New Age: From Crisis Theology to Christian Atheism; Jesus Christ: Fundamentals of Christology**.

# Biographical Information